THE PRACTICE OF DIASPORA

THE PRACTICE OF DIASPORA

Literature, Translation, and the Rise

of Black Internationalism

BRENT HAYES EDWARDS

HARVARD UNIVERSITY PRESS

Cambridge, Massachusetts and London, England   2003

Library of Congress Cataloging-in-Publication Data
Edwards, Brent Hayes.
The practice of diaspora : literature, translation, and the rise of
Black internationalism / Brent Hayes Edwards.
p.   cm.
Includes bibliographical references and index.
ISBN 0-674-01022-1 (cloth)
ISBN 0-674-01103-1 (paper)
1. Literature—Black authors—History and criticism.   2. Literature, Modern—20th
century—History and criticism. 3. Paris (France)—Intellectual life—20th century. I. Title.
PN841.E38 2003
809′.8896′0904—dc21   2002038813

"Jazz Band in a Parisian Cabaret" from *The Collected Poems of Langston Hughes* by
Langston Hughes, copyright © 1994 by The Estate of Langston Hughes. Used
by permission of Alfred A. Knopf, a division of Random House, Inc.

Quotations from Claude McKay's works courtesy of the Literary Representative for
the Works of Claude McKay, Schomburg Center for Research in Black Culture,
The New York Public Library, Astor, Lenox and Tilden Foundations.

FOR MY PARENTS

CONTENTS

ILLUSTRATIONS

PROLOGUE

At the dawn of the last century, W. E. B. Du Bois coined a phrase that was at once a prophecy and a preface. In July 1900, he came to London from France, where he had helped install the American Negro exhibit at the grandiose *bilan du siècle* of the Paris Universal Exposition on the banks of the Seine. Du Bois crossed the Channel to join such figures as African American feminist Anna Julia Cooper, Haitian politician Benito Sylvain, black British composer Samuel Coleridge-Taylor, and well-known former slave Henry "Box" Brown at the Pan-African Conference organized by Trinidadian lawyer Henry Sylvester Williams. In the final sessions of the conference in Westminster Town Hall, Du Bois gave a speech titled "To the Nations of the World" that opened with a stunning paragraph:

> In the metropolis of the modern world, in this closing year of the nineteenth century there has been assembled a congress of men and women of African blood, to deliberate solemnly upon the present situation and outlook of the darker races of mankind. The problem of the twentieth century is the problem of the colour line, the question as to how far differences of race . . . are going to be made, hereafter, the basis of denying to over half the world the right of sharing to their utmost ability the opportunities and privileges of modern civilisation.[1]

The second sentence ("the problem of the twentieth century is the problem of the colour line") would reverberate three years later in the famous "Forethought" to Du Bois's masterwork, *The Souls of Black Folk,* in a formulation that is often considered an inauguration for thinking about the significance of race in the modern world.[2]

Reading *The Souls of Black Folk* as an echo of the prior usage at the Pan-African Conference necessitates coming to terms with the ways that the phrase emphatically frames the "color line" not in the U.S. debates and civil rights struggles that are commonly taken to be its arena, but in the much broader sphere of "modern civilization" as a whole. This preface addresses "the nations of the world," but from the setting and in the name of a transnational gathering of men and women. Although the conference gathered intellectuals of African descent, it aimed to "deliberate" on and even speak for a larger population of the colonized and oppressed, the "darker races of the world." Or as Du Bois would underline again and again in the next few years, the "Negro problem" in the United States is only a "local phase" of a much greater problem: "the color line belts the world."[3]

If the Pan-African Conference was an ephemeral organization with little lasting impact, still Du Bois's phrase set the tone for the eruption of black expressive culture and political initiatives in the 1920s. As he put it later, a "world view" on the color line was all the more indispensable in the wake of a series of earthshaking events in the second decade of the century, most of all "that great event of these great years, the World War."[4] What Nathan Huggins terms the "post-war effort to thrust Negro social thought into an international arena" is a constant thread in the work of black intellectuals of the period no matter what their ideological outlook, whether Du Bois or Marcus Garvey, whether Jessie Fauset or W. A. Domingo, whether Claude McKay or Lamine Senghor.[5] The cosmopolite Howard University philosophy professor Alain Locke claimed in the introduction to his 1925 anthology *The New Negro* that his title was partly an allusion to the Negro's "new internationalism," which represented one of the few "constructive channels" for black cultural institution building beyond the "cramped horizons" of postwar U.S. racism and segregation.[6] With very different aims, the brilliant black socialist orator Hubert Harrison picked up the internationalist implications of Du Bois's "color line" right after the war, calling for attention to the self-determination struggles of the peoples of Egypt, India, China, and Africa, and prescribing that "before the Negroes of the Western world can play any effective part they must first acquaint themselves with what is taking place in that larger world whose millions are in motion. . . . If our problem here is really a part of a great world-wide problem, we must make our attempts to solve our part link up with the attempts being made elsewhere to solve the other parts."[7]

To note that the "New Negro" movement is at the same time a "new" black internationalism is to move against the grain of much of the scholarship on African American culture in the 1920s, which has tended to emphasize U.S.-bound themes of cultural nationalism, civil rights protest, and uplift in the literary culture of the "Harlem Renaissance."[8] This book is an attempt to come to terms with the reminders of a handful of scholars such as Robert Stepto, Michel Fabre, and Melvin Dixon that "the Renaissance was international in scale both in terms of where its contributors came from and in terms of its being merely the North American component of something larger and grander."[9] This approach means not only tracking the transnational contours of black expression between the world wars, but also accounting for the ways that expression was molded through attempts to appropriate and transform the discourses of internationalism that seemed to center "the destinies of mankind," as Du Bois put it in 1919—the discourse of international civil society as embodied in the League of Nations, the counter-universalism of proletarian revolution envisioned by the Communist International, and the globe-carving discourse of European colonialism.[10]

One approach to the stirrings of the cultures of black internationalism is to consider the ways that during and after the war, metropolitan France was one of the key places where African Americans, Antilleans, and Africans were able to "link up." During World War I, about 370,000 African Americans served in the segregated American Expeditionary Force in France, in both service and combat units. Along with a warm reception from French civilians, African American soldiers encountered the tangible presence of soldiers of color from throughout the French Empire. During the war, the French conscripted nearly 620,000 soldiers from the colonies, including approximately 250,000 from Senegal and the Sudan and 30,000 from the French Caribbean. France simultaneously imported a labor force of nearly 300,000, both from elsewhere in Europe and from the colonies. Although France repatriated the great majority of the "native" troops, in 1926 there were still at least 10,000 Caribbean students and workers and 1,500 black African workers in Paris alone, along with hundreds of African American visitors and expatriates.[11] After the war, tales of encounter and connection, forged in the trenches and on the docks, traveled back to the United States with the American fighting forces. Some U.S. blacks stayed in France to study or to perform, most gravitating to Paris—for Paris had simultaneously come to appreciate jazz and *l'art nègre,* partly through the performances of military music units like James Reese Europe's 369th Infantry

Regiment "Hellfighters" Band and postwar musicians including Palmer Jones's International Five, Louis Mitchell, Arthur Briggs, Cricket Smith, Eugene Bullard, Ada Smith, and Florence Embry Jones.[12] Looking just at the culture makers usually identified with the "Harlem Renaissance," it is striking that the exceptions are those who remained in the United States. Not even to mention visual artists, almost all of the major literary figures of the period, including Anna Julia Cooper, Claude McKay, Walter White, Gwendolyn Bennett, Countee Cullen, Langston Hughes, Alain Locke, James Weldon Johnson, Jessie Fauset, J. A. Rogers, Jean Toomer, Eric Walrond, and Nella Larsen, spent time abroad and especially in Paris in the 1920s. It is often overlooked that many early Francophone Antillean and African intellectuals (such as René Maran, Kojo Tovalou Houénou, Louis Achille, Léo Sajous, and Léon-Gontran Damas) were equally mobile in the period, in Europe, Africa, and in some cases the United States as well.

Still, these numbers are nowhere near the concentration of peoples of African descent in Harlem. It is important to recognize that the significance of Paris in this period is not a question of sheer population size. Instead, as Raymond Williams has argued, the European metropole after the war provided a special sort of vibrant, cosmopolitan space for interaction that was available neither in the United States nor in the colonies. It allowed "a complexity and a sophistication of social relations, supplemented in the most important cases—Paris, above all—by exceptional liberties of expression. . . . [W]ithin the new kind of open, complex and mobile society, small groups in any form of divergence or dissent could find some kind of foothold."[13] Paris is crucial because it allowed boundary crossing, conversations, and collaborations that were available nowhere else to the same degree.

At the same time the city resonates in the cultures of black internationalism because it came to *represent* certain kinds of crossings, certain extensions of the horizon, even for populations that did not travel. I will discuss this point in more detail later with regard to a variety of genres, but to sketch its implications quickly, one might note—just in terms of interwar black U.S. novelistic production alone—that to ask about the function of Paris is to ask a broader set of interrelated questions about the role of outernational sites even in texts that are putatively the canonical literature of "Harlem." It is as though certain moves, certain arguments and epiphanies, can only be staged beyond the confines of the United States, and even sometimes in languages other than English. In other words, why does James Weldon Johnson's *The Autobiography of an Ex-Colored Man* (which predates the war, but only becomes a key text after its reprinting in the 1920s) place in Berlin the narrator's realization about using folk materials in classical composition? Why does Jessie Fauset's *Plum Bun* need that Paris ending; why is the last third of her *Comedy: American Style* set in the South of France? One thinks equally of Nella Larsen's *Quicksand,* with its crucial scenes in Copenhagen, Claude McKay's *Banjo* set in Marseilles, Du Bois's *Dark Princess,* so fascinated with the corridors of international power and intrigue, or Eric Walrond's *Tropic Death,* unraveling the intricacies of imperialism and labor migration in the Caribbean basin.

Many of the black literati invested in one way or another in the notion of Harlem as a worldwide black culture capital, and yet many of them came to view Paris as a special space for black transnational interaction, exchange, and dialogue. For African American intellectuals in particular, as Tyler Stovall phrases it, the role of Paris

> was both fascinating and deeply ironic. After all, the city was the seat of one of the world's great colonial empires, a place where anonymous French officials supervised the subjugation of millions of black Africans. . . . Outside of Marseilles, London, and some other British cities, one could not find a more diverse black population anywhere in Europe. More so than in the United States, even New York, African Americans found that in Paris the abstract ideal of worldwide black unity and culture became a tangible reality. . . . French colonialism and primitivism thus paradoxically combined to foster a vision of pan-African unity.[14]

A vision of internationalism, perhaps, though not exactly "worldwide black unity": in these transnational circuits, black modern expression takes form not as a single thread, but through the often uneasy encounters of peoples of African descent with each other. The cultures of black internationalism are formed only within the "paradoxes" Stovall mentions, with the result that—as much as they allow new and unforeseen alliances and interventions on a global stage—they also are characterized by unavoidable misapprehensions and misreadings, persistent blindnesses and solipsisms, self-defeating and abortive collaborations, a failure to translate even a basic grammar of blackness.

In part, as Stovall points out, black and brown encounters on the Seine were uneasy due to the African American habit of thinking about Paris as liberatory and "free of racism" precisely at the height of French colonial exploitation. Claude McKay took the "Renaissance" literati to task on this issue:

> The good treatment of individuals by those whom they meet in France is valued so highly by Negroes that they are beginning to forget about the exploitation of Africans by the French. . . . Thus the sympathy of the Negro intelligentsia is completely on the side of France. It is well-informed about the barbarous acts of the Belgians in the Congo but it knows nothing at all about the barbarous acts of the French in Senegal, about the organized robbery of native workers, about the forced enlistment of recruits, about the fact that the population is reduced to extreme poverty and hunger, or about the total annihilation of tribes. It is possible that the Negro intelligentsia does not want to know about all this, inasmuch as it can loosely generalize about the differences in the treatment of Negroes in bourgeois France and in plutocratic America.[15]

This blindness allowed the "Harlem Renaissance" intelligentsia to bask in its own vanguardist myths, as it employed the putative universality of the French "Rights of Man" to decry U.S. racism. In effect, transnational black solidarity is traded in for a certain kind of national currency, an anti-racism in one country. In this configuration, the very notion of *"Paris noir"* is paradoxical because it represents the elision of black French culture in all its forms, whether that of the Francophone African and Antillian workers, performers, and students in the metropole, or that of the expressive traditions and struggles of the populations in the French colonies themselves.

What is seldom recognized in the many condemnations of the New Negro movement as a "failure"—as myopic, elitist, or insufficiently radical—is the degree to which the paradoxes of black Paris are in fact constitutive of black modern expression in general, which is shaped to a significant degree by what Kenneth Warren has termed the "necessary misrecognitions" of diasporic discourse.[16] Attempts to articulate the "race problem as a world problem," in Locke's phrase—to foster links among populations of African descent in order to organize the "darker peoples of the world" across the boundaries of nation-states and languages—are necessarily skewed by those same boundaries.[17] That is, the level of the international is accessed unevenly by subjects with different historical relations to the nation (for instance, in a collaboration between a U.S. citizen marked by a context of violent racist exclusion, disenfranchisement, and segregation of a minority population, and a French West African citizen marked by a context of colonialism, invasive subjugation of a majority population, and Eurocentric structures of privilege and mobility). Thus, if the cultures of black internationalism are shaped by the imperatives of what Edward Said has called "adversarial internationalizations" (attempts at organizing alliances to challenge the prevailing discourses of Western universalism), those cultures are equally "adversarial" to themselves, highlighting differences and disagreements among black populations on a number of registers.[18]

Another way to put this point is to note that the cultures of black internationalism can be seen only *in translation.* It is not possible to take up the question of "diaspora" without taking account of the fact that the great majority of peoples of African descent do not speak or write in English. I have outlined some of the reasons that it makes sense to situate this question in particular through the dialogues and encounters facilitated in the French metropole between the world wars; if, as I argue, that space is privileged and richly varied, it is by no means the exclusive prism of linguistic exchange. The larger point is that one can approach such a project only by attending to the ways that discourses of internationalism *travel,* the ways they are translated, disseminated, reformulated, and debated in transnational contexts marked by difference.

It should be evident that undertaking such a project necessitates unearthing and articulating an *archive,* in the sense not so much of a site or mode of preservation of a national, institutional, or individual past, but instead of a "generative system": in other words, a discursive system that governs the possibilities, forms, appearance, and regularity of particular statements, objects, and practices—or, on the simplest level, that determines "what can and cannot be said."[19] In terms of the cultures of black internationalism between the world wars, one must consider a great variety of texts: fiction, poetry, journalism, criticism, position papers, circulars, manifestoes, anthologies, correspondence, surveillance reports. One can come to terms with what archivist Robert Hill calls the "*stratification* of the deposits" in such a discursive field only by taking stock of not just the most durable and widely circulated, but also the most fleeting—the most time-bound—modes of expressive production.[20]

This particular archive turns especially on the multilayered, high-stakes efforts between the wars to document the "fact" of blackness itself—to frame race as an object of knowledge production in the service of a range of adversarial internationalizations. Writing in the mid-1920s, Walter Benjamin comments in one of the orchestrated fragments of *Einbahnstrasse* that

> [t]he construction of life is at present in the power far more of facts than of convictions, and of such facts as have scarcely ever become the basis of convictions. Under these circumstances, true literary activity cannot aspire to take place within a literary framework; that is, rather, the habitual expression of its sterility. Significant literary effectiveness can come into being only in a strict alternation between doing and writing; it must nurture the inconspicuous forms that fit its influence in active communities better than does the pretentious, universal gesture of the book—in leaflets, brochures, articles, and placards. Only this prompt language shows itself actively equal to the moment. Opinions are to the vast apparatus of social existence what oil is to machines: one does not go up to a turbine and pour machine oil over it; one applies a little to hidden spindles and joints [*Nieten und Fugen*] that one has to know.[21]

The "spindles and joints" of a print culture that aims to construct the "fact" of blackness, that attempts to intervene in conditions of great suffering and social upheaval, that strains to be "actively equal" to the exigencies of crisis and advocacy, are located above all at the stratum of periodical culture. Not surprisingly, the periodical print cultures of black internationalism were robust and extremely diverse on all sides of the Atlantic. If the list of journals and newspapers in the United States during the 1920s and 1930s was better known (including the *Negro World,* the *Messenger,* the *Crisis,* the *Crusader, Opportunity,* the *Emancipator,* the *Voice of the Negro, Fire!!,* the *Chicago Defender,* and the *Amsterdam News*), their counterparts in France and Africa (one might begin with *Le Paria, L'Action coloniale, Les Continents, La Voix des Nègres, La Race nègre, Le Courrier des Noirs, La Dépêche africaine, Légitime Défense, La Revue du monde noir, Le Cri des Nègres, L'Etudiant martiniquais, L'Etudiant noir,* and *Africa*) were quite keen to "link up" with English-language sources and just as energetic, albeit more ephemeral.

Taking up questions of the travels of discourses of black internationalism requires investigating in particular the multiplicity of translation practices—and transnational coverage more generally—that are so crucial to the fabric of this transatlantic print culture. A significant subset of these practices is the bilingualism espoused so frequently by black periodicals in this period. In Europe, the *Negro Worker* circulated a mimeographed French edition; in New York, the *Negro World* published a French page edited by Theodore Stephens and a Spanish page edited by M. A. Figueroa; in Paris, a number of venues *(La Revue du monde noir, Les Continents, La Dépêche africaine)* tried to publish an English-language section. If translations are in the most basic sense the practice of linguistic connection—if, in other words, translation is one of the ways the "turbine" of the cultures of black internationalism is lubricated—then it is no coincidence that this situation caused such disproportionate consternation among French and British colonial authorities. In June 1928, to take one example, an internal correspondence from the political affairs branch of the French West African colonies to the Ministère des Colonies in Paris reported that *La Dépêche africaine,* published out of the French capital, had been reaching Senegal, Guinea, and the Ivory Coast. The administrator counseled that the relatively moderate periodical should continue on the list of "suspect publications" and added that *La Dépêche africaine,* "containing a page of articles in English, could be treated a priori much more rigorously than publications only in the French language."[22] In other words, black periodicals were a threat above all because of the transnational and anti-imperialist linkages and alliances they practiced: carrying "facts" from one colony to another, from the French colonial system to the British, from Africa to the United States.

This is not to claim that what follows is an exhaustive survey of these issues. I elaborate a limited set of U.S.-Francophone conjunctures that involve especial concentrations of exchange and translation (as in the links between *Les Continents* in Paris and *Opportunity* or the *Negro World* in New York), but one could pursue them just as fruitfully in a range of periodical contexts I hardly touch, whether the *Diario de la Marina* in Havana or *Justice* in Fort-de-France, *La Voix du Dahomey* in Cotonou or *Wasu* in London, *La Revue indigène* in Port-au-Prince or *Le Périscope africain* in Dakar.

In New York, one could turn also to the *Messenger*, whose early issues are likewise shot through with a pervasive concern with the potential of black internationalism.[23] Nor is this to claim that France and the French colonies are the *only* privileged site of black transnational interaction, exchange, and translation. It would be equally possible to investigate links between Harlem and Port-au-Prince during this period (when the United States was occupying Haiti), through the work of anthropologists such as Jean Price-Mars and Zora Neale Hurston and the correspondence of intellectuals and activists including James Weldon Johnson, Dantès Bellegarde, and Georges Sylvain. Or one could consider Liberia as a flash point for black internationalism, with scheming and heated squabbles among a number of intellectuals, including W. E. B. Du Bois, Marcus Garvey, George Schuyler, George Padmore, and the Haitian Léo Sajous. (Any given examples would overlap in different ways, of course: these two possible lines of inquiry underline the ways that in the interwar period, discourses about black *national* autonomy—especially as filtered through the passionate interest in the three independent black states, Haiti, Liberia, and Ethiopia—played a formative role in the formulation of black *internationalist* initiatives.)

Michel Foucault has suggested that the analysis of the archive involves a "privileged region" that is in fact the "border" *(bordure)* of the present we inhabit. The archive starts at the outside of our own social language practices *(langage)*, and thus reading it "deprives us of our continuities; it dissipates that temporal identity in which we are pleased to look at ourselves when we wish to exorcise the discontinuities of history." Reading the archive must not serve to buttress the pretensions and mystifications of the present self or the current community, in other words. The archive instead "establishes that we are difference, that . . . difference, far from being the forgotten and recovered origin, is the dispersion that we are and make."[24] If this book tracks such an edge of history, it hopes to trace in shadow the possibilities of adversarial internationalism in the current conjuncture. This book is written with "something of the fever and the fret"[25] of a moment when discourses of internationalism and globalization are resurgent, but the unending exploitation of the "darker peoples of the world" is too often ignored or dismissed fatalistically. In a time when the notion of an efficacious black internationalism seems but the pipe dream of a few haggard lobbyists and scattered radicals, this book attempts to hear the border of another future of black internationalism in the archive of its past.

Elsewhere I have noted the paradox that the term *diaspora* is not taken up in the cultures of black internationalism until the mid-1950s. I have attempted to sketch a genealogy of the term, an intellectual history of the reasons it is adopted at a particular moment in the African historiography of scholars such as George Shepperson and Joseph Harris.[26] That genealogy is not my task here. I do however take up the term *diaspora* in what follows as a term of analysis in the spirit of what I consider to be its particular intervention: it makes possible an analysis of the institutional formations of black internationalism that attends to their constitutive differences. Diaspora is a term that marks the ways that internationalism is pursued by translation. This is not to say that internationalism is doomed to failure, but instead to note that it necessarily involves a process of linking or connecting across gaps—a practice we might term *articulation*.

Stuart Hall's work offers the most suggestive theoretical elaboration of articulation in relation to the particular archive at stake here. His well-known 1980 essay "Race, Articulation, and Societies Structured in Dominance" attempts to theorize the function of difference in a global capitalist mode of production. To understand capitalist production on a "global scale," Hall writes (drawing on the work of Louis Althusser and Ernesto Laclau), that Marx began to theorize

> an articulation [*Gliederung*] between two modes of production, the one "capitalist" in the true sense, the other only "formally" so: the two combined through an articulating principle, mechanism, or set of relations, because, as Marx observed, "its beneficiaries participate in a world market in which the dominant productive sectors are already capitalist." That is, the object of inquiry must be treated as a complex articulated structure which is, itself, "structured in dominance."[27]

Articulation here functions as a concept-metaphor that allows us to consider relations of "difference within unity," non-naturalizable patterns of linkage between disparate societal elements. The functional "unity" of specific and strategically conjoined structures, then, is emphatically

> not that of an identity, where one structure perfectly recapitulates or reproduces or even "expresses" another; or where each is reducible to the other. . . .

The unity formed by this combination or articulation is always, necessarily, a "complex structure," a structure in which things are related, as much through their differences as through their similarities. This requires that the mechanisms which connect dissimilar features must be shown—since no "necessary correspondence" or expressive homology can be assumed as given. It also means—since the combination is a structure (an articulated combination) and not a random association—that there will be structured relations between its parts, i.e., relations of dominance and subordination.[28]

The notion of articulation is crucial not just because it combines the structural and the discursive but also because it has a flip side: such "societies structured in dominance" are also the ground of cultural resistance. Hall, following Antonio Gramsci, contends that ideology must be considered the key site of *struggle* over competing articulations.[29] In a transnational circuit, then, articulation offers the means to account for the diversity of black takes on *diaspora,* which Hall himself explicitly begins to theorize in the late 1980s as a frame of cultural identity determined not through "return" but through difference: "not by essence or purity, but by the recognition of a necessary heterogeneity and diversity; by a conception of 'identity' which lives with and through, not despite, difference."[30]

Another way to make this point is to note that a discourse of diaspora functions simultaneously as abstraction and as anti-abstraction. We have generally come to make recourse unquestioningly to its level of abstraction, grounding identity claims and transnational initiatives in a history of "scattering of Africans" that supposedly offers a principle of unity—as Paul Gilroy phrases it, "purity and invariant sameness"—to those dispersed populations.[31] I am arguing here neither to disclaim this history of dispersal nor to substitute another abstraction (an alternative principle of continuity, such as the oceanic frame offered by Gilroy's *Atlantic*). Instead, I am emphasizing the anti-abstractionist uses of *diaspora.* This is an ideological task that cannot be simply "won"—it is continually necessary to attend to the ways the term always can be re-articulated and abstracted into evocations of untroubled essentialism or inviolate roots. Read as an anti-abstractionist term, *diaspora* points to difference not only internally (the ways transnational black groupings are fractured by nation, class, gender, sexuality, and language) but also externally: in appropriating a term so closely associated with Jewish thought, we are forced to think not in terms of some closed or

autonomous system of African dispersal but explicitly in terms of a complex past of forced migrations and racialization—what Earl Lewis has called
a history of "overlapping diasporas."[32] The use of the term *diaspora,* I am
suggesting, implies neither that it offers the comfort of abstraction, an easy
recourse to origins, nor that it provides a foolproof anti-essentialism: instead, it forces us to articulate discourses of cultural and political linkage
only through and across difference in full view of the risks of that endeavor.

If a discourse of diaspora articulates difference, then one must consider the status of that difference—not just linguistic difference but, more
broadly, the trace or the residue, perhaps, of what resists or escapes translation. Whenever the African diaspora is articulated (just as when black
transnational projects are deferred, aborted, or declined), these social forces
leave subtle but indelible effects. Such an unevenness or differentiation
marks a constitutive *décalage* in the very weave of the culture, one that cannot be either dismissed or pulled out. Léopold Senghor has written suggestively about the differences and influences between U.S. blacks and African
blacks as spun out across such a gap:

> Le différend entre Négro-Américains et Négro-Africains est plus léger
> malgré les apparences. Il s'agit, en réalité, d'un simple décalage—dans
> le temps et dans l'espace.[33]

> Despite appearances, the difference between Negro-Americans and
> Negro-Africans is more slight. In reality it involves a simple *déca-
> lage*—in time and in space.

Décalage is one of the many French words that resists translation into
English; to signal that resistance and, moreover, to endorse the way that
this term marks a resistance to crossing over, I will keep the term in French
here.[34] It can be translated as "gap," "discrepancy," "time-lag," or "interval";
it is also the term that French speakers sometimes use to translate "jet lag."
In other words, a *décalage* is either a difference or gap in time (advancing or
delaying a schedule) *or* in space (shifting or displacing an object). I would
suggest, reading somewhat against the grain of Senghor's text, that there is a
possibility here in the phrase "in time *and* in space [italics added]" of a
"light" *(léger)* and subtly innovative model to read the structure of such unevenness in the African diaspora.

The verb *caler* means "to prop up or wedge" something (as when one leg on a table is uneven). So *décalage* in its etymological sense refers to the removal of such an added prop or wedge. *Décalage* indicates the reestablishment of a prior unevenness or diversity; it alludes to the taking away of something that was added in the first place, something artificial, a stone or piece of wood that served to fill some gap or to rectify some imbalance. This black diasporic *décalage* among African Americans and Africans, then, is not simply geographical distance, nor is it simply difference in evolution or consciousness; instead it is a different kind of interface that might not be susceptible to expression in the oppositional terminology of the "vanguard" and the "backward." In other words, *décalage* is the kernel of precisely that which cannot be transferred or exchanged, the received biases that refuse to pass over when one crosses the water. It is a changing core of difference; it is the work of "differences within unity,"[35] an unidentifiable point that is incessantly touched and fingered and pressed.

Is it possible to rethink the workings of "race" in the cultures of black internationalism through a model of *décalage?* Any articulation of diaspora in such a model would be inherently *décalé,* or disjointed, by a host of factors. Like a table with legs of different lengths, or a tilted bookcase, diaspora can be discursively propped up *(calé)* into an artificially "even" or "balanced" state of "racial" belonging. But such props, of rhetoric, strategy, or organization, are always articulations of unity or globalism, ones that can be "mobilized" for a variety of purposes but can never be definitive: they are always prosthetic. In this sense, *décalage* is proper to the structure of a diasporic "racial" formation, and its return in the form of *disarticulation*—the points of misunderstanding, bad faith, unhappy translation—must be considered a necessary haunting. This reads against the grain of Senghor, if one can consider his Négritude one influential variety of this diasporic propping up. Instead of reading for the *efficacy* of the prosthesis, this orientation would look for the *effects* of such an operation, for the traces of such haunting, reading them as constitutive to the structure of any articulation of diaspora.

Recall that Hall points out the word *articulation* has two meanings: "both 'joining up' (as in the limbs of the body, or an anatomical structure) and 'giving expression to.'"[36] He suggests that the term is most useful in the study of the workings of race in social formations when it is pushed away from the latter implication, of an "expressive link" (which would imply a predetermined hierarchy, a situation where one factor makes another "speak"), and toward its etymology as a metaphor of the body. Then the relationship between factors is not predetermined; it offers a more ambivalent, more elusive model. What does it mean to say, for example, that one *articulates a joint?* The connection speaks. Such "speaking" is functional, of course: the arm bends at the elbow to reach down to the table, the leg swivels at the hip to take the next step. But the joint is a curious place, as it is both the point of separation (the forearm from the upper arm, for example) and the point of linkage. Rather than a model of ultimate debilitation or of predetermined retardation, then, *décalage,* in providing a model for what resists or escapes translation through the African diaspora, alludes to this strange "two-ness" of the joint. It directs our attention to the "antithetical structure" of the term *diaspora,* its risky intervention. My contention, finally, is that articulations of diaspora demand to be approached this way, through their *décalage.* For paradoxically, it is exactly such a haunting gap or discrepancy that allows the African diaspora to "step" and "move" in various articulations. Articulation is always a strange and ambivalent gesture, because finally, in the body it is *only* difference—the separation between bones or members—that allows movement.

CHAPTER 1

VARIATIONS ON
A PREFACE

In December 1927, a Martinican student in classics at the Sorbonne named Jane Nardal wrote to Dr. Alain Locke at Howard University in Washington, D.C., requesting permission to translate his 1925 collection *The New Negro* into French. She had proposed the project to the Parisian publisher Payot and noted that her sister Paulette (who held a degree in English from the Sorbonne) would be assisting her in the preparation of the volume. The publisher and the Nardals had already agreed that *The New Negro* would have to be abridged for a French edition. She adds, "As an Afro-Latin [*en ma qualité d'Afro-Latine*], I was well positioned to tell him, on his request, the excerpts that might interest the French public, generally so out of touch with what is happening outside of France."[1] The letter asks Locke for advice about these choices, commenting optimistically: "For a book written by American Negroes to be translated by French Negroes, wouldn't that be an obvious sign of the workings of that Negro internationalism [*cet internationalisme noir en marche*] that Mr. Burghardt Du Bois speaks about so prophetically in his masterful exposé, 'Worlds of Color'?" Nardal is alluding to the essay that concludes *The New Negro*, "The Negro Mind Reaches Out," in which Du Bois sketches the possibility of an alliance of intellectuals of African descent that might "shadow" and speak against the creeping domination of European imperialism around the world. "Led by American Negroes," Du Bois writes, "the Negroes of the world are reaching out hands toward each other to know, to sympathize, to inquire."[2]

Locke responded favorably, offering to compose a new introduction for the French version. He adds that he would "gladly rewrite the whole thing in a connected story of the new movement of the American Negro Renaissance, using excerpts of poetry, short stories, and several folk tales. And I

Jane Nardal. From *La Dépêche africaine* 1 (February 1928). Bibliothèque Nationale, Paris.

send this as a counter proposal to you and M. Payot." In the meantime, he suggests, the Nardals might start—perhaps with the assistance of the Martinican novelist René Maran, with whom Locke had been corresponding for years—translating his prefatory essays in *The New Negro,* as well as some of the poems and Du Bois's piece, since all would "undoubtedly be included either in an abbreviated translation . . . or in what I would rewrite as a new book on this movement."[3]

Jane Nardal mentions in her letter that she would be able to publicize the translation through her connections to a number of Parisian newspapers, including *Le Soir* and *La Dépêche africaine,* a new periodical founded by a Guadeloupean named Maurice Satineau. In fact, she says, she has just written an essay for the latter's inaugural issue. But she neglects to inform Locke that her contribution to Satineau's paper—whose masthead trumpeted the subtitle "grande organe républicain indépendant de correspondence entre les Noirs" ("major independent republican journal of correspondence among Negroes")—was in fact the source of the phrase she used in describing Du Bois. Nardal's essay "L'internationalisme noir" appeared in February 1928, opening with a forceful invocation of the world-straddling political ambitions that emerged after World War I:

L'on abaisse ou plutôt l'on tente d'abaisser en cet après-guerre les barrières qui existent entre les pays. Les frontières, les douanes, les préjugés, les mœurs, les religions, les langues diverses permettront-ils jamais de réaliser ce projet? Nous voulons l'espérer, nous autres qui constatons la naissance dans le même temps d'un mouvement qui ne s'oppose nullement au premier. Des noirs de toutes origines, de nationalités, de mœurs, de religions différentes sentent vaguement qu'ils appartiennent malgré tout à une seule et même race.

In this postwar period, the barriers that exist between countries are being lowered, or are being pulled down. Will the diversity of frontiers, tariffs, prejudices, customs, religions, and languages ever allow the realization of this project? We would like to hope so, we who affirm the birth at the same time of another movement which is in no way opposed to the first. Negroes of all origins and nationalities, with different customs and religions, vaguely sense that they belong in spite of everything to a single and same race.[4]

Whereas previously, there had been only mutual miscomprehension—with the "more favored" populations in the Americas looking down on Africans as savages, and the Africans themselves thinking of New World blacks as no more than slaves, subjugated "cattle" *(bétail)*—in the 1920s another kind of consciousness began to become possible, Nardal claims, largely due to transnational circuits of expressive culture: the advent of the *vogue nègre* in France and the increasing popularity of the spirituals, jazz, and African art. She concludes her summary history with an espousal of the "birth of racial spirit" in the metropolitan Negro intellectual: "Dorénavant, il y aurait quelque intérêt, quelque originalité, quelque fierté à être nègre, à se retourner vers l'Afrique, berceau des nègres, à se souvenir d'une commune origine. Le nègre aurait peut-être à faire sa partie dans le concert des races où jusqu'à présent, faible et intimidé, il se taisait" ("From now on, there will be a certain interest, a certain originality, a certain pride in being black, in turning back toward Africa, cradle of the blacks, in recalling a common origin. The Negro will perhaps have to do his part in the concert of races, where until now, weak and intimidated, he has been silent").

In theorizing this *internationalisme noir,* however, Nardal is not willing to turn to a rhetoric of rootless racial belonging that would deny her background and upbringing—what her sister Paulette elsewhere termed her "Latin education" *(formation latine).*[5] And thus Jane Nardal turns to a neologism:

> A idées nouvelles, mots nouveaux, d'où la création significative des vocables: Afro-Américains, Afro-Latins. Ils confirment notre thèse tout en jetant une lueur nouvelle sur la nature de cet internationalisme noir. Si le nègre veut être lui-même, affirmer sa personnalité, ne pas être la copie de tel ou tel type d'une autre race (ce qui lui vaut souvent mépris et railleries) il ne s'ensuit pourtant pas qu'il devienne résolument hostile à tout apport d'une autre race. Il lui faut, au contraire, profiter de l'expérience acquise, des richesses intellectuelles, par d'autres, mais pour mieux se connaître, et affirmer sa personnalité. Etre Afro-Americain, être Afro-Latin, cela veut dire être un encouragement, un réconfort, un exemple pour les noirs d'Afrique en leur montrant que certains bienfaits de la civilisation blanche ne conduisent pas forcément à renier sa race.

> For new ideas, new words are required, and thus the meaningful creation of terms: Afro-Americans, Afro-Latins. These confirm our thesis while throwing a new light on the nature of this Negro internationalism. If the black wants to be himself, to affirm his personality, not to be the copy of some type of another race (as often brings him resentment and mockery), it still does not follow that he becomes resolutely hostile to any element from another race. On the contrary, he must profit from acquired experience, from intellectual riches, through others, but in order to better understand himself, to assert his own personality. To be Afro-American, to be Afro-Latin, means to be an encouragement, a comfort, an example for the Negroes of Africa by showing them that certain benefits of white civilization do not necessarily drive them to deny their race.

One notes the ingenuity of the term "Afro-Latin," which strikes an intriguing parallel to "Afro-American." The neologism is not a direct profession of loyalty to a nation-state or empire, but instead an appropriation of a wider cultural heritage of which republican France is a part. Oddly, though, it implies that "American" and "Latin" are parallel terms—apparently, as simultaneously regional and cultural distinctions within a broader Western space. Nardal does not espouse biological assimilation or miscegenation

("Afro-Americans" and "Afro-Latins" share a "racial" identity as *nègres*) but one of acculturation within a context of colony-metropole migration ("certain benefits of white civilization do not necessarily drive them to deny their race"). Although Jane Nardal was not a colonial apologist, as were many of the other contributors to *La Dépêche africaine,* her invention of "Afro-Latin" gives voice to a political moderation that she shared with the circle around Satineau's organization. She shies away from anything approaching Du Bois's fierce condemnation of colonial exploitation and racism, his flat pronouncement that "modern imperialism and modern industrialism are one and the same system."[6] As one might expect, Nardal's brand of *internationalisme noir* may be most closely attuned to the internationalist thread in the writings of Alain Locke—above all, in its emphasis on cultural exchange and in its persistent New World Negro vanguardism.

I open with Nardal's initiative not because it was successful. Although *The New Negro* in its original edition remained a touchstone text for Francophone intellectuals in the late 1920s and early 1930s, a full translation never appeared in French. In 1931, the leftist journal *Europe* finally published a version of Locke's introductory essay, now translated by Louis and Renée Guilloux, under the title "Le Nègre nouveau."[7] What I want to highlight is precisely the semantic shifts in this bilingual flood of racial appellations and adjectives, the transformations enacted through what Nardal terms "la création significative des vocables." Not a linear chain, but a field through which are carried signifiers of "racial identity": *New Negro, internationalisme noir, Afro-Latin, noirs américains, nègres, Afro-American, nègre nouveau.* I emphasize the multiplicity of this field to point out that in this regard, the practice of translation is indispensable to the pursuit of any project of internationalism, any "correspondence" that would connect intellectuals or populations of African descent around the world. If translation is a "poietic social practice that institutes a relation at the site of incommensurability," then reading the specifics of that practice are the only way to gauge the ensuing "relation" that is articulated across *décalage.*[8] This is also to point out that translation is not just the arena of any possible institutionalization of internationalism, but also the arena of ideological argument over its particular contours and applications.

To read this field, one must come to terms with the heterological slippage among vocables such as *nègre* and *noir.* What difference does it make to translate *The New Negro* as *Le Nègre nouveau* instead of *Le Nouveau noir?* Of course, a term such as *Negro* is already contested in English alone. Thus critics such as Henry Louis Gates, Jr., and Lawrence Levine have identified a struggle around the political valence of *New Negro* among U.S. black intellectuals in the 1920s: the socialist journal the *Messenger* espoused A. Philip Randolph's vision of an irrepressible, militant New Negro, while the journal *Opportunity* came to adopt a very different version of that phrase in the image of Alain Locke's cultural sophisticate.[9] But both these competing formations simultaneously insist on inflecting their differing definitions of the *New Negro* toward internationalism—whether the *Messenger's* socialist anticolonialism or *Opportunity's* "Talented Tenth" cosmopolitanism. In other words, to comprehend the internationalist aspirations among intellectuals of African descent after World War I, it is necessary to read evocations of *Negro* in the U.S. context next to the simultaneous debates around the applications and connotations of terms such as *nègre* in French. The space of any possible *internationalisme noir* is the place these (and other) contexts come into contact: in discrete if variable instances of translation.

To undertake such an inquiry is in part to follow the suggestions of Raymond Williams in the introduction to *Keywords* regarding one of the limitations of that work. Except in a few cases (as with the terms *alienation* and *culture*), Williams's book does not offer any comparative linguistic analysis of the "vocabulary" it sketches, what he calls the "shared body of words and meaning in our most general discussions, in English, of the practices and institutions which we group as *culture* and *society.*" Such comparative studies would be helpful, he admits, since "many of the most important words that I have worked on either developed key meanings in languages other than English, or went through a complicated and interactive development in a number of major languages."[10]

Characteristically, Williams lets that "we" drift, effectively allowing the contours of his envisioned community of vocabulary sharers to remain assumed, undefined, and uncontested. *Keywords* opens with another characteristic gesture: the invocation of Williams's "working class family in Wales," his service in the army, and his years studying at Cambridge. The common phrase "we just don't speak the same language" becomes in this field of experience the key to a consideration of the social dynamics of what might be termed the heteroglossia of "Englishness":

> When we come to say "we just don't speak the same language" we
> mean something more general: that we have different immediate val-
> ues or different kinds of valuation, or that we are aware, often intan-
> gibly, of different formations and distributions of energy and interest.
> In such a case, each group is speaking its native language, but its uses
> are significantly different, and especially when strong feelings or im-
> portant ideas are in question. No single group is "wrong" by any lin-
> guistic criterion, though a temporarily dominant group may try to
> enforce its own uses as "correct."[11]

But what if "we just don't speak the same language" is the literal—instead
of the figurative—ground of heteroglossia? It is to encounter a situation
where, indeed, "no single group is 'wrong' by any linguistic standard" but
any alliance across those differences (of values, of formations, of energy, of
interest, and of language itself) will be skewed by the peculiarities of interaction. It is to ask about the ramifications of semantic transformations in
such a situation, since as Williams comments elsewhere, pursuing such an
issue "across language" would demonstrate that "certain shifts of meaning
indicate very interesting periods of confusion and contradiction of out-
come, latencies in decision, and other processes of a real social history,
which can be located rather precisely in this other way, and put alongside
more familiar kinds of evidence."[12]

    The discontinuities and disjunctures in any translation, the unavoidable
skewing in any institutionalization of *internationalisme noir,* might be best
described not as predetermined failure but as the rich complexity of a modern cultural practice characterized above all by what Edouard Glissant calls
"detour." He suggests that populations formed through forced exportation
and exploitation are traumatically wrenched away from their habitual social
forms and into a specific kind of colonial context: not one formed by hostile incursion into a homeland, but one of "uprooting" *(déracinement).*
Glissant contrasts *retour* and *détour* as two strategic cultural responses to
such uprooting. "Return," he writes, "is the obsession with the One: one
must not alter being. To return is to consecrate permanence, non-rela-
tion."[13] Detour, on the other hand, is a turning away first of all from such
an obsession with roots and singular genealogy. In Glissant's words:

> Detour is the ultimate resort of a population whose domination by an
> Other is concealed: it then must search *elsewhere* for the principle of

domination, which is not evident in the country itself: because the mode of domination (assimilation) is the best of camouflages, because the materiality of the domination (which is not only exploitation, which is not only poverty, which is not only underdevelopment, but actually the complete eradication of the economic entity) is not directly visible. (32/20, modified)

The great utility of such a model is that it allows us to consider the work of figures such as Aimé Césaire and Frantz Fanon without recourse to simplistic models of expatriation and exile, working instead with a paradigm in which indirection can be functional—can indeed be strategically necessary in certain conditions.

Thus detour is helpful in considering the complexities of internationalism, the sometimes "camouflaged" dynamics of formations in which two or more differently positioned populations attempt to counter a transnational "system of domination"—one thinks back to Du Bois's phrase: the incursions of "modern imperialism and modern industrialism" in the broadest sense—by organizing around a common "elsewhere," a shared logic of collaboration and coordination at a level beyond particular nation-states. For intellectuals such as Nardal, Locke, and Du Bois, black internationalism aims to translate "race" as the vehicle of that detour, as the shared and shifting ground of that "elsewhere." Unfortunately, Glissant's discussion of detour in *Le Discours antillais* tends to fall back on the nation-state and the national community as the final points of entanglement, the end of the road. Admittedly, he writes, it is necessary to come to terms with the African roots of Martinican culture. And familiar modern black transnational projects—he cites Marcus Garvey's Back-to-Africa movement and Négritude—exemplify the necessity in detour to "go somewhere," in the ways that they usefully "link a possible solution of the insoluble to the resolution other peoples have achieved" (35/23). Still, these examples are "singular" evidence of the difficulties of moving beyond borders; as Glissant notes with irony, intellectuals such as Césaire, Fanon, and the Trinidadian radical George Padmore are much better known in Africa than in their home countries in the Caribbean—in other words, their detours are "camouflaged or sublimated variants of the return to Africa" (35/24). It requires "an intense effort of generalization" for Africans and Antilleans to share the common ground of some internationalist project, with the result that a formation such as the Négritude movement remained abstract, ineffectual, unable to "take particular situations into account."

This dismissal of the "generalizing" drive of detour is unfortunate, because it defuses the term's capacity as a tool to theorize the position of populations undergoing "modes of domination" that exceed the nation-state— whether continuing and pervasive patterns of conflict-driven refugee movement (in contemporary Central Africa, for instance), economically compelled migration (in Mexico or Haiti), marginalization or eradication on national frontiers (as with the Kurds or the Basques), and involuntary exile (as with the Palestinians or Algerian secular intellectuals and feminists). Glissant's wariness of "generalization" relegates such diverse transnational or extranational flows of populations to the status of exceptions—or what he terms, in the case of Fanon, the "radical break" *(coupure radicale)* with the properly national context (36/25). Glissant is careful not to claim that intellectuals such as Césaire and Fanon are irresponsible or "abstract," but there appears to be little use to their "generalizing":

> The plans [*tracés*] of Négritude and the revolutionary theory of *The Wretched of the Earth* are generalizing, however. . . . They illustrate and demonstrate the landscape of a shared Elsewhere. One must return to the site [*Il faut revenir au lieu*]. Detour is not a useful ploy unless it is nourished by return: not a return to the dream of origin, to the immobile One of Being, but a return to the point of entanglement [*point d'intrication*], from which one was forcefully turned away; that is where it is ultimately necessary to set to work the elements of Relation, or perish. (36/26, modified)

What appears unthinkable in this conclusion is the possibility that detour may be the only strategy in certain situations: that the *point d'intrication* may in fact be "elsewhere" rather than in what Glissant refers to as the "pays natal," the native homeland.

In what follows, I take up the role of a particular set of "elsewheres" in the formulation and translation of black internationalist initiatives during the 1920s and 1930s. To take one, Paris represents a different detour for African Americans (whether soldiers, musicians, artists, or the New Negro intelligentsia), for Antilleans, and for Africans. Traveling to Paris is obviously a detour for the African American, a voyage considered an escape (even if partial, even if temporary) from the outrages and frustrations of racism in the United States. But it must be considered another sort of detour even for the Francophone citizen or subject traveling from colony to metropole—if only because that move allows certain unpredictable kinds of boundary crossings and encounters. There is a multiple detour, in other words, in the way that, arguably more than anywhere in the world, Paris functions as a space of interaction among populations of African descent. In 1929, Franck Schoell argued in one of the first French-language overviews of the "Harlem Renaissance" that Paris had played a crucial role as transnational meeting ground:

> For it is France, it is England, it is Belgium that for a number of years have offered if not the first, then at least the most fruitful possibilities for real [*effectif*] contact among African blacks and American blacks [*Nègres d'Afrique et Nègres d'Amérique*]. If a Du Bois, a Langston Hughes has visited West Africa, it is through Europe that they passed to get there—in all the senses of the phrase. It is in the *quartier* of Pigalle and in the cafés of Montmartre, even in the cafés of Montparnasse, that the first encounters between Harlemites and Dahomeans were formed [*nouées*].[14]

Critics Tyler Stovall and Michel Fabre have more recently concurred that diasporic encounters possible in Paris were unparalleled in the interwar period.[15] Of course, some African Americans (including Du Bois and Hughes) went directly to West Africa in the 1920s, just as some Africans (Kwame Nkrumah and Kojo Tovalou Houénou, for example) went directly to the United States. Nevertheless, the European metropole was the privileged point of encounter, particularly in the small, ephemeral organizations and periodicals that sprung up throughout the interwar period in Paris and attempted to pursue internationalist alliances with similarly oriented groups in Harlem or in Kingston, in Fort-de-France or in Porto-Novo.

Translating the Word *Nègre*

If any *point d'intrication* is necessarily shared—necessarily also a crossroads, a point where linguistically and ideologically heterogeneous detours meet —then a consideration of the internationalist projects enabled in those meetings must begin by grappling with the semantic shifts and altered vocables they occasion. To gain a sense of the paleonomy of *Negro* and *nègre* in the context of American racism and European colonialism, one would have to turn to a work such as Jack Forbes's impressive study *Africans and Native Americans: The Language of Race and the Evolution of Red-Black Peoples,* a painstaking archival inquiry into the sedimentation of terms of racial designation through the period of slavery and colonization in the Americas.[16] Forbes's argument is far-reaching in its implications: after Columbus's nearly genocidal initial incursion, the process of re-populating the New World (especially throughout the Caribbean basin) was not characterized by the "replacement of Americans by Africans and African-European mixed-bloods" as has been often assumed, but instead by the incorporation of native Americans into the general slave population (269). This merging, Forbes argues, was concealed by the use of increasingly racialized terms of identity, which disenfranchised this "colored" labor force by imposing a "caste regime" system of social exclusion, thereby erasing what was in fact the highly varied background of populations throughout the Americas. Forbes informs us that he uses "the term 'American' for Indians in the colonial era and 'African' rather than 'negro' for presumably unmixed sub-Saharan Africans" (192); this basic premise must slowly but radically alter our sense of the phrase "African American" throughout his book.

Because *Africans and Native Americans* is structured around multi-linguistic etymological studies of the use of various racial terms (*negro, mulat(t)o, mestizo, pardo, loro, moor,* and *mustee*), the work is especially instructive about the historical relationship between *Negro* and *nègre*. In French, the first translations of African narratives of the early Spanish and Portuguese explorers and slave traders in the mid-sixteenth century almost exclusively used *noir* for the Spanish or Portuguese *negro* (meaning "black," the color), which was read as representing solely a color description. Only in the late 1500s and early 1600s did there begin to develop an understanding of *negro* that considered the term to represent a particular people and to mark their "difference." Other linguists including Simone Delesalle and Lucette Valensi have charted the way the word *nègre* came to be used in French to represent that specific alterity. As the French entered the slave trade (the Code Noir, the legal basis of the trade in France, was established in 1685), there developed an association between *nègre* and *esclave* ("slave") as synonyms, cemented in early dictionaries including Savary's *Dictionnaire universel de commerce* (1723), the work that single-handedly defined the French conception of Africans as a "race of slaves" in a phrasing copied in almost all the dictionaries of the next two hundred years.[17] Forbes argues that a crucial feature of the development of this logic of racialization was the invention of "miscegenation" terms such as *mulat(t)o, mestizo,* and *mulâtre,* which were used to extend the regime of exclusion and to control the access to civil rights and privileges (269). The spread of these terms over the next century served to impose racial difference as singular, distinguishing between only "black" Africans and "white" Europeans (125–130). The term *Negro* in English was adopted only relatively late from *negro* and *nègre* in Spanish and French, which were understood not as simple color designations but as variations on the term "slave" (84–85).[18]

Interestingly, in French the development of *nègre* had relatively little impact on the color designation *noir,* and thus we find French abolitionists adopting the latter term as a proper noun in the late eighteenth and early nineteenth century, attempting to invest it with connotations of humanity and citizenship. As Serge Daget notes, "With the word *Noir,* the abolitionist considered himself the master of a relatively new term, one which he would consider capable of introducing ideological substratums into his literature of combat."[19] This set of circumstances helps to explain the reasons black French citizens in the early twentieth century tended to describe themselves as "Noirs"—which indeed was second only to "hommes de couleur" as a self-designation among the elite. The connotations these terms held in the 1920s and 1930s has most famously been described by Frantz Fanon:

> The African, for his part, was in Africa the real representative of the black race [*la race nègre*]. As a matter of fact, when a boss made too great demands on a Martinican in a work situation, he would sometimes be told: "If it's a nigger [*nègre*] you want, go and look for him in Africa," meaning thereby that slaves and forced labor had to be recruited elsewhere. Over there, where the niggers [*nègres*] were.
>
> The African, on the other hand, apart from a few rare "evolved" [*évolués*] individuals, was looked down upon, despised, confined within the labyrinth of his epidermis. As we see, the positions were clear-cut: on the one hand, the black [*nègre*], the African; on the other, the European and the Antillean. The Antillean was a Negro [*noir*], but the black [*nègre*] was in Africa.[20]

In English, on the other hand, there is no such separation between *black* and *Negro,* both of which were taken after the Civil War to refer to a predominantly African-derived emancipated population, and both of which retained (in different degrees) the stereotypical baggage of *nègre* in French. In Forbes's account, this is due, again, to the pervasive "Africanization" of the slave population in the United States. Toni Morrison has described this process in terms of the U.S. literary imagination with the neologism "American Africanism," a phrase which indicates the common invocation of a "real or fabricated Africanist presence" as a means to consolidate the "white" citizen-subject in American fiction.[21] For Forbes, moreover, the civil rights initiatives of African American intellectuals and activists in the modern period do not serve to challenge the core assumptions of linguistic racialization—on the contrary they risk buttressing and even extending them (262). This is not to suggest that Forbes is consequently hostile to civil rights, but his work does make clear that the African American "legitimation by reversal"[22] of terms of racial designation during the 1920s and 1930s—one example is Du Bois's defense of the capitalized word "Negro" as a proper appellation—is a project fraught with risks.[23]

Let us return to the Francophone context after World War One. The very suggestion that the French word *nègre* translates English words such as *Negro* and *black* during the 1920s may seem odd, since one of the long-standing assumptions of Francophone literary criticism is that the noun *nègre* is not rehabilitated until much later. *Nègre* still had extremely negative connotations in the early 1920s, and a number of sympathetic French commentators refused to use the term at all. Thus Lucie Cousturier, who wrote a fascinating book about teaching French to West African soldiers stationed in Provence during the war, shudders at *nègre,* calling it an offensive word "that doesn't apply to real objects."[24] It is commonly supposed that Aimé Césaire is the first writer of African descent to claim the term *nègre* as a positive appellation: as one critic phrases it, Césaire "must be credited with being the first black intellectual outside Africa to have taken the humiliating term *nigger* and boldly transformed it into the proud term *black.*"[25] However, notwithstanding the remarkable intervention of Césaire's neologism "Négritude" on the eve of World War II, he is by no means the first to appropriate the noun *nègre.*

In January 1927, Lamine Senghor published an essay called "Le Mot 'Nègre'" (The word "Nègre") in the first issue of a newspaper call *La Voix des Nègres,* the organ of his group the Comité de Défense de la Race Nègre. Born on September 15, 1889, Senghor was the most charismatic and elo-

Lamine Senghor at the
Brussels Congress of the
League Against Imperial-
ism (February 1927).
From *Survey* 58, no. 9
(August 1, 1927).

quent black Marxist of the interwar era during the few years that he was active in the metropole. He apparently volunteered for service among the
West African recruits *(tirailleurs sénégalais)* in the French Army during
World War I and was gassed in action at the front. Repatriated to Senegal,
he moved again to France in 1921, working as a postal clerk and informally
auditing classes at the Sorbonne. By the summer of 1924, he had joined the
Union Intercoloniale, the unit of the French Communist Party that had
been formed to sponsor rebellion throughout the French colonies (other
members included the Antillean Max Clainville Bloncourt, the Haitian
Camille Saint-Jacques, Samuel Stéphany from Madagascar, Jacques
Barquisseau from the island of Reunion, the Algerian Hadj Ali Abdelkader,
and a young Indochinese intellectual named Nguyen Ai Quoc, who would
later be better known as Ho Chi Minh). Around this time, Senghor married a white Frenchwoman and had two children; although his family lived
in Fréjus, in the south of France, he spent most of his time working for radical causes in the capital.

In March 1926, sensing like the other African and Antillean members of

the Union Intercoloniale that the Party was paying too much attention to
the Riff war in Morocco and rebellions in Indochina, and too little to
struggles in West Africa and the Caribbean, Senghor left the Communist
Party to found the Comité de Défense de la Race Nègre (CDRN). *La Voix
des Nègres* published only two issues in January and March 1927 before
there occurred a split in the group between Senghor's supporters (the hard-
line activists and unbending anticolonialists committed to labor organizing) and a circle around Maurice Satineau, the Guadeloupean who would
found *La Dépêche africaine* the next winter. Senghor and Tiemoko Garan
Kouyaté brought together a new group called the Ligue de Défense de
la Race Nègre, which founded a new periodical called *La Race nègre*. In
February 1927, Senghor attended the inaugural congress in Brussels of
the League Against Imperialism, organized by the German Marxist Willi
Munzenberg (attendees included the Indian Jawarharlal Nehru, the Algerian Messali Hadj, the Barbadian Richard B. Moore, and Max Clainville
Bloncourt). There, Senghor gave a stunning, impassioned speech that was
highly influential and widely reprinted.[26] Senghor was arrested in 1927 in
Cannes for his agitation activities and imprisoned in Draguignan for part
of the spring. His war injuries, already quite serious, were aggravated during the imprisonment, and he died in November 1927 at his home in
Fréjus.[27]

Senghor's "Le Mot 'Nègre'" is an extraordinary and scathing analysis of
linguistic colonialism through the terminology of racialization in French.[28]
The word *Nègre*, Senghor opens, "is the dirty word of our times; it is the
word by which some of our race brothers no longer wish to be called." He
continues:

> [t]he dominators of the peoples of the *race nègre*, those who divided
> up Africa for themselves under the pretext of civilizing the *nègres*, are
> employing an abominable divisive maneuver in order to better reign
> over them. In addition to the primitive division of caste, of tribes and
> religions, which they exploit in their favor in our lands, the imperial-
> ists are working to break the very unity of the race so as to keep us
> eternally in the state of slavery where we have been held by force for
> centuries.
>
> To accomplish this, they are extracting two new words out of the
> word *nègre*, in order to divide the race into three different categories,

Première année N° 1.　　　　　LE NUMÉRO : 50 CENTIMES　　　　　JANVIER 1927

LA VOIX DES NÈGRES

Rédaction, Administration :
43, rue du Simplon
PARIS (18°)

ORGANE MENSUEL DU COMITÉ
DE DÉFENSE DE LA RACE NÈGRE

ABONNEMENTS
France et Colonies .. 3. » 6. »
Étranger .... 4. » 7. »

A TOUS NOS FRÈRES !
A TOUS LES NEGRES DU MONDE !
A TOUS LES HUMANITAIRES DU MONDE !
A TOUS CEUX QUI S'INTERESSENT A LA RACE NÈGRE !

Le Comité de Défense de la Race Nègre :

Considérant que parmi les déshérités de la terre d'Afrique ;

La Race Nègre qui forme la cinquième partie de la population du Globe, est la plus humiliée de toutes les races humaines ;

Que les centaines de millions d'hommes qui la composent sont un immense monde opprimé ;

Que toutes les nations africaines, anéanties au cours des siècles, doivent se relever et refleurir afin de réoccuper leur place dans les conseils de tous les peuples ;

Considérant que l'expérience démontre que l'émancipation des nègres sera l'œuvre des nègres eux-mêmes, que la lumière, le progrès et le colonialisme sont incompatibles ;

Que le premier principe de la dignité humaine est qu'elle est faite pour tous les hommes ;

A l'honneur de vous informer qu'il a pris l'initiative de publier à Paris LA VOIX DES NÈGRES.

Nous faisons un pressant appel à toutes et à tous. Que personne ne soit retenu par le doute de l'inutilité de ses efforts, car nul ne saurait mesurer l'étendue des son action dans cette œuvre :

LE COMITÉ.

LE MOT « NÈGRE »

C'est le gros mot du jour, c'est le mot que certains de nos *frères* de race ne veulent plus être appelés ainsi.

Les dominateurs des peuples de race nègre, ceux qui se sont partagé l'Afrique sous prétexte de civiliser les nègres, s'en piquent à une abominable manœuvre divisionnaire pour mieux régner chez eux. En plus de la division primitive de caste, de tribus et de religions, qu'ils exploitent et leur donnent au sein de nous-mêmes, les impérialistes s'emploient à briser l'unité même de la race pour nous maintenir éternellement dans l'état d'esclavage auquel nous sommes contraints par la force de rester depuis plusieurs siècles.

Pour arriver à cela, ils sortent du mot nègre deux autres mots nouveaux, afin de diviser la race en trois catégories différentes, savoir : « hommes de couleur », « noirs » — tout court — et nègres. On fait croire aux uns qu'ils sont des « hommes de couleur », et non noirs ni nègres (première catégorie) ; aux autres, qu'ils sont des « noirs » (deuxième catégorie). Quant aux « restes », ce sont des nègres (troisième catégorie).

Que veut dire « hommes de couleur » ? Nous affirmons que ce nom désigne tous les hommes de la terre. La preuve : il n'y a pas un seul homme, dans ce monde, qui ne soit pas d'une couleur ou de l'autre. Donc, nous ne pouvons prendre, pour nous seuls, ce qui appartient à tous. Et « noir » ? Pour le mot noir, nous ne croyons pas qu'il puisse servir pour désigner tous les nègres du monde. Étant donné que tous les nègres d'Afrique reconnaissent eux-mêmes qu'ils existe, dans divers points du continent, des nègres aussi blancs que certains blancs d'Europe, et qui n'ont de nègre que les traits et la chevelure. Nous refusons donc d'admettre que, sauf, ceux qui vivent aux fins fonds des brousses sénégalaises, ceux que l'on exploite dans la culture cotonnière de la vallée du Niger, les coupeurs de cannes à sucre dans les champs des domaines de la Martinique et de la Guadeloupe soient des nègres. Tandis qu'un de nos frères titulaire d'un brevet des écoles de hautes études européennes — l'intellectuel — serait un homme de couleur, et que celui qui n'a pu arriver à ce degré, mais qui exerce le même métier qu'un blanc et qui s'adapte comme les blancs à leur vie et à leurs mœurs et usages — l'ouvrier — serait un « noir » tout court.

Non, messieurs les diviseurs pour régner !

Permettez-nous de vous rappeler que les derniers sont les descendants des premiers.

Les jeunesses du C. D. R. N. se sont fait un devoir de ramasser ce nom dans la boue où vous le traînez, pour en faire un symbole. Ce nom n'est celui de notre race, nos droits et notre liberté ne nous appartiennent plus, nous nous cramponnons sur ce qui, avec l'éclat de la couleur épiderme sont les seuls biens qui nous restent de l'héritage de nos aïeux. Ce nom est à nous ; nous sommes à lui ! Il est nôtre comme nous sommes siens ! De là, avec nettons tout notre honneur et toute notre foi de défendre notre race. Oui, messieurs, vous avez voulu voulu servir de ce nom comme mot d'ordre scissionniste. Voilà pour vous comme mot d'ordre de ralliement : le flambeau ! Nous nous faisons honneur et gloire de nous appeler Nègres, avec un N majuscule en tête. C'est notre race nègre que nous voulons guider sur la voie de sa libération totale du joug esclavagiste qu'elle subit. Nous voulons imposer le respect dû à notre race, ainsi que son égalité avec toutes les races du monde, ce qui est son droit et notre devoir, et nous appelons Nègres!

Le Comité.

Ce qu'est notre Comité
de Défense de la Race Nègre

Certains journaux français et étrangers ont demandé à plusieurs reprises ce qu'était le « Comité de Défense de la Race Nègre ». Pour satisfaire leur curiosité, notre secrétaire général a eu deux fois l'occasion de déposer sur les bureaux de l'agence Havas, à Paris, une *déclaration officielle du Comité* (juillet 1920) et un ordre du jour voté par notre assemblée générale du 31 octobre 1926 à Paris, mais nous constatons avec regret que ces quêteurs de nouvelles ont préféré garder le silence plutôt que de publier ces deux notes.

Cependant, quelques journaux français ont voulu, le 1er novembre dernier (le lendemain de notre assemblée générale), à tout prix, donner des renseignements (à leur façon) à leurs lecteurs sur ce qu'ils croyaient être notre Comité. L'*Écho de Paris* est fait plus particulièrement remarquer ; ce journal nous gratifie d'un esprit du pur nationalisme français en publiant : « Les nègres sont des Français et veulent servir la France... » (?). Or, rien n'est aussi faux que cette affirmation ! Les nègres ne sont d'aucune nationalité européenne et ne veulent servir les intérêts d'aucun impérialisme contre un autre impérialisme.

Au sein du Comité de Défense de la Race Nègre, il n'y a pas de distinction entre les nègres soumis au joug de l'impérialisme français [...] nous sommes tous des frères du fait d'un esclavage [...] nous subissons le même sort (sous différentes formes, bien entendu) esclavagiste par l'impérialisme international.

« *L'esclavagisme est aboli* », crie-t-on à travers l'univers.

Voyons cela ! Les colonialistes internationaux se sont emparés de nos territoires et de nous-mêmes ; puis, ils se les ont partagés. Pendant plusieurs siècles, ils se sont livrés à la traite des nègres, en nous vendant au nom acheteur comme de la marchandise. Aujourd'hui, ils prétendent avoir aboli l'esclavage cependant qu'ils s'octroient « démocratiquement » — les droits de vendre et d'acheter un peuple tout entier sans demander l'avis de ce dernier... Quelle hypocrisie ! Quel mensonge ! La vérité est que le nom se débat et que les nègres sont la vente en gros est permise, mais tandis que la vente au détail est interdite.

C'est contre toutes ces iniquités que nous nous sommes groupés, sans distinction de nationalité ethnique ni de nationalité de nos maîtres, pour combattre la haine de race, démontrer à tous ceux qui nous opprime qu'à l'envi de ce que nous sommes capables de faire et que nous ne pas avoir moins d'autres dignes d'être, en société, faisant ne pas venir droit à l'égalité à toucher du doigt notre droit d'égalité à tous.

[...] les races humaines. Pour ne pas salir cette noble œuvre, nous refusons catégoriquement de servir les ambitions d'une nation colonisatrice quelconque, car nous sommes toujours les victimes, en fin de compte !

Les jeunesses nègres, réunies au sein du Comité de Défense de la Race Nègre ont la ferme volonté de suivre la voie que leur ont tracée les milliers de nègres conscients et de blancs humanitaires qui ont hésité, devant le sacrifice de leur vie, de leur fortune et, très souvent, de leur liberté, pour la libération totale et l'émancipation de la race nègre. Ils sauront donc être solidaires les uns des autres pour mener la lutte contre le régime spécial auquel leur race est soumise, sans toutefois perdre de vue que tous les blancs ne sont pas des impérialistes et que des colonisateurs. Ils feront au contraire voir à l'unité que ils savent combien leur sort est lié avec celui des milliers de travailleurs manuels et intellectuels des nations européennes.

Les jeunesses patriotes de la Race (Alpes-Maritimes), à leur assemblée générale du 6 novembre dernier ont consacré tout leur temps sur la nécessité d'étendre leur propagande sur les réservoirs d'hommes, c'est-à-dire sur les colonies françaises. Ah ! Quel retard ! Ils ne songent pas que les nègres auront maintenant, aussi bien qu'eux, le rôle lamentables que l'on voudrait leur faire jouer [...]

[...] leur propre pays, leurs propres nationaux. Et bien, non ! Les nègres ne marcheront pas. Ils sont l'unique fauteur de la misère universelle : l'impérialisme international.

En résumé, le Comité s'est assigné :
1° La tâche de combattre avec la dernière énergie *la haine de race* ;
2° Travailler pour l'évolution sociale de la Race Nègre ;
3° Refuser de renforcer l'appareil d'oppression dans les colonies dirigé contre la Race Nègre ou contre toute autre race humaine, et travailler à briser plutôt cet appareil ;
4° Collaboration permanente avec les organisations qui luttent véritablement pour la libération des peuples opprimés et pour la révolution mondiale.

Enfin et pour tout : Lutte sans merci contre le colonialisme, contre tous les impérialistes du monde, de quelque couleur soient-ils.

L. SENGHOR,
*Président du Comité de Défense
de la Race Nègre.*

Nègres, en garde !

Nos adversaires, nos ennemis nous guettent. Tout sera utilisé pour empêcher votre Comité, si bien parti de se développer.

Leurs moyens sont nombreux. Le premier, le principal, faire le silence sur votre organisation, silence presque général de la presse. De bouche à oreille, la calomnie. Infiltration dans nos rangs d'éléments de désagrégation. Voilà pour les principaux et contre lesquels vous tiendrez en garde.

Nègres! la lutte sourde et méprisable de nos ennemis est pour vous un sûr garant que nous sommes dans la bonne voie.

Groupons-nous plus que jamais autour de notre Comité et à la honte de ceux qui font la conspiration du silence, nous vaincrons toutes les difficultés et le triomphe est certain.

LE BUREAU EXÉCUTIF.

CIVILISATION !

Il paraît que l'occupation de l'Afrique noire n'a été faite que dans un but de civilisation. Parmi les bienfaits apportés, il y a celui de servir sous les drapeaux de la « Patrie d'adoption ». Cet honneur nous l'avons connu pendant la grande guerre et nous savons ce qu'il nous a coûté. On a brogé du non de paquets. M. Diagne et le général Mangin en connaissent quelque chose ; Ils ont aussi contribué au recrutement ! Mais il est bon de rappeler les moyens employés, pour bien situer le sens réel de cette « civilisation » tant vantée par les civilisateurs, et nous publions, sans commentaires, des extraits du rapport d'un administrateur colonial.

Les faits qu'il relate ont été publiés [...]

namely: *"hommes de couleur," "noirs"*—simply—and *Nègres.* The former are made to believe that they are *"hommes de couleur"* and neither *noirs* nor *nègres* (first category); the others are made to believe that they are *"noirs"* simply and not *nègres* (second category). As for the "leftovers" [*Quant aux "restes"*], they are *nègres* (third category).

There are a number of remarkable moves in this passage. First, rather than contesting or historicizing the term itself, Senghor starts by assuming *la race nègre* to be a valid descriptive. *Nègre* is in fact the unmarked category here, in linguistic terms. Thus *"hommes de couleur"* ("men of color") and *"noirs"* are marked off by quotation marks as colonial impositions, terms that "divide and conquer." The analysis understands these terms to be related in a socially imposed hierarchy that achieves through nominalized racialization what Forbes calls a "caste" system of exclusion "with each successive layer from top to bottom experiencing a greater degree of exclusion than the one above it."[29]

The essay's schema breaks down the function of an imposed tripartite system of racialized designation in French colonization. In this sense, it is especially notable that Senghor does not dawdle in the then-current debates around assimilation. He refrains from an attack against collaborationist politicians such as the legislators Blaise Diagne and Gratien Candace—who commonly insisted they were "Black Frenchmen" *(noirs français)*—or reformist defenders of the empire such as Maurice Satineau (when he left the CDRN, Satineau founded a group significantly named the Comité de Défense des Intérêts de la Race *Noire*). Senghor instead wrenches open the chromaticism of *"hommes de couleur"* and *"noir"* with more than a little humor, not to squabble but to close ranks. He contends that even persons claiming to fall under those "extracted" categories are actually *nègres:*

What does *"hommes de couleur"* mean? We contend that this name designates all the men of the earth. The proof: there isn't a single man in the world who is not of one color or another. Thus, we cannot take for ourselves alone what belongs to all. And *"noir"?* We do not think that the word *"noir"* can serve to designate all the *nègres* in the world, given that all African *nègres* recognize with us that there exist, in various points of the continent, *nègres* as white as some European whites, *nègres* who have nothing *nègre* aside from their features and hair. We thus refuse to admit that only those who live in the depths of the

Senegalese jungle, those who are exploited in the cotton fields of the Niger valley, the sugarcane cutters in the plantation fields of Martinique and Guadeloupe, are *nègres*. Whereas one of our brothers holding a diploma from a European institution of higher learning would be a *homme de couleur*, and another who hasn't reached that level, but who works the same job as a white man and who adapts like white men to their life and their customs—the worker—would be simply a *"noir."*

No, Mr. Divide-and-Conquer!

Senghor closes with a clarion call to arms around exactly that term which had been the most derogatory designation for African diasporic populations under colonialism and slavery:

> The youth of the Comité de Défense de la Race Nègre have made it their duty to take this name out of the mud where you are dragging it, so as to make of it a symbol. This name is the name of our race. Our lands, our rights and our liberty no longer ours, we cling to that which, along with the radiance of our skin color, is all that remains of the inheritance of our ancestors. . . . Yes, sirs, you have tried to use this word as a tool to divide. But we use it as a rallying cry: a torch! [*Nous, nous en servons comme mot d'ordre de ralliement: un flambeau!*] We do ourselves honor and glory by calling ourselves *Nègres,* with a capital N. It is our *race nègre* that we want to guide on the path of total liberation from its suffering under a yoke of enslavement. We want to demand the respect due to our race, as well as its equality with all the other races of the world, as is its right and our duty, and we call ourselves *Nègres!*

Christopher Miller has pointed out that in the way it reclaims *Nègre,* a word dragged in the mud of history, this argument is a "space-clearing gesture" that is "radical in the etymological sense: it attacks the roots of domination."[30] The strategy is not to undo the term's naturalized racialism (*Nègre* is still "the name of our race") but to "rally" and realign the term in the ideological "service" (*nous, nous en servons comme mot d'ordre de ralliement)* of a new anti-imperialist solidarity.

With a sense of the complexity of this field of signifiers, we are left with the question: how would we translate *Nègre* in Senghor's usage into English? Turning to contemporary literature in English, one thinks of Du Bois's propaganda campaign to capitalize *Negro*—but is this term then equivalent to Senghor's capitalized *Nègre?* One might also think of Carl Van Vechten's 1926 *Nigger Heaven* (translated into French as *Le Paradis des Nègres*), a novel that caused considerable controversy not only because its author was white, but also because of its title, with readers debating whether the phrase was simply an intentionally outrageous advertising ploy or an "honest" attempt to employ *nigger* as a "non-derogatory" appellation for African American urban characters.[31] Another work to note is U.S. Southern writer Roark Bradford's 1928 *Ol' Man Adam an' His Chillun,* a collection of folktales in which we encounter a seemingly similar three-tier typology of the African American population.[32] In the foreword to this "personal study of the black race," Bradford notes that he has somewhat informally "divided it into three general groups: The 'nigger,' the 'colored person,' and the Negro—upper case N."[33] Again, we are presented with a hierarchy, but here uncritically as a natural typology of the race—invested with all the familiar paternalistic baggage of stereotypes. So the "Negro" "is . . . a man of character and understanding who realizes that his people could not possibly have acquired in two hundred years the same particular brand of civilization that the white people built up in thousands of years," whereas the "colored person" is simply "tragic," "neither fish nor fowl."[34] The "nigger," as one might expect, interests Bradford "more than the rest." Rather than Senghor's biting etymology, we are offered an abstract litany of "traits": the "nigger" is uninterested in work but highly loyal, irresponsible but responsive to any stimuli, intuitively and endlessly creative within the confines of a fading rural folk culture.[35] Do the *niggers* in Van Vechten and Bradford (not necessarily the same figures, of course) jibe with Senghor's *Nègre,* a more or less rehabilitated term of derision?

It should be evident that it is difficult to match up any such hierarchy of social usage in the two contexts. I will risk constructing a shorthand, as follows: in the interwar period, the various ideological accentuations of this group of signifiers share a ground-level connotation that *Negro* in English functions most like *noir* in French (both are adopted by assimilationists and civil rights activists; both aim at a certain "respectability" on the national front). At the same time, the function of *nègre* in French—while not unlike that of *nigger* in English—may be closest to the word *black,* a derogatory appellation in the 1920s (both are terms that populist radicals such as

Lamine Senghor in French and Marcus Garvey in English were keen to re-habilitate in the service of a certain nationalism). The best "translation" of *nègre,* though, might not be a literal translation at all, but a linguistic nu-ance, an effect achieved in a particular nongeneralizable discursive instance. Consider this anecdote from Langston Hughes's autobiography *The Big Sea,* a hilarious recounting of his encounter with the woman who would re-place him as an English teacher in Mexico:

> Professor Tovar had neglected to tell the new teacher that I was an *americano de color,* brown as a Mexican, and nineteen years old. So when she walked into the room with him, she kept looking around for the American teacher. No doubt she thought I was one of the stu-dents, chalk in hand, standing at the board. But when she was in-troduced to me, her mouth fell open, and she said: "Why, Ah-Ah thought you was an American."
>
> I said: "I am American!"
>
> She said: "Oh, Ah mean a white American!" Her voice had a south-ern drawl.
>
> I grinned.
>
> At the end of the first day, she said: "Ah never come across an edu-cated Ne-gre before." (Southerners often make that word a slur be-tween *nigger* and *Negro.*)
>
> I said: "They have a large state college for colored people in Arkan-sas, so there must be some educated ones there."
>
> She said: "Ah reckon so, but Ah just never saw one before." And she continued to gaze at me as her first example of an educated Negro.[36]

Hughes's cutting commentary on the woman's racism is coy and formalis-tic. His phonetic transcription of her accent simply relegates her first per-son singular to the level of a stammer ("Ah-Ah"), and that record of her idi-ocy defuses any derogatory force her slurred "Ne-gre" might have carried. But as an accentuation "between *nigger* and *Negro,*" "Ne-gre," as described by Hughes, places its nominal force close to that of *nègre* in French both phonetically and ideologically.

Some of the most intriguing moments in the interwar period occurred when these racialized terms were re-accentuated back toward what Forbes describes as their "originary" sense of "multi-raciality," alluding to the mixture of disenfranchised populations in transatlantic patterns of dispersion. What is perhaps most suggestive about this occurrence is that it established a means of historicizing transnational formations, or as Gayatri Spivak puts it, "'inter-nationalizing' subalternist work from below."[37] Thus when Forbes cites the 1854 case where the California State Supreme Court "sought to bar all non-Caucasians from equal citizenship and rights" by creating a catchall term "Black," a designation designed to include not just all "Negroes" but also all the other "non-white" races as well, we should read this term in subtle resonance with the uses of "Black" to refer to Africans, Caribbeans, and Southeast Asians in post-World War II Britain—uses which have made possible at certain moments during the past twenty years a number of progressive "inter-national" alliances there.[38] This historical etymology should also resonate when we attempt to come to terms with current usage in France, where interestingly enough, the chosen self-designation of the younger generation of Africans and Antilleans is sometimes *les Noirs,* but just as often *les blacks*—a term adopted from English in the past thirty years.

Likewise, there may be similar possibilities in the history of French usage of *nègre,* an epithet that at isolated moments during the history of the French Empire was applied liberally to a variety of populations. It should be clear that Lamine Senghor's claiming of the word *Nègre* is not an argument for *return,* in Glissant's terminology. It does not propose a usable originary blackness or a single African identity, but instead begins by accepting the historical fact of colonization and the contemporary racialized ideologies of exploitation in order to construct an appeal for solidarity. What's fascinating is that other Francophone radicals were at certain moments going even further: attempting to wrench the term *nègre* into the service of anti-imperialist alliances among what W. E. B. Du Bois called "the darker peoples of the world."

One instance is the contribution by Martinican poet and schoolteacher Gilbert Gratiant to the single issue of the journal *L'Etudiant noir,* which appeared in March 1935. Apparently the young students who were assembling *L'Etudiant noir* (including Aimé Césaire and Léopold Sédar Senghor) asked Gratiant to write a response to the attacks that had been launched against him, especially in the predecessor student journal *Légitime Défense* (1932). His essay, "Mulâtres . . . pour le bien et le mal," is ultimately a defense of his unique political position and his own understanding of "creole" culture in the French Caribbean.[39] Gratiant clarifies that in writing about creole culture, he is not at all denying the African roots of the "black soul" (*âme nègre*) and the importance of African cultural forces in present-day Antillean life. He does argue, however, that the Caribbean is a mixed-race population from the beginning and that its cultural issues cannot be neatly packaged using inapplicable racialist dividing lines. The word *nègre,* Gratiant contends, has no "real" referent in some population linked by common roots. It can be employed only as a discursive strategy, an act of language to mark certain historical and material relations of domination and suffering. The position is significant, not least because Gratiant articulates it from a strong Marxist standpoint (specifically commending the work in Paris of the Communist Party–affiliated journal, *Le Cri des Nègres*). He advises conserving the use of *nègre* for that revolutionary context, which goes beyond a racial designation:

> [I]f the fact of proclaiming: *I am nègre!* [*je suis nègre!*] is the record of the limited historical fact I have tried to analyze, then I proclaim it, but that proclamation has no value elsewhere. If one wants to understand thereby that, recognizing that there subsists in me a *nègre* soul, in its creole form, or more vaguely in its unawakened forms, I am publicly paying tribute to that wonderful fact, I cry with a joyful wonder: *je suis nègre,* but the cry is not an exclusive one and my joy is just as deep at feeling myself a Martinican mulatto or just simply French in Vendômois, the Vendômois of the sweet Loire valley, that of my childhood, my friends, my brother's daughters. If, with this cry launched in defiance, one wants to understand a courageous and vehement support for the cause of the persecuted, my brothers in opprobrium whose skin is black, martyrs of race hatred, martyrs of villainous imperialisms: then I show my solidarity and shout: *je suis nègre!*[40]

In this limited sense, Gratiant accepts the word being brandished by the young students. But he refuses to take up what he sees as its racialist mystifications: even in underlining the survivals of African cultural forms in the French Caribbean, Gratiant insists on the other forces and factors that have shaped "creole" identity. But if the word *nègre* is a term of "solidarity" that is not essentialist, that is "not exclusive," then it allows something beyond a racial nationalism: for Gratiant, it is the lever of an anti-imperialist rallying cry that is articulated as an internationalism, a "support for the cause of the persecuted" in a more generalizable sense.

The Frame of Blackness

Claiming the term *nègre,* investing it with particular signifying content, and then deploying it as a link to another context (using it to translate *Negro,* for instance) are clearly practices with implications that go beyond the "simply" linguistic. In a larger sense, these are all *framing* gestures. Thus the divergent interventions of Lamine Senghor and Gilbert Gratiant, for example, do not just *define* the word *nègre.* They also frame it: positioning, delimiting, or extending its range of application; articulating it in relation to a discursive field, to a variety of derived or opposed signifiers *(homme de couleur, noir);* fleshing out its history of use; and imagining its scope of implication, its uses, its "future." It is not coincidental that the interventions I have outlined so far take place in a particular limited range of sites within print culture, sites that imply a certain transitionality or instability if not rupture. Framing gestures work the edges, in other words: in the manifesto, in the impassioned response or open letter, in the broadside, in the editorial or position paper that stakes out ground in the inaugural issue of a newspaper. In the 1920s and 1930s, they emerge most emphatically in concerted efforts to "preface blackness" in all the senses of that phrase, particularly in introductions to books, collections, and anthologies.[41] As David Scott has recently noted, an introduction *"frames* a text by *placing* it in relation to its conditions of enunciability, and in relation to the system of discursivity that governs the production and organization of its statements. An introduction shows how a text occupies a certain space of problems, a particular context of questions, a distinctive domain of arguments. In short, it shows what the relations are to that background of knowledge—the archive—that sustains it."[42] Here I will briefly elaborate this broader sense of framing race, in order to argue that internationalist initiatives during the interwar period make recourse to certain strategies of literary formalism—and in particular, to certain practices of the preface.

Literary critics and historians including Robert Stepto, Henry Louis Gates, Jr., John Blassingame, and William Andrews have demonstrated in work on the slave narrative tradition in the nineteenth century that the emergence of African American narrative involves an inescapable grappling with the politics of literary form. Narratives by former slaves were a persistently *framed* mode of production: they are almost always supported and sometimes suffocated by a mass of documentary and verifying material serving to "authenticate" the Negro subject's discourse by positioning and explicating it. This material includes prefaces and postfaces from prominent abolitionists, the signature of the former slave on the frontispiece, photographs, avowed and unavowed editorial addendums and elisions, guarantees and testimonials to the former slave's upstanding character, ancillary tales or narratives, appended letters, and explanatory notes.[43] In particular, Stepto's 1979 study *From behind the Veil* argues convincingly that the representation of the black modern subject relies on the control over the framing apparatus even after the slave narratives, as works including Booker T. Washington's *Up from Slavery* (1901), Du Bois's *The Souls of Black Folk* (1903), James Weldon Johnson's *The Autobiography of an Ex-Colored Man* (1912), and Ralph Ellison's *Invisible Man* (1952) represent a variety of "archetypes" of black identity through the manipulation of framing structures and especially prefatory material.

On the one hand, Du Bois's *The Souls of Black Folk* attains this effect through a set of operations one might term "allegories of reading," which articulate the various levels of the text—their shifting, carefully calibrated points of entry to an "inside" marked as "Negro"—in a manner that stands in for social and epistemological access to the multiple layers and "deeper recesses" of the "world in which ten thousand thousand Americans live and strive." Thus it is on the textual border, in the book's "Forethought," that Du Bois announces that "herein lie buried many things which if read with patience may show the strange meaning of being black here in the dawning of the Twentieth Century."[44] At the same time, the book draws not just on formal strategies of the "authenticating frame" but also on the figurative rhetoric characteristic of the slave narratives. The most obvious example is the trope of the "veil." This trope does not commence with Du Bois but in fact recurs throughout the slave narrative tradition, in works by Frederick Douglass, Olaudah Equiano, Harriet Jacobs, and Mary Prince, usually deployed at moments of great narrative stress to mark the excesses of slavery that are in some sense "unspeakable." The veil is a metaphor for a particular kind of border, both rhetorical and moral. Toni Morrison, whose 1987 novel *Beloved* may indeed be read as a more recent elaboration of this same inherited trope, has discussed the veil's prevalence and its implications as a particular kind of silence that shapes the tradition: "Over and over, the writers pull the narrative up short with a phrase such as, 'But let us drop a veil over these proceedings too terrible to relate.' In shaping the experience to make it palatable to those who were in a position to alleviate it, they were silent about many things, and they 'forgot' many things. There was a careful selection of the instances that they would record and a careful rendering of those that they chose to describe."[45]

The Souls of Black Folk rearticulates the trope of the veil to indicate the frontier of a black counterculture of modernity in a manner that allows the text to authenticate itself—to invest the narrator's first person with authority over that social and epistemological boundary. As the "Forethought" announces: "Leaving, then, the world of the white man, I have stepped within the Veil, raising it that you may view faintly its deeper recesses,—the meaning of its religion, the passion of its human sorrow, and the struggle of its greater souls."[46] For Stepto, Du Bois's text not only puts pressure on its joints in this way, but also multiplies its framing gestures into an "orchestration" of every possible register.[47] Thus the "Forethought" and "Afterthought" are echoed at another level by the epigraphic structure of each chapter, where the prose is preceded by an ambiguous pairing of a quote from a European-language poem and a fragment of a musical score of a Negro spiritual (without the lyrics).[48] *The Souls of Black Folk,* which manipulates many kinds of data, facts, and evidence about blackness and which "weaves" together "varying modes of formal writing, including historiography, autobiography, eulogy, and . . . fiction," is a "new way of thinking about documentary writing and about what constitutes authenticating evidence."[49] The book continually shifts the epistemology of race through its complex layering of frames.

Many critics have noted the debts of James Weldon Johnson's 1912 *The Autobiography of an Ex-Colored Man* to Du Bois's work.[50] I would add that the importance of the novel is intimately linked to the ways it applies and revises the framing strategies of *The Souls of Black Folk. The Autobiography* is the "first sophisticated structural exploration," as Richard Yarborough has suggested, "of the generic fluidity underlying much of Afro-American autobiographical writing . . . and the first successful attempt to exploit this generic fluidity as an apt representation of the psychological tensions . . . inherent in the black experience."[51] One might push this insight even further and note that the novel explores this "generic fluidity" most prominently through a reformulation of the relation between preface and text.

Like the "Forethought" to *The Souls of Black Folk,* the preface to *The Autobiography* promises sociological facts and documentation to come in the text: it claims that the book will be a "human document," one which "shows in a dispassionate, though sympathetic, manner conditions as they actually exist between whites and blacks today."[52] It takes up the trope of the veil as well, marking a textual border as allegory: "In these pages it is as though a veil has been drawn aside: the reader is given a view of the inner life of the Negro in America, is initiated into the freemasonry, as it were, of the race" (xl). But this preface (written by Johnson, but signed "The Publishers")—combined with the novel's anonymous publication—signals a small but crucial shift of authority.[53] The Negro world is not a "prison-house" as it is described in *The Souls of Black Folk,* nor is "double consciousness" at once a gift and a deprivation that is conferred or imposed from without.[54] Instead, it is the white readership that is shut out, and which must by implication undergo a transformation, an initiation "into the freemasonry" of the Negro race, in order to cross what now seems to be a much more unsettling frontier. The sensationalism has been inverted, in other words—the book offers not the thrill of access to a "veiled" world, but the threat of incomprehension, of indistinguishable limits. So the preface here is not a door or frontier, but a kind of parodic "hinge" both opening and closing an "impossible text." As Aldon Nielsen describes it, *The Autobiography of an Ex-Colored Man* "produces the impossibility of a stable reading of its own narrative as exemplary of the instability, the impossibility, of American racial definition."[55] As in George Schuyler's 1931 novel *Black No More,* sociology becomes a kind of joke on the reader, since the "color line" is exposed not as a tragic American fact but as the paradigmatic American fiction. When the narrator comments near the end of *The Autobiography* that he is "an ordinarily successful white man who has made a little money" (211), one realizes that Johnson's novel is less a revelation of "veiled" blackness than a critical exposure of normative American "whiteness." In the end, the narrative is nothing other than what Nielsen calls "the tale of the creation of an ordinary white man."[56]

It is sometimes overlooked that the rearticulation of framing strategies in *The Autobiography of an Ex-Colored Man* is anchored not just in the form of the novel but also by its transatlantic journey out of the nation-space. Although the preface promises a "vivid and startlingly new picture of conditions brought about by the race question in the United States" (xxxix), the unnamed narrator's most trenchant epiphany about race takes place during a trip to Europe with his wealthy patron. At the beginning of chapter 9, on the ocean liner to the old continent, the narrator comments that the ship "ran in close proximity to a large iceberg. I was curious enough to get up and look at it, and I was fully repaid for my pains. The sun was shining full upon it, and it glistened like a mammoth diamond, cut with a million facets. As we passed, it constantly changed its shape; at each different angle of vision it assumed new and astonishing forms of beauty" (126–127). It is as though the reader is being offered an optic image to replace the binarism and simplicity of the veil—a reminder that the "color line" must be comprehended in its subtle "facets" (and in international waters). It is a "constantly changing," "mammoth" whiteness at once beguiling and glisteningly treacherous. The so-called "Negro problem," as Johnson would later put it (taking his point of departure from *The Souls of Black Folk*'s famous rhetorical query, "How does it feel to be a problem?"), is "not a problem in the sense of being a fixed proposition involving certain invariable factors and waiting to be worked out according to certain defined rules. It is not a static condition; rather, it is and always has been a series of shifting interracial situations, never precisely the same."[57]

The Ex-Colored Man's epiphany about black popular music, inspired by a German pianist at a party in Berlin, is the same kind of realization:

> My millionaire planned, in the midst of the discussion on music, to have me play the "new American music" and astonish everybody present. The result was that I was more astonished than anyone else. I went to the piano and played the most intricate rag-time piece I knew. Before there was time for anybody to express an opinion on what I had done, a big bespectacled, bushy-headed man rushed over, and, shoving me out of the chair, exclaimed: "'Get up! Get up!" He seated himself at the piano, and, taking the theme of my rag-time, played it through first in straight chords; then varied and developed it through every known musical form. I sat amazed. I had been turning classic music into rag-time, a comparatively easy task; and this man had taken rag-time and made it classic. The thought came across me like a flash—It can be done, why can't I do it? From that moment my mind was made up. (141–142)

The German brusquely pushes the narrator away from the piano to prove that musically, too, the "line" shifts, that it can be crossed both ways. The scene shows in microcosm what the novel as a whole achieves: the troubling, ambiguous framing of blackness, the performance of a "state of suspension between racial realms of cognition."[58]

But why does this scene need to be set in Berlin? In its staged syncretism, it is almost a kind of dramatization of the Germanic predilections of *The Souls of Black Folk*, in which Du Bois (who had himself studied in Berlin) quotes lyrics from Wagner's opera *Lohengrin*, or places a musical snippet from a Negro spiritual beneath a poem by Schiller. But even more pointedly, the contention in *The Autobiography of an Ex-Colored Man* is that a transnational foray is necessary to undo the "fixed" and "static" nature of the "Negro question" in the United States. The "flash" is predicated on a confrontation, on the violence of a "shove" and a re-voicing of a "theme," on a "shifting interracial situation." The scene of two pianists in a party, jousting with improvised variations, is a scene where heterogeneous detours intersect at yet another *point d'intrication*—in this case the transnational circulation of African American music ("rag-time") in the European metropolis. In other words, the epiphany can be framed only as another sort of translation.

Race and the Modern Anthology

Gerald Early has recently made the provocative assertion that "the book that really kicked off the phase of the New Negro Movement known as the Harlem Renaissance—the phase that tried to produce a school or an identifiable discipline of black American letters—was not Jean Toomer's *Cane* (1923) or Claude McKay's *Spring in New Hampshire* (1922), it was James Weldon Johnson's 1922 anthology *The Book of American Negro Poetry*, the first collection of its type but surely not the last to display a considerable obsession in anthologizing the Negro."[59] The extension of formalist strategies from the slave narratives into African American literature in the twentieth century is evident not just in generically hybrid, subtly prefaced books by Du Bois, Johnson, and others. It is also, perhaps most importantly, evident in the Negro anthologies that seemed to be pouring out of publishing houses on both sides of the Atlantic in the early 1920s. For the first time— and in a rush that with hindsight is astonishing—there was great interest in

researching, notating, transcribing, assembling, and packaging almost anything having to do with populations of African descent. Because the com-
pulsively documentary New Negro movement coincides with the *vogue
nègre* (the acquisition-minded European fascination with black performance and artifacts) and with the institutionalization of anthropology as a
discipline, there appears to be an almost overnight explosion of textual collections after the war. It is possible to cite literally dozens and dozens of anthologies around black themes, from Blaise Cendrars's *Anthologie Nègre*
(1921) in Paris and Johnson's *Book of American Negro Poetry* (1922) in New
York all the way through the next decade.[60]

To note this flood of energy in modern print culture is to raise the question of the particular way an anthology frames race, the particular way it articulates an epistemology of blackness. As Theodore O. Mason, Jr., has
pointed out in a smart treatment of the history of African American anthologizing efforts, it is also to highlight the perhaps surprising and perhaps
ironic function that the anthology plays—not in confirming the canon, not
in a backward-looking survey of the high points in a trajectory, but instead
in founding and enabling the very tradition it documents, "at the beginning rather than the end of literary history making."[61] At the same time, it
is crucial to place a text such as *The Book of American Negro Poetry* within
this much wider, multilingual, Western rush to anthologize blackness, even
if James Weldon Johnson's concerns and motivations are not at all consonant with the aims of V. F. Calverton, not to mention Cendrars, Maurice
Delafosse, or Leo Frobenius. Such a juxtaposition makes clear the high
stakes of framing the black subject in the 1920s, which is not just a national issue. The anthology is a means more broadly to grapple with *modernity* itself: the form serves to "mark time," whether for the purposes of racialist retrenchment (positioning the Negro as paradigmatically backward
and primitive, innocent and unlettered, as in many of the European colonial and anthropological texts) or racialist vindication (positioning the Negro as paradigmatically modern and up to date, historical and literate, as in
the anthologies that emerge during the Harlem Renaissance).

The anthology takes on such a central role in this period of "considerable obsession" with the Negro partly because the form is above all a way of
accounting for a given cultural conjuncture. It delimits the borders of an
expressive mode or field, determining its beginning and end points, its local
or global resonance, its communities of participants and audiences. In do-

ing so it necessarily "presumes some idea of *difference*" (whether national, linguistic, generic, thematic, or identity-based) and aims to present the specific contours of that difference, in a way that both articulates it—makes it speak—and marks it off.[62] The anthology's expressive force is concentrated not just in the contents of a given collection or in its apparatus (its bibliography, its illustrations) or in its methodology (the sources it admits, the notational techniques it prefers, the way it limits its scope and pursues its assemblage). Most strikingly, the power of the anthology is concentrated in its discursive frame—in its preface, introduction, or opening statement. It should be no surprise that in a form so intimately concerned with framing, the preface becomes a point of great tension: the frame of the frame, as it were, the place where the collection itself is collected.

The allographic preface of the anthology "speaks before" *(prae-fatio)* what it collates.[63] A preface is always early or late, always a mask or a coda. It conditions the protocols of reception for the documents it presents. It purports to strike a path, to point the reader through a door or over a horizon, but paradoxically is usually written only after the text has been assembled. If the preface functions as a frame, we should recall that a frame in the etymological sense (as in the phrase "to frame an idea") refers both to the materiality of the limits or the edges of an object and to the interior force that gives it shape, that gives it life—not just the container but also the contained, not just the skin but also the blood or the skeleton. As a formal device, the preface speaks double in this way: it is outside, it marks what is not within the book, it precedes the book's "speaking," but it is also the very force that animates the book, that opens it for us and shows its contents. The preface therefore is a frame not always easily separable from the artifact itself, even as it rhetorically holds itself to be distinct from and prior to what it introduces.[64]

Let us consider in more detail James Weldon Johnson's anthology *The Book of American Negro Poetry.* The successful 1922 collection not only was the first gathering of Negro verse handled by a major U.S. publisher, but also was distinguished by its preface, a forty-two page essay on "The Creative Genius of the Negro" that, as Johnson put it a dozen years later, forcefully "called attention to the American Negro as a folk artist, and pointed out his vital contributions, as such, to our national culture."[65] Like Du Bois, Alain Locke, Charles S. Johnson, and Carter G. Woodson, Johnson hoped to provide overwhelming proof of the vitality, modernity, and historical depth of black expressive culture with the aim of reshaping the parameters of "the Negro question" in the United States. The famous declaration on the first page of the preface is characteristic: to varying degrees, these culture-framers shared Johnson's belief that nothing would accomplish more to change the "national mental attitude toward the race . . . than a demonstration of intellectual parity by the Negro through the production of literature and art."[66]

Johnson's effort to "demonstrate" parity through culture is above all a concern with the "universality" of black modernity. It is clear from the first page of the preface that *The Book of American Negro Poetry* aims to note how a black culture is distinctive, while at the same time lays claim to what Johnson terms black culture's "universal appeal." The rhetorical appeal to universality is by no means an unfamiliar strategy. Immanuel Wallerstein has pointed out that any project of cultural resistance necessarily must contest "the ideology of the system by appealing to antecedent, broader ideologies (that is, more 'universal' values)," which in effect accepts "the terms of the debate as defined by the dominant forces."[67] Johnson attempts to walk this tightrope when he begins the preface to *The Book of American Negro Poetry* with the oft-cited sweeping statement that "[a] people become great through many means, but there is only one measure by which its greatness is recognized and acknowledged. The final measure of the greatness of all people is the amount and standard of the literature and art they have produced. The world does not know that a people is great until that people produces great literature and art" (9). He takes on the parameters of culture as they have been defined by the very defenders of the Western high cultural tradition who would dismiss Negro American expression as formless or infantile.

But after these grand opening gestures, Johnson moves into a preface that seems at times to contradict this announcement about universality and "greatness." Ostensibly the preface frames black U.S. literature, but on the second page, Johnson indulges in an extended digression on the "creative genius of the Negro" *not* in terms of literature, not through the poetry collected in the anthology, but instead in terms of African American vernacular art: folklore ("the Uncle Remus stories"), music ("the 'spirituals' or slave songs"), dancing ("the cakewalk"), and popular commercialized music ("ragtime") (10–20). If the goal is to argue the achievements of African Americans in "high art," then why does the preface commence with a passionate defense of the "vital spark" of "lower forms" (15, 17)? In the end, the preface is most remarkable in that it digresses precisely in order to contend that Negro expression is both constitutive of the American "cultural store" and excessive to it—what Paul Gilroy terms a "counterculture," but one that simultaneously defines the core of national culture.[68] Indeed, Johnson worries not that U.S. culture will absorb or consume African American culture, but in fact that the latter has so fully defined the national culture that its origins have gone unrecognized (13).

More specifically, Johnson argues that it is the Negro's "transfusive quality" that places black expression in a privileged relation to the "national spirit" as the predominant voice of "our common cultural store" (3). The Negro is "the creator of the only things artistic that have yet sprung from American soil and been universally acknowledged as distinctive American products" (10). But that "transfusive quality" is not a characteristic limited to the populations of African descent on U.S. territory. It is instead a "racial gift" that expresses itself wherever Negroes are found: "This power of the Negro to suck up the national spirit from the soil and create something artistic and original, which, at the same time, possesses the note of universal appeal, is due to a remarkable racial gift of adaptability; it is more than adaptability, it is a transfusive quality. And the Negro has exercised this transfusive quality not only here in America, where the race lives in large numbers, but in European countries, where the number has been almost infinitesimal" (20). With this move, Johnson is able to position black culture as the defining American culture without limiting black creativity to a national origin. It eludes the frame of the nation, even as it indelibly defines what is "universally recognized" as national.

When the preface finally does get to poetry, it goes "a little afield" again, this time geographically, discussing the literature as a phenomenon that straddles the entire hemisphere. Johnson includes Claude McKay (from Jamaica) and George Reginald Margetson (from St. Kitts) in the collection along with the many poets from the United States. In his autobiography, Johnson explains that his preface "went a little afield and mentioned some of the Negro poets of the West Indies and South America, giving most space to Plácido, the popular poet of Cuba. My selections for the anthology proper increased to three or four times the number I had originally planned for, but I felt that in the case of this particular book, there was more to be gained by being comprehensive than would be lost by not being exclusive."[69] It should be noted that this shift is enacted with a shift in terminology, another "creation of vocables." In the first pages of the preface, Johnson writes of the "Negro" or "American Negro poets." As he moves "afield" at the end of his discussion of Paul Laurence Dunbar, he introduces a new racial appellation: "Aframerican" (36). Although Dunbar "is the most outstanding figure in literature among the Aframericans of the United States, he does not stand alone among the Aframericans of the whole Western world. There are Plácido and Manzano in Cuba; Vieux and Durand in Haiti; Machado de Assis in Brazil, and others still that might be mentioned, who stand on a plane with or even above Dunbar" (37). This word is a transport term in that it allows Johnson to extend the definition of "American" in another fashion beyond the borders of the U.S. nation, for "Aframerican" designates, as he puts it, "Negroes of . . . North America, South America, or the West Indies."[70] Part of the accomplishment of the preface is making proper this expanded sense of racial identity; by the discussion of "Negro dialect" toward the end of the preface, it is no longer so striking that he defines black culture as exorbitant to the nation, with the result that the nation is the subset of a larger regional space, as in references to "Aframerican poets in the United States" (42).

Functionally, a preface differs from an introduction in that the latter is unique, with "a more systematic, less historical, less circumstantial link with the logic of the book."[71] Prefaces "are multiplied from edition to edition and take into account a more empirical historicity," and so it is worth noting that in the preface to the revised 1931 edition of *The Book of American Negro Poetry*, Johnson seems to include the term "Aframerican" in his contention that, in the intervening decade, the claims of the preface to the first edition had been accepted as "facts," a matter of "historical data."[72] The second edition is often considered the more authoritative, because it includes the poetry of what Johnson calls the "World War group": the younger generation of talented New Negro poets who emerged in the mid-1920s including Langston Hughes, Sterling Brown, Helene Johnson, Arna Bontemps, Gwendolyn Bennett, Frank Horne, and Waring Cuney—as well as Johnson's own experiments in vernacular poetry in his 1927 *God's Trombones*.[73] In the new edition's shorter preface, Johnson now uses "Aframerican" interchangeably with "Negro."

In the first edition, the term "Aframerican" allows the preface to frame Negro expressive culture as exceeding the U.S. nation in yet another, even more remarkable manner. Johnson concludes his move "afield" with an extraordinary subversive gesture that mobilizes the new word:

> In considering the Aframerican poets of the Latin languages I am impelled to think that, as up to this time the colored poets of greater universality have come out of the Latin-American countries rather than out of the United States, they will continue to do so for a good many years. . . . The colored poet in the United States labors within limitations which he cannot easily pass over. He is always on the defensive or the offensive. . . . I think it probable that the first world-acknowledged Aframerican poet will come out of Latin America. (39–40)

In an anthology titled *The Book of American Negro Poetry* that claims a certain "universality" for that poetry, this can only be called a startling departure. One might best characterize this move as what Jacques Derrida terms a "textual feint," a way of using the preface that undermines the very pretensions of the anthology form.[74] It is also of course still a certain framing of blackness, even if the frame here ends by undoing itself, by demonstrating the instability—even the impossibility—of framing within national bounds.

The Book of American Negro Poetry does not simply tip the scale the other way, of course. It is *not* an anthology of "Aframerican" poetry in the sense of an exhaustive, or even vaguely representative, collection of poetry by writers of African descent throughout the Americas. In fact, Johnson declines to abstract the generalizing drive of the term "Aframerican" and, on the contrary, emphasizes the differences between the placement of the Cuban poet Plácido and any of the black U.S. poets. "Over against the probability" that the first "world-acknowledged Aframerican" poet will emerge from Latin America, he thus writes, is "the great advantage possessed by the colored poet in the United States of writing in the world-conquering English language" (40). Johnson is looking for an uneasy balance here in which a racial generalization or internationalism will not trump American nationalism. The sooner that "Aframerican poets in the United States" write "*American* poetry spontaneously, the better," and the primary referent remains national even though the descriptive "American" is thrown into question or opened up suggestively.

In terms of its content, the anthology pursues this shuttling or ambivalence in the significance of "Aframerican" in at least two ways. The poetry in the body of the text is itself *geographically* transnational, as I have pointed out, due to the inclusion of Margetson and McKay from the Anglophone Caribbean. Although there are no foreign-language poets featured in the anthology, it demonstrates the *linguistic* diversity implied by "Aframerican" first by undercutting its interior (the section of work by Jessie Fauset includes her translation of "Oblivion," by the Haitian poet Massilon Coicou [208]) and then by proliferating its edges: providing a single poem by Plácido not in the body of the text, but in an appendix to the book. The Spanish evidence of "Aframerican" writing sits at the back door, not quite counted in the body of *American Negro Poetry,* not quite exterior to it. Even this closing frame is itself split, for Johnson includes Plácido's original Spanish of "Despida a Mi Madre" followed by *two* quite different translations of the poem, one by William Cullen Bryant and another by Johnson himself (293–294). The anthology breaks and breaks again, as though to make *décalage* manifest in an open set of overlapping spaces. It invests in the signifier "Negro" and then extends it with "Aframerican"; it writes in English and then supplements it with Spanish; it carries the Spanish back to English and then translates it again. It is impossible to sew this fraying into some seamless space of common blackness. So if *The Book of American Negro Poetry* frames its particular motivating difference by overflowing the nation-state—even while defining national culture through a "racial gift"— the same framing overflows itself, extending and questioning the limits of its difference. The book splits its own binding.

Border Work

I do not mean to suggest that such strategies cannot be located in Francophone literary culture in the 1920s. The French black drive to document and anthologize was not comparable to the activities in Harlem, and not simply because the black presence in France (although vibrant and visible) was much smaller. Nor was the problem that Francophone intellectuals were unconcerned with collecting Negro culture (as we have already seen with Jane Nardal's approach to Alain Locke). Even in the midst of the *vogue nègre,* the circuits of financing and patronage that supported the Harlem intelligentsia until the onset of the Depression were never available in Paris. Still, black intellectuals in Paris were reading works such as *The Book of*

American Negro Poetry and *The New Negro,* and it is possible to track—in other forms—a Francophone engagement with and reformulation of framing practices.

At times in Francophone periodical print culture, one might read instances of framing in effects of juxtaposition: departures from a context (whether translations, articles by an unlikely source, or pieces in a different tone) that are equally insertions into that context. I am thinking for instance of an exceptional document that was inserted into the first issue of *La Race nègre,* the newspaper that in June 1927 succeeded *La Voix des Nègres* as the organ of Lamine Senghor's Ligue de Défense de la Race Nègre. Titled "Réponse d'un ancient tirailleur sénégalais à M. Paul Boncour" (Response of a former African soldier to M. Paul Boncour), the piece is the testimony of a soldier from the Sudan named Baba Diarra concerning the harsh treatment of African recruits during the war. But unlike the pieces that surround it in the issue, Diarra's text is composed not in standard French but in a transcription of the version of French called *petit nègre,* which was spoken by many soldiers. It opens:

> 1912 moi ngasi volontaire partir la guerre Moroco pasqui mon commandant mon cercle li promi boucou bons quand moi y a bien travailler pour Lafranci tuer boucou Morocains. Moi venir 2e régiment Kati, Ayéyé-yéye! Mon boucou maloré plus que esclave. Caporani y a frapper moi, sergent y a toujours manigolo . . . Y a pas bon, y a pas boucou manger . . . 1914, la guerre Lafrance avec bochi y a comenser, moi vinir encore . . . moi gagné gallon caporani. 1916 moi gagne sagent. Mais sagent ropéen parler moi comme lui y a parler tirailleur 2e classe. Gradé ropéens y a compter nous comme sauvasi, comme plus mauvais chien encore. Si nous faire clamison ficiers y a dire nous, vous pas droit, vous pas citouin français, vous . . . ndigènes.[75]

In 1912 I volunteered to go to the war in Morocco because the commandant of my district promised great rewards if I worked well for France and killed many Moroccans. I came in the second Kati regiment [from Bamako], Ayéyé-yéye! I suffered a great deal, more than a slave. The corporal hit me, the sergeant always had his cudgel . . . It wasn't good, there wasn't much to eat . . . 1914, the war between

France and the Germans started, and I came back again . . . I earned my corporal's stripes. But the European sergeant spoke to me like he spoke to a private second class. Europeans consider us savages, even worse than dogs. If we complain to the officers they tell us, you have no rights, you aren't a French citizen: you're . . . natives.

I have provided a relatively straightforward English translation of the passage, because there is no way to reproduce the effect the passage has in the original. In *La Race nègre,* Diarra's "response" is not introduced, explained, or translated in any manner, and it confronts a French reader with its unfamiliar syntax and vocabulary *(Ayéyé, manigolo, sauvasi, ficiers).*

Historian Philippe de Witte has noted that the inclusion of this document in *La Race nègre* attempts "to elevate a 'patois' to the rank of a language of communication" and that as a result "an infantilized, ridiculed, and humiliating language [*langue*] becomes . . . a popular language, rich and full of images."[76] Another critic who has considered the piece, Christopher Miller, is certainly correct to point out that *petit nègre* functions here as a "means of resistance."[77] But it is necessary to clarify that *petit nègre* is not precisely a patois, and—as Frantz Fanon recognized—nor is it a creole.[78] In fact, *petit nègre* is one of the strangest legacies of World War I: it was a simplified, deformed version of French that the military codified and deliberately *taught* to African soldiers as they came to fight in Europe, as a means both to infantilize them and to control their modes of interaction with their mainly white French commanding officers. It is no coincidence that the same issue of *La Race nègre* excerpts a passage from Lucie Cousturier's 1920 *Des Inconnus chez moi,* which is the first text in metropolitan France to take issue with the policy of *petit nègre* instruction in training camps:

> The instructors were able to generalize an esperanto, or *"petit nègre,"* proper to the fabrication and the delivery of soldiers through the quickest possible means. The instructors' role was restricted to this end; they did not at all anticipate that these soldiers might want to speak French in France. This is the proof of a military machine's perfection: not to make life easier, but . . . to destroy it.
>
> Suppose that having to teach our language to an Englishman, we carefully took note of all the deformations his first attempts inflict on French pronunciation and syntax, and that from then on, we draw

on them to present him with a French reduced to his English compat-
ibilities.[79]

As de Witte comments, were Diarra's account "translated into Parisian
French or into communist jargon, the indictment would have lost a good
deal of its force."[80] But one might add that the text's "force" is located *in
its form:* linguistically, *petit nègre* makes the same critique as the narrative itself. It implies that the proper mode of critique is a spoken vernacular
(since *petit nègre* is not a written language, the text points to a certain
orality, whether Diarra wrote it himself or whether it was transcribed from
his speech). The text gains its "force" not only because it represents a populist gesture of inclusion in a black metropolitan periodical, but also because *petit nègre* is itself evidence—the framed documentation, confronting the reader—of the mistreatment of French West African soldiers during
the war.

My second example is a singular novel published in 1924, the Guadeloupean Suzanne Lacascade's *Claire-Solange, âme africaine.* The story
takes place in "that period of internationalism" just before World War I, as
a successful colonial administrator named Etienne Hucquart arrives in the
metropole from Fort-de-France with his daughter Claire-Solange.[81] Set in
Paris, the novel follows the unfolding of a love affair between the young
mulâtresse (Claire-Solange is the product of Etienne's marriage to an Antillean woman) and Jacques Danzel, a distant cousin. The title character is
one of the more remarkable characters in early Francophone fiction: impul-
sive, highly educated, and fiercely proud of her African ancestry. At one
point, as the extended household is discussing the evils of prejudice in the
modern world, an aunt asks Claire-Solange if she is anti-Semitic. She responds defiantly: "Papa has traveled around the world, fighting against
prejudices; and how could I despise another oppressed race, I who am *nègre*
[*moi qui suis nègre*]" (36). When her aunt, appalled at the word *nègre,* tries
to dismiss this declaration as folly, Claire-Solange launches into a soliloquy:

Look my frizzy hair. I couldn't smooth it down into tresses against my
cheeks, like the Jews of Aden; I couldn't lift it up into a 1830 *chignon*
bun. . . . My *nègre* hair must be separated with headbands, twisted for
better or worse against the nape of my neck. . . . In order to deny my
African origin, I would have to live under a veil, hiding both my eyes

and my nose from view. . . . Come on, aunt, smile. Accept as she is a woman of color, who will give some variety to the family. (36–37)

Elsewhere she declares that her hobby *(marotte)* is to "protect and glorify the Negro race [*la race noire*]." "I am African," she proclaims, "African, through atavism and despite my paternal heritage!" offering a fanciful enumeration of the royal lineage of her African family line (65–66). Claire-Solange—whose mother perished when she caught a chill on a visit to Europe—even advances a sort of continental climatology, contending that her maternal "African" side is genetically far superior to her "cold," "artificial," "dull" European heritage.

Claire-Solange eventually falls in love with Jacques and, despite her abhorrence of the European winter, decides to stay with him in the metropole as the war breaks out, offering him the "unique love of an African woman" (220). Her choice to remain in Paris is both the result of Jacques "conquering" her "African pride" and the result of her own patriotism as a French citizen herself: "This city that I didn't love, this city is all of France, it's the honor of the country, it's you, it's my life. . . . My pride as an African woman [*orgueil d'Africaine*] has been conquered by you, Jacques, my pride as a Frenchwoman [*orgueil de Française*] remains intact" (170). As Maryse Condé has pointed out, this *dénouement* is an all-too-familiar stereotype of the "hot-blooded" Antillean woman surrendering as erotic object, even if for once she is rewarded with a French husband rather than a temporary colonial lover.[82] Still, *Claire-Solange*'s racialist rhetoric, its strong female characterization, and its rich portrait of creole popular culture were apparently radical enough that the book aroused great indignation in the Caribbean, with the result that Lacascade was forced to leave Guadeloupe.[83]

Claire-Solange, âme africaine is particularly innovative in its depiction of Caribbean vernacular culture and music. The novel contains a great deal of Creole, which is usually explicated or contextualized in French although not always fully translated, in passages such as the one when an Antillean servant comes into the room where Claire-Solange and Jacques are talking; the servant, who was supposed to do Claire-Solange's hair, and has been looking for the young woman all over the house, complains, "*Man jouque croué ou bliez moin, tit fille. . . .* Je commence à croire que vous m'oubliez" ("I'm starting to think that you're forgetting about me"). Claire-Solange chides her with a vulgarity, but then refuses to translate it for Jacques: "*Pas*

fais guiolle kiou poule, da chè. . . . Oh! Monsieur Danzel, je ne me risque pas
à traduire. . . . Le créole en ces mots brave l'honnêteté. . . . Il me faut vous
quitter pour un étrange devoir. Je dois prêter ma tête à ma bonne" (*"Pas fais
guiolle kiou poule, da chè.* . . . Oh! Monsieur Danzel, I don't dare translate. . . . The Creole in these words defies respectability. . . . I have to leave
you for a strange fate. I have to lend my head to my maid") (47).[84] Over
and over, the text performs the edges of Caribbean vernacular culture,
pointing at all that cannot be carried over. This is often a way of figuring
Claire-Solange's "mixed" parentage, as in the amusing scene when she sits
down at the piano in the parlor to play Schumann's *Carnaval* and impro-
vises away from the theme into "strange, nostalgic cadences, brief complaints, hoarse joys—a tam-tam of sorrowful drunkenness, whose syncopa-
tions tear the fevered soul: it is Ramadan, the African Carnival. Then the
rhythm, starting to skip, creating a youthful gaiety, recalls a habanera." *"Le
Mardi Gras à Fort-de-France,"* Claire-Solange announces, and starts to sing
a lyric in Creole (31). *Carnaval* is a significant choice, since Schumann's
1835 suite is already virtuosic and polyvocal, with each section of the suite
designed to represent what the composer called the "many different mental
states" brought about by his marriage (drawing on a coded musical tone se-
quence based on the letters of his wife's birthplace). Schumann sometimes
referred to it as a *Maskentanz,* a masked ball, and the piece was inspired not
just by what he considered to be the pieces of his personality (two sections
are called *Florestan* and *Eusebius,* Schumann's imaginary names for the "two
sides" of his nature), but also by the European improvisational tradition:
many of the fragments are titled after characters in the *commedia del l'arte*
and other figures from the popular theater *(Pierrot, Arlequin, Pantalon et
Colombine).*[85] So for Claire-Solange to play this particular piece "with originality" (31) and then to transport it across the Atlantic toward another Carnival tradition *(Le Mardi Gras à Fort-de-France)* is an excursion at least as
suggestive as the epiphany in Johnson's *The Autobiography of an Ex-Colored
Man.*

But if music figures mixed heritage through cultural transport in *Claire-
Solange,* it also comes to mark a certain inaccessibility, a certain part of
an "African" heritage that remains elusive and unconquered. At one point,
depressed on a cold, rainy day, Claire-Solange stays in the house, trying
to soothe herself with music: "Anguish agitates her moving nostrils, makes
her eyelids heavy, but the tears do not fall: Africans, you should know,

conceal their impressions; if they cannot contain their suffering, they sing passionately. This is what the *mulâtresse* did." There follows a short indented refrain:

> Tchah, béhoué, kika, kika
> Tchah, béhoué, kika!
> Krinon-no-no-no-no béhoué
> Ahah, béhoué, ahah (43)

The tune is described as "a tune of savage revolt, it cracks like the blow of the lash on the naked back of Negro slaves [*esclaves noirs*], it is repeated indefinitely . . ." (44). When her father, standing in the doorway *(sur le seuil)*, says that he doesn't recognize it, she explains, "it's what that servant boy was singing in Zanzibar, on the N'Gamba bridge, the day when he stopped traffic with his contortions; no one dared to pass [*personne n'osait plus passer*], thinking that he was possessed."

Strikingly, this is a moment when the text multiplies its own thresholds *(seuils)*. The indented lyrics are footnoted with the following sentence: "L'auteur a entendu ces paroles dans des circonstances analogues à celle que relate Claire-Solange, mais personne n'a pu, ou n'a voulu lui en donner le sens" ("The author heard these words in circumstances analogous to those that Claire-Solange relates, but no one could, or would, give her their meaning") (43). The gesture is immediately reminiscent of W. E. B. Du Bois's repeated telling—in each of his four principal autobiographies—of a story about his "grandfather's grandmother," who used to sing an old Bantu song that no one could translate into English: *Do ba-na co-ba, ge-ne me, ge-ne me! / Ben d'nu-li, nu-li, nu-li, nu-li, den d'le.* It had been passed down through the generations, and "we sing it to our children," Du Bois writes, "knowing as little as our fathers what its words may mean, but knowing well the meaning of its music."[86] The song in *Claire-Solange* similarly figures a link to an African past. She tells her father, accepting his embrace, "Don't worry, I'm just going through a little bout of nostalgia [*Je traverse un petit accès de nostalgie*]" (44). However, this moment is slightly different in significance from Du Bois's familial anecdote. Claire-Solange's song is not an ancestral hand-me-down, representing both a possessed heritage and that heritage's inherent distance in unfamiliar, untranslatable words. Hers is a personal memory of an individual past in a ambiguous position in Africa, as the daughter of a colonial administrator with some imagined "access" *(accès)* to an "African" identity, but with constant reminders of what separates her from the "natives." "No one could, or would, give her [the words'] meaning," as the footnote puts it. The footnote claims to provide a "documentary" source and confirms the song through the "analogue" of autobiography, although the note's insertion is both a way of indicating the entrance of an authorial voice into the text and at the same time a way of marking a distance between author and character (since the circumstances are "analogous" but not identical).

The explanatory footnote makes the text generically hybrid in another sense, since it confers an ethnographic rhetoric of citation around the song's use in the fiction. In fact, this rhetoric—what "the author heard" herself— is given a certain privilege as a recording, because it is distinguished from the pretensions of European colonial travel literature and anthropology. A few pages later, remarking that spring is arriving in Paris, Claire-Solange explains to Jacques, "I imagined the spring, and France itself, from your literature, yes, just as you imagine the colonies from the lying tales of explorers [*d'après les récits mensonges des explorateurs*]" (46). Lacascade's own artifact is apparently meant to convey knowledge about Africa in a mode different from the old *récits mensonges*—though intriguingly, it discovers that mode not in travel narrative or anthropology per se, but in a "mixed" form that appends or grafts a musical document into the "imagined" space of the novel. The footnote, in other words, attempts to articulate itself as a fact within a fiction, a framing that tells a certain truth about colonialism with the evidence of a recorded music of "savage revolt," a remembered music that is insistent and repeated in a manner that metaphorically represents "the blow of the lash on the naked back of Negro slaves." As with Du Bois, what makes the music powerful as evidence is precisely that it cannot be translated—that it marks a certain inaccessibility, a space of expression exterior to the colonial system, a certain resistance that "no one dares to pass."

Even as it is transcribed, even as it is "authenticated" by Lacascade's footnote, the song remains elusive. Perhaps it is truthful evidence about colonialism not just in that it represents African resistance through its own resistance to translation, but also in the sense that no one dares to pass it *on*—Lacascade transmits it to the reader only as something that *cannot* be transmitted as evidence in any disciplinary sense, as something that can appear only in this oblique, layered space in a fiction. This point is emphasized by a countergesture at the end of the book: Lacascade includes an ap-

"Mardi-Gras." Suzanne Lacascade, *Claire-Solange, âme africaine* (Paris: Eugène Figuière, 1924). Beinecke Rare Book and Manuscript Library, Yale University.

pendix of "Trois Bel-Airs Des Antilles" (Three Tunes from the Antilles), handwritten manuscripts that the text indicates were harmonized by Joseph Salmon. The scores provide the lyrics, melody, and musical accompaniment of three songs that appear in the novel: "Le Clair Solange," "Dis-Moi Doudou," and "Mardi-Gras" (the tune *Le Mardi Gras à Fort-de-France* that Claire-Solange segues into during her performance of Schumann's *Carnaval*). There are other interwar examples of Francophone writers appending ethnographic data or texts to their fictions—one thinks for instance of Ousmane Socé's 1935 *Karim, roman sénégalais,* which includes a ninety-page appendix of nine "Contes et légendes d'Afrique noire" (Negro African tales and legends) at the end of the novel.[87] What's different about Lacascade's book, of course, is that the appendix does not include that strange, untranslatable, footnoted song sung by the servant boy in Zanzibar. If the appendix as a framing gesture represents a certain documentary impulse with regard to Antillean vernacular culture, it also closes *Claire-Solange, âme africaine* by pointing the reader to an impassable "record" of colonialism that remains outside the book's grasp.

A Blues Note

I close with one more variation, one more take on these framing strategies in yet another genre. It would be possible to devote an entire study to the uses of framing in Langston Hughes's oeuvre, especially in his work as a translator and editor. If we should recall that both Aimé Césaire and Léopold Sédar Senghor published translations of African American poetry early in their careers, we should equally recognize that Hughes is the most prolific black poet-translator of the twentieth century (publishing versions of Léon-Gontran Damas, Jacques Roumain, Nicolás Guillén, Regino Pedroso, Gabriela Mistral, David Diop, and Jean-Joseph Rabéarivelo, among many others) and at the same time a prodigious and groundbreaking anthologist in his own right.[88] Here, however, I will focus solely on framing practices and translation aesthetics in Hughes's poetry itself. His second book, *Fine Clothes to the Jew* (1927), was one of the more controversial black publishing events of the second half of the decade, a lightning rod for impassioned reviews both positive and negative.[89] The *Pittsburgh Courier* judged that Hughes's new book was "trash," while the headline in the New York *Amsterdam News* proclaimed, "Langston Hughes—The Sewer Dweller." Another paper called him "the poet lowrate of Harlem," punning in derision of the writer who would later be fondly referred to as the "Negro poet laureate." Critic Benjamin Brawley averred that "it would have been just as well, perhaps better, if the book had never been published. No other ever issued reflects more fully the abandon and the vulgarity of its age."[90] Another array of intellectuals, including James Weldon Johnson, Margaret Larkin, and Alice Dunbar-Nelson attempted to argue for the book's significance. Howard Mumford Jones went so far as to contend that with his "blues poems," Hughes "has contributed a really new verse form to the English language," in an accomplishment reminiscent of the experiments with the spoken vernacular in the *Lyrical Ballads* composed by Wordsworth and Coleridge at the turn of the nineteenth century.[91] But it is only much more recently that critics have begun to come to terms with *Fine Clothes,* which Arnold Rampersad rightly calls Hughes's "finest achievement in language" and "one of the most astonishing books of verse ever published in the United States."[92]

The oft-noted innovation in Hughes's new poetry is that, in contrast to the rhetorical distancing in earlier efforts such as "The Weary Blues"—in which an ambivalently placed speaker reports that he "heard a Negro play" in Harlem "the other night," and then describes and quotes the lyrics of the singer's music—the poems in *Fine Clothes* are unmediated: blues lyrics recorded directly on the page with no intervening or exterior voice.[93] The lines are enjambed at the caesura, so that the A-A'-B structure of the twelve-bar blues forms a six-line stanza, as in "Young Gal's Blues," which concludes as follows:

> When love is gone what
> Can a young gal do?
> When love is gone, O,
> What can a young gal do?
> Keep on a-lovin' me, daddy,
> Cause I don't want to be blue.[94]

The blues poems allude to recording not just in their parallels to blues structure, but also in their length, which is always either three or four stanzas—just like the songs of Ma Rainey, Bessie Smith, and Ida Cox. As Martin Williams has noted, the limitations of the ten-inch record (which allowed a singer only about three minutes, enough time to sing four blues stanzas) were a crucial factor in the expressive possibilities of early blues recordings, and Hughes's blues poems operate within the constraints of the recorded form.[95]

The unmediated quality of the poems has an effect that is often stunning, especially since they are sung or spoken mainly in the voices of young black women. The reader encounters stark, unleavened voices of the black working class not just in the performance situations of the blues but also in everyday, domestic moments. The poem "Baby" is no more or less than the voice of a parent yelling at her child: "Albert! / Hey, Albert! / Don't you play in the road." The most radically minimalist poem in this vein is "Shout," which in its entirety runs three lines: "Listen to yo' prophets, / Little Jesus! / Listen to yo' saints!"[96] These poems attain the economy of haiku, but the aesthetic is not so much concerned with observation and distillation as it is with what one might call the technologies of recording: capturing the varied and fragmented soundscape of black Memphis or Washington, D.C., in a roving aural sampling that includes sung blues as well as splintered, seemingly overheard exclamations and exchanges. What is striking is the implied proposition that the spoken black vernacular can provide the material of a modernist lyric poetics—without mediation, without elevation, without any of the rarefied quirks that are so often taken to connote "poetry."

This is not to say that *Fine Clothes* abandons framing devices. The book opens with a prefatory gesture, "A Note on the Blues" designed to instruct the reader in the peculiarities of the form:

> The first eight and the last nine poems in this book are written after the manner of the Negro folks-songs known as *Blues*. The *Blues*, unlike the *Spirituals*, have a strict poetic pattern: one long line repeated and a third line to rhyme with the first two. Sometimes the second line in repetition is slightly changed and sometimes, but very seldom, it is omitted. The mood of the *Blues* is almost always despondency, but when they are sung people laugh.

The preface announces the structure of the book to be itself framed by the blues poems it contains, a form whose "inescapable persistence" returns at the end of the volume.[97] This framing is itself doubled, since the first poem ("Hey!") and the last poem ("Hey! Hey!") in *Fine Clothes* are succinct companion pieces that frame the book within the temporal space of a single night: "Sun's a settin' . . . Wonder what the blues'll bring?" opens the first, whereas the second echoes, "Sun's a risin', / This is gonna be my song."[98] Since the unmediated blues poems imply a certain recording or transcription of a performance, it is important that the "Note" emphasizes that the poems are "written after the manner of" the blues—not ethnographic reproductions of a given blues context, but a written form that aims at the "mood" of that context in a way that may have a complex and even transformative relation to it. That is, if the blues poem suggests a transcription, it also suggests the graphic particularities of a musical score: a writing that precedes and structures a performance rather than follows and records it. One might add that the blues involves a split between affect and reception: its "mood" is sorrow—or more precisely melancholia, as Jahan Ramazani argues—but its performance triggers the release of laughter in the audience.[99]

In his autobiography *The Big Sea* (1940), Hughes explains that *Fine Clothes* was mainly about black working class culture: its voices are those of "workers, roustabouts, and singers, and job hunters on Lenox Avenue in New York, or Seventh Street in Washington or South State in Chicago—

people up today and down tomorrow, working this week and fired the next, beaten and baffled, but determined not to be wholly beaten, buying furniture on the installment plan, filling the house with roomers to help pay the rent, hoping to get a new suit for Easter—and pawning that suit before the Fourth of July."[100] The book moves through five sections (titled "Blues," "Railroad Avenue," "Glory! Hallelujah!," "Beale Street Love," "From the Georgia Roads," "And Blues"), traveling through what Robert Stepto terms the "symbolic geography" of sacred and secular, urban and rural spaces in African American life in the first decades of the twentieth century. Even in this controlled progress, though, *Fine Clothes* jumps and skips at various points, shifting register, articulating a black symbolic geography in unexpected ways. Hughes would write elsewhere that the blues are paradigmatically "songs you sing alone."[101] But a number of the poems in the volume (including "Closing Time," "Brass Spittoons," and "Mulatto") depart from the single-voiced blues lyrics and experiment with many-voiced interwoven constructions.

On a larger scale, the individual poems are situated in a broader polyvocality precisely through their contrasts—the interpoem "conversations" the book performs in the way it is arranged. So one of the most controversial pieces in the book, "Red Silk Stockings" (in which an unidentified speaker instructs, "Put on yo' red silk stockings, / Black gal / Go out an' let de white boys / Look at yo' legs / . . . An' tomorrow's chile'll / Be a high yaller") is undeniably inflammatory when taken as an isolated statement. But it is provocative in a different manner when it is read next to the poem that precedes it, "Mulatto" (with its repeated refrain—*"I am your son, white man!"*—interspersed with the father's rejection—*"You are my son! / Like hell!"*—and another gnawing, intermittent voice—*"What's the body of your mother?"*). And the confrontation in "Mulatto" is tempered in turn by the subtle ethics of the poem that comes before it, "Magnolia Flowers." There a speaker searches for "flowers" but instead finds "this corner / Full of ugliness." The description of the search for magnolias is interrupted by a repeated plea for forgiveness ("'Scuse me, / I didn't mean to stump ma toe on you, lady") that seems to form—even as it interrupts, or "stumps its toe" on the body of the poem—a fragile model for ethical interaction in a context of gendered violence.[102] In other words, the dynamics of framing operate simultaneously at the level of the book (its prefaces and divisions), between poems (in contrast, juxtaposition, or echoing), and within poems (in carefully layered polyvocality).

These three poems all appear in the section of *Fine Clothes* called "From the Georgia Roads." The poem that follows "Red Silk Stockings" appears to break dramatically from that context, and indeed to break the frame of the book as a whole. Rather than the blues context of violence and labor in the U.S. South, we are offered "Jazz Band in a Parisian Cabaret":

> Play that thing,
> Jazz band!
> Play it for the lords and ladies,
> For the dukes and counts,
> For the whores and gigolos,
> For the American millionaires,
> And the school teachers
> Out for a spree.
> Play it,
> Jazz band!
> You know that tune
> That laughs and cries at the same time.
> You know it.
>   May I?
>   Mais oui.
>   Mein Gott!
>   Parece una rumba.
> Play it, jazz band!
> You've got seven languages to speak in
> And then some,
> Even if you do come from Georgia.
>   Can I go home wid yuh, sweetie?
>   Sure.[103]

Apparently Hughes wrote the poem in early 1924, when he was a twenty-two year old expatriate scraping by in Paris working as a dishwasher at a club in Montmartre called Le Grand Duc. Founded three years earlier, Le Grand Duc had been purchased that winter by the African American boxer and sometimes drummer Eugene Bullard, who had joined the French

Légion Etrangère to fight in World War I (eventually becoming the only black pilot in the Lafayette Escadrille, a squadron of U.S. fighter pilots fighting for the French), and then stayed in Paris. When the headliner, African American singer Florence Embry Jones, left that spring to open a new club down the street called Chez Florence, Bullard hired a relative unknown from Harlem named Ada Smith, who would soon be one of the most famous entertainers in Paris, performing under a nickname that paid tribute to her red hair: "Bricktop." Le Grand Duc became known as an after-hours joint: "when all the other clubs were closed," Hughes explains, "the best of the musicians and entertainers from various other smart places would often drop into the Grand Duc, and there'd be a jam session until seven or eight in the morning—only in 1924 they had no such name for it."[104] The musicians included the trumpeter Cricket Smith, the drummer Buddy Gilmore, pianist Arthur "Dooley" Wilson, violinist Louis Jones, singers Mabel Mercer and Sophie Tucker, the dancer Louis Douglas, and pianist Palmer Jones (Florence's husband). The audiences at Le Grand Duc seemingly drew every celebrity in Paris: Mistinguett, Louis Aragon, the Prince of Wales, Fred Astaire, Charlie Chaplin, Fatty Arbuckle, Gloria Swanson, Nora Baynes, Fannie Ward, Nancy Cunard, Jimmy Walker, Ernest Hemingway, F. Scott Fitzgerald, Robert McAlmon, Cole Porter, Man Ray, Kiki, and Kojo Tovalou Houénou.[105]

"Jazz Band in a Parisian Cabaret" is a singular evocation of Hughes's expatriate experience. But what is it doing in *Fine Clothes?* First of all, the poem links jazz as a music—"that tune that laughs and cries at the same time"—to the doubled-edged description of blues in the book's prefatory "Note." It reminds us that the two forms were not always easily distinguishable in the 1920s. Indeed, in recounting his months working in Le Grand Duc, Hughes's autobiography refers to the jazz musicians who played at the club, but calls their music *blues:*

> Blues in the rue Pigalle. Black and laughing, heartbreaking blues in the Paris dawn, pounding like a pulse-beat, moving like the Mississippi! . . .
>
> Play it, Mister Palmer Jones! Lawd! Lawd! Lawd! Play it, Buddy Gilmore! What you doin' to them drums? Man, you gonna bust your diamond studs in a minute![106]

The new word "jazz" pulls the blues poems of *Fine Clothes* out of their frame, out of the confines of black performance spaces in the United States. In other words, if poems such as "Railroad Avenue" and "Bound No'th Blues" articulate a migrancy particular to U.S. spaces, "Jazz Band in a Parisian Cabaret"—with its "new vocable" for the music—tugs that allusion to black modern mobility into another register, now transnational. The cabaret is an "amphibious space" of situational, temporary mobility in a number of senses: not only in nationality and language, but also class (allowing interaction and seduction among the European aristocracy, new American "millionaires," middle-class professionals "out for a spree," and the musicians themselves).[107] That mobility is at the same time a quality *in* the music as well, mirrored in jazz's ability to change its affective implications, to "laugh and cry at the same time."

The indented lines in four languages can be read on a number of levels. On the one hand, they are a recording:

> May I?
> Mais oui.
> Mein Gott!
> Parece una rumba.

Four voices in the audience of a cosmopolitan cabaret like Le Grand Duc—disparate responses, sounded: an English speaker inviting someone to dance or requesting a cigarette; a French speaker's affirmative reply; a German speaker's exclamation of shock or surprise ("My God!"); an analysis and re-contextualization in Spanish ("It sounds like a rumba"). This polyvocal strategy is one that Hughes experimented with in a few other poems around the same time, all in an effort to capture the particular aural overload of a club scene. The best known may be another poem evoking the late-night jam sessions in Le Grand Duc, "The Cat and the Saxophone (2 A.M.)," which appeared in Hughes's first book, *The Weary Blues* (1926). It interweaves the lyric transcription of a dialogue with lines from the 1924 song "Everybody Loves My Baby, But My Baby Don't Love Nobody But Me," written by Jack Palmer and Spencer Williams:

> Say!
> EVERYBODY

> Yes?
> WANTS MY BABY
> I'm your
> BUT MY BABY
> sweetie, ain't I?
> DON'T WANT NOBODY
> Sure.[108]

But like the lines in "The Cat and the Saxophone," the multilingualism in "Jazz Band" may be an effort not just to capture a conversation, but also to *describe* the workings of the music itself. In this poetics, jazz is defined as "communication," as Hughes puts it elsewhere: the lyric draws on many languages to represent the music's dialogic qualities (thus, each language figures the specific intonation and expressive mode of a given instrument in the music's fabric).[109] The many languages in the poem are a means of apprehending a music so intimately concerned with dialogue and exchange among a group of performers and the audience that it can be approached only through a kind of critical multilingualism.[110] As Duke Ellington writes in his foreword to *The Encyclopedia of Jazz:* "I don't think there are enough words in the English language to do all of this right, and unless a man has a grasp of other languages it may be impossible for him to find the nuances and subtleties, the varying degrees of quality, in music."[111]

This is also a poetics of universality, to return to the terms of Johnson's preface to *The Book of American Negro Poetry.* Jazz "plays it" for a range of audiences that is wide, if not potentially unbounded: "You've got seven languages to speak in / And then some." Or as Hughes writes about the blues, the music has "something that goes beyond race or sectional limits, that appeals to the ear and heart of people everywhere."[112] At the same time, the music embodies the particular: if it speaks to everyone, it also always speaks for the place it "come[s] from." And that place inescapably carries certain connotations in the midst of what Bricktop called *le tumulte noir,* the exoticist craze in Paris for all things black. Thus the somewhat sneering tone to the qualifier that follows: "Even if you do come from Georgia." This is of course another sort of framing. (It may also be a way of moving from the figurative register back to the descriptive: the lines may be a reminder that Eugene Bullard himself was originally from Georgia—a reminder that the poem speaks to a particular context, *a* Parisian Cabaret and only one: Le Grand Duc. This may likewise be the reason that the next line is the only moment in the poem that implies a black Southern vernacular: "Can I go home *wid yuh,* sweetie?") But like the other framings I have elaborated, the poem undoes the very frame it sets up, since it places "Georgia" in Paris. It articulates the "blues in the rue Pigalle" that are "moving like the Mississippi." These imaginative shifts transform and expand the contours of the symbolic geography of black modern culture that *Fine Clothes* articulates.

Also indented, the last lines of the poem can be read as a recording, too. "Can I go home wid yuh, sweetie? / Sure": the transcription of two voices in a successful seduction, a mutual agreement to "go home" together. But they are also an approach to the music, in a poem that is first of all an apostrophe—a form of lyric that calls out to the lyric, words that demand and beckon music ("Play it, jazz band"). The poem performs the intimacy, the erotics, of a sound that travels: what in the music takes you "home," and goes "home" with you. In other words, these last lines attempt to hold at least two things together in a fragile balance: on the one hand, an individual listener's affective connection to the music, and, on the other, the collectivity of listeners the music allows, the connections it fosters.

Does "Jazz Band in a Parisian Cabaret" imagine that collectivity in any broader sense? Does it represent anything that might approach Jane Nardal's *internationalisme noir?* To ask such a question, of course, is to suggest a complex articulation of the disparate instances of formalist strategies I have outlined here: to suggest a link among discursive practices that aim (at a wide variety of points in a transnational print culture) to frame blackness as an object of knowledge beyond the nation-state. Next to the polemics of Senghor and Johnson, the diasporic gestures of Lacascade and Hughes seem no more than whispers: a footnote in a novel, a few lines of a lyric. In "Jazz Band," one might say that the smallest frame is just a hint, even a mishearing: the possibility that in the first two indented lines of the poem ("May I?/Mais oui"), the English reader is asked to hallucinate the joint of collectivity in a bilingual pun. "May I?" might also ask us to mishear the next line, written in French, as its English homophone: *May we.* We are back where we started, with the complexities of linguistic difference. This effect would be the smallest hint of a broader coming together in the popular good-time spaces of the *vogue nègre,* in the guise of a corrective: don't ask for yourself alone ("May I?")—we're going to dance *together.* Even if the poem is written in many languages, this hint can be heard only by its primary readership: it is audible only for an English speaker because it is produced by *partage,* a nonsignifying difference between languages.[113] But for an English-speaking audience, in the "yes" *(oui)* there is at once a fore-shadowing of community—the sound of the affirmation that brings "us" together, the articulation of a connection across difference—and also the kernel of what cannot be carried over: the sound of another tongue. At the smallest level, then, in the play of that productive ambivalence where "Jazz Band" breaks the book's frame to reach Paris "from the Georgia roads," the possibility of black internationalism is heard to be a matter of music.

CHAPTER 2

ON RECIPROCITY:
RENÉ MARAN AND ALAIN LOCKE

In the fall of 1921, *Batouala,* the first novel by an obscure Martinican poet named René Maran, was awarded the Prix Goncourt, the most prestigious literary prize in France.[1] The next year a rather unhappy translation by Adele Seltzer was published in New York, and the novel garnered a rush of attention particularly in the African American press, even though—as Hubert Harrison lamented in one review—"the fine Gallic flavor of *Batouala* has evaporated from the English version."[2] What is remarkable about the black U.S. reception of *Batouala* is that it received rave reviews from all quarters of the "New Negro" movement. Charles Chesnutt called the novel a "triumph"; Alain Locke extolled its "bold realism," and later added that its influence was "educative and emancipating" for the "younger generation" of African American writers.[3] The inaugural issue of *Opportunity* in January 1923 boasted that the journal would tell "more about René Maran." In the *Crisis* (which featured a portrait of Maran on its May 1922 cover), Jessie Fauset praised the "almost cinema-like sharpness" of this "great novel," commenting that Maran—who had been working since 1909 as an administrator in the French Central African colony of Ubangi-Shari (in what is now the Central African Republic)—had "lived with these people many years and he tells with a wealth of detail and great plainness what he has seen."[4] Another notice in the *Crisis* gushed, "The whole world is reading it!"[5] At the same time, Robert Machray, William H. Ferris, J. A. Rogers, and Hubert Harrison lauded *Batouala* in Marcus Garvey's newspaper, the *Negro World,* and Garvey himself opened the 1922 convention of the Universal Negro Improvement Association by citing Maran's book as proof of "the universality of the dissatisfaction that now exists among far-seeing, self-respecting Negroes, over the mis-Government and exploitation that is carried on in Africa."[6] Two years later, W. E. B. Du Bois would echo his nationalist nemesis, writing that Maran's "attack on

France" in *Batouala* "marks an era. Never before have Negroes criticized the work of the French in Africa."[7]

To take account of the impact of *Batouala* at the dawn of the "Harlem Renaissance" would mean reconfiguring the accepted cartography of black literary modernism. It would mean coming to terms with a black New York journalistic reception that took a French Caribbean colonial bureaucrat for an "'African' point of reference" *(point de répère africain),* as Michel Fabre phrases it.[8] It would mean considering Maran's own adamant articulation of diaspora, his insistence—in the preface to *Batouala*—that his fiction would have relevance because prejudice and violence in the U.S. South (as well as the postwar debates about the presence of French African soldiers guarding the German front) had made "the Negro question" apropos: "Mon livre n'est pas de polémique. Il vient, par hasard, à son heure. La question nègre est 'actuelle.' Qui a voulu qu'il en fût ainsi? Mais les Américains. Mais les campagnes des journaux d'outre-Rhin" ("My book is not a polemic. It comes, by chance, when its hour strikes. The Negro question is 'of the moment.' Who made it thus? Why, the Americans. Why, the press campaigns on the other side of the Rhine").[9] It would mean asking, indeed, how a book that proclaims itself timely, a book written in Africa that links itself to America and to Europe, a book that claims a certain applicability to "la question nègre" might *not* be "polemic." It would mean theorizing a Francophone mode of framing blackness, a Caribbean approach to the formalist manipulation of the preface.

It would also mean taking account of the peculiar role of Maran's novel in its particular literary field, in the development of what came to be called "colonial literature" in France, an emergent tradition that African American critics such as Locke and Fauset were following with great interest. How much do *Batouala*'s internationalist take on "the Negro question" and its critique of colonialism stand out in French literature of the period? How exceptional is Maran's book? In fact, although early colonial anthologies in French such as Blaise Cendrars's 1921 *Anthologie nègre* are obviously transnational in the simplest sense, in that they extend their gaze beyond the borders of France itself, it is possible to argue that in this orientation they are nonetheless not international, for they begin and end obsessed with the modernity of France, peering out at what is imagined to be an African Other. The colonies, in other words, are presented at best as a culture or "backward" civilization and put more or less directly in juxtaposition to the modernity of the French national culture. (In this operation, African civilizations are never described as having anything in common with the modern European nation-state.) So the possibility of internationality is at best a lacuna. But as Toni Morrison has pointed out, "invisible things are not necessarily 'not there'. . . . [C]ertain absences are so stressed, so ornate, so planned, they call attention to themselves; arrest us with intentionality and purpose, like neighborhoods that are defined by the population held away from them."[10]

In French colonial literature, internationality is this kind of "arresting," constitutive gap. It is not a passive absence, but the force that must be pushed away and controlled in the service of a greater project: the cultural representation of France to the French. Colonial literature turns its attention to the colonies with the aim of "worlding a world," in Gayatri Chakravorty Spivak's phrase—shaping a blank and indefinite *France d'outre mer* into the inscribed and definite entity of *la plus grande France*. Internationality and difference must be swallowed in the service of an expansive, anthropophagic nationalism. This is an epistemic violence because it must take for granted that the ground it claims is history-less, is uninscribed.[11] And any articulation that attempts to demonstrate otherwise—to argue that Africa or Asia already is inscribed by culture or that natives be framed in other ways (by race sentiment or by class consciousness)—is an immediate challenge to such a project. Thus, just as the competing British empire represents a threat to the linguistic and cultural dominance of France over its colonies, likewise any hint of black internationalism represents another kind of threat to this dominance—perhaps even more of a threat, in the end, since black internationalism imperiled not just France's colonial possessions, but also one of France's main ways of defining itself. So it should be noted that the framing gestures of the early anthologies such as Cendrars's, which present African culture as primitive and studiously ignore *les nègres* elsewhere in the world, are the other side of the coin of the colonial administration's efforts to prevent black U.S. papers such as Marcus Garvey's *Negro World* from seeping into the colonies.

Cendrars's *Anthologie nègre* is the direct descendant of nineteenth-century European travel narratives and early ethnography.[12] René Maran later would term the approach of such work *anthroponégrisme:* the vulgar collection of black cultural and biological "data," with a prevailing and almost bureaucratic pretension to objectivity, in a manner that at once exoticizes and distances the black subject into a premodern or infantile specimen.[13] Often this anthropologizing frame amounts to no more than the most crude Western technique of distancing or retarding black culture in order to consolidate certain ideas of a racialized European modernity—in this sense, it is not unconnected to strategies that Edward Said has categorized with the term *Orientalism*.[14] The innovative French ethnographer and autobiographer Michel Leiris wrote later that Cendrars's book was one of the opening forays of the *vogue nègre* in the 1920s: "More than a book, this was an act," Leiris proclaimed.[15] And the *Anthologie nègre* is as sensationalist as this statement suggests: it is composed of already-published, sloppily translated, poorly organized "facts" and documents (often of questionable validity in the first place) culled from travel journals and collections by previous European voyagers in Africa. The anthology's success speaks more to the demands of the period for any "exotic" material at all than for any quality in the book itself.

Cendrars's preface is almost amusingly thin. In a page and a half, he makes no effort at all to collate his jumbled excerpts or to situate the reader and, in fact, opens inauspiciously by apologizing that the translations are so poor. "The present volume is a compilation," he explains. "I have reproduced these tales just as the missionaries and explorers brought them back to us in Europe and just as they published them. They are not always the most original versions, nor the most faithful translations."[16] But what becomes evident in the somewhat surprising lack in the book of any mention of black art or culture in the United States or in the Americas in general is indeed the very purpose of this "act." Paul Morand, another popular French writer on exotic subjects in the 1920s, punctuated his review of the *Anthologie nègre* by noting that it "brought back to black art [*l'art nègre*] a public that other manifestations had distanced."[17] Cendrars's framing not only projects its own disorganization onto its subject's "primitivism," but moreover is also concerned to battle against those "other manifestations": the emerging evidence of a transnational black modern culture. So the very possibility of a black internationalism plays a central role in the *Anthologie nègre* in the way it is not voiced, in the way it is silenced. This compilation, in other words, even as it plays a part in the *vogue nègre* right alongside early jazz, African art, and emergent Francophone and Harlem Renaissance literature, quite deliberately attempts to push out of the picture the "manifestations" of a black modern expressive culture that had scandalized, titillated, and ultimately "distanced" the French public—precisely because the proximity and influence of that culture posed an immediate threat to the tradition of imagining a reassuringly distant and backward African.

A different debate started to develop, though, in the medium of such framing gestures, about the efficacy of the old French colonial policy of *assimilation,* which, unlike the British policy, actively tried to cultivate a native elite harvested from the best and brightest black French citizens of West African society. Inhabitants of the Four Communes of Dakar, Saint Louis, Gorée, and Rufisque in Senegal were given voting privileges and citizenship rights, but the overwhelming majority of French West African "natives" *(indigènes)* were disenfranchised "subjects" and actually fell under a different, harsher set of legal strictures—the notorious *indigénat*—than black or white French citizens.[18] Increasingly the black African elite had been brought to the metropole to be educated in French schools. Although the policy of assimilation depended on an unwieldy centralization of the colonial administration and on the exploitation of the African peasantry through forced labor in extravagant "public" construction projects and forced conscription in World War I, the French collaboration with the native elite allowed France to claim that it was antiracist in philosophy and practice and that it was "civilizing" the natives as quickly as possible.

But in the wake of Colonial Minister Albert Sarraut's project for the "Mise en Valeur" of the African colonies, announced in early 1921, which envisioned a great wave of construction of ports, railroads, highways, and irrigation systems in order to increase the economic yield of the possessions, critiques of French "native policy" became louder and louder.[19] The critique emanated from an odd couple: a loose and shifting alliance of former and current French colonial administrators (Pierre Mille, André Demaison, Gaston Joseph) and, later on, the early French ethnographers (especially students of Marcel Mauss and Lucien Levy-Bruhl), fast becoming an academic force in their own right.[20] This coalition was institutionalized with the creation of the Institut d'Ethnologie in 1925 and led directly to the re-formation (carried out by Georges Henri Rivière and Paul Rivet) of the Musée d'Ethnologie-Trocadéro into the Musée de l'Homme in the 1930s.[21] These scholars and administrators began to argue that Africans were not unformed savages to be molded into Frenchmen, but instead people with a long history and a rich civilization, albeit a primitive or "backward" one. For example, Maurice Delafosse, another former colonial minister who published a number of books on African culture and civilization in the 1920s, wrote: "We now have a much clearer and broader idea of the existence, alongside and outside of our society, of other societies, each of whom has its civilization, its own aspirations, its special needs as we do ourselves; and no one can now deny to these societies, however different they may be from French society, the right to maintain their civilization, to realize their aspirations, to provide for their needs, according to their genius [*génie*] and temperament."[22] As Raymond Leslie Buell noted a few years later in *The Native Problem in Africa:* "There is a growing recognition in France, as well as elsewhere, that because of environment and heredity, it is impossible to convert a native into a Frenchman simply by teaching him the French language and by giving him a few years in a French school."[23]

The weight of publications supporting this revisionist culturalist argument accrued in the early part of the decade, with increasingly comprehensive and encyclopedic works by authors including Delafosse, Demaison, Louis Huot, Lucien Levy-Bruhl, Robert Delavignette, and Leo Frobenius appearing in Paris in rapid-fire succession.[24] This social science attack on the philosophy behind assimilation led to calls for drastic reform, for a "new native policy," as Delafosse put it, which

> will take as a point of departure the accurate and profound recognition of native societies and as an aim the maintenance and the reinforcement of these societies and of everything in their institutions and moral development, it being well understood that this development will have as a corollary the development of our own civilization.
>
> The rights of native groups on the soil which they occupy should be recognized; these groups should be given every necessary guarantee that they may enjoy these rights in liberty and security. Respect should be accorded to their traditional customs in everything that is not contrary, not to *our* ideal of civilization, but to the welfare of the native societies themselves; native law should be justly applied to local tradition, education should be adapted to native needs and aspirations, and this policy should be accompanied by necessary measures for the improvement of the native health and for native economic development.[25]

Such a seemingly generous concept of "indirect rule" or *association* did not transform colonial policy in French West Africa—the economic stakes were too high, first of all, and the racist ideology that required a "backward" African other was too deeply entrenched.

Ironically, this reformist assault met some of its toughest resistance from many of the *évolués*—the "evolved" African and Antillean elite—who had both a vested interest and an ideological commitment to a colonialism based on the principle of making a small and privileged minority of black "natives" into Frenchmen. A number of scholars have pointed out the paradoxes of the shift in French policy from assimilation to association, and some have asserted that indeed the anthropological argument was only incidental to more basic imperial concerns: "France's reassessment was motivated more by a desire to contain the *évolués* in particular, and to re-establish authority among their subjects in general, than by any intrinsic interest in either African civilizations or democratization."[26] So association in practice came to refer to a shift in emphasis away from the education of the *évolués*, who were considered too independent and "undisciplined," threatening both traditional social structures and colonial power, and toward a renewed cooperation with the old African elites—religious authorities, chieftains, and ruling notables—whom the French attempted to use as intermediaries in the colonial exploitation of the masses.

It is seldom noticed that the colonial administration's wariness of the *évolués* was a reaction to the Pan-African Congress movement in the early 1920s as much as a result of French ethnographic scholarship. The French were worried that the Pan-African Congresses could foment new revolts, especially in the West African colonies, and the policy decision around assimilation and association was largely hashed out in communiqués between Paris and Dakar in the wake of black internationalist stirrings. The administration often viewed Pan-Africanism as a force effectively in collusion with international communism, which was already attempting to aid anticolonial movements in the European colonies. In one such memo from the fall of 1921, the Governor General wrote that

[t]he ideas of emancipation, which the backers of the anti-European movement are attempting to spread in Africa, are obviously destined to create illusions among the young educated blacks [*les jeunes noirs lettrés*], agents of the administration or of commerce, who desire to equal the white man. . . . On the other hand, new impressions have been stimulated amongst the masses, who up until now have stayed

attached to the land and to their ancient customs, by the accounts of liberated soldiers or of soldiers returned from trips to the metropole or to the coastal cities. . . . It thus behooves us to confront these unhealthy stimuli [*excitations malsaines*] with the notions of order and social discipline, which should direct the evolution of the black races [*des races noires*] and preserve Africa from upheavals, whose certain effect would be to annihilate the work of civilization that has begun, returning the continent to its ancient barbarism.[27]

The Ministre des Colonies was so fearful that news of the Pan-African gathering in particular might reach "the natives" that a memo was sent to each of the colonial governors in Africa, asking for reports on the effects of the congress and on the "state of mind" *(état d'esprit)* of the masses.[28]

Even within the parameters of such a debate on colonial policy, then, the very idea of a particular black modern culture remains a lacuna, still the possibility that must be concealed or pushed away. Writing in 1931, André Demaison insists that there once existed an African literature, not just oral but written, but describes only the far-off "classical" literature written centuries earlier in Arabic and a few West African languages, for example, without noting that Africans had begun to write in European languages as well.[29] In the 1922 *Les Noirs de l'Afrique,* one of the first works synthesizing the material on the history of African civilization, Maurice Delafosse goes so far as to present his book as a possible "preface" to a black modernity—but that possibility is necessarily out of the book's scope, displaced to some unspecified future moment. First and foremost, one must consider the question of the origins of African civilization, Delafosse says. In fact, his opening chapter goes on to argue that the black populations originated in Oceania and only later migrated to Africa—so "African culture" is not even originally African. Then he quickly limits the scope of his inquiry, saying that he will not be writing about the "important role" played by "the white race" *(la race blanche)* in the history of North Africa or about Islamic influences on African societies. He frames his object as a "pure" and purely *continental* black culture: "the civilizations and the material, intellectual, and social characters of Negro populations [*populations de race noire*] living on the African continent." This means of course that the book will not speak of other parts of the world that "possess blacks [*Nègres*]," in particular "the countries, such as America, where the appearance of the Negro race [*la race noire*] only occurred in a recent era, following the generally involuntary migrations whose genesis and circumstances we know."[30]

Delafosse dispenses with this single mention of forced migration and the slave trade on the second page and never suggests that this history "whose genesis and circumstances we know" might have any impact on the African civilization he goes on to describe so neatly. On the contrary, he then is conveniently able to describe African civilization as "isolated" in a manner that consolidates French modernity even as it laments African history as distant and divorced from the world, sadly deprived of cultural contact aside from the Arab and European slave trades, which were invasive and oppressive and thus not conducive to growth:

> But the Negroes of Africa [*les Noirs de l'Afrique*], through no fault of their own, have had the disastrous misfortune of not being able to evolve as the other great human races have. Whereas, for centuries, the descendants of our ancestors the Gauls found themselves constantly in contact with populations more evolved or differently evolved than themselves, but from a civilization contemporary to their own, and they were able, taking from some, being inspired by others, to become the French of today, during the same period the unfortunate blacks [*les malheureux Nègres*] were almost completely isolated from humanity.[31]

So Delafosse's own rhetorical dismissal of the disparate cultural influences on Africa becomes a sign of European sophistication, on the one hand, and more slyly an apology for reformed colonialism (as an avenue for Africa to the cultural "contact" necessary for "evolution"). At this point, at the other end, he can close his work with the following paragraph, a remarkable twist in French colonial strategies of framing:

> The isolation in which natural barriers have shut off the environment of the blacks of Africa [*des Nègres de l'Afrique*] for too long has made them backward [*des arriérés*] or, more precisely, belated [*des attardés*] in relation to the more favored Europeans: they have lost a great deal of time, and will not be able to catch up in a day or even in a century. But they certainly have not said their last word, and their history is not finished. Perhaps it is only beginning, and this book is but a

preface [*Peut-être ne fait-elle que commencer et ce livre n'est-il qu'une préface*].[32]

This notion of African civilization as stunted due to isolation is an argument that depends to a large degree on Delafosse's opening moves to shut out any consideration of syncretism or cultural cross-fertilization. Of course Africa is isolated if one cuts out Egypt, Islam, and Greece and declines to discuss the slave trade! The book not only frames the history of traditional African civilization with this gesture, but also concludes by framing itself. Here are the origins, it says, here is the history—but the story is not over. It may be just beginning. But if Delafosse's book serves as a "preface" to black modernity, that modernity is thereby distanced, deferred, a time to come. "They will not be able to catch up in a day, or even in a century": the book thus firmly closes its frame to any contemporary black modern culture through the very underhanded gesture which patronizingly admits the possibility of such an "unfinished" history.

Raoul Girardet has argued that the increasingly nuanced claims expounded in such works of early French ethnology and colonial reform were not only supported by the cultural waves of the *vogue nègre,* but in fact preceded and introduced by the first stirrings of the "colonial novel" even before the war, with works such as Victor Segalen's *Les Immémoriaux* (1907) and the Tharaud brothers' *La Fête arabe* (1912).[33] René Maran, in a 1929 entry on "French African Literature" for the *Encyclopaedia Britannica,* makes no mention of the few Africans who had published in French (Ahmadou Mapaté Diagne, Kojo Tovalou Houénou, Bakary Diallo, Lamine Senghor), but instead basically offers a list of colonial literature, of what might more accurately be termed "French Literature about Africa," including not just novels but also nonfiction such as Lucie Cousturier's *Des Inconnus chez moi* (1920) and André Gide's *Voyage au Congo* (1928). He notes moreover that fiction like his own work and that of the Tharaud brothers, Gaston Joseph, Demaison, and the Leblonds has "also contributed to the researches of such men as Delafosse, Bruel and missionaries of all classes, lay, military, commercial and religious."[34] "French African Literature" is defined here, then, neither as African nor as simply fiction: it indicates a cross-genre compendium of writings about the dark continent.

What becomes apparent in such material might be described as a facet of a cultural field even broader than Maran's already broad definition. In the

1920s, there developed a multidisciplinary and relatively flexible apparatus for framing *les nègres,* combining popular cultural and administrative and academic techniques. The novel approaches social science, anthropology flirts with fiction, and jazz itself is viewed even by the most perceptive Parisian listeners not as an expression of a "black counterculture of modernity," but more as an "African" ethnographic event, even as a sort of religious possession ceremony. In this sleight of hand, American jazz—whether Mitchell's Jazz Kings holding court at the Casino de Paris from 1919 to 1923; or Ada "Bricktop" Smith wowing the Prince of Wales with "Insufficient Sweetie" and "Miss Otis Regrets" at the Grand Duc; or Sydney Bechet's arrival on the scene in 1920 at the Théâtre de l'Apollo in Montmartre with the Southern Syncopated Orchestra; or Copeland and MacHenry playing the old Jockey Bar in Montmartre in 1923; or Josephine Baker and Bechet in the legendary "Revue Nègre" at the Théâtre des Champs-Elysées in 1925—in any version, becomes a document of Africa.

For this reason, the group of French ethnographers who emerged in the 1920s had a singularly odd relationship to jazz. Looking back at his nights spent roaming the Montmartre jazz clubs with Georges Bataille, Michel Leiris would later comment famously that he considered jazz in Paris to be the "première manifestation des *nègres,* mythe des édens de couleur qui devait me mener jusqu'en Afrique et, par-delà l'Afrique, jusqu'à l'ethnographie" ("first manifestation of the *blacks,* myth of colored Edens which were to lead me all the way to Africa, and, beyond Africa, to ethnography").[35] Other French intellectuals had more complex and more direct relations to black expressive culture in the 1920s, complicating the framing of jazz as ethnographic document. For instance, Georges Henri Rivière, the driving force in French museology and the emergence of the Musée de l'Homme, was a passable pianist who often played at jam sessions at the infamous jazz club Le Boeuf sur le Toit. In 1926 Rivière even penned a frivolous tune for Josephine Baker, who was performing at the Folies-Bergère. While Baker danced, a singer dressed as an "academic" sighed, "Et ma tête matin et soir / Est pleine d'idées noires / Tout'les femmes veulent prendre l'air / De Joséphine Baker. . . ." ("And morning and night, my head / is full of black ideas / All the women want to assume the airs / of Josephine Baker").[36] Most significantly, in 1924 Rivière also served as the "music critic" *(critique musical)* for *Les Continents,* the short-lived newspaper founded and edited by Kojo Tovalou Houénou with René Maran, contrib-

Josephine Baker and Georges Henri Rivière at the Musée de l'Homme, 1933 (photo by Lipnitski). Collection Musée de l'Homme, Paris.

uting a couple of articles including a review of a classical concert by the African American singer Roland Hayes.[37] But by 1928 Rivière stopped playing music in public to concentrate on his museum work, entering the institution that would become the Musée de l'Homme "as one enters a religion."[38]

The best-known hint of Rivière's prior diversions is a series of notably strange photos taken in 1933, where Rivière and Josephine Baker flirt among African artifacts and musical instruments brought back by the Mission Dakar-Djibouti. In the photos, Rivière seems to offer Baker the instruments in poses that at once frame her as female, black Other—"putting her under glass" *(en vitrine)* as one commentator phrases it—and simultaneously envision the space of the museum as a space of play for two old friends snickering at the erotic stereotypes of anthropological exoticism.[39] But this complexity stands outside the general tenor of the times—except in the way its racial spectacle cobbles together unlikely faces and unlikely spaces in the metropole. Overall, the history of the *vogue nègre* in the 1920s

can be read as instances of the articulation of an unwieldy framing apparatus—discontinuous and contradictory ones, at times announced with great
force and at times announced in ways that were awkward, if not sophomoric and downright ludicrous. René Maran's *Batouala* enters this mine-
field with a bang of its own.

Véritable Roman Nègre

Maran's *Batouala* was described by one critic as "by no means a work of
art," but another cultural artifact to be placed alongside early African
American jazz in Europe, galas of modernist primitivism such as the Fêtes
Nègres produced by the Comte de Beaumont after the war, avant-garde
music such as Poulenc's *Rhapsodie nègre* (1917) and Stravinsky's *Ragtime
pour onze instruments* (1918), exoticist literature including Robert Goffin's
jazz-inspired poems, and the early exhibitions of African and Oceanic art
arranged by collectors such as Paul Guillaume. In this extended field,
Batouala was original only because it was a novel "écrit et pensé en nègre"
("written and thought in *nègre*"). "We should have expected it," the critic
continues. "After the invasion into our orchestras of that epileptic cacoph-
ony called jazz-band, where the mooing of car horns and the howls of delir-
ious darkies [*moricauds en délire*] are jumbled together; after the expositions
of puerile drawings and formless black statues [*informes statues nègres*], the
black novel [*roman nègre*] had to have its turn."[40]

It should come as no surprise that so much critical energy swirled
around Maran—not just in Harlem, but in Paris as well—when *Batouala*
was awarded the Prix Goncourt on December 14, 1921. For *Batouala* represents both the inception of the tradition of the colonial novel and the
great exception to that tradition. It is both formative and exorbitant for one
simple reason: because René Maran was, in the words of another journalist,
"lui-même, paraît-il, un homme de couleur" ("himself, it would seem, a
man of color").[41] Maran's novel is not a rupture because it is especially radical in its style or insights. The conundrum and the provocation is packaged
in the book's subtitle: "véritable roman nègre." This seemingly innocuous
phrase speaks double, not exactly in the vocabulary of "double consciousness" elaborated by Du Bois and Johnson, but in a manner that one might
term particularly Francophone.

On the one hand, the novel is *véritable* in the sense of being "true." This
pretension to verisimilitude imposes parameters that become definitive for

the genre: an obsession for absolute "cultural truth" that approaches a kind of "psychological naturalism," as Raoul Girardet puts it, often one with explicit claims to something like social science. Gaston Joseph's *Koffi, roman vrai d'un Noir* (1922), a portrait of an obsequious "native" who works as assistant and interpreter for a French colonial official, was considered to be the official "anti-*Batouala*" novel and was coronated as such in 1924 with the first Grand Prix de la Littérature Coloniale—a new prize expressly concocted to counter Maran's Goncourt win.[42] Nevertheless Joseph was forced to challenge *Batouala* on Maran's terms, the oxymoronic paradigm of the "true novel." As described in the preface by Gabriel Angoulvant, a former governor of the colonies, *Koffi* is "as its title indicates, the *Novel of a Black Man* [*le Roman d'un Noir*], and I am tempted to say the History [*l'Histoire*], because this is a true story [*une histoire vraie*], lived, exact in the smallest details: there is not one characteristic, one expression, one incident, one adventure, that the author did not capture and note from life, on the spot [*sur le vif et sur place*]."[43] This compulsion is echoed without exception throughout the genre, as stressed for example in the preface by Jean and Jérôme Tharaud to André Demaison's 1923 *Diato,* another novel filled to the brim with "authentic" African tales, songs, and proverbs.[44] Maurice Delafosse's incensed review of *Batouala* focuses precisely on the novel's claims to "truth." He contends that Maran would never have won the Goncourt if he were white; indeed, he would have been prosecuted by the colonial administration for his libelous fabrications about the colonial situation. "Some people," Delafosse snarls, "are quite lucky to be *nègres.*"[45] There were even a number of anthropological works that sold themselves as "correctives" to *Batouala*'s excesses, again purporting to offer the "truth" about conditions in the colonies.[46]

But on the other hand, *Batouala* is also *véritable* in that it is seen as being "written in *nègre*"—it is the first celebrated novel in French published by a writer of African descent.[47] The problem with *Batouala,* however, is not that it expresses some essential blackness or even some creole identity. The problem is more simple: this very double "veritable-ness" challenges the main assumption behind the multifaceted efforts at framing blackness, as laid out in works such as Cendrars's *Anthologie,* which works so hard to position *les nègres* as distant, primitive, isolated, and above all silent—anthropological objects that never talk back. *Batouala* is a counter-"act" because Maran's novel is considered to represent *the black modern speaking himself*—

a black voice that intervenes and that is inescapably metropolitan, current, and independent.

In France, then, the double entendre of Maran's subtitle stirred up a great deal of consternation since the gesture was perceived as an intervention and shift. As with the Pan-African movement, a number of commentators accused *Batouala* of anti-colonial "propaganda," even charging that the novel aimed to provoke rebellion in Africa.[48] It is interesting to note in contrast that in the black U.S. press the valence of Maran's phrase was either blatantly misunderstood by the reviewers (a surprising number) who simply assumed that Maran himself was a "contemporary African"[49] or taken at face value by reviewers such as Locke and Fauset. The latter wrote guilelessly that "*Batouala* is really what its sub-title indicates, a story of actual Negro life *(véritable roman nègre)*," not seeming to notice that her translation does not at all capture the ambiguity of the French phrase.[50]

The subtlety of Maran's gesture is a radical departure in the history of colonial literature, and in the *vogue nègre*. Still, *Batouala* confounded French critics also because Maran himself claimed repeatedly throughout his career to have been wholly unaware of the radical implications of his "act" in publishing the novel. Almost forty years later, it is still with some puzzlement that Maran describes *Batouala*'s "non-conformisme, dont je ne me rendais pas compte" ("non-conformity, which I did not realize").[51] Although many French critics read the book as a troubling expression of black modernity—and worse, as a dangerous expression of diasporic solidarity between educated French Caribbean citizens and peasant French African subjects—what is exceptional about *Batouala*'s exceptionalism is precisely the discrepancy between the novel's orientation and its reception. Maran does not identify himself as a "nègre" in the preface. Although he certainly intends his novel both as a political intervention (into debates around colonial reform) and as a stylistic shift (rejecting any romanticism in the colonial novel), he does not seem to anticipate that the very specter of him—an *évolué* Martinican colonial administrator, after all—writing about Africa will be received as blasphemy and threat.

It must be emphasized that *Batouala*'s doubleness is reinforced at a *formal* level. The fulcrum of the discrepancy lies in the often-noted shift in tone and seeming shift in argument between the book's preface, a fierce diatribe against French colonial abuses, and the story itself, in which the focus is wholly placed on a decaying African traditional culture.[52] Compared to the tale of the chief Batouala's betrayal at the hands of his favorite wife Yassiguindiji and his best friend Bissibingui, Maran's preface hits hard, describing in excruciating detail the devastation of the Kemo region of Ubangui-Shari in French Equatorial Africa caused by persistent famine and forced labor:

> Civilisation, civilisation, orgueil des Européens, et leur charnier d'innocents. . . . Tu bâtis ton royaume sur des cadavres. Quoi que tu veuilles, quoi que tu fasses, tu te meus dans le mensonge. A ta vue, les larmes de sourdre et la douleur de crier. Tu es la force qui prime le droit. Tu n'es pas un flambeau, mais un incendie. Tout ce à quoi tu touches, tu le consumes. . . . (11)

> Civilization, civilization, pride of the Europeans, and their slaughterhouse of innocents. . . . You build your kingdom on top of corpses. Whatever you want, whatever you do, you are mired in lies. At the mere sight of you, eyes well up with tears and cries break out. You are the force that supersedes right. You are not a torch, but a conflagration. You consume whatever you touch. . . .

To French readers used to the romantic exoticism of Pierre Mille and Pierre Bonardi, these words were a slap in the face. When *Batouala* became a bestseller and was awarded the Goncourt—which Proust's *A l'ombre des jeunes filles en fleurs* had won two years earlier—this canonized affront, considered to be the first literary attack on the French system, with its complaints about the excessive drinking, "intellectual anemia," and "moral asthenia" of colonial administrators (14), escalated into a full-fledged scandal.

Even in the preface, though, Maran is never simply accusatory. He is engaged in the project of framing the "colonial question" in highly striking terms, but throughout, he remains a reformer, not a revolutionary. He chooses to stake out a certain distance from the Africans he portrays, even when his reformist aims are most explicit. Thus he insists, for example, on a version of what Talal Asad has called "cultural translation"—a trope that also becomes pivotal to the emerging colonial novel genre's articulation of itself as a kind of social science.[53] "J'ai mis six ans à le parfaire" ("I have spent six years perfecting it"), Maran tells us:

J'ai mis six ans à y traduire ce que j'avais, là-bas, entendu, à y décrire ce que j'avais vu.

Au cours de ces six années, pas un moment je n'ai cédé à la tentation de dire mon mot. J'ai poussée la conscience objective jusqu'à supprimer des réflexions qu'on aurait pu m'attribuer. (9)

I have taken six years to translate what I had heard, there, and to describe what I had seen.

In the course of those six years, I never yielded a single moment to the temptation of saying my own word. I have pushed objective consciousness to the point of suppressing reflections which might have been attributable to me.

Such a translating frame necessarily installs cultural distance, posing the novelistic "translator" as a mediating figure. It is a trope that reappears often in colonial literature: Demaison, for one, is said to "translate the complication that naturally escapes the notice of the visitor simply passing through [*au regard du simple passant*]," and the Tharaud brothers offer a longer passage with the same flavor in their preface to *La Randonnée de Samba Diouf,* describing a conversation with Demaison:

We imagined this tale [*récit*] while listening to you talk, and you gave us the thousand details necessary to give it life—details as much in the language of the Wolofs as in that of the Mandingos, both of which you speak with the same ease as the patois of Périgord. "Ah! dear friend," I said to you once, "truly, your Negroes [*Noirs*] express themselves like academics!" "My word, yes," you responded. "But what would you have me do? I am translating what they say, word for word. If their languages [*langues*] are supple and rich, and capable of rendering the most subtle nuances, it is simply testimony that these people of West Africa are not at all the brutes that a mediocre colonial literature likes to represent to us. A beautiful language [*un beau langage*] is a collective and unconscious masterpiece. These Negroes would not speak this way if there were not a civilization behind them, a very simple one, but a civilization all the same."[54]

Speaking of translation in these prefaces becomes a way of representing a frontier. When one speaks of "translating" a culture, one rhetorically posits it both to be discrete and to be inaccessible without mediation—and so the work of translating is the work of carrying it across that linguistic border, bringing it closer to a home audience. This of course privileges the translator as an agent of cultural commerce with absolute authority.

Translation *turns* here, as all tropes do, for there is a continual slippage in the use of this term: sometimes (as when Cendrars or Delafosse writes of translating myths or folktales, or when the Tharaud brothers describe Demaison as speaking Wolof and Mandingo "with the same ease as the patois of Périgord") the term alludes to linguistic translation, to the knowledge of an African language. But sometimes (as with the Tharauds themselves) it alludes to metaphoric translation—one "translates" a culture into some form comprehensible to the European audience. In other words, the translation metaphor represents not just a trope of authority, but also a particular kind of invasive gesture, one that works by eliding the difference between anthropological and linguistic studies, as Talal Asad has pointed out:

> One difference between the anthropologist and the linguist in the matter of translation is perhaps this: that whereas the latter is immediately faced with a specific piece of discourse produced within the society studied, a discourse that is *then* textualized, the former must construct the discourse *as* a cultural text in terms of meanings *implicit* in a range of practices. The construction of cultural discourse and its translation thus seem to be facets of a single act.[55]

In purporting to read what Asad calls "the *implicit* in alien cultures" (or what Demaison terms "the collective and unconscious masterpieces" of African expression), the colonial novelist as cultural translator actively *constructs* a discursive image of the other culture, while crouching behind the alibi that he is only "passively" translating—that is, letting the object culture "speak for itself."

The trope serves three functions, then: first, it acts to mark off cultural difference by emphasizing linguistic difference, in a move that simultaneously distances *les nègres* and confers absolute interpretative power on the author—only through his expertise can their complexity be understood. Second, it latches onto an argument then becoming widespread in social linguistics—that a language reflects a particular way of comprehending the world—to support its anti-assimilationist project. Africans would not speak in such supple, rich, nuanced ways "if there were not a civilization behind them," so one should not try to transform them into Frenchmen. And third, it adds to the social science allure of the enterprise of colonial novel writing. Thus the profusion of phrases such as "word for word" and "painstaking." Using a metaphor of translation, writers such as Maran and Tharaud take advantage of the trappings of literal translation to paint themselves as engaged in a sort of precise, "objective" craft.

Maran's approach to translation is all the more complex because despite the claims in the preface, the many African words in the novel itself (*tourougou, kouloungoulou, ga'nzas, koufrou, bazi'nguérs, boundjouvoukou*) are not translated directly.[56] At most *Batouala* offers what in ethnolinguistics is termed *contextualization,* or *cushioning:* a brief explanatory phrase in the target language that allows the reader to infer the meaning of the African-language words or phrases describing "culturally bound objects or occurrences," as they are "sprinkled" through the prose.[57] (Maran increased his use of cushioning to some extent in the "definitive" 1938 revision of Batouala partly in response to criticism about the many untranslated words.) Thus at one ceremony, we learn that there are "'bangaos' ou patates douces" ("'bangaos' or sweet potatoes") (65); in the opening pages of the novel, dawn breaks to the accompaniment of animals crying in the forest, including "l'appel rauque des 'bacouyas,' singes au museau allongé comme celui du chien" ("the hoarse call of 'bacouyas,' monkeys with elongated muzzles like dogs") (20). If anything, this approach to "translation" in *Batouala* ultimately serves to emphasize Maran's authoritative positioning, as the text continually re-marks the linguistic barriers of cultural alterity.

As though to be sure to avoid any confusion, the preface to *Batouala* quickly goes beyond the habitual translator's alibi, adding a vivid image of disjunction. Maran describes writing the novel over a six-year period while serving in the administration of the Central African colony of Ubangui-Shari. The book is "completely objective," he explains, emphasizing the *décalage* between him and "les nègres de l'Afrique Equatoriale":

Ce roman est donc tout objectif. Il ne tâche même pas à expliquer: il constate. Il ne s'indigne pas: il enregistre. Il ne pouvait en être autrement. Par les soirs de lune, allongé en ma chaise longue, de ma véranda, j'écoutais les conversations de ces pauvres gens. Leurs plaisanteries prouvaient leur résignation. Ils souffraient et riaient de souffrir. (10)

This novel is thus completely objective. It does not even attempt to explain: it states. It does not become indignant: it registers. It could not have been otherwise. On moonlit evenings, stretched out on the chaise lounge on my veranda, I listened to the conversations of these poor people. Their jokes gave proof of their resignation. They suffered and laughed at their suffering.

What is surprising, considering the way the book is received, is that there is no black internationalist consciousness expressed here, much less an expression of solidarity. This is on the contrary a clear image of distinction: Maran the administrator on his veranda, unseen, listening in the half-light to the conversations and laughter of the Africans below. At best it continues the claim of anthropological objectivity, and at worse it is a rather plain admission of Maran's posturing as an *homme de couleur*—an odd sort of parasite, literally and figuratively above *les nègres*. Maran goes further in this direction in a letter to one critic who had written an especially unfavorable review of *Batouala*:

Au cours de ce laps de temps, j'ai étudié quotidiennement l'indigène, je l'ai fait parler. . . . Si j'ai reproduit, traduit les doléances indigènes, si je me suis efforcé de rendre tangible leur mentalité, je ne peux admettre que l'on veuille m'imputer ce qu'ils pensent vraiment et ce qu'ils disent *lorsqu'ils croient qu'on ne les entend pas.* Mon livre, la préface mise à part, ne contient rien de mes idées. Je n'ai été là qu'un appareil à enregistrer.[58]

During this period, I studied the native every day; I made him speak. . . . If I have reproduced, translated the sorrows of the natives, if I have striven to render their mentality tangible, I cannot allow that people impute to me what the natives really think, and what they say *when they think that no one hears them.* My book, the preface aside, contains none of my ideas. In it, I have only been a recording device.

The aesthetic of overhearing is troubling, to say the least. What does it mean to insist that one has recorded what the natives say "when they think that no one hears them"? The claim is an extension of the familiar insistence on "objectivity," that the novel "contains none of my ideas": Maran has provided his readers a record of what the Africans "really think" when they are among themselves, when they are not mollifying French officials by masking their real impressions. There is not exactly an insinuation of sympathy with the "natives" here, and no suggestion that Maran has slipped even slightly in his loyalty to the French colonial project. On the contrary: it is difficult not to wonder whether Maran is not positioning himself—as a black colonial administrator—as a special kind of funnel, a privileged conduit of "native" information imbued with insight precisely because of his racial status, which somehow places him closer to the Africans, better able to hear and "translate" even as he lounges above them. Even though this recording recalls the aesthetic of Langston Hughes's blues poems, Maran's rhetoric of self-distancing and orientation in framing (always "translating" the native "mentality" for a privileged metropolitan French colonial audience) clearly distinguish the positioning in *Batouala* from the populist lyricism of *Fine Clothes to the Jew*.

One striking feature of Maran's language in these passages is his insistence that he has "never yielded to the temptation to say his own word," that he is in fact, curiously, "only a recording instrument." Alain Locke, in his *Opportunity* review of "The Colonial Literature of France," uses similar language as he describes the contours of the genre, emphasizing the stylistic advances of Maran's novel. Compared to the "tainted or inartistic sources" of traditional colonial literature, carelessly jotted down by "the exploiting charlatans, the incompetent romancers, and the moralistic missionaries," Maran's work represents a huge leap forward toward "realism," Locke argues.[59] Locke reads colonial literature in 1923 as standing at a kind of generic crossroads, choosing between the popular romance of the Tharaud brothers, the enlightened humanitarianism of Gaston Joseph, and the "aesthetically objective" approach of Maran.[60] Significantly, when Locke argues that Maran's work represents this crucial new stylistic development—and a black modern expression, as well—he turns to a similar kind of "recording" metaphor:

Even more so than in the American school of fiction was the native in colonial literature merely a dark note by which the false high-lights of the painting were keyed up. . . . But the public mind, with its predilection for fake and lurid chromos, by this brilliant, daring etching of Maran's has been, so to speak, resurfaced for a new impression, at

once more artistic and true. . . . It was heroic work—and required to
be done by the Negro himself—this revolutionary change from sentimentality to realism, from caricature to portraiture.[61]

Here, the recording metaphor is phrased in terms of the visual arts—apparently Locke is expanding on a phrase on the first page of Maran's preface
("Il n'est, à vrai dire, qu'une succession d'eaux-fortes" ["To tell the truth, it
is only a succession of etchings"] (9)). Maran abandons this visual metaphor and concentrates on aural tropes of recording, but Locke runs with
this first image, with a contradictory flourish: *Batouala* is an "etching" that,
in being carved into the *tabula rasa* of the "public mind," has "resurfaced"
that material and prepared it for a new, truer impression. It is rhetoric that
is reminiscent, say, of Freud's "Mystic Writing Pad" essay a year later,
though here somewhat muddled: for it is unclear how an etching can clean
or erase the surface it marks.[62] And while they are an intriguing transatlantic stretch, Locke's words about "the Negro" ring slightly off key, as well:
there is no mention of Maran's self-positioning in relation to the Africans in
Ubangui-Shari, and Locke's sentence ends up more a chest-swelling boast
of pride in The Race than a serious reflection on the literary representation
of differently positioned populations of African descent. This tone continues throughout the essay, as in the following passage: "We can take much
satisfaction in the fact that the path to candid portraiture of the colonial
system and of native life has been shown by one from whom it was least of
all expected, but through whom it comes with the greatest acceptability—
an educated Negro colonial official" (334).

In Maran's hands, though, the "recording instrument" metaphor seems
to be doing more complicated work. It seems possible that he is alluding
here to the recording technology that would develop as a medium both for
the so-called Race Records boom in the mid- and late-1920s and for the
first efforts at anthropological documentation of black culture (for instance, the French excursion that traveled from Dakar to Djibouti from
1931 to 1933 included recording technician Eric Lutten and musicologist
André Schaeffner, who attempted to document musical performances).
The metaphor of the "recording instrument"—a stylus carving grooves into
a disc?—also marks the interface between the oral and the written, for the
relatively new technology in principle allowed a listener to preserve the spe-

cifics of a sonic performance: the inflections of the voice, the dynamics and singular timbre of an instrument, the precise intervals of a scale.

But the syntax of Maran's metaphor ("I *am* an apparatus for recording") might imply something more subtle than a reference to modern technology. It is possible, in other words, that this image of the black administrator as recording apparatus is a striking example of what Bruce Robbins has termed an "allegory of vocation."[63] If Maran is accused of the treason of racial solidarity, then perhaps his defense is also inflected by a racial logic. What is fascinating is that he attempts to erase his identity altogether, making no reference to "race" at all, and claiming moreover that he "does not speak" at all in his novel. In this formulation, the *évolué* Antillean colonial administrator is singularly placed: as an implicitly modern, new "technology," but only a technology, only a tool serving to register the African, offering a clear and untainted reflection of the white European's black African Other. It is a strange triangulation, because here the "recording instrument" insists loudly that it does not speak; this modern technology claims not to speak its own modernity.

This twisted metaphor recalls the well-known characterization of the Antillean in Frantz Fanon's 1952 *Peau noire, masques blancs*. Fanon describes the French Caribbean subject as a sort of ontological void: "*Nègres* are comparison. First truth. . . . Every time they find themselves in contact with another, it is a question of value, of merit. Antilleans have no proper value; they are always tributaries of the apparition of the Other."[64] But the triangulation here goes even further: for Maran, the Antillean is the "tributary" for the apparition not just generally of the black Other, but specifically of the "true" African Other. The Antillean functionary "evolves" only to echo his darker brother for European ears. Locke is correct when he writes that "Maran's real thrust is more anti-romantic and anti-sentimentalist than anti-imperialist; it is the literary traducers whom he would annihilate."[65] But when read with attention to the way Maran places himself in relation to the Africans he claims to "record," *Batouala's* "real thrust" goes beyond issues of style: it is a complex kind of diasporic positioning.

I should note that even in the awkward phrasing of Locke's metaphor—"so weakly winding round and round and getting nowhere," as Claude McKay once described Locke's prose—there is still a hint of this more subtle reading.[66] For Locke, in writing of an "etching" that somehow erases a surface in the very process of inscription, may be attempting to catch the specific sense in Maran's language of a recording instrument that, in doing its work, is silent—that declines to speak, itself. If this image indeed represents an effort to capture the harsh quality of Maran's metaphorology, still it must be considered a failure. Saying that *Batouala* is an "etching" that clears a surface is not the same as saying that "Je n'ai été là qu'un appareil à enregistrer." Not only does Locke's formula lack a sense of the way Maran's preface is an articulation of diaspora, but it is also unable to account for Maran's anthropological aims, his approach to modern technologies of cultural recording. This novel is work "required to be done by the Negro himself"—but for Maran, it is "required" because the job calls for an Antillean whose *évolution,* whose entrance through the revolving doors of modernity, allows the novel to be an instrument of "impersonal observation" (18), not erasing prior "impressions," but erasing the very positionality of the author in the process. In the end, it is because he is a modern black subject that he "only" records: as though it is precisely Maran's modernity that silences him, that makes him a monstrous mute "apparatus" *(appareil).*

Maran claims that he "does not speak" at all in his novel—"the preface aside" *(la préface mise à part).* And this is the knot at the heart of *Batouala.* The preface frames the novel, and—however "objective" it may be—conditions its reception. To put it another way, the contradiction is that Maran, in employing the metaphor of the "recording instrument," thereby speaks, and speaks as a black modern voice, figuring himself even as he claims with the same gesture to be silent. Though Maran does not seem to anticipate it, this two-step is what French critics respond to in *Batouala.* And the critical response, as much as it attempts to defend French colonial policy, also attempts to control Maran, this confusing figure both black and French, both mute and modern. The favorable reviews from the left journals, such as *L'Humanité* and *Le Populaire,* simply ignore the complexity of Maran's stance and celebrate him as condemning the entire enterprise of colonialism.[67] And the more numerous negative reviews perform the familiar dance of racism: either *Batouala* is artless propaganda, a book so intent to slander colonialism that it gladly castigates "heathen" Africans as well in the process, or the novel is inherently flawed, poorly written, a sign of Maran's natural inferiority and of his failed attempt to assimilate to European culture.[68] Either Maran is portrayed as *exceptional*—a talented stylist who somehow eluded the normative stupidity of blacks (an exception formed, of course, through a French education)—or he is portrayed as *atavistic*—an innate *nègre,* as a savage who might show signs of civilization but is still essentially a savage.

A "Black Logic" of the Preface

One example of the latter and more common response is an essay called "La Logique Noire," which appeared in the conservative daily *Le Temps* after *Batouala* won the Prix Goncourt.[69] The critic, J. L., who usually wrote political commentary for the paper, allows that there is something noteworthy in the novel, though it may be more of an anthropological curiosity than a literary event: "Without doubt, it is the first work in the French language written by a black man [*nègre*] where one recognizes an artistic sensibility perceptible to our sensibility. And that is a 'case' for the ethnographers, as well as for the literary critics." The attack centers on the supposed gap in orientation between the preface and the novel itself. The former is "a sort of political manifesto; in it, a black man [*nègre*] denounces the faults and even the crimes of the 'whites.'" But although one expects to find "frightening revelations about the savagery of the civilized" in the novel that follows, in fact "all of *Batouala* is a tableau of black savagery [*barbarie nègre*]. . . . It is dark realism [*réalisme sombre*], in all the senses of the word." The critic uses this distinction to conclude with the following comment, turning again on an "instrument" metaphor:

> But why, in composing this sincere work, did M. René Maran comment on it with a preface that contradicts it? It is that our novelist is a black man [*nègre*]; it is that he lacks, as blacks do, logic and measure. His gods, assisted by Bordeaux professors, conferred on him the talent of writing; they refused him the talent of reason. The brain of the blacks [*nègres*] is still an intermittently functioning mechanism; but it is not futile to hope that the culture of our ideas will perfect this primitive and maladjusted instrument.

With wicked humor, J. L. uses the "objective" rhetoric of modern science to proclaim Maran's black brain to be an "intermittently functioning mechanism," unable to produce a clear and uncorrupted recording because it is "primitive and maladjusted." This reading of a "black logic" of course relies on the critic's characterization of *Batouala* as utterly split ("Ce livre est double," he writes), and J. L. conveniently ignores all evidence to the contrary—the few passages in the novel itself that seem to echo the critique of colonialism in the preface.[70] The question remains, in any case, how one might counter J. L.'s accusation that if Maran is a "recording device," then that "mechanism" functions only "intermittently," forcefully anti-imperialist at one moment and exoticist or sensationalist the next. And more important, why does Maran stress over and over that his voice is heard "only" in the preface? If *Batouala*'s formalist turn—its "black logic"—is an important innovation, as Locke argues, rather than the halting squeamishness of a colonial bureaucrat, then exactly how does the strategy work?

Léopold Sédar Senghor, like a number of Francophone literary critics, also describes Maran in terms of a "black logic" of doubleness.[71] For Senghor, it would be perhaps more appropriately termed a "Logique Nègre," though. He reads Maran as the first to express the "âme noire, avec le style nègre, en français" ("Negro soul, with black style, in French"), in a way that leads directly to the Négritude movement. But Senghor's description of *Batouala*'s contradictions is relevant here:

> Here he is engaged as an *administrator* and as a *Nègre,* here he is engaged in a *situation* full of *contradictions.* As an administrator, he must serve Colonization, firmly, at times harshly, in applying the Justice of the Colonizer. As a *Nègre,* he cannot avoid sensing that there is a law superior to colonial policy: French Law [*le Droit français*]. And superior to that, the Rights of Man [*les Droits de l'Homme*] invoked by the *Nègres* held away from the Residence of the "Commandant." How are these contradictions surmounted? The *Writer* will do it for the Man.[72]

Rather than evade these "contradictions" of his awkward positionality, then, Maran aestheticizes and formalizes them. As Senghor puts it, Maran "fut le premier à refuser de choisir" ("was the first to refuse to choose"), attempting to inhabit the seemingly paradoxical position where one could both claim French citizenship and articulate a reformist critique of French colonization. As I have argued with respect to the phrase *véritable roman nègre,* "race" itself is the hinge of this "situation full of contradictions," the force that must be managed (through the appropriation of "impersonal" modern discourses of ethnographic translation and recording technology) in order to straddle this force.

In one arena, Maran does elaborate a rhetoric that parallels these readings of doubleness. Not in his novels or his autobiographical efforts, but in-stead, interestingly enough, in his more explicitly "polemic" works of re-formist journalism. His essays continually describe French colonialism itself as double, as "Janus-faced" or as having "two countenances."[73] In a 1924 essay, Maran argues that there exists a "true France," the republican France of the Rights of Man, "whom all who come to see and know love, and love eternally." But this ideal is jeopardized by "official France," the scheming and imperialist France represented in its colonies by its colonial administra-tion, which attempts to conceal its abuses to the world with the "conjurer's mirage" of the ideal image. Maran warns against buying into the idea of a kinder, gentler French colonial policy, calling the *indigénat* "codified slav-ery."[74] The doubleness of the French nation-state for Maran is finally a split between metropole and empire: "Perhaps it is not too late . . . to place colo-nial France in opposition to metropolitan France, in order to show that the first, through measures and intolerance which anger as much as they con-tradict its most eloquent affirmations, is alienating little by little the true af-fection for the latter that colored populations are glad to affirm."[75] The convoluted phrasing of this passage gives evidence of the tortured rhetoric provoked by such characterizations in Maran's essays.

Again, although Maran displays a kind of solidarity with the African subjects, with phrases like "nos frères noirs," he continually steps away from any affirmation of black internationalist consciousness that seems too strong by emphasizing that he is mainly interested in the treatment of black French *citizens*—Antillean or African—like himself, working in the colo-nial service. "We are tolerated here, it is true," he sighs, "as one can espe-cially realize who considers how on account of the decline of French man-power, they have increasing need of us. We are tolerated perhaps because, submerged in the mass, we pass almost negligibly. But that has not hin-dered France up to the very present from using every method to block our way to posts of prime importance."[76] At times he comes close to speaking for French blacks in general: in a 1923 article, he contends that "it would be a lie to assert about *nègres,* as it is proclaimed to the four winds, that they love their conquerors. In truth, vaguely resigned to their obscure destiny, they observe them, curiously, hiding their deep thoughts as much as possi-ble." But immediately, the article pulls back with a disclaimer, limiting the scope of the complaint to the mistreatment of French black citizens in the colonies and to the glass ceiling they face in the colonial service: "Today I only want to occupy myself with the *French blacks* [*des nègres français*]— Antillean, Guyanese, Senegalese, and Reunionais—who are the object of the deep hatred of the Central Colonial Administration, a hatred actively seconded by most of the colonial governors and administrators."[77] The preface to *Batouala* takes a similar stance when Maran follows his condemnation of French imperial "civilization" with a call addressed not to his fellow "natives"—much less any invocation of racial alliance or proletarian revolution—but instead to his "brothers in spirit" *(frères en esprit),* his fellow French writers, who must take up the "beautiful task" of condemning colonial abuses in the interests of "the nation of which you are the keepers" (13, 15).

Clearly this is no anticolonialist stance. But as Senghor points out, it *is* a political aesthetic: Maran considers it the task of colonial literature to undo this duplicity, this two-faced countenance of metropolitan and colonial France, with the harsh truths of the pen.[78] But this implies neither anti-imperialism nor an inherent sympathy for the "natives." As he told one journalist (anticipating the title of one of his later novels, *Un Homme pareil aux autres*): "The *nègre* is a man like other men [*un homme comme les autres*]; by that I mean that he is fundamentally malicious. And far from spicing up my tale, I weakened it [*loin de corser mon récit, je l'ai anémié*]."[79] In this quote one gets a sense of Maran's unique stance: his reformist intentions are wholly polemic, but his literary aesthetic refuses any polemicism, insisting that human decadence is universal and in a sense beyond "race" and region. Again, this is not just a stylistic but also a political stance.

In other words, Maran's rhetoric *is* indeed "doubled": it moves toward a kind of solidarity with *les nègres,* as he invokes the Rights of Man and rails against colonial abuses, but then it tacks in the opposite direction with a proclamation of fidelity to the French empire. Finally, here, black internationalism (an espoused link between the Antillean administrator Maran and his African "subjects") can be imagined only as a potential within the embrace of *la plus grande France,* as a common assimilation into the greater imperialist nation. As he concludes one article:

"Colonialism" as it is practiced only engenders disaffection or passivity. Its law is founded on force. The day when its latent hatred and its dissimulated malice become negligible, the *nègres,* understanding that their destiny is linked to the destiny of France, will run voluntarily to die for her—even those who are not yet *"assimilated Europeans."*[80]

Thus, in "speaking his word" in the preface to *Batouala,* Maran attempts to create a doubled effect in a manner both formally reminiscent of and ideologically divergent from the preface-work of African American intellectuals such as Du Bois and Johnson. Maran attempts to mobilize the structural divergence between preface and text to manage "race" in the ways I have suggested, articulating a discourse in which a gesture of black solidarity is re-coded as the "true" promise of the colonial endeavor. He seems to move toward a rhetoric of black internationalism, but only in the service of a greater nationalism—a greater France finally animated by the republican principles of the Rights of Man.

It is a particularly Francophone version of a formalized double consciousness, in which what Du Bois terms the "gift of second sight" is never a suggestion of a possible racial identity, but is always inherently a vision of the true potential of the nation-state. But in *Batouala's* reception, this articulation, so painstakingly elaborated and formalized, is invisible. It is simply overwhelmed by the force of a discursive context that insists on reading any expression of the black modern as a threat—for as I have pointed out, the modern self-construction of France relies on an array of representational strategies to distance the *nègre* as silent Other, as well as political strategies to mitigate against any black internationalist alliance undermining the smooth borders of the nation. In Paris, Maran's *Batouala* falls in this trap. And in the United States, its particular version of doubleness, potentially in dialogue with "New Negro" work, is misunderstood by a black intelligentsia that knew little about Africa and less about the Francophone world. In later writings, it is clear that Maran recognizes that his preface-work has been misread—that it was in fact perhaps unreadable in the sensationalized context of the *vogue nègre* in the early 1920s. In an interview, he laments: "Because of the Goncourt Prize, my preface is given a significance [*une portée*] beyond what my own thinking had given it; it reaches colonial officials who once respected me, and now they turn their backs, thinking that I was describing them."[81] Significantly, when he left his post in the colonial administration, disgraced by the "L'Affaire *Batouala,*" and moved to Paris

René Maran in Ubangui-
Shari. From *Bingo, l'illustré
africain* 73 (February 1959).

to write full-time, he also abandoned this formal strategy, this attempt to
articulate a particularly Francophone version of the black modern. None of
his subsequent works possessed any sort of sustained preface.

Paris, Heart of the Negro Race

Maran's wariness of any explicit project of black internationalism should
not be construed as isolationism. In fact, from the publication of *Batouala*
throughout the interwar period, Maran may be the Francophone intellectual in closest contact with his African American counterparts in New York
and Washington, D.C. He corresponded or interacted with almost all the
significant participants in the "Harlem Renaissance," including Langston
Hughes, Countee Cullen, Gwendolyn Bennett, Jessie Fauset, Claude
McKay, and Rayford Logan.[82] In 1927, he was closely involved in the effort
by Paulette and Jane Nardal to translate Alain Locke's anthology *The New*

Negro, and the next year he was instrumental in the publication of a French version of Walter White's 1924 novel *The Fire in the Flint.*[83]

The key conduit of Maran's dialogue with black U.S. intellectuals was a periodical, the Paris-based *Les Continents,* which—even though it only lasted from May until December 1924—was a crucial forum for debates around black modernity and Pan-Africanism in Francophone circles, influencing many of its successors in the French metropole *(La Race nègre, La Dépêche africaine, Le Cri des Nègres).*[84] Founded by the Dahomean philosopher, lawyer, and brazen social climber Kojo Tovalou Houénou, *Les Continents* was linked with two groups he attempted to organize in the mid-1920s, first a "solidarity association" called L'Amitié Franco-Dahoméenne, and then a group oriented more toward questions of colonial reform and black internationalism, the Ligue Universelle pour la Défense de la Race Noire (LUDRN)—a title which may well reflect Tovalou Houénou's admiration for Marcus Garvey's Universal Negro Improvement Association (UNIA). The day-to-day operations of the bimonthly paper were run by Tovalou Houénou and the white French critic Jean Fangeat, but Maran played a crucial role in shaping its contents, both as a regular contributor and in editorial decisions. *Les Continents* was forced to cease publication when it was sued for libel by Blaise Diagne, after the paper printed an article (unsigned, but almost certainly written by Maran) contending that the Senegalese legislator was a master of "the art of selling his brothers" who had been paid "a certain commission for each solider recruited" in French West Africa during World War I.[85] Notably, the trial occasioned the first appearance in the public record of a former *tirailleur sénégalais* who would go on to found the more radical papers *La Voix des Nègres* and *La Race nègre* two years later. Lamine Senghor spoke briefly about the tribulations of his fellow African soldiers during the war and testified to the widespread dislike for Diagne, whom he estimated "was paid well enough not to need twenty *sous* for each recruit."[86]

In almost every issue, *Les Continents* boasted of its echoes across the Atlantic, noting for instance that a portrait of Tovalou Houénou had been published in the *Crisis* or pointing its readers to his contributions in *Opportunity.* As we shall see, it also published an article by Alain Locke, as well as poems in English by Countee Cullen and Langston Hughes.[87] One might assume that this was meant to highlight the paper's transnational resonance for a French readership, but in fact *Les Continents*—as implied by the plural title—had ambitions of transatlantic distribution and toward the end of its run attempted to begin publishing a second English-language section.[88] Even before then, it was read regularly by the members of the New Negro intelligentsia who had a command of French (including Du Bois, Locke, Fauset, and Gwendolyn Bennett). So when *Les Continents* commented on "La Presse Noire d'Amérique," it was above all because it was attempting to articulate itself as part of a broader multilingual diasporic dialogue about the shape and direction of black modern culture.[89]

This interest likewise shaped the activities of the LUDRN, which attempted to foster links between black cultural forms across the Atlantic. The small group of intellectuals around *Les Continents* combined a critical attention to French colonialism in Africa with coverage of black expressive culture in the metropole, and the paper actively promoted African American music and literature. In late May and early June 1924, Tovalou Houénou hosted two *soirées* of "musique nègre américano-africaine" featuring jazz and spirituals (by musicians including the singers Florence Jones and Ada "Bricktop" Smith, the vocal duo Crutcher and Evans, and the drummer Buddy Gilmore), as well as a classical pianist (the Cuban Gloria de la Cuesta).[90] Later in the summer, Roland Hayes gave a benefit concert for the LUDRN at the Salle Gaveau, singing Schubert and Debussy as well as a selection of spirituals.[91]

That summer, Tovalou Houénou visited the United States, undertaking a speaking tour during the second half of the year in an attempt both to publicize *Les Continents* and to extend its black internationalist connections. Maran put him in contact with W. E. B. Du Bois at the offices of the *Crisis*.[92] The two men never met, in part because Du Bois was irritated that Tovalou Houénou dared contact him and Marcus Garvey simultaneously. "One thing has happened which we do not like," Du Bois wrote to Maran with characteristic imperiousness. "He is visiting the Garvey convention and associating with Garvey. We want to be as charitable as possible and we gladly receive all difference of opinion but there is absolutely no doubt that Marcus Garvey is a scoundrel and a thief and is using all the arts of the low demagogue to deceive his ignorant followers."[93] Tovalou Houénou, a charismatic Dahomean "about six feet, well-formed, straight as a birch" with "long, black fingers like a musician's and fine lacquer-black complexion" (as Claude McKay described him in the *Crisis*), was indeed the featured guest at the annual convention of the UNIA, wooing Harlem in a white suit.[94]

G. O. Marke, Kojo Tovalou Houénou, and Marcus Garvey in Harlem, August 1924 (photo by James VanDerZee). Courtesy of Mrs. Donna Mussenden VanDerZee.

Tovalou Houénou had adopted the title "Prince"—claiming to be related to Behanzin, the king of Dahomey who had been ousted by the French— and the spectacle of "authentic" African royalty was irresistible in the UNIA atmosphere of regal pomp. At the convention banquet, he was toasted by

Garvey himself, and they were photographed on a Harlem rooftop by James VanDerZee.[95]

On August 18, Tovalou Houénou's speech in French to the convention audience was translated by Theodore Stephens, the spokesman of the Haitian delegation of the UNIA (as well as the editor of the French section of the *Negro World*).[96] Welcomed by the "lively" *(vibrant)* crowd with a standing ovation, he told Garvey that the UNIA was "the Zionism of the Negro Race [*la Race Noire*]" and said that he spoke "in the name of millions of Africans" to tell the organization that "our cities [*cités*] are ready to welcome you!" A once and future king, beaming from the stage in Liberty Hall—the vision did nothing to counter the ways that for a vindicationist Harlem audience, "Africa is always imagined in retrospect—as the place one has come from—or in a retrospective prospect—as the home one is going to."[97] But if his welcoming words seemed to be exactly what the audience wanted to hear, what Tovalou Houénou proposed next must have come as a surprise. The "goal" of black political groupings around the world must be "diversité dans l'action" ("diversity in action"), differently placed organizations "contributing to the work of redemption according to their methods, their disciplines, their resources, their activities." But the LUDRN in Paris was prepared to play the central role in coordinating this variety. Tovalou Houénou proposed his group as an umbrella organization to "rally in federation all the existing societies" in order to present "our claims" to the League of Nations. Why the fledgling LUDRN? Why Paris? As Tovalou Houénou opined:

> The choice of Paris as the center for our activities seems to me to offer the highest advantages. Paris is the capital of France, which shares with England almost the whole of Africa. Paris is six hours from London and Brussels; closer to New York than any other capital of Europe; the artistic and intellectual center of the world; the diplomatic capital and the capital of great reformist ideas [*grandes idées rénovatrices*]. And what interests us most is that France is the only country that not only has no race prejudice itself, but also fights for its disappearance.[98]

If, as I suggested earlier, coming to terms with the work of René Maran necessitates remapping the parameters of black modernity, then Tovalou Houénou announces another version of that task—right on the stage of

Liberty Hall in Harlem, with a proposition at once stunningly radical and hopelessly naive. At the closing session of the Convention, Tovalou Houénou spoke again, praising the UNIA's work for the "redemption of Africa" and adding that "the problem of the race in toto is not national, but international."[99] In a *mélange* as peculiar as Maran's brand of colonial reformism, Tovalou Houénou's ardor for black internationalism was matched only by his ideological innocence—he held the simplistic notion that all intellectuals of African descent are ultimately working toward the same end. Before undertaking a speaking tour in the Midwest (Philadelphia, Buffalo, Gary, Detroit, and Chicago, where he made a point of taking a bouquet of flowers to Lincoln's grave), Tovalou Houénou wrote to Du Bois in French, expressing regret that they hadn't been able to meet. Tovalou Houénou wanted to have it both ways, to have it "double" in a different sense. He told Du Bois that "I knew about the serious and profound disagreements that separate you from Mr. Garvey. In Paris I was told to choose between two brothers who are enemies [*deux frères ennemis*]. I refused. I am for all parties who are interested in Negroes [*noirs*]. . . . Any place where a fellow Negro [*un congénère*] creates a movement favorable to the evolution of the race, he will be my friend, I'll be on his side."[100]

At the same time it is important to recognize that this episode did have an effect on the UNIA. Tovalou Houénou's visit was one of the key points of contact between the Garvey movement and the black Francophone world—one of the elements of the UNIA that remains understudied. The impact was reflected in the *Negro World,* whose French section is particularly active during this period: the paper not only published Alain Locke's aforementioned article on "The Colonial Literature of France" (which appeared nearly simultaneously in *Opportunity*), but also reprinted articles from a wide variety of French-language periodicals: *Le Temps de Paris, Le Journal Schoelcher, L'Action coloniale, Le Courrier haïtien,* and especially *Les Continents.*[101] Thus *Les Continents* directly shaped the discourse of the UNIA, the Francophone contours of the "Universal Negro" pursued in its own periodical. This theme does not vanish from the movement, even after Garvey's prison sentence. In 1928, Garvey was still leaning toward Francophone connections, announcing to readers of the *Negro World* during his trip through Europe that "we have already cemented a working plan with the French Negro by which we hope to carry out the great ideals of the UNIA."[102]

In the fall of 1928, Garvey visited Paris and gave a speech at the Club du Faubourg that attracted an audience of more than 1,500. Garvey said that France, as "the only country which offers to the Negro legal equality and the humane rights of citizenship," must "continue to aid the Negro in his ambition to establish his own country and his own government in Africa."[103] At the conclusion of the speech there was a barrage of hostile questions—"vehement accusers, defenders without conviction, subtle denigrators"—and, reported the conservative French newspaper *La Dépêche coloniale,* a couple of sly queries from the "father of *Batouala.*" "Is it out of love for France that American Negroes [*noirs*] came to fight on her soil, or were they convinced by the promises of liberation they'd been given?" Maran asked. "In America, aren't there clubs for light-skinned Negroes [*noirs peu colorés*] that deny entry to dogs and to full Negroes [*noirs intégraux*]"? Apparently Garvey did not answer.

After a number of lengthy attacks and aggressive challenges, another black man arose, this time "a prince" whose "tender name" *(nom caressant),* the newspaper reported, was "Novalou" [*sic*]. In a "soft voice," the dapper Tovalou Houénou tried to play the peacemaker, "invit[ing] the whites, whose fashion of dress [*système vestimentaire*] he borrows tastefully, to love and to liberate" his Negro "brothers." But Maran interrupted once again, declaring that he saw "hardly any difference between the European colonizers—even if he'd admit that the French beat the blacks [*bat les nègres*] a little less than the Americans or the English."[104] Two weeks later, Maran wrote to Alain Locke, saying he'd taken on "that dark visionary [*cet obscur illuminé*], the illustrious Marcus Garvey." As though something had been apparent in the exchange besides what *La Dépêche coloniale* called the realization that "between intellectual and civilized Negroes [*noirs*] there exist profound dissensions," Maran crowed: "doubtlessly your newspapers have already informed you that I was excessively brilliant."[105]

Encounter on the Rhine

The correspondence between Maran and Locke is the single most extensive point of contact in the 1920s between the "Harlem Renaissance" culture framers and the Francophone intelligentsia. I will now turn to one portion of their dialogue from the middle of the decade in order to consider the links between *Les Continents* and another of the most influential Harlem journals, *Opportunity.* In the January 1924 issue of *Opportunity,* Locke published an article called "The Black Watch on the Rhine," a report of his visit to see French African troops guarding the border with Germany after World War I.[106] "My title is no misnomer," he begins, and immediately goes on to make extravagant claims for the significance of the *tirailleurs sénégalais* watching over the frontier: "[T]he first troops I saw on entering the occupied territory, and the last I saw on leaving, were colored—and a very impartial observer, let us say the traditional martian, would have jotted down in his diary that a polyglot, polyracial African nation had in alliance with France conquered Germany" (6). Locke, surprised at the sight of such a large contingent of integrated African and Antillean soldiers comporting themselves responsibly and with more autonomy than would be imaginable in the U.S. armed forces, gushes in the article about the putative nonracist policies of France in relation to its colonies. He writes:

> [M]ere social miracle as it may seem to the Anglo-Saxon eye, they are not merely French soldiers, they are French citizens, comrades not only in arms but in all the basic human relationships. . . .
>
> The instinctive social logicality of the French mind has made a clean sweep of the whole field [of prejudice], and in spite of its handicaps of militarism and colonial imperialism, France has here worked out a practical technique of human relationships which may very possibly earn for her world-mastery as over against her apparently more experienced and better equipped competitors. (8)

Moreover, Locke commends the "human quality" of the French military ("other armies are machines, the French is human" [8]), noting with pleasure the diversity tolerated in its colonial ranks. The barracks in Caseme Hoche in Mayence, Locke writes,

> was a medley of types, costumes and manners—more like a bazaar than a garrison: here natives in French uniforms, there French in adapted native uniforms—and pervading all a good fellowship that was amazing. And if in an army barracks one could get the unmistakable impression of freedom of life and respect for alien customs—and at times this impression was strong enough for one to imagine himself already across on the other side of the Mediterranean—then it was quite to be understood how different the French colonial attitude is

from all others. Instead of imposing her civilization and culture, France super-imposes them. (9)

Latin justice and tolerance is set implicitly against the racism and segregation of the U.S. "Anglo-Saxon" military model (6), as might be expected, in what is ultimately a propaganda piece in the context of U.S. civil rights and antilynching struggles. Of course, the choice of example itself is significant, because in the early 1920s, German propaganda (and parts of the international media) had been attempting to incite U.S. opposition to the French occupation of the Rhine by portraying the African soldiers there as "savages" and "rapists"—with a logic explicitly indebted to U.S. lynch mobs. But Locke wants not only to dispel racist myths about the comportment of black soldiers in Europe, but also to criticize the resurgence of racism in the United States after the war. Slyly, Locke writes, "I am not going to discuss motives in this article—(that makes another article, if you please)" (6), and yet his own motives are nonetheless clear. Above all, his discussion of the ways "Anglo-Saxon and Latin ways . . . differ widely" uses a fawning depiction of French military "humanism" to decry—indirectly, by juxtaposition—the terrors and inequities of racial oppression across the Atlantic.

Later that year, *Opportunity* published a remarkable exchange of letters stemming from Locke's article. Maran wrote an "Open Letter to Professor Alain Leroy Locke," initially published in the June 15 issue of *Les Continents* and then translated for *Opportunity* in September.[107] Maran, writing that "it grieves me to shatter your illusions," critiques the blindnesses of Locke's "Rhine" piece, repeating his argument about the "double countenance" of French colonialism. "The benevolence of France toward subject races," Maran remarks bitingly, "is a matter of theory and official pretense. It is little more than a subterfuge" (261). One shouldn't be confused about the conditions of "codified slavery" in the colonies, nor about the violent history of forced conscription and forced labor instigated by the French during the war (262). Maran suggests that Locke "take pains to read" critiques of French colonial policy such as Lucie Cousturier's *Des Inconnus chez moi* and colonial literature such as the Tharaud brothers' 1922 *La Randonnée de Samba Diouf.*[108] "Reading them," he continues,

> will make clear our position and creed. . . . You will then understand that the black, brown and yellow soldiers [*les volontaires noirs ou jaunes*] did not come to the French colors as the little children come

to Jesus. Far from it. On the contrary, either by express order, or at least with the tacit approval of the Colonial Administration, in certain of the colonies government officials under one pretext or other of recruiting actually engaged in seizure and man-hunting.

Thus, summarily, do the official representatives of France superimpose civilization. France well understands that job. (262)

Maran concludes by calling for an international strategy of collaboration to expose the hypocrisy of the French colonial system: "Europeans, Asiatics, Negroes [nègres], we must work assiduously in the same cause. We must gather, bit by bit, the evidence of these things in irrefutable fact. And one by one they will be exposed in the French parliament" (262). While this call is notable in itself, we should not overlook the tenor of Maran's critique: his "Open Letter" is a way of telling Locke not to use blacks "elsewhere" in the service of African American civil rights struggles in the United States. It contests Locke's articulation of diaspora in his argument, which prioritizes national integration over international antiracism and anti-imperialism. In this sense, Maran's letter is the "flip" side of Locke's flippant "watch on the Rhine"—the diaspora writing back, as it were.

Locke, scrambling mightily, admits his narrow motives in his reply, which is addressed to Maran as "Dear Friend and Kinsman" (262). Retreating from the claims of his article, Locke explains that his "firing-range was set from our own trenches and for a very special purpose. I was not discussing French policy in Africa, but merely the French treatment of her Negro soldiers in Europe. At the time I was primarily concerned with contrasting this treatment of the man of color in the armies of France with that of our own American army" (262). The military metaphor is pressed to the breaking point as a means of claiming "common" purpose between them:

> The need for international coordination among us is imperative; that is why, no matter what you might say, the very sound of your voice is welcome. . . . But the essential thing, my dear Maran, is not that we should have common tactics, but common counsel. We cannot all wear the uniform of the same national loyalty, or carry the weapons of the same social philosophy. But we can and must coordinate our efforts, and share our burdens as we hope also to share our victories. (262)

The military metaphor seems oddly inappropriate in a discussion of military policy toward troops of color. In fact, it allows Locke the seemingly active discourse of "commands" and "enlistments" and "barrages" while at the same time excusing him from the possibility of discussing an international alliance that would place global democratic rights and anti-imperialism before civil rights in one country—such a step is "impossible," for "we cannot all wear the uniform of the same national loyalty."

In many ways, Maran's "Open Letter" calls the bluff of another article published by Locke in *Opportunity*, the February 1924 "Apropos of Africa," in which Locke had called for the attention of African Americans to the educational, economic, and political affairs of Africa in the postwar period. "American Negroes," Locke writes, are "culturally the heirs of the entire continent" of Africa. He goes on to claim that "as the physical composite of eighty-five per cent at least of the African stocks, the American Negro is in a real sense the true Pan-African."[109] Although the "Africa interest" among African Americans is a kind of necessary vanguardism for Locke, it is important to recognize that it is also a kind of necessary anti-Americanism, an emphatic privileging of black internationalism over and above nationalism: "[I]t is rather *against* than within the wish of the interested governments, that the American Negro must reach out toward his rightful share in the solution of African problems and the development of Africa's resources."[110] This pronounced theme in Locke's work is seldom noted, but it is one of the more influential articulations of internationalism in the "New Negro" period—an argument in the vein of what Locke, in the essay titled "The Colonial Literature of France," terms "cosmopolitan humanism."[111] Even as Locke writes in the service of civil rights in the United States, he is hedging his bets, arguing for an explicit strategy that would use the channels of international arbitration available after World War I to influence and override U.S. racial debates. Locke, not surprisingly, is specifically fascinated by the possibilities of the League of Nations and the mandates commission that had placed the former German colonies under international control after the war. He claims that

> [m]inorities have as their best protection today the court of world opinion; if they do not live on an international scale and in the eyes of the world, they are doomed even in the twentieth century to medieval conditions and hardships. . . . [T]he Jew has been made interna-

tional by persecution and forced dispersion,—and so, potentially, have we. . . . [A]s a minority threatened here and there, its only intelligent safe-guard has been international appeal and international organization. . . .

   We have for the present, in spite of Mr. Garvey's hectic efforts, no Zionistic hope or intention. But for protection and mutual development, we must develop the race mind and race interest on an international scale. For that reason, we should be most vitally interested in the idea of the League of Nations and all kindred movements.[112]

In one interview, Locke went so far as to describe the seat of the League, Geneva, as "the Mecca of the liberal and progressive elements of all nations."[113]

In the most remarkable section of this essay, however, Locke not only advocates such a black internationalism but also begins to temper his vanguardism with a call for what he terms "reciprocity" in African diasporic politics.[114] In his view, the "best channels of cooperative effort" lie in educational exchanges and economic investment projects, precisely because black internationalism in politics gives rise to "inevitable contentiousness and suspicions."[115] The "spirit" of emerging black *political* internationalism, then, must for Locke be "reciprocal," rather than provincial or condescending (the notion of some "civilizing mission"), because that internationalism is necessarily a politics of difference—a dialogue among blacks placed unevenly in transnational political environments, or something like what Tovalou Houénou terms "diversité dans l'action." "We must realize that in some respects we need what Africa has to give us as much as, or even more than, Africa needs what we in turn have to give her," Locke instructs:

   [U]nless we approach Africa in the spirit of the finest reciprocity, our efforts will be ineffectual or harmful. . . . [T]he meeting of mind between the African and the Afro-American is dependent upon a broadening of vision and a dropping of prejudices from both sides. The African must dismiss his provincialism, his political-mindedness, his pride of clan; the Afro-American, his missionary condescension, his religious parochialism, and his pride of place. The meeting of the two will mean the inauguration of a new era for both.[116]

As he envisions this model for a truly "Pan-African" politics, Locke argues that mainly through the work of the Garvey movement, "the first great span in the archway" has already in large part been established: "communication, exchange of thought and information between American Negroes and their brothers in the West Indies."[117] But Maran's "Open Letter" stakes out a challenge to this model from the perspective of the Caribbean, in the voice of a Martinican intellectual, around the issue of the African presence in the French military (and from a Parisian newspaper run by a West African, Tovalou Houénou), by criticizing Locke's strategic misrecognition of French colonialism. In *this* case of black international politics, Maran reminds Locke, there is no way to consider the "American Negro" to be "the most disinterested party," as Locke would have it.[118] Locke's commitment to civil rights in the United States is as context-bound, as "provincial," as Maran's commitment to the ideals of French universalist humanism.

Maran's intervention is black internationalism as reciprocity, in other words. One should note that reciprocity is not quite the same as "call and response," that structure of antiphony we so often associate with black expression. Reciprocity is less an originating appeal that is answered than a structure of mutual answerability: articulations of diaspora in tension and in dissonance, without necessary resolution or synthesis. As Kenneth Warren has argued, diasporic thought is marked by ambiguities and contradictions that exceed capture by any one individual or text, but it is "perhaps most of all, a desire to speak these contradictions in a single voice. Yet . . . this voice could not be single but was, and is, poignantly dependent on getting an answer from invisible shores."[119] In this sense, diaspora can be conceived only as the uneasy and unfinished *practice* of such dialogue—where each text both fulfills the demand of the other's "call" and at the same time exposes its necessary "misrecognitions," its particular distortions of the way race travels beyond the borders of nation and language.

What are the effects of this debate? In fact, there are deep reverberations from what is at first glance a moment of mishearing and miscommunication—from this exchange of articulations, "takes" on the diaspora, different invocations of blacks elsewhere. Early in 1925, Maran's work began to be translated regularly for publication in *Opportunity,* and Locke would strive unsuccessfully in later years to have Maran's novels (including *Le Roman d'un Nègre* and *Djouma, chien de la brousse*) published in English.[120]

Through Maran and Paulette Nardal, Locke would meet the younger generation of Francophone students in Paris.

Moreover, this dialogue had important consequences for the shape of *Opportunity* itself. Scholars of the journal such as David Levering Lewis, Abby Arthur Johnson, and Ronald Maberry Johnson have noted a shift in the magazine's focus during its second year of existence, a transformation usually linked to the influence of the famous March 1924 Civic Club dinner (in celebration of the publication of Jessie Fauset's novel *There Is Confusion*), which the journal's editor, Charles S. Johnson, and Locke used to inaugurate the "New Negro" movement. In Lewis's view, this shift was the result of Johnson's new editorial emphasis on literary material in the journal, moving away from the previously dominant sociological vision of Urban League directors George Edmund Haynes and Eugene Kinckle Jones:

> Until late 1924, most of *Opportunity*'s articles had read like chapters from Johnson's *The Negro in Chicago:* Horace Mann Bond's analysis of wartime army intelligence testing; E. Franklin Frazier's discussions of Negro education; Melville Herskovits's statistical conclusions about racial variations in physiology; Joseph A. Hill's study of migration to the cities; and Monroe W. Work's study of rural and urban demography. Now, following the Civic Club affair, the magazine's literary content began to grow rapidly.[121]

It is just as important, though, to consider this shift in terms of diasporic issues in the wake of Maran's "Open Letter." Since its first issue in January 1923, *Opportunity* had always evidenced an interest in transnational black culture, reporting on a wide variety of topics: Claude McKay's attendance at the meetings of the Communist International, the publication of Maran's *Batouala,* sociological studies and fiction in French on "Negro" topics, the racism of American tourists in France, and the condition of Africa after World War I.[122] This interest was certainly reflected in the May 1924 issue of the journal, which focused on "African art," and included essays by Locke, Albert C. Barnes, and the French art critic and collector Paul Guillaume, as well as an essay by Carl Van Doren introducing the "younger school of Negro writers." We should not ignore the fact that two of the three poems included as examples of the emergent school (Claude McKay's

"Africa" and Lewis Alexander's "Africa") are thematically not "Harlem" poems, but works reflecting the "Africa interest" of the issue.[123]

It may not be possible to separate the turn to literature in *Opportunity* from the turn to the diasporic, in other words. The clearest example is indeed the first time the journal decides to publish creative material, in April 1923. One of the two poems in the issue is Countee Cullen's "The Dance of Love (After Reading René Maran's *Batouala*)."[124] It is one of Cullen's weaker efforts, certainly, apparently inspired by one of the controversial erotic scenes in Maran's novel: "All night we danced upon our windy hill, / Your dress a cloud of tangled midnight hair, / And love was much too much for me to wear / My leaves; the killer roared above his kill, / But we danced on. . . ." But it is also surely significant that the journal chose this expressly intertexual poem in particular as one of its first forays into publishing poetry.

Even more interestingly, Cullen's exoticist poem goes on to become part of the initial batch of material exchanged between *Opportunity* and *Les Continents* in the wake of Maran's "Open Letter." During the summer of 1924, as Locke was composing his response to Maran's critique, other material was exchanged as well: for instance, Kojo Tovalou Houénou's "The Problem of Negroes in French Colonial Africa" appeared in the July *Opportunity,* preceding his arrival in New York by a few weeks.[125] And the exchange was reciprocal: in the September *Les Continents,* there was a feature on the new generation of U.S. black poets, which reprinted Cullen's "The Dance of Love" as its centerpiece. It seems that Tovalou Houénou and Maran asked Locke to provide a brief statement on the "younger" New Negro poets, such as McKay, Hughes, and Cullen. In the Parisian journal, "The Dance of Love" is published in English, but Locke's brief introduction is translated into French under the title "La jeune poésie africo-américaine."[126]

Locke's statement is notable, not only because it is one of the first descriptions of the younger Harlem "Renaissance" generation published anywhere, but also for the way the translation introduces yet another racial appellation ("Africo-Americans")—another instance of the awkward ways black modern thought is translated, often in such novel and oddly formulated vocables. It is tempting to read the term as a trace of the sea changes that any racial representation must undergo in the process of dissemination: the ways that translation always involves not just a transport of content but a "regulated transformation."[127] Locke prefaces the Cullen poem with these words:

> La plus jeune génération de la culture Africo-Américaine est brillamment représentée par toute une pléiade de jeunes poètes noirs: Claude Mac-Kay, Jean Tosmer [*sic*], Langston Hughes, et Countee Cullen, à qui nous devons le poème suivant. Chez tous ceux-ci on reconnaît sans peine un beau résultat acquis et un espoir justifié, chose triplement significative au point de vue personnel, national et racial. Il est permis d'insister sur ce dernier trait, l'importance au point de vue racial, car il semble démontré que le mouvement dénommé par les alarmistes réactionnaires "la marée montante du péril noir" est plus vraisemblablement destiné à rendre la culture plus profonde et plus vaste, et non à embourber et engloutir la civilisation. Le poème sur le "Batouala" de René Maran n'implique-t-il pas en lui-même le futur enrichissement de l'art par ce nouveau mouvement du génie africain, par ce nouveau commerce intellectuel entre les continents?

> The youngest generation of Africo-American culture is brilliantly represented by a whole host of young Negro poets: Claude McKay, Jean Toomer, Langston Hughes, and Countee Cullen, to whom we owe the poem that follows. In all of them, one easily recognizes great accomplishment and a fulfilled hope, something triply significant, from a point of view at once personal, national and racial. We may insist on this last characteristic, their importance from a racial point of view, because it seems to have demonstrated that the movement called "the rising tide of the black peril" by reactionary alarmists is destined not to bog down and engulf civilization, but more realistically to render culture deeper and broader. Doesn't the poem about René Maran's "Batouala" itself imply the future enrichment of art by this new movement of the African genius, by this new intellectual commerce between the continents?

Locke introduces a notion of an increasing universalization of "culture," which is here understood as inherently cosmopolitan and diverse, rather than as the paradigmatic self-representation of a particular civilization. In fact, Locke returned often to this call for a strategic disjuncture between culture and civilization, which should be understood in its most robust sense, as an early and salutary attempt to think beyond the pitfalls of what Edward Said has more recently helped us comprehend as the "cultures of imperialism."[128]

As Locke puts it in a 1925 essay on internationalism and art: "Our cultural relations, especially with widely divergent cultures, have thus been in the mood of imperialism, and with the more closely related bodies of art there has been too much of the spirit of exclusive proprietary claims and too little of the feeling of equivalent human expressions."[129] In this piece, Locke argues that the contemporary establishment of "culture-capitals" such as Harlem might not be either balkanizing or nationalist at all. The development of particular cultural expression, Locke claims, can foster not "reactionary political nationalisms" but instead "progressive cultural nationalism," leading somewhat paradoxically to an "internationalization of culture" wholly consistent with universalist humanism. Citing the philosopher George Santayana, Locke prophesies that "civilization and culture [will] come to a parting of the ways, when development of the one must proceed in the direction of an ever-spreading unity and uniformity, and of the other in the opposite and non-competitive direction of an increased and enriched diversity." Locke suggests that not art itself, but criticism (the ideological positioning and interpretation of expressive culture) must be dislodged from "reactionary" political nationalisms:

> Cutting across the established lines of cleavage, springing up within the borders of the old nationalisms, [cultural diversifications] are already irreconcilable with the old order, but the clash which approaches holds doom not for nationalism in art but for chauvinism in criticism. Not much longer shall we be able to make jingoes of our poets, propaganda of our art, and stalking-horses of our cultural inheritances. Purged of chauvinistic motives and ideals, national and racial expression, as cultural individualities, will have scope and incentive to develop more freely and with sounder values. (75)

In other words, the unification of international *civil* society foreshadowed in the League of Nations does not preclude the increasing variety of particular cultural expressive forms.

What is especially interesting about "La jeune poésie africo-américaine" is that Locke finds evidence of a cultural "enrichment" in Cullen's poem, as an example of black "intellectual commerce between the continents." Left unsaid, but implicit in the positioning of the passage, is that Locke considered his own exchanges with Maran and *Les Continents* to be equally felicitous commerce—a diasporic movement "of the African genius" that deepens and broadens art, even as it explores a "racially" specific literary expression. Moreover, a reading of *Opportunity* demonstrates the degree to which Locke considered translation to be the necessary mode of such exchange. The many translations subsequently published in the journal by some of the major "Renaissance" intellectuals (Jessie Fauset, Mercer Cook, Rayford Logan, Countee Cullen) may indeed be the major legacy of the Maran/Locke encounter.[130]

The Practice of Diaspora

My argument about the dynamics of print culture between Harlem and Paris recalls Benedict Anderson's well-known suggestion that the "steady onward clocking of homogenous, empty time" in the newspaper is one of the pivotal means by which an "imagined community" is represented. The "profound fictiveness" of the newspaper is based in its reliance on "essential literary convention": the "inclusion and juxtaposition" of events that are "linked" above all by their coincidence in time, their simultaneous surfacing in a given moment in a serial mass publication.[131] Here, though, I diverge from Anderson in asking whether the periodical can function not simply as the "technical means for 're-presenting' the *kind* of imagined community that is the nation," but more complexly, *also and at the same time* as the "technical means" for representing the imagined community of a diaspora.[132]

More specifically, this means asking about the function of translation in publications such as *Opportunity,* the *Negro World,* or *Les Continents.* What exactly is being "imagined" when one periodical translates an article originally written in a different language in another periodical in a different nation-state? On the one hand, since almost all the articles translated in these publications are current (not historical or archival), part of the work performed has to do with what Anderson calls "simultaneity"—the sense of reading *now* what peoples of African descent are doing or thinking elsewhere. On the other hand, Anderson's emphasis on "anonymity" seems less useful in this context, since translations so regularly highlight the specificity and irreducibility of difference: particular examples of "black" people elsewhere doing different things, or the same things in different ways. A transnational community of "race" structured by *décalage* involves a special sort of imaginative work, in other words.

If the practice of translation is first of all the "simple miming of the responsibility to the trace of the other in the self," then translation plays a peculiar role in the imagining of "racial" identity.[133] It is a role that is necessarily "double-edged," as Lawrence Venuti puts it: designed for a particular constituency, bringing outside material "in" to a domestic context, but at the same time transforming that domestic "inside" with the inhabiting of an "outside" or "foreign" voice.[134] This is particularly true for publications geared to frame black modern identity. For as "foreign" as it might be (in terms of language, perspective, ideology), a French article, say, on *tirailleurs sénégalais* or on *biguine* in Martinique in the end aims differently at the same discursive formation as *Opportunity*: the framing of modern identity under the sign of race. The "double-edge" is that translation both provides support for the "domestic" agenda and continually threatens to undermine it or reconfigure it. Translations of Francophone material in the "Harlem Renaissance" give evidence of black modernity and perhaps most important show the ways that "race" actually *transcends* the nation-state: if the color line is global, if people of African descent are persecuted around the world, then the black U.S. intellectual can lay claim to a discourse of universality, and can gain purchase on the institutionalization of universality represented by international civil society. But at the same time, translations open "race" to the influence of an exterior, pulling and tugging at that same signified in an interminable practice of difference, through an unclosed field of signifiers (*Negro, noir, black, nègre, Afro-American, Aframerican, Africo-American, Afro-Latin,* etc.) whose shifts inescapably reshape the possibilities of what black modern culture might be.

The exchange between Maran and Locke theorizes a way to inhabit, even collaborate, in this uneasy space of diaspora. "Reciprocity," in demanding not just mutual attention, mutual translation, but also mutual answerability, aims toward a practice of imagining diaspora in print culture that would be structured through what Kenneth Warren terms "the imaginative contemporaneity of Africa and the 'West' and of black elites and masses."[135] Anderson's "simultaneity" may not suffice here, since the notion that each segment in the diasporic imagined community is simply "out there" ("moving along quietly, awaiting its next reappearance in the plot") can also serve as an alibi for silencing, ignoring what is outside a given horizon of competence or predilection. A better term might be *coevalness,* which for Johannes Fabian covers both the synchronous ("events occurring at the same physical time") and the contemporary ("co-occurrence in . . . typological time"), and moreover connotes answerability: "a common, active 'occupation,' or sharing, of time."[136] As a model for dialogue and exchange, reciprocity would attend to the *décalage* of diaspora by ensuring coevalness in the very structure of any black internationalist endeavor.

It should already be evident, even from the contrast between the correspondence of *Les Continents* with the *Negro World* and with *Opportunity,* that this model is a structure *for* the political articulation of black internationalism, rather than a structure that would install some predetermined politics. We should not overlook the fact that Maran and Locke find common ground in a commitment to an elitist (and sexist) black vanguardism. They are "stretched out" on different "chaise lounges" on different "verandas," but both assume the impossibility of black internationalism as any sort of popular project, as anything but a correspondence among the *évolués* and the Talented Tenth.[137] Thus, theorizing the practice of diaspora through reciprocity does not evade the kind of complaint that the Guyanese writer Léon-Gontran Damas, for example, still finds it necessary to voice in 1939, in an essay titled "Misère Noire" (Black Misery).[138] "It is ridiculous to pretend that the American Negro [*nègre américain*] is not, materially, the most privileged in the world," Damas writes. "In no other country has the Negro race [*la race noire*] had as many economic and financial possibilities. . . . In no other country has the Negro race been able to develop in a racial sense [*développer dans le sens de sa race*] to the same degree" (341). Still, Damas laments the "incomprehension that threatens to slip into the international relations between blacks" [*incompréhension qui risque de se glisser dans les rapports internationaux entre nègres*] (342). He tells of a conversation in Paris between a "special envoy" from black American newspapers and a Caribbean man who had been living in Africa for the prior ten years. The black American was impressed to see Blaise Diagne, the first African to be elected to the French legislature (and at that time the vice president of the Chambre des Députés), preside over a session of the legislative body, whereas the Caribbean man was impressed by the black journalist's friendly, respectful reception from the mainstream French newspapers. They talked over and around each other's heads. And meanwhile, Damas complains, although all the world knew about the horrors of lynching in the United States, no one paid attention to French colonial abuses in Africa; no one paid attention to Diagne's remark in the Chambre that education in African colonies was "excessive." For Damas, such skewed patterns of perception are intimately linked to the shape of print culture: noting the brief history of the bilingual journal *La Revue du monde noir,* Damas argues that part of the problem is there has never been a specifically black literary vehicle *(publication nègre)* appearing with any consistency or duration in French.

Such "misery," such mutual incomprehension, may well be constitutive in the elaboration of black modernity as a transnational phenomenon, even in a structure of reciprocity. In other words, the ambiguities of diaspora do not resolve. As Fabian comments, coevalness is not a thing or a state with certain properties, but a "mode of temporal relations" that is necessarily "embedded in culturally organized praxis."[139] In this sense, black internationalism is above all *practiced* in the multilayered and convoluted exchanges between periodicals such as *Opportunity* and *Les Continents,* in their sometimes uneasy and sometimes misdirected attempts to carry blackness beyond the boundaries of nation and language, to read the race problem as a world problem. In this sense, diasporic reciprocity is above all a call to translate.

CHAPTER 3

FEMINISM AND *L'INTERNATIONALISME NOIR:*
PAULETTE NARDAL

n the summer of 1931, a Martinican student named Paulette Nardal and a Haitian dentist named Léo Sajous founded *La Revue du monde noir,* a French-English bilingual literary journal that, during its six-issue run until the following spring, became a crucial focal point for African diasporic arts and the growing movement of African and Caribbean intellectuals in Paris. Paulette Nardal would later explain that the *Revue* "was Dr. Sajous' idea originally. He had noticed that there was very little community of tastes between Negroes of different nations, and in different parts of the world; he felt if he could found a common journal of some kind, to include all sorts of articles, scientific, literary, geographical, etc., and a correspondence page on which all kinds of questions from Negroes everywhere could be answered, it would help draw Negroes all over the world together."[1] Sajous is a crucial interwar figure whose role has not been fully appreciated: he was active both in the anticolonialist and communist organizations such as Lamine Senghor's Ligue de Défense de la Race Nègre (Sajous offered free dental service to black workers in his offices in Ménilmontant) and in more moderate groups associated with Maurice Satineau's *La Dépêche africaine.* But Nardal's role, as editor, translator, and contributor, was at least as important as Sajous's. The roots of *La Revue du monde noir* lie not just in the periodicals that preceded it in the previous decade (*Les Continents* and especially *La Dépêche africaine*), but also in the weekly salons hosted by Nardal and her three sisters in their home in Clamart, just outside Paris, or by their cousin Louis Thomas-Achille in his apartment at 51, rue Geoffrey St. Hilaire, overlooking the Jardin des Plantes, or by René Maran in his apartment on rue Bonaparte. With her fluent English, Paulette Nardal became the most important connection between the "Harlem Renaissance" writers and the Francophone university students who would become the core of the Négritude movement.

Léopold Senghor and the editorial collective of *La Revue du monde noir* (June 26, 1932). Paulette Nardal is on the far right, Clara Shepard is sixth from the right, and Senghor is third from the right. Bibliothèque Nationale, Paris.

More than any other interwar periodical, *La Revue du monde noir* systematically strove to practice black internationalism as *bilingualism,* running English and French in parallel columns throughout every issue. This approach comprehends the link among intellectuals of African descent to be paradigmatically a link across linguistic difference, and thus it is first and foremost the journal's translations that attempt to "create among the Negroes [*les Noirs*] of the entire world, regardless of nationality, an intellectual and moral bond [*lien*] that will permit them to know each other better, to love one another fraternally, to defend their collective interests more effectively, and to glorify their Race."[2] Nardal's interest in creating "bonds" among black intellectuals carried over into her salon, where she served as a "cultural intermediary," introducing the young Léopold Sédar Senghor not just to Maran but also to Claude McKay, Mercer Cook, Carter G. Woodson, Alain Locke, Countee Cullen, and Hale Woodruff.[3]

The narrative of the emergence of Négritude has been a story of "representative colored men": Senghor, Léon-Gontran Damas, and Aimé Césaire. The symbology of the movement is sung not only though Léopold Sédar Senghor's hymns to the "Black Woman" *(Femme Noire),* but equally through a range of commentary on the black woman's role that systematically overlooks the direct contributions of women like Nardal to the movement's emergence.[4] We are left with more or less explicit metaphors of the "fathers of Négritude" that frame its birth as a special kind of immaculate conception. In a 1972 interview, for example, Damas told Keith Warner:

> In Vermont at the Conference on Black Francophone Literature, they asked me, "Who is the father of Négritude?" I said, "I'm fed up of all that. I don't understand why Négritude needs so many fathers." Anyway I recalled an African proverb. I said that in Africa we don't know our fathers, we know our mothers. Now, the man who coined the word "Négritude" was Aimé Césaire, and Senghor has been obliged to admit this. But, for many reasons, Senghor is first now, the father of Négritude. In Vermont they asked me who I was among the three. I said, "Perhaps I'm the Holy Spirit."[5]

What's fascinating about this passage is the way Damas moves slyly from matrifocal foundation ("we don't know our fathers, we know our mothers") to paternal *dénouement* ("Senghor is . . . the father of Négritude"), from "Mama's Baby, Papa's Maybe" to the Trinity. Although both Césaire and Senghor would pay tribute to Paulette Nardal after her death in 1985,[6] there has never been a thorough attempt to take account of her work during the fifteen years she lived in Paris—arriving in the metropole in the mid-1920s to pursue a *licence* degree in English (she wrote a thesis on Stowe's *Uncle Tom's Cabin*), taking up a pivotal role in black periodical culture while she was completing her studies (she contributed to *La Dépêche africaine, Le Soir, La Revue du monde noir, L'Etudiant noir, France-Outremer,* and *Le Cri des Nègres* among other venues), participating in the demonstrations that erupted in Paris following the Italian invasion of Ethiopia in 1935, and finally departing to return to Martinique on the eve of World War II. What becomes clear is that the history of this impossibility is also the question of whether such an erasure is constitutive in the elaboration of a Négritude aesthetic, and moreover whether it might indeed be concomitant with the forgetting of a more avowedly anticolonial black politics in the 1920s and 1930s, represented in the work of intellectuals including Sajous, Lamine Senghor, and Tiemoko Garan Kouyaté.

Paulette Nardal complained in 1963 in a letter to Jacques Hymans, one of the biographers of Léopold Senghor, that a complete "silence was maintained for a long period" about her activities in the 1930s. She wrote that her sister Jane Nardal was the first "promoter of this movement of ideas, so broadly exploited later," and that Senghor and Césaire "took up the ideas tossed out by us and expressed them with more flash and brio. . . . [W]e were but women, real pioneers—let's say that we blazed the trail for them."[7] What would it mean, though, to stake out a "silenced" genealogy of Négritude through the transnational intellectual circuits of African American and Caribbean women during the interwar period? What would it mean to theorize a feminist articulation of diaspora?

In the last issue of *La Revue du monde noir*, Nardal asserted that Francophone women in particular had instigated the "awakening" of black cultural interest and correspondence. Her essay "Eveil de la conscience de race" ("Awakening of Race Consciousness") may be the single most significant work to be published in the journal. It is often overlooked that her evocation of an emergent black cultural internationalism is linked to an equally nascent feminism—a critical understanding of the particular positioning of upwardly mobile women of African descent in the metropole, and a consideration of the relations between Caribbean men and women in migration. Among the Caribbean communities in Paris *(les Noirs Antillais),* she contends, there have been momentous shifts in attitude toward "questions of race" in the wake of the International Colonial Exposition in the summer of 1931:

> Il y a à peine quelques années, on pourrait même dire quelques mois, certains sujets étaient tabous à la Martinique. Malheur à qui osait y toucher: on ne pouvait parler d'esclavage ni proclamer sa fierté d'être descendante de Noirs Africains sans faire figure d'exaltée ou tout au moins d'originale.

> A few years ago, we might even say a few months ago, certain questions were simply tabooed in Martinica. Woe to those who dared to approach them! One could not speak about slavery, or proclaim his

pride of being of African descent without being considered as an over-
excited or at least as an odd person.[8]

The English translation of "Awakening of Race Consciousness"—as with all
the articles in *La Revue*—is by Nardal herself and the African American
schoolteacher Clara Shepard, living in Paris at the time. It is worth considering the complexities of this bilingual, collaborative practice, despite the
minor slips and idiosyncrasies in their English. In this passage, for instance,
it should be noted that the French "descendante" is feminine. Thus the
phrase might be rendered more faithfully: "One could not speak about slavery, or proclaim one's pride in being a woman of African descent without
being considered reckless, or at least eccentric."

Nardal contrasts this shift in Antillean attitudes with the more historically rooted racial consciousness among African Americans, offering a brief
survey of black U.S. history and literature. With language that evidences
the influence of both James Weldon Johnson's preface to *The Book of American Negro Poetry* and Langston Hughes's 1926 essay "The Negro Artist
and the Racial Mountain," Nardal argues that "without abandoning black
themes [*thèmes nègres*] and the emotional contribution due to their ancestral sufferings," modern African American writers

> en font le point de départ de leur inspiration, les universalisent, et,
> chose plus importante encore, abandonnent les moyens d'expression
> spécifiquement nègres, pour employer les formes et les symboles de la
> littérature traditionnelle. Nos lecteurs ont eu, par les vers de Claude
> Mac Kay, un aperçu de cette nouvelle attitude et plus récemment en-
> core, par les poèmes de Langston Hughes, ils ont pu constater que les
> américains, ayant écarté tout complexe d'infériorité, expriment tran-
> quillement leur "être individuel à la peau noire, sans crainte et sans
> honte."

took them as the starting point of their inspiration and gave them a
universal purport. It is important to note that they abandonned [*sic*]
the Negro dialect in favour of the forms and symbols of traditional
literature. The poems of Claude Mac-Kay which were published in
this Review have acquainted our readers with this new attitude, and
more recently, those of Langston Hughes have shown how the young

Negro writers, rejecting all inferiority complex, "intend to express their individual dark-skinned selves without fear or shame." (27)

Nardal advances the conjecture that the French colonial policy of assimilation kept previous generations of Antillean writers from making the same progression and traces the rise of a black modern Francophone intellectual culture through work such as Maran's *Batouala,* the newspapers *Les Continents* and *La Dépêche africaine,* and the Guyanese writer Leo Cressan's 1928 *Heimatlos.* Although exile and "uprooting" *(déracinement)* gives much of this work "en dépit de leur formation latine, une âme nègre" ("a real Negro soul, in spite of the authors' Latin education") (25), Nardal makes a strong case that *La Revue du monde noir* represents a break in this tradition. Unlike the Francophone literature in the 1920s, *La Revue* conceives black culture as an autonomous and transnational tradition rather than a subset of French colonial history. The predecessor works in the 1920s remained "tributaries of Latin culture" rather than attempts at studying the "Negro question" on its own terms *(la question noire en elle-même):* "Aucun d'entre eux n'exprime la foi en l'avenir de la race, et la nécessité de créer un sentiment de solidarité entre les différents groupements noirs disséminés par le monde" ("In none of them do we find the expression of a sincere faith in the future of the race and the necessity of creating a feeling of solidarity between the different groups of Negroes living throughout the globe") (29).

Notably, Nardal locates this break in modern Francophone culture specifically in the group of Antillean *women* students living in the metropole after World War I:

> Pourtant, parallèlement aux efforts isolés cités plus haut s'affirmaient chez un groupe d'étudiantes antillaises à Paris les aspirations qui devaient se cristalliser autour de la Revue du Monde noir. Les femmes de couleur vivant seules à la métropole moins favorisées jusqu'à l'Exposition coloniale que leurs congénères masculins aux faciles succès, ont ressenti bien avant eux le besoin d'une solidarité raciale qui ne serait pas seulement d'ordre matériel: c'est ainsi qu'elles se sont éveillées à la conscience de race. Le sentiment de déracinement . . . aura été le point de départ de leur évolution.

However, parallel to the isolated efforts above mentioned, the aspirations which were to be crystallized around "The Review of the Black World" asserted themselves among a group of Antillean women students in Paris. Until the Colonial Exposition, the coloured women living alone in the metropolis have certainly been less favoured than coloured men who are content with a certain easy success. Long before the latter, they have felt the need of a racial solidarity that would not be merely material. They were thus aroused to race consciousness. The feeling of uprooting which they experienced . . . was the starting point of their evolution. (29)

This chapter is an attempt not only to reconsider Nardal's work, but also to elaborate the theoretical implications of the suggestion that black internationalism in Paris has a historical origin among migrant communities of women of African descent. Nardal goes on to record the number of Francophone women students who had turned to the study of issues of race *(la race noire)*, mentioning not only her own study of Stowe's *Uncle Tom's Cabin,* but also other students' theses on subjects including Lafcadio Hearn, Père Labat, and, more recently, "les écrivains afro-américains" (30). She hopes that these female pioneers will influence future students, male or female *(étudiants),* to follow such paths of inquiry. "Au cours de leur évolution," she comments,

> leur curiosité intellectuelle s'est tournée vers l'histoire de leur race et de leurs pays respectifs. . . . Au lieu de mépriser leurs congénères attardés ou de désespérer de voir jamais la race noire arriver à égaler la race aryenne, elles se sont mises à l'étude. . . . Espérons que les étudiants qui préparent des licences d'histoire et de géographie tireront parti des richesses que leur offrent le passé de la race noire et le continent africain. . . .

> In the course of their evolution, their intellectual curiosity applied itself to the history of their race and of their respective countries. . . . Instead of despising their retarded brothers [*sic*] or laying aside all hope of about [*sic*] the possibility of the black race ever being on a par with the Aryans, they began to study. . . . Let us hope that the students coming up for degrees in History and Geography will avail

themselves of the riches which the black race and the African continent offer to them. (29–30)[9]

With these lines, Paulette Nardal is alluding not just to her own thesis and to her published journalism, translations, essays, and short stories, but also to the work of other women. In her letter to Hymans, she mentions her sister Jane, who returned to the Caribbean in late 1928 but contributed a number of influential articles to Maurice Satineau's *La Dépêche africaine,* including her aforementioned "L'internationalisme noir" in the newspaper's first issue. In the words of Paulette Nardal, the black Caribbean women in Paris,

> après s'être docilement mises à l'école de leurs modèles blancs, peut-être ont-elles passé, comme leurs frères noirs américains, par une période de révolte. Mais, plus mûres, elles sont devenues moins sévères, moins intransigeantes, puisque tout est relatif. Leur position actuelle est le juste milieu.

> after a period of obedient imitation of their white models, they may have passed through their period of revolt, just as [*sic*] their American brothers. But, as they grew older, they became less strict, less ultra, since they have understood the relativity of all things. At present their position is the middle ground. (29)

To begin to sketch out this circuit of activity, we might first return to the letter Jane Nardal wrote in French to Alain Locke in December 1927 asking permission to translate *The New Negro.* Nardal's note opens with a significant anecdote: "More than two years ago," she writes, "I attended the dissertation defense of Mrs. JJ Cooper."[10] Despite the erroneous first initial, Nardal is clearly alluding here to the open session on March 23, 1925, at which the great African American feminist Anna Julia Cooper took an unapproved leave of absence from her job teaching at Dunbar High School in Washington to defend her Ph.D. dissertation at the Sorbonne on the subject of "L'attitude de la France dans la question de l'esclavage entre 1789 et 1848."[11] Cooper was the fourth black American woman to receive the Ph.D. She was 65 years old at the time.[12] Nardal continues:

> Connue, en ma qualité d'étudiante noire, j'allais la complimenter, une dame de ses amies, me demanda si j'allais, moi aussi, faire

Alice Nardal and Jane Nardal (c. 1950). Courtesy of Christiane Eda-Pierre.

quelque chose pour "my niggers." Pas précisément, lui répondis-je, en toute sincérité; en bonne négresse française, je ne voyais rien que de négligeable et de gênant dans le passé de notre race. Pourtant, ma curiosité, mon intérêt déjà sollicité par d'autres faits nègres, commençaient à s'éveiller. Ce serait abuser de votre attention que de vous raconter par quelle série d'expériences je passai avant de découvrir, tout au fond du creuset, l'esprit de race, entièrement enseveli sous l'éducation et l'instruction françaises qui m'avaient été données, conformément au travail d'assimilation auquel on s'est attelé, depuis 1848, dans les colonies françaises. Car je ne vous écris pour vous faire "l'Autobiography of a Re-Coloured Woman," mais pour essayer, moi aussi, de faire œuvre utile à ma race.

Known in my status as a Negro student, I went up to compliment her, and one of her friends asked me if I, too, was going to do something for "my niggers." Not exactly, I told her in all sincerity; a good French negress, I did not see anything beyond the negligible and the painful in the past of our race. Yet, all the same, my curiosity, my interest, already captured by other things *nègre,* began to awaken. It would be an abuse of your time to recount the entire series of experiences through which I discovered, down at the bottom of the crucible, my racial spirit, completely shrouded under the French education and instruction given to me, in accordance with the work of assimilation that we have been buckling down to since 1848 in the French colonies. For I am not writing to tell you the "Autobiography of a Re-Colored Woman," but instead to attempt, in my turn, to do work useful to my race.

One can only imagine Alain Locke, perusing his daily correspondence in some quaintly decorous office in Howard University, coming to the phrase "faire quelque chose pour 'my niggers'"! On the one hand, Nardal may have misheard the accent of an English-speaking friend of Anna Julia Cooper who was saying the word "Negroes." On the other hand, this may be Nardal's (mis)translation of the French word *nègres,* which she most likely would have considered a derogatory term in 1925 (this would explain the use of *nègre* later on: she is pointing out her "awakening racial consciousness," her reconception of the term in the preceding few years). At the same time, Jane Nardal possessed more than a streak of sarcasm: it is possible that she is trying to use the phrase to joke with Locke, not quite understanding its weight in English. After all, Jane Nardal had taken a degree in Classics at the Sorbonne, not in English like her sister. Reading it as awkward humor would make sense in light of the rest of the passage: her tongue-in-cheek descriptions of the ways Antilleans "buckled down" to the task of assimilation, and her more successful joke with the title of James Weldon Johnson's *The Autobiography of an Ex-Colored Man.* All we can say with some certainty, I think, is that it seems unlikely that Cooper's friend is a lonely harbinger of late-twentieth century rehabilitations of "nigger" in casual black U.S. speech and hip-hop culture.

After this remarkable introduction, she moves to the business of her letter, requesting permission to translate Locke's collection *The New Negro* with Paulette for the French publisher Payot. She requests Locke's advice about editing down the volume for an abridged French publication, noting that such a task is difficult for her, as she cares so deeply for the work of so many of the authors:

Pourtant mon embarras fut grand: il me fallait choisir entre tous ces auteurs qui me sont déjà de vieilles connaissances (car je suis une lectrice assidue d'Opportunity que Miss Nellie Bright a l'obligeance de nous envoyer, à ses amies et à moi). Comment ne pas réduire les noms et les articles de W. White, A. Locke, W. Pickens, Domingo, Mrs. MacDougal, Burghart Du Bois, les poèmes de C. MacKay, Lanston Hughes, Jean Toomer, etc.? (Je cite de mémoire.) J'ai été aussi particulièrement charmée par l'artistique présentation de "The New Negro," par les illustrations si modernes et si caractéristiques. . . .

Yet my consternation was great: I had to choose among all these authors who are already old acquaintances (for I am an assiduous reader of *Opportunity,* which Miss Nellie Bright is kind enough to send us, her friends and me). How to trim the names and articles of W. White, A. Locke, W. Pickens, Domingo, Mrs. MacDougal, Burghart Du Bois, the poems of C. McKay, Langston Hughes, Jean Toomer, etc.? (I cite from memory.) I have also been charmed in particular by the artistic presentation of *The New Negro,* by the illustrations, so modern and so characteristic. . . .

The quote is fascinating as much for its matter-of-fact evocation of a transnational community of interaction and interest among black women in Paris (Francophone women going to support Anna Julia Cooper at her defense; Nellie Bright regularly sending Jane Nardal copies of *Opportunity* in Paris) as for its enthusiasm about *The New Negro.*

Gender in Black Paris

Unfortunately, we have only a scattered sense of the travels of black women intellectuals and artists in the first part of the twentieth century. Cooper was one of three black women to address the World's Congress of Representative Women in 1893 and one of the few women to attend the 1900 Pan-African Conference in London.[13] There are fragmented records of the transnational voyages, both physical and fictional, of Bright, Mary Church Terrell, Jessie Fauset, Nella Larsen, Gwendolyn Bennett, Zora Neale Hurston, and others.[14] There is a good deal of recent scholarship on international feminism in the interwar period and on women in France, particularly in the suffrage movement. Yet one is hard-pressed to find work on French feminism that includes any discussion of feminist participation in debates around French colonialism in the interwar period.[15] Even the brief commentaries on Josephine Baker in some work on French women between the wars tend to read her as a sort of inconsequential stage alien, untethered to the world around her. On the one hand, the performer the French called "La Baker" is portrayed as exceptional, with no links to the community of black performers in France. At the same time, there is no attempt to account for the earth-shattering impact of her image on notions of French femininity during the period. As Countee Cullen remarked, Josephine Baker was "like Cinderella touched with a magic wand—only this Cinderella balked at clothes. And Paris is in a state of violent hysteria over her; there are Josephine Baker perfumes, costumes, bobs, statuettes; in fact, she sets the pace. All that remains now is for her to try on the glass slipper and marry the prince."[16] The scholarship has generally failed to consider the ways both French feminism in particular and ideologies of gender in general were molded by notions of race in the very period when European colonialism was at its apex and Baker "set the pace" of fashion for Parisian women.

It is relatively uncommon to find work on French feminism such as Joan Wallach Scott's essay on Olympe de Gouges, in which Scott argues that in considering the ideological construction of French citizenship, we cannot overlook the ways that race has intersected with gender *from the beginning*—thus complicating any discussion of suffrage, *la garçonne,* or "depopulation" in interwar France. "Feminism was not a sign of the benign and progressive operations of liberal individualism, but rather a symptom of its constitutive contradictions," Scott writes, and she attempts to demonstrate that these contradictions were articulated around a variety of ideological sites including citizenship, colonialism, class, revolutionary struggle, sexuality, and gender itself. Scott recounts a resonant story from the official record of the National Convention in 1794, when slavery was temporarily abolished in the French colonies by the revolutionaries in Paris. When the legislature made its emancipation proclamation, the two colored representatives in the French assembly approached the tribune to accept a presidential embrace of goodwill. Another legislator, Pierre-Joseph Cambon, then took the floor to announce that "a citizeness [*citoyenne*] of color who regularly attends the sittings of the Convention has just felt so keen a joy at see-

ing us give liberty to all her brethren that she has fainted. (Applause) I demand that this fact be mentioned in the minutes, and that this citizeness be
admitted to the sitting and receive at least this much recognition for her
civic virtues." Scott comments:

> The woman was allowed to sit near the president for the rest of the
> session; as she took her place, brushing tears from her eyes, she was
> greeted with cheers and applause. The woman's "civic virtue" con-
> sisted in her outpouring of gratitude to legislators, who had acted on
> her behalf by permitting the men of her race to represent her. It was
> no accident that Cambon seized on this moment of fraternal inclu-
> sion to make a black woman the sign of the entry of black men into
> the ranks of citizenship. The men's difference from women served to
> eradicate differences of skin color and race among men; the universal-
> ity of the abstract individual was in this way and at this moment es-
> tablished as a common maleness.[17]

I would rephrase the last sentence in a slightly different direction. The
point is not simply that any "difference—for purposes of defining the individuality that conferred political citizenship—was equated with sexual difference," as Scott puts it. Such an approach would iron out the very complexity of the anecdote, as though race simply stands in for gender, when in
fact both are at work in the spectacle of the tearful *citoyenne de couleur*
seated at the head of the assembly. It would be more useful to note that a
racial articulation always *necessarily underlies* this construction of the "universality of the abstract individual" as a "common maleness." Still, Scott's
use of this vignette is a break from trends in French feminist history, for it
shifts the ground of inquiry from a single axis (what Scott terms the fallacy
of choosing *either* gender equality *or* gender difference) to a varied, shifting
foundation where race and gender cannot necessarily even be thought of as
separate categories, where we will no longer be able to read the suffrage
movement in post–World War I France without placing it in the historical
context of the apotheosis of French colonialism.

Likewise, with regard to the United States, while there is a growing body
of discussion of the "profeminist" politics of W. E. B. Du Bois, there is little
scholarship on the transnational work both of radical black women intellectuals such as Amy Jacques Garvey and of more moderate figures including
Mary Church Terrell, Adelaide Casely-Hayford, and Fauset.[18] There is a

woeful lack of information on the Fourth Pan-African Congress in New York in 1927, which is usually considered to be the least significant Congress politically, but which was almost exclusively organized by black U.S. women such as Mrs. A. W. Hunton and the women of the Circle of Peace and Foreign Relations, who brought in speakers such as the Haitian politician Dantès Bellegarde, the anthropologist Melville Herskovits, Leo Hansberry, and Chief Amoah III of the Gold Coast.[19] We know that the National Association of Colored Women, after being represented by Mary Church Terrell at the 1904 Berlin Congress of the International Council of Women, decided that the global feminist organization paid too little attention to racial issues and founded a sister group called the International Council of Women of the Darker Races, which functioned in the early 1920s.[20] Still much recent work on women in the "Harlem Renaissance" period tends to take it for granted that, for the black female writer, "journey, . . . though at times touching the political and social, is basically a personal and psychological journey. The female character in the works of Black women is in a state of becoming a 'part of an evolutionary spiral, moving from victimization to consciousness.'"[21] These kinds of facile assumptions are still all too common, often leading to insipid, depoliticized readings that indiscriminately "psychologize" black women's expression—this despite the more recent injunctions of critics such as Cheryl Wall that "metaphors of travel recur in writing by Harlem Renaissance women. Despite the restrictions against it, they traveled widely in fact and in imagination."[22]

The necessity of rethinking the imbrication of gender and black internationalism is immediately evident when one attends to the periodical print culture of the period. A number of African American women published their most significant work in the small journals and newspapers that were to a large extent the vehicles of the New Negro movement. The essays of Gwendolyn Bennett, for instance, often demystify the common African American mythology of a lack of prejudice in France, and some of her stories such as "Tokens" and "Wedding Day" explore black expatriate life in Paris, where she lived in the middle of the decade.[23] From 1926 to 1928, with her column "The Ebony Flute" in *Opportunity,* Bennett was one of a group of writers including Countee Cullen, Alain Locke, J. A. Rogers, and Jessie Fauset who wrote extensively and often about events and publications in French, commenting on "attempts at the unification of Negroes throughout the world."[24] It is revelatory to recognize just how closely these supposedly Harlem-obsessed figures followed events in the Francophone world, even ones that have been considered relatively obscure. Bennett not only wrote on Josephine Baker, but also followed Francophone left-wing newspapers such as Lamine Senghor's short-lived *La Voix des Nègres* in 1927 and the spin-off publication edited by Camille Saint-Jacques (another member of the Ligue de Défense de la Race Nègre) called *Le Courrier des Noirs*.[25] Bennett generally offers sanguine appraisals of the potential for black transnational organizing, emphasizing the differences and difficulties of understanding between African American expatriates and Francophone communities in Paris. In one column, for example, she notes that René Maran "is extremely interested in the American situation, and is constantly writing in French journals and magazines critical notes on the recent literature and cultural advance of the American Negro." When Bennett met him in Paris, Maran "brought out a copy of a current French news sheet and showed an article on lynching. . . . He, himself, was incensed at the idea of such barbarity and told me that in a like manner the white Frenchman could in no way understand the toleration of such cruelty in a civilized country." But her conclusion is sharply noncommittal: "It was a beautiful thing to note the kindredship that existed in his heart because of the irradicable black of our skins."[26] For Bennett, Maran's race consciousness is at best a "beautiful thing," a sort of sentimental chromaticist quirk, rather than the foundation of an internationalist project.

While Gwendolyn Bennett's published writings in sum do not raise issues of gender in an international frame, her journals during her year studying in Paris from June 1925 through the summer of 1926 and her *Opportunity* columns confirm that there were extensive connections between black U.S. women intellectuals and their black Francophone counterparts throughout the late 1920s and early 1930s.[27] Unfortunately, even in scholarship whose specific goal is to sketch a "Black Atlantic" imaginary, there is little attempt to consider not just the way black women travel, but more important, the ways the ideological uses and abuses of gender always undergird any articulation of diaspora—the ways evocations of black populations elsewhere are always shaped by the representation of reproduction, motherhood, and the relations between men and women.[28] It is precisely through the lens of this kind of inquiry into "Black Atlantic" modernity, however, that we should read the work not only of Paulette Nardal, but also of her U.S. counterparts such as Bennett and Jessie Fauset, who served as literary editor of the *Crisis* under W. E. B. Du Bois from 1919 until 1926.

Like Paulette Nardal with regard to Négritude, Jessie Fauset has been famously described as a "midwife" of Harlem cultural activity—that is, as an editor and supportive elder intellectual who facilitated the careers of emerging writers including Langston Hughes and Claude McKay, but who by implication was secondary or ancillary in the conception of the "Renaissance" moment.[29] Fauset is also often characterized as a "paradox," an intellectual whose tastes were squeamish and proper, and whose own novels were mainly ideological propaganda for the new black middle class, but who provided crucial support as an editor for many of the more politically radical and so-called primitivist writers in the New Negro movement. Critic Robert Bone banishes Fauset (along with Nella Larsen) to what he calls the bourgeois idealistic "Rear Guard" of black modern fiction, and adds that "her novels are uniformly sophomoric, trivial, and dull." But Bone concludes his brief overview of her career with the caveat that Fauset represents "something of a paradox, for in her editorial work on the *Crisis* she often championed the young rebels of the Harlem School. Unlike Du Bois, who was a Philistine and objected to the Harlem School on moral grounds, she showed a genuine interest in the development of Negro art even when its main current ran counter to her own social prejudices."[30]

Cheryl Wall has argued that we must turn our attention to a certain degree away from Fauset's novels to her essays, which together form an impressive body of work comparable to the criticism and journalism of Alain Locke or George Schuyler.[31] With translations from the French, book reviews, historical portraits, and travel narratives of her voyages to Europe and North Africa, Fauset's work in the *Crisis* was instrumental in casting the New Negro movement in a transnational frame. Her vision of metropolitan black culture strives to articulate connections and correspondences among intellectuals of African descent throughout the Western world. Even in Fauset's New York salon, the currents constantly blew in from points distant. Langston Hughes jokes in his autobiography that

> [a]t the novelist, Jessie Fauset's, parties there was always quite a different atmosphere from that at most other Harlem good-time gatherings. At Miss Fauset's, a good time was shared by talking literature and reading poetry aloud and perhaps enjoying some conversation in

French. . . . At her house one would usually meet editors and students, writers and social workers, and serious people who liked books and the British Museum, and had perhaps been to Florence. (Italy, not Alabama.)[32]

Reading her essays as evidence of this persistent and pervasive internationalist outlook, it is evident that Fauset cannot be easily pigeonholed as solely an apologist for the urban U.S. black bourgeoisie. Most of Fauset's articles in the *Crisis* make no mention of U.S. black urban class tensions: instead, they focus on the beginnings of the Great War (Fauset was in France in the summer of 1914), or Fauset's visit to Algiers in the mid-1920s, or nationalism and Egypt.[33] In such work we discover a different Fauset than the one we have been taught to expect by criticism on *Plum Bun* and her other novels. In the essays, the historical analysis is clear and cogent, and the anti-imperialist commitment is pronounced. In the piece on Egypt, she offers a remarkably detailed account of the rise of rebellion and nationalist propaganda in the wake of Britain's 1882 establishment of a "veiled protectorate," which dominated Egyptian internal affairs through the first decades of this century. She reads the independence movement as a long-smoldering fire that had been "fanned" after World War I "by the wonderful pronouncements, made during the war, on the rights of small nations to self-determination."[34] Explaining the violent reaction to the official recognition of the British protectorate during the Versailles Peace Conference, Fauset concludes: "Egypt is thoroughly aroused now. She sees English motives clearly and estimates their worth. . . . Who doubts that Egypt is really speaking for the whole dark world? Thus is the scene being staged for the greatest and most lasting conflict of peoples."[35]

Many of Fauset's essays clearly evidence the influence of Du Bois, especially in their consistent commitment to the Pan-African project and their anti-imperialism. Yet in the place of Du Bois's grand pronouncements and sometimes overblown romantic internationalism, we find Fauset more often turning her eye to the telling detail, to the elaboration of the nuances of an encounter, to the everyday lives of her subjects. As critics such as Wall, Deborah McDowell, and Gloria Hull have pointed out, Fauset's authority at the *Crisis* was almost exclusively editorial: she had no access to institutional funding or the patronage that underwrote so many of the male Harlem writers.[36] Before and after her stint with the NAACP journal, she taught French and Latin at the M Street (Dunbar) High School in Washington, D.C.—where she fostered ties to other educator-writers such as Anna Julia Cooper, Georgia Douglas Johnson, and Angelina Grimké. It is not surprising then that she manifested a teacher's attentiveness to what she describes as "breathing-spells, in-between spaces where colored men and women work and love and go their ways with no thought of the 'problem.'"[37]

Those "in-between spaces" are also sometimes the result of diasporic *décalage,* the traces of significant difference in black internationalist efforts. Take for instance the piece she wrote on the Second Pan-African Congress in 1921, after she had accompanied Du Bois to the meetings in London, Brussels, and Paris.[38] Fauset's coverage is suffused by the optimism and enthusiasm of the moment, and it gushes in admiration of Du Bois's charisma and leadership. Nevertheless, Fauset offers a number of perspicacious observations that amount to a take on the congress wholly her own.[39] Describing the Brussels session, where an argument broke out between the U.S. delegates led by Du Bois and the Francophone constituency led by the Senegalese *député* Blaise Diagne concerning the discussion of the French African colonies in the congress's final resolutions, Fauset bluntly lays out the colonial economics at stake in the collusion between Diagne and the Belgians. Noting that there were more Europeans present for the meetings than there had been for the first sessions in London, she comments:

> [I]t was not long before we realized that their interest was deeper, more immediately significant than that of the white people we had found elsewhere. . . . Any interference with the natives might result in an interference with the sources from which so many Belgian capitalists drew their prosperity. . . .
>
> After we visited the Congo Museum we were better able to understand the unspoken determination of the Belgians to let nothing interfere with their dominion in the Congo. Such treasures! Such illimitable riches! What a store-house it must plainly be for them. . . . Small wonder that the Belgian men and women watched us with careful eyes. (371–372)

In this hostile context, the strategy of the U.S. delegation was relatively straightforward: "We knew the tremendous power of capital organized to exploit the Congo, but despite this we proposed before the Congress was over to voice the wrongs of Negroes temperately but clearly" (374). What is new about Fauset's version of the events is that she is one of the first participants in the Pan-African movement to lay out the political differences among representatives from Africa and the Americas that continually threatened the stability and structure of the organization. By the third session of meetings in Paris, Fauset had turned sober about the movement's potential: "Already we had realized that the black colonial's problem while the same intrinsically, wore on the face of it a different aspect from that of the black Americans" (376).

At the end of her description of the meetings in Brussels, where the U.S. delegation compromised, allowing Diagne to jam through a mild resolution "stating that Negroes were 'susceptible' of education and pledging co-operation of the Pan-African congress with the international movement in Belgium" (374), but successfully retaining the more progressive London resolutions on the table for consideration in Paris, Fauset recorded a small act that she felt encapsulated the entire conflict—the forced silences, the high stakes between colonial exploitation and international justice, the minuscule gestures that can carry immense weight:

> How great was this smothering power which made it impossible for men even in a scientific Congress to be frank and to express their inmost desires? Not one word, for instance, had been said during the Congress by Belgian white or black, or French presiding officer which would lead one to suspect that Leopold and his tribe had ever been other than the Congo's tutelary angels. Apparently not even an improvement could be hinted at. And the few Africans who were present said nothing. But at that last meeting just before we left, a Congolese came forward and fastened the button of the Congo Union in Dr. Du Bois' coat.
>
> What lay behind that impassive face? (375)

Fauset's original contribution in her political and historical essays is to capture this kind of "translation of hitherto unsyllabled, unuttered prayers" (378), the seemingly minor and unrecorded signifying acts that in such situations can in fact comprise the real work of communication across difference.

Unfortunately, whereas Fauset's essays are unprecedented in the ways they introduce gender issues, they never sustain this approach toward an articulation of diaspora that would combine anti-imperialism with a feminist critique. In one sense, this is due to Fauset's habitual self-effacement: for example, although she herself gave a speech about the status and activities of African American women at the meetings of the 1921 Congress, Fauset does not use this material in her summary of the events. Nor does she wonder how her own insights might be linked to the political issues at stake. She flatly puts herself in the third person, without elaboration: "Miss Fauset told of the colored graduates in the United States and showed the pictures of the first women who had obtained the degree of Doctor of Philosophy" (373). In another article which offers a survey of all the European press coverage of the Pan-African Congress, she only allows her own contributions to be described tangentially, as in the quote from an article in the Scottish *Glasgow Herald:* "Miss Fauset, of Philadelphia, literary editor of the *Crisis,* spoke on the subject of the colored women in America, who, she said, had been a great moving force behind all the movements for emancipation."[40]

This kind of reticence carries over into Fauset's essays on poverty and everyday life in Europe: the portraits of women in her articles—about France on the brink of war, about the Clignancourt flea market, about lodging houses *(pensions)* in France—never push issues of gender as far as they might. Even the critic Deborah McDowell, who strains to argue that Fauset's fiction uses the "convention of the novel of manners" not in the spirit of the ultimately conservative aesthetic that most critics have identified, but instead "as protective mimicry, a kind of deflecting mask for her more challenging concerns," concludes by admitting that Fauset ends up with only an "oblique and ambivalent treatment of feminism."[41] The essays, like the fiction, are full of subtle descriptive passages that fall mute or close off prematurely, such as the following section from a piece Fauset wrote after weeks of living in the cheapest *pensions* in Paris:

In the pension a line from a melancholy hymn of my Presbyterian childhood comes back to me: "Change and decay in all around I see." . . . And about the boarders there was this same air of desiccation. An old, old lady, a widow I judged from her deep black and her son of perhaps 55; another old lady, once the matron I should say of some frightfully corrective institution, erect and with a terrible, raucous voice; four or five depressed young men, bookkeepers, clerks, hopelessly nondescript. The food was nondescript too.[42]

Where one might expect this to lead to a consideration of her cloistered upbringing in Philadelphia, or to a sketch of the ancient Frenchwoman boarder, Fauset tumbles back onto an easy generalization in the next paragraph: "Life in a pension is not French life only; it is life everywhere in similar environment." Cheryl Wall has observed that this kind of writing "often works to deny the difference that is its most promising subject. In the end, the [essays'] too-easy universalism is the clearest evidence of the constraints that constructions of race and gender impose upon Fauset's work."[43]

Similarly, in "This Way to the Flea Market," her 1925 essay on the well-known *marché aux puces* at the northern tip of Paris, Fauset presents a vivid rumination on life at the border of urban economic existence: the diverse crowd ("representatives of the poorer groups of all those nationalities with which Paris teems"), the petty haggling, the obsessive puttering through piles of "gee-gaws" and trinkets, the resolute will to survive, signified in small acts of buying and selling. Describing a tough bargain negotiated between her guide and a woman merchant, she writes that the "hard and stratified" qualities in the French character are evidenced "nowhere more plainly than in the poor and middle-class French woman. It is an extension of that instinct which makes the small and cornered animal fight so bitterly, converting him finally into a truly formidable opponent. Woman being the weaker creature must harden herself proportionately just that much more to meet the exigencies of her existence."[44] But this is as far as Fauset can go—and she seems incapable of extrapolating on this characterization, or linking it to other moments of her visit when gender (and race) come into play, as when for instance a boy with a "box of shoe-blacking" approaches as they are leaving the market and sarcastically suggests that Fauset could use some to augment the color of her light-brown skin ("you'd better buy some for mademoiselle!" the boy says to Fauset's friend, holding open the polish).[45] Fauset makes no comment on this last confrontation. She simply takes comfort in regaining the interior of Paris: "Behind us curved and closed the fortifications; viewed from this side they emanated security, protection. 'Pass in,' they murmured, 'You are safe!'" (163) And thus the shroud of bourgeois respectability and comfort falls back over her, even as she dares to peek through its seams.

Paris seems to attract Fauset in part because she is able there to test what she recognizes in herself as a reluctance to broach issues concerning the interconnections of class, race, and gender. Not surprisingly, she professes the common reasons of U.S. black expatriates to visit France: "I like Paris because I find something here, something of integrity, which I seem to have strangely lost in my own country. It is simplest of all to say that I like to live among people and surroundings where I am not always conscious of 'thou shalt not.'"[46] What is peculiar about Fauset is that the "thou shalt not" is above all an internalized injunction, not the more explicit discrimination that black artists from William Wells Brown to James Baldwin have eloquently expressed a need to escape. Fauset confesses,

> I am somewhat tired, pardonably so, I think, by the unnatural restraint imposed when both races meet, and this restraint is mostly my own. It manifests itself in my personal behavior because I am conscious of belonging to another race. In order to offset criticism, the refined colored woman must not laugh too loudly, she must not stare—in general she must stiffen her self-control even though she can no longer humanly contain herself. (47)

There is thus justification to Cheryl Wall's assessment that Fauset was a "reluctant explorer," since "the potential risk was too great, as much to the image she reflected as a proper Negro woman as to herself."[47] The risk of crossing barriers is a recurring theme in Fauset's career, as when she declined to translate René Maran's *Batouala* in 1922 and wrote in sheepish explanation to Joel Spingarn that "Alas, alack, I know my own milieu too well. If I should translate that book over my name, I'd never be considered 'respectable' again."[48]

It is not useful, however, to overemphasize Fauset's conservatism to the point that we no longer recognize the originality of her work on Pan-Africanism and European life. Hazel Carby is correct to posit a link between the novels of Fauset and Nella Larsen—both are inventive in their treatment of class conflict in northern cities, a focus that departs from the obsession with reconstructing what she terms "folk authenticity" in other literature of the "Harlem Renaissance."[49] But Carby may be too quick to insist on a firm distinction between Fauset's strategy of "adapting" the romance genre without radically transforming it and Larsen's more resolved refusals of the standard of middle-class respectability in *Quicksand*.[50] Most important, it must be recognized that the fiction of Larsen and Fauset shares a common critique of the ways the black modernist modes of imagining expatriation and migration are always gendered. In Larsen's 1928 *Quicksand,* Helga Crane travels to Copenhagen only to discover—through Axel Olsen's courtship of her as no more than an exotic sexual creature—that while she can consume, she can always become a gendered object of consumption as well.[51] Europe, supposedly free of prejudice, does not allow Helga an escape from a gendered economy of race relations; as Farah Griffin has described it, "Her body becomes the text on which the narrative of a sexualized other is written."[52] Fauset's often-overlooked 1933 novel *Comedy: American Style* makes a similar point when the Philadelphian Teresa Cary marries Aristide Pailleron, her white French phonetics teacher at the University of Toulouse, and assumes she will easily "pass" into the comfort of French middle-class life. With terrible irony, she comes to learn that she is effectively stranded in the south of France with her new husband, who turns out to be a hardened racist and a ridiculous miser to boot. "She did not know what to make of her life. It was so strange, so different from anything she had anticipated. Was she to spend it thus forever with her vapid, unimaginative man, her scolding mother-in-law, her petty household duties? . . . Gradually her expectation of a change died away and she settled down into an existence that was colorless, bleak and futile."[53] Both *Quicksand* and *Comedy: American Style,* placing "race" in a transnational context, emphasize the way black modern migrancy is always gendered, in ways that inescapably constrain the paths open to black women. Both are an implicit critique of the painless expatriation commonly portrayed in novels from Johnson's *The Autobiography of an Ex-Colored Man* throughout the period: the fiction of Larsen and Fauset argues against the view that would articulate black transnational migrancy as a simple escape from U.S. racism without taking into account sexism, European exoticism, or class barriers.

Even in this critique of black modern migrancy, however, Fauset's work tends to retrench its own limitations and to reproduce its own injunctions, especially by recourse to a rhetoric of sentimentality. Her vision of black internationalism, as sharp-sighted as it can be in her essays on the Pan-African Congress, curdles into a discourse of *nostalgia* as it strains to elide or compensate for the very gaps and discrepancies it uncovers. Fauset introduces what will become a key term for her writing in "Nostalgia," a 1921 essay published in the *Crisis*.[54] "Love of fatherland," Fauset writes, is "nostalgia's cause." The piece encompasses four vignettes. Three are centered on the longings of U.S. immigrants for "home": Fauset talks with the Greek owner of a fruit shop on Seventh Avenue in New York, the Italian cobbler on 12th Street, and a Romanian girl named Rachel, whose father is a Zionist. The fourth anecdote departs from the pattern: an old Philadelphia acquaintance, a "colored boy whom [Fauset] used to know at the Art School," comes back after serving in the war and living in France. He tells her, "I never knew what home was until I went to France" (156). But then he announces that ever since returning to the States, his only desire has been to get away from American racism and go back to Europe. Citing Du Bois's anecdote about the untranslatable, haunting old Bantu song his ancestress sang, Fauset argues that the "American Negro" is afflicted with a special kind of "spiritual nostalgia" due to what Edouard Glissant would call his radical "uprooting" (*déracinement*) from his African "fatherland" (157). "The black American," Fauset writes, "is something entirely new under the sun" (158), unable to translate—to carry over into a new context—the African cultural inheritance. The homeland that haunts the black American psyche is not Africa, finally, but an imaginary and, one might add, an entirely *exegetical* ideal:

> In the main, the American Negro is without ties and the traditions that throw back. Instead, he has built unconsciously from his childhood a dream-country, and yet surely no dream country [*sic*] since it is founded on that document which most realizes and sets forth the primal and unchanging needs of man—the Constitution of the United States.
>
> Where the Greek dreams of his statues, he dreams of Justice; where the Italian yearns for his opera, he yearns for Opportunity; and where the Jewish visionary longs for freedom of sect, he cries out for an escape from Peonage. (157)

The passage seems at once incisive and inane. In a sense, it expresses perfectly the civil rights figure of the "New Negro" as envisioned by the *Crisis* and the NAACP after World War I, a figure that attempts to bring into being the "dream country" of American constitutional democracy. With the

same stroke, the notion of "spiritual nostalgia" is exemplary of the ultimately phantasmic nature of the "New Negro" paradigm. In the words of
Henry Louis Gates, Jr., "just as *utopia* signifies 'no-place,' so does 'New Negro' signify a 'black person who lives at no place,' and no time. It is a bold
and audacious act of language, signifying the will to power, to dare to recre-
ate a race by renaming it, despite the dubiousness of the venture." Fauset's
version of black internationalism is unique in that it continually produces a
rhetorical tension between what Gates calls "the weary black dream of a
perfect state of being, with no history in particular detail" on the one hand
and "the search for a group of black and especial historical entities" on the
other.[55] Hers is a rhetoric that always resolves this tension in favor of nostalgia, in favor of the easy universalism that—as evidenced by the acquaintance from Art School, who finally doesn't know where he wants to be, except that he doesn't want to be *here*—resides in perpetual unfulfillment, a
"sadness without an object."[56] At the same time, this resolution acquiesces
to the implicit gendering of the "New Negro." Although Fauset provocatively describes nostalgia in reference to maternity, arguing that it "is as universal a phenomenon as that of possessing a mother," she then defines the
term as longing for a "fatherland"—unlike Du Bois himself, who explores
the possibility of theorizing diaspora as scattered or broken maternity by arguing that Africa might be "perhaps better" termed his "motherland."[57]
Fauset's essay describes nostalgia with a portrait of a male figure in longing,
refusing to extend the theme to her own stays in France, and never intimat-
ing whether she might share her acquaintance's sentiment.

Extending these issues to the context of Francophone intellectuals in
Paris during this period would necessitate coming to terms with the
décalage between the literary imaginings of African American expatriates
and black Francophone migrants. One might juxtapose Fauset's rhetoric of
nostalgia with a Francophone instance such as the short story called "En
Exil" (In exile) that Paulette Nardal published in *La Dépêche africaine* in
December 1929.[58] It is a brief account of an Antillean woman named Elisa
on her way home from work as a maid, day-dreaming of her "native town"
(bourg natal), Sainte-Marie in Martinique. As she walks through the rain
down the windswept rue des Ecoles to catch the bus, she thinks to herself:
"This country really doesn't suit an old Negress [*une vieille négresse*] already
weighed down by age and stiff with rheumatism." Her only wish is that her
son, who has been "trying his fortune" for the past five years in Colomb

(Algeria), will comes back with a little money so that she can return "to her country" *(au pays)*, which "she should have never exchanged for the mirage of Paris."[59] Her imagination "had almost personified" the French winter, a "cruel and implacable enemy," but it also delivers her from the drudgery of her journey. With a "distant look" *(regard lointain)* on her face, she day-dreams she is back in the Sainte-Marie of her youth:

> After a day of ironing, she sits down on a worm-eaten bench in front of the door of her low-roofed house, attracted by the chatter of friends who, like her, are savoring the salty air. . . . Someone starts to "tell tales" [*conter contes*], not forgetting the traditional opening formulas: "Titime?" "Bois sec."—"Trois fois bel conte." As always, it's the adventures of Brer Rabbit [*Compère Lapin*] . . . African tales adapted to the Antillean soul.

Drums off in the distance "ring out like an anguished call," and for Elisa "it is all the soul of old Africa that passes in that Antillean tam-tam, awakening an obscure emotion in the talkers, who are now suddenly attentive."[60] Her "rêverie" is finally torn *(déchiré)* by the "brutal" voice of the driver calling out her stop: "Rue de Rennes!" But at her building on the boulevard Pasteur, the concièrge hands her a letter from Colomb: her son writes that "the Americans bought his leatherware business for a good price" and that he'll be coming soon to take her back home. Weeping with "unexpected joy," Elisa bounds up the six flights of stairs with newfound energy as the story concludes: "[T]he neighbors, who pity her every night hearing her wearily climb the worn steps, no longer recognize this light footfall, and ask themselves who it could be humming that strange refrain with its staccato rhythm, with its guttural and soft syllables [*ce refrain étrange, au rythme saccadée, aux syllabes gutturales et douces*]. . . ."

Clearly the story is not structured around the rhetorical "non-place" of Fauset's nostalgia. Here, Elisa is not drifting in abstract "homesickness," but on the contrary is emphatically "in exile." The condition of migration is exilic for the colonial subject, and she dreams of return to a particular New World home. At the same time, Martinique is defined outside or beyond the logic of colonialism: Elisa recalls the rhythms of dusk in Sainte-Marie, the "languid" chatting and tale-telling of friends, and above all the African roots of Caribbean popular life.

This fictional rendering of migration, longing, music, and gender identity is a common theme in the interwar period, not just in early Francophone literature but also in conventional and commercial French imaginings of the Caribbean. Take for instance the introductory text accompanying a 1930 catalog of Odéon Records (one of the companies keen to profit from the Parisian craze for Caribbean music such as the Martinican beguine). Titled "L'ame nègre en exil . . . au bal antillais" (The *nègre* soul in exile . . . at the Antillean ball), the text draws on language immediately reminiscent of Nardal's piece, but used for entirely different purposes:

> These powerful and sweet blacks [*nègres puissants et doux*] left in France by the war, these naive *négresses* with sparkling smiles who have come to "serve" in our families, have retained a nostalgia for their wonderful distant country. And they've communicated it to us! [*Et ils nous l'ont communiquée!*]
>
> One of them, wearing a hat covered in yellow cockleshells that reigned over the Vaugirard sidewalk, suddenly announced that she was leaving her mistress. "What?" cried the latter. "Aren't you satisfied?"—"Yes, yes," protested the dark child, "me real happy here with Madame" [*moi, bien content ici avec madame*]. Then, with a smile at once happy and sorrowful, she added:—"But I have a *traveling soul. . . .*" [*Mais j'ai l'âme voyageur. . . .*]
>
> How many others who aren't able to leave Paris are going to make that beautiful, long voyage in their dreams, in one of the black popular dance halls [*bals populaires nègres*] on the left bank of the Seine, which have recently been so much in vogue, and which are indeed so curious?
>
> Close your eyes, spin the record [*Fermez les yeux, faites tourner le disque*].[61]

The catalog, with its narrative of the gendered Antillean "traveling soul," attempts to commodify the expressive longing of the subject trapped in migration, dreaming of home in a metropolitan dance hall as Martinican music wafts through the "curious" space. In the rhetoric of this text, it is the record itself that holds or carries the "communication" of black nostalgia, and thus having the record allows the listener access to those sounds. As Theodor Adorno pointed out a few years later, the phonograph record is the "first means of musical presentation that can be possessed as a thing."[62]

In a certain sense, the record here is represented as a peculiar kind of souvenir, an object that "speaks to a context of origin through a language of longing, for it is not an object arising out of need or use value; it is an object arising out of the necessarily insatiable demands of nostalgia."[63] It is peculiar, of course, because the record as object is the souvenir of someone else's nostalgia—indeed, the souvenir of the nostalgia of those "nègres puissants et doux," those "négresses naïves à l'éclatant sourire," who have come to work for "our" families. So the commodification of recorded beguine is simultaneously the commodification of the colonies, of "native" homesickness: another way for the European to appropriate *La France d'outre-mer.* In other words, the beguine record serves as a reminder that commodities are indeed above all "sensuous things which are at the same time suprasensible or social," the reflection of "the definite social relation between men" (the system of colonization itself) in a "fantastic" or "mysterious" form.[64] That form explicitly works by an operation of metaphor, a "troping" or "turning" (*Fermez les yeux, faites tourner le disque*) that links the listener's possession of the object to France's possession of the colonies.

One might remark that in "En Exil" Nardal writes directly against such a rhetoric of appropriation, even if—or precisely because—she draws on the same set of figures. The story attempts to practice a mode not of commodifiable nostalgia but instead of elusive *exile.* In so doing, it never loses sight of the politics of colonial labor, however: thus Elisa's reverie takes place on the bus ride home from a difficult day at work "serving" a European family. Even in the Caribbean context of "nostalgia," Elisa imagines passing the day "ironing." The story very subtly broaches an internationalist representation at the same time, since her upwardly mobile son has traveled to "try his fortune" in Algeria. In fact, it is not the grace of France, but the aggressive finance capital of another imperial power lately stretching its influence into the region ("the Americans") that finally provides Elisa's son the money to realize her dream, to fetch her and take her home. This is not a critique of colonialism in general but a critique of the ways that the longings of a bourgeois Antillean *évoluée* are necessarily bound up with a globe-girdling system of expansion: *exploitation* in the double sense of that word in French (both "making a profit from" and "taking advantage of"). What is elusive about exile in Nardal's story is that its "means of musical presentation" cannot be grasped, cannot be "turned" to the service of the colonial

project. The story points us at what can't be caught in Elisa's musical reverie, the sound of its "strange refrain."

Feminism and *La Dépêche Africaine*

In the scholarship on the emergence of the Négritude movement, there is a
common assumption that the group around Paulette Nardal and her sisters
was simply "assimilationist" and therefore to be dismissed, representative of
the "stage of consciousness" that an intellectual such as Aimé Césaire had
to pass through or bypass in order to reach his formulation of a new
Négritude aesthetic. The group around *La Revue du monde noir,* even if it
pursued an interest in an African heritage with unprecedented verve, remained at best politically reformist and "superficial," celebrating the triumphant exoticism of the 1931 Colonial Exposition in Paris and working ultimately to "preserve the status quo while exhibiting the relative prestige and
the advantages of a colored elite. This group prided itself on what it
thought to be its perfect assimilation into French society."[65] These kinds of
assumptions are fueled not just by Césaire's few disparaging statements
about Nardal's salon, but also by the usual failure to link intellectual groups
and journals in the early 1930s, such as *La Revue du monde noir,* to their
predecessors, such as *La Dépêche africaine* and *Les Continents.*

The most pernicious version of this trend in the historical literature ends
by racializing the development of Négritude, arguing that the movement
was produced out of a conflict between one group of "mixed" Antillean students and intellectuals—who espoused not just cultural assimilation into *la
plus grande France* but moreover racial miscegenation—and another group
of more radical, "pure Negro" Africans. For instance, the Belgian critic
Martin Steins, accepting without question the racialist presuppositions of
terms such as *métis* ("half caste") and *mulâtre* ("mulatto"), argues summarily that "in the history of the movement that concerns us here, analysis
of the relationship between mulattos and blacks [*la relation mulâtres-nègres*]
has almost always been avoided. But, from all evidence, this relationship is
at the core of the question; it even seems that the Négritude movement was
born out of a change in the attitude of the Antillean *métis.*"[66] Steins goes so
far as to extend this kind of racialism to black modernist cultural politics
more broadly, writing that a "mixed-blood International" *(Internationale
métisse)* dominated the interwar period "on both sides of the Atlantic."[67]

Even more strangely, he identifies racial miscegenation as the "driving idea" of the New Negro movement in Harlem.[68] Even granting the many U.S. debates around "passing" after World War I, it is plainly foolish to argue that all the culture framers of the New Negro movement—Du Bois, Locke, James Weldon Johnson, and Charles Johnson, among others—were by any stretch of the imagination calling for intermarriage or "whitening the race" as the central civil rights strategy. Steins furthermore assumes that all the *mulâtre* intellectuals from Martinique, Guadeloupe, and French Guyana who were in Paris in the 1920s shared the same outlook: "As their American counterparts [*sic*], they thought that the burning problems of the race would eventually brown out: the Negro's soul would mate with the genius of France and give birth to a creole culture, a promising hybrid that would animate the imperial community. Both concepts, the one cultural, the other political, were of a somehow-mulatto type."[69] Interestingly, beginning with the Martinican journal *Lucioles* and the work of Gilbert Gratiant in the mid-1920s, there were in fact intellectuals who elaborated a position that Caribbean culture was "creole." But even for Gratiant, this position was more a kind of regionalism, an attempt to come to terms with the specificity of the Antillean experience, articulated in connection with Gratiant's firm Marxist politics, and never a simple proposition for "racial" amalgamation.[70]

Steins conflates the work of Gratiant in Martinique with the activities of figures such as the Nardals in Paris and cites Jane Nardal's neologism *Afro-Latin* as exemplary of "the 'brown' solution."[71] In fact, though, as we have seen, Jane Nardal deliberately uses the term *nègre* in her article "L'internationalisme noir" and makes no call for miscegenation. On the contrary, *Afro-Latin* is a term specifically geared to approximate or translate what Nardal considers the racial consciousness inherent in the appellation "Afro-American" in the interest of a larger project of black internationalism. It should be evident that Nardal's article is not concerned with either cultural or racial assimilation to a French standard, but with the elaboration of a transnational circuit of black modern culture among intellectuals whose "American" or "Latin" education has "not necessarily driven them to deny their race."[72]

If nothing else, the circles of black intellectual activity among Caribbean, African, and U.S. migrants in Paris in the 1920s and 1930s were heterogeneous and volatile. At every turn, we encounter a wide range of interconnected cultural work, contentious debates, and shifting positions. In no way can this context be reduced to either a cultural or a racial schema that would pit "brown" against "black," "bourgeois" against "proletariat." A number of the most conservative proponents of the French imperialist system were "dark-skinned"; a number of the most radical anti-imperial and Communist intellectuals were "brown" Antilleans originally of petit bourgeois origins. A number of intellectuals, most notably Léo Sajous, but also Kojo Tovalou Houénou, Tiemoko Garan Kouyaté, Jules-Marcel Monnerot, and Emile Faure, shifted political positions and affiliations and served as links especially between the more hard-line Communist groups and the more reformist cultural groups. Even with regard to *La Dépêche africaine*—which overall is without a doubt the most conservative of the interwar Francophone journals in the metropole—it is difficult to agree with Steins that the newspaper represents the "*depoliticization* of the black question; the desire for collaboration between French and native with the *Empire . . .* and the defense of racial and cultural *cross-breeding.*"[73] In *La Dépêche africaine,* as in other black Parisian periodicals (and as in U.S. journals such as the *Crisis* and *Opportunity*), there is never a single, consistent party line, but a variety of political positions, in varying degrees of accordance with one another. There is a significant distance between Maurice Satineau's editorials defending the French imperial system and celebrating the economic exploitation of the African colonies, art collector Paul Guillaume's articles lauding "primitive" African sculpture as the "sperme vivificateur du vingtième siècle spirituel" ("life-giving sperm of the spiritual twentieth century"), African American bandleader Noble Sissle's explanation of "Why Jazz Has Conquered the World," the Dahomean Félix Couchoro's pastoral African tales, Charles Bellan's calls for education and development in the African colonies, Dantès Bellegarde's essay criticizing the U.S. occupation of Haiti, the numerous reports on "Harlem Renaissance" cultural activity and African American artists in Paris, and Paulette Nardal's cultural criticism.[74]

There is an equally striking range among the contributions to *La Dépêche africaine* that make claim to a feminist stance. Madame Winter Frappier de Montbenoît, from the island of Réunion, was the founder of a group called "La Française Créole" (The Creole Frenchwoman) and was especially concerned to protect the interests of "mixed-race" *(métis)* citizens in the French colonies. In one essay, she argues that this issue should be para-

La Dépêche africaine 31
(December 1930).
Collection of the author.

mount in colonial policy: whereas illegitimate children of the fleeting relations between French men and "native" women were scorned in the colonies, Montbenoît claims (against all historical evidence, and against her
own patronizing anecdote of subjugation) that black populations *(les
nègres)* had always been well respected:

> There exists an enormous difference between the *nègre* in the United
> States, the *nègre* who is an English subject, and the *nègre* of the old
> French colonies. The first, whom the Americans boycott in the ways
> we already know, are only tolerated as inferiors. I am irritated when I
> observe their exhibitions, for in Réunion and the French Antilles, the
> *nègre* has always enjoyed on the contrary the greatest esteem. My fa-
> ther always used to give his Negro [*noirs*] servants dangerous mis-
> sions, certain they would carry them out wonderfully.[75]

Montbenoît is less interested in suffrage for women than in equal social treatment. Thus she makes the relatively radical suggestion that to overcome discrimination against the *métis* in the French colonies, family descent and inheritance should be defined as matrilineal, rather than dependent on the absent or reluctant white father.

Another feminist, Marcelle Besson, wrote for *La Dépêche africaine* about French women in colonial affairs, not by calling for suffrage or solidarity but by taking up another argument familiar in French feminism of the period: that the proper role of woman is to spread her positive "moral" influence. With "a clear head and a large heart," Besson argues, the French woman can help by working to stop the disease and pestilence devastating colonized populations, by advising politicians on policies to "hasten the evolution" of "primitive peoples," or by combating exploitation in colonial policy "to a certain extent." This variety of conservative feminism is not a call for social equality, but an argument for the strategic use of woman's "indirect" authority. Besson contends that "each of us can, in fact, indirectly manage our country in suggesting ideas to relatives, friends, and acquaintances who hold effective control."[76]

The articles of Jane and Paulette Nardal in *La Dépêche africaine* move in yet another direction. I point out the diversity of this work in the journal in the spirit of Joan Scott's argument that French feminism necessarily operates within a paradox, articulating claims from the seemingly universal ground of "woman" even while critiquing in various ways the very founding discourses of rights, citizenship, and individuality that had worked and naturalized a split between the categories of man and woman. Rather than reading feminism simply as an autonomous and singular political stance, then, one must comprehend feminism through difference, as the plural and shifting "legacy" of this paradox, "reading the repetitions and conflicts of feminism as symptoms of contradictions in the political discourses that produced feminism and that it appealed to and challenged at the same time."[77] We are often accustomed to thinking the other way around: thus Sylvia Wynter, in one of the better-known essays on black diasporic feminism, aims to construct a narrative in which "race" is a term, a "variable," which troubles the intervention of black women into feminism, in the same way that feminism had earlier inserted the term of gender into the supposedly "universal" doctrines of Western liberal humanism and Marxism.[78] But the multifaceted feminist work in *La Dépêche africaine* may offer another possible trajectory of development—one that will be echoed, say, in Etienne Balibar's formulation that racism always "presupposes" sexism.[79] This is to take Paulette Nardal's claim about the origins of "racial" consciousness among Francophone women intellectuals in the metropole as a serious theoretical position rather than a simple historicist point of order. The point is not that "race" troubles the supposed universality of feminism—for there are only feminisms, plural and interested articulations of that legacy of paradox—but instead that "race" and gender are always inextricably interwoven. The possibility therefore opens that in a transnational cultural context, feminism, as one strategic unraveling of that weave, may precede and lead to black internationalist consciousness.

Salons and *Cercles d'Amis*

Interestingly, one of the only biographical portraits of Paulette Nardal was written by Eslanda Goode Robeson, the wife of actor and activist Paul Robeson. She penned two articles about "Black Paris" for the journal *Challenge* in the 1930s. The article on Nardal opens: "Paulette Nardal is beautiful. Her lovely clear dark-brown skin has bronze lights in it; her face is full of intelligence and repose; her voice is low and soft, cultured and controlled, and her diction faultless. She is equally fluent in French, her mother tongue, and in English. She has poise and charm. She carries herself with quiet unselfish dignity like some magnificent dusky queen."[80]

Paulette Nardal was born in the town of François, Martinique, on October 12, 1896. Her father, Paul Nardal, was an important construction engineer from St. Pierre who had been trained in France and who served as the unofficial manager of construction on the whole island. Relatively "dark-skinned" like his daughters, Paul Nardal faced a good deal of color prejudice in the Martinican government despite his talent and expertise. Robeson writes that the "[g]overnment never formally recognized his position. . . . It is said, had he been a mulatto, the Government would probably have appointed him; but being a pure Negro, they considered it bad policy for him to hold such a position."[81] His wife Louise Achille was a government piano teacher who never left the island. (It was through their mother's father, originally from Guadeloupe, that the Nardal sisters were related to their cousin Louis-Thomas Achille, who like them came to study at the Sorbonne and who later would teach at Howard University in Washington,

Paulette Nardal (c. 1970).
Bibliothèque Nationale,
Paris.

D.C.) The portrait of Martinique that Paulette Nardal gave Robeson during their interview demonstrates not just a keen sense of the historical in-
terrelations of race and class, but also a sense of the particular difficulties af-
fecting Antillean women:

> It is almost impossible for Negroes to accumulate money, because all
> the land in Martinique belongs to the white plantation owners; the
> peasants, Negroes, are merely workmen, civil officers, and a few have
> small unimportant businesses. . . .
> Until nearly twenty years ago, the Negro girls in Martinique did
> not work, but remained at home and waited for a husband.[82]

Four of the seven Nardal sisters were among the first generation to go to
France to study to qualify for government positions in teaching and the
civil service. Alice Nardal became a professor of music; Jane, with her degree in classics, returned to the Caribbean to teach high school Latin at the

Basse-Terre Lycée in Guadeloupe; and Cécyl, trained as a midwife, opened a practice in Guadeloupe with Jane's husband, who was a doctor.[83]

Paulette Nardal began her higher education at the Colonial College for Girls in Martinique and then spent some time in the British West Indies to perfect her English. She won a competitive scholarship to study for a graduate degree in Paris at the Sorbonne in the early 1920s; after returning to Martinique for a year to teach English, she moved to Paris and worked as a journalist and translator for a number of publications, including *Le Soir* and *La Dépêche africaine*. After she founded *La Revue du monde noir* in 1931, Paulette was commissioned to write a tourist guidebook to Martinique later that year.[84] As we shall see, she retained close ties to Antillean students in Paris through organizations such as the Association des Etudiants Martiniquais and the journal *L'Etudiant noir*. Nardal was equally active on the feminist front, working with moderate groups including Ad Lucem Per Caritatem and the Union Féminine Civique et Sociale. Even so, she found time throughout the 1930s to meet the many U.S. black artists and intellectuals who visited Paris. When John Paynter was in Paris in 1936, for instance, staying with Louis-Thomas Achille, Nardal "was on several occasions the cheerful medium of conversation, particularly at the always enjoyable dinner hour." She took Paynter on a tour of the Palais Royale and the Place de la Concorde, and they went to see Josephine Baker and the African dancer Feral Benga at the Folies Bergère one night. Paynter writes,

> Later, through the entree to this kindly family, I had the pleasure of an afternoon and evening with Mlle. Paulette Nardal as my charming guide. It was not strange, perhaps, that—with her unusual Parisian charm, yet with a richly dark complexion, so decidedly strange in contrast with the native Parisienne—she, and even her escort, who was decidedly not native though less attractive, should win some unusual attention from the passers-by. But it was an attention of polite and restrained curiosity, French to the core. However, Mlle. Nardal was, or seemed, oblivious; concerned with only where to go and how to get there.[85]

When she was forced to flee France in 1939 on the eve of the war, Paulette Nardal had been working for some time as the secretary to Galandou Diouf, the Senegalese *Député* who had replaced Blaise Diagne in the French

Assembly. She went on to pursue a long and celebrated career in Martinique until her death in 1985, both in feminist work (founding the Rassemblement Féminin there in 1945 and editing a journal titled *La Femme dans la cité*), and in cultural endeavors, especially through her choir, "La Joie de Chanter" (The Joy of Singing), which in 1954 presented the first concert of "Negro spirituals" in Martinique and also performed Nardal's own arrangements of creole folk tunes.[86]

The history of the first generation of Antillean and African students to study in the metropole after World War I remains to be written. Eslanda Robeson contends that the black women Francophone students in Paris had a very different experience of the metropole than the men:

> They did not have a happy time in Paris. There are usually about two hundred and fifty Negro students in Paris, mostly boys from Guadeloupe, Martinique, Africa, and a very few from America. The Negro boys often have great success, and are sometimes lionized by the French girls; the mulatto is often successful, too. But the Negro girls of the better class, often proud and sensitive, have a difficult time; their own boys are much more interested in making conquests in the new field, and leave them sadly alone; and French boys are not interested in them, except as friends.[87]

The constellation of intellectuals that gathered around the Nardal sisters is characterized above all by a concerted effort to establish new and independent intellectual institutions, support groups for discussion and publication, and even performing arts networks. Although historians acknowledge the role of this loose-knit group in introducing black luminaries in the pre-Négritude period, their weekly meetings and concerts (not to mention their extensive work as literary and musical critics, musicians, journalists, translators, editors, and activists) are almost always quickly dismissed as no more than a "salon" in the traditional French bourgeois model. But on closer inspection, the group around the Nardals might not be best described as a salon at all. Indeed, perhaps to distinguish her own aims, Paulette Nardal preferred to call her gatherings a "cercle d'amis" ("circle of friends") instead.[88] In a recent reflection on the period, Louis-Thomas Achille has attested to the singularity of the Sunday *cercle d'amis* that met at the Nardal house at 7 rue Hébert in Clamart, a suburb of Paris:

A dominant feminine mood ruled the tone and the rituals of these convivial afternoons, not at all like a business circle or a masculine club. The furniture of the two connecting rooms, the living room and the dining room, did not reproduce in any way the decor of a salon of the traditional bourgeoisie of France or of the Antilles. Some English armchairs, airy, comfortable and light, furnished the accommodations for the conversation, which took place rather naturally also in English. There was neither wine, nor beer, nor French cider, nor whisky, nor exotic coffee, nor even creole *ti-punch* to refresh the throat. Only English tea cut into these meetings, which never went beyond the dinner hour. . . .[89]

I wonder whether the quick urge of Césaire to dismiss this space as "superficial" and as ultimately tangential to the birth of the Négritude movement is not in fact another kind of reaction, directed more at the dominant figures of the Nardals as women—and in particular as religious women—than at the class forces that shaped the environment.[90]

It is crucial to recognize the experimentalism and innovation in this institution building, in this effort to create a new kind of migrant black communal space in Paris—a space sometimes identifiable as "bourgeois," sometimes identifiable as "feminist," sometimes identifiable as "intellectual," sometimes identifiable as "Anglophile," but more generally characterizable as shifting and subtly defiant to our anticipations. Moreover, the Nardal *cercle* amounts to an argument that *l'internationalisme noir* requires what we might term the institutionalization of reciprocity: the creation of open, informal spaces designed to allow certain kinds of transnational, translinguistic dialogue rather than to voice any particular social doxology.

In terms of New Negro activity on the other side of the Atlantic, Achille's evocation of the *cercle d'amis* is immediately reminiscent of the salons led by black U.S. female intellectuals such as Jessie Fauset, Regina Anderson, and Ethel Ray Nance in New York and Georgia Douglas Johnson in Washington, D.C.[91] Johnson's "Saturday Nighters," hosted at her home at the corner of S and 15th Streets in Washington, are perhaps the best known.[92] African American salons had been held in Washington as early as 1905 by the Mu-So-Lit Club and then after World War I by Edward C. Williams's Literary Lovers.[93] But in the 1920s it was Johnson's "Saturday Nighters" (originally Jean Toomer's idea) that gathered the widest range of the East Coast black literati including Langston Hughes, Zora Neale Hurston, Bruce Nugent, Angelina Grimké, Jessie Fauset, Alain Locke, Alice Dunbar Nelson, Kelly Miller, Wallace Thurman, and Sterling Brown. Other intellectuals and writers such as Gwendolyn Bennett, Countee Cullen, James Weldon Johnson, Charles S. Johnson, A. Philip Randolph, and Carter G. Woodson sometimes made plans to stop by Johnson's house when they came to visit Washington, D.C.[94] Bruce Nugent would tell an interviewer later that "Georgia Douglas Johnson's salon was the most unique one because it was almost like a throwback to ancient days when salons were the property of women. Women always had salons. Nobody went to Georgia's to meet writers, you went there to meet people."[95] The evenings attracted "a freewheeling jumble of the gifted, famous, and odd," and chances were that the crowd would even include some of the well-known white literary figures who passed through black circles, such as Vachel Lindsay, Edna St. Vincent Millay, Waldo Frank, and H. G. Wells.[96]

Although I am suggesting that the innovative dialogic spaces assembled by black women played an often underappreciated role in transnational cultural circuits during the interwar period, it is necessary to add that the salons led by black U.S. women such as Georgia Douglas Johnson differed in important ways from the Nardals' *cercle d'amis* in Paris. The New York and Washington gatherings were first of all less cosmopolitan, less spaces of translation, less geared to foster links in a vision of black internationalism. And while the Paris circuits constructed a diasporic cultural space within a mostly indifferent European milieu, the New York and Washington groupings constructed a supportive network within a mostly hostile black middle class context. The point of Johnson's group was not belletristic pretentiousness or "Saturday night adventures in tidy parlors, among mostly tidy-minded literati."[97] As Ronald M. Johnson has pointed out, the gatherings functioned on the contrary as a haven for "Harlem Renaissance" intellectuals and artists, a buttress against isolation in an insufferable middle-class black climate. The "Saturday Nighters," Johnson writes, "brought together an isolated and otherwise ignored group of individuals. Here they read their works, exchanged criticisms, and argued views on literature, art, and politics; here they found the nurture, encouragement, and reception that black Washington seemed unwilling to extend."[98] Langston Hughes, for example, singled out the literary community as one of the few high points of his time in Washington, which were "unhappy years, except for poetry and the friends I made through poetry." His assessment of the class obsessions of the segregated black community in D.C. is particularly resentful: "the 'better class' Washington colored people," he writes, "were on the whole as unbearable and snobbish a group of people as I have ever come in contact with anywhere."[99]

Although there were certainly readings during the "Saturday Nighters" in Washington, the gatherings run by the Nardal sisters seemed much more open to a wide variety of participatory performance. Whereas the Washington sessions sometimes centered on political discussions about the history of slavery or miscegenation, Louis-Thomas Achille's description of the Paris cercles d'amis highlights their communal and improvised engagement with a variety of black expressive forms: "Alternating with the piano, readings or recitations of Antillean poems by Daniel Thaly and E. Flavia Léopold, or poems by Gilbert Gratiant written in Creole, provided a literary interlude. Sometimes a chorus formed on the spur of the moment to read through Negro American 'spirituals' or 'blues.'"[100] Such a juxtaposition—which again may not be representative of the range of practices in either locale—implies that the Nardals' gatherings focused on performance, whereas the discussions in the living rooms of Jessie Fauset or Georgia Douglas Johnson were spaces of casual interaction and debate.

What is especially important and particularly unique about the circle around the Nardal sisters is that it cleared space for a kind of feminist practice that otherwise was not possible in the midst of the vogue nègre in Paris. If as Joan Scott contends, feminism "is produced, differently at different moments, at sites of difficult, historically specific discursive contradiction,"[101] then the work of the Nardal sisters as cultural critics is significant in the way it strives to contend with its particular historical "contradiction": the pernicious framing of black Francophone women in the gendered metaphors of colonial exoticism, travel, and desire specific to the modern European imagination. Hortense Spillers has famously described an "American grammar book" of tropes conscribing black U.S. women, a "locus of confounded identities, a meeting ground of investments and privations in the national treasury of rhetorical wealth."[102] The work of the Nardals is in part a feminist response to what we should understand to be a transnational modern "treasury of rhetorical wealth," which exploited stereotypes of "dark" and "dusky" women from around the globe.

This discursive field has deep roots in French colonial history, which critic Régis Antoine has partially traced through readings of the figure of the *doudou,* an image as integral to the French imperial imagination as that of the grinning Senegalese soldier in Banania advertisements. French discourse around the *vieilles colonies* in the Antilles consistently describes the islands with phrases such as "l'île enchanteresse" ("the enchanting isle"), "une colonie heureuse de son sort" ("a colony happy with its fate"), phrases about the "wonders" of Martinique or the "luxuriant" and "transporting" verdure of Guadeloupe. This metaphorology contributed not just to the exoticization but also to what Antoine terms the "hyper-feminization" of the islands.[103] As early as 1769, the popular song *Adieu foulards, adieu madras,* attributed to M. de Bouillé, then gouverneur of Guadeloupe, immortalized this set of tropes with a highly charged narrative of desire, which introduced a female "type" that came to be termed *la doudou.* The lyrics tell a tale of a Caribbean woman separated from her French lover, in a formula that "took on a symbolic function, *ad nauseam,* as the ideal representation of an amorous relation projected onto the political backdrop between the Antilles and France."[104] By the late nineteenth century the *doudou* was commonly understood both in the Antilles and in metropolitan France to be any "smiling, sexually available black or colored woman (usually the latter) who gives herself heart, mind, and body to a visiting Frenchman (usually a soldier or colonial official) and is left desolate when her lover abandons her to return to France, having, of course, refused to marry her though often leaving her with a child who will at least 'lighten the race.'"[105]

By the turn of the twentieth century this figure had begun to extend or "unfurl" into the literary arena, in a subset of colonial literature that came to be termed *la littérature doudou* or *doudouisme.* In the depiction of the Antillean context, Antoine explains, "The young woman of color and her heartaches effectively became a motif inseparable from the countryside motif [*motif paysage*].[106] Providing the mythical foundation for any number of poems, sentimental novels, and travel narratives, the figure of the *doudou* came to serve as a reservoir of immediately recognizable tropes to inscribe the "wonderful islands" and to propel readerly desire. By World War I, the literary *doudou* presented an "an erotic object obligingly proposed for the consumption—the textual consumption—of metropolitan readers, by Antillean writers themselves as well as by French voyagers."[107]

This particularly Antillean "grammar book" worked against other possible characterizations of the islands, helping to elide the racialized specificity of class relations and labor exploitation in the French Caribbean. At the same time, the mystification whereby the *doudou* came to stand in allegorically for the islands served to elide other possible resistant or anti-imperialist images of Antillean women.[108] There were a few scattered attempts just after the war to challenge this complex metaphorical field around Antillean femininity. One thinks of Suzanne Lacascade's aforementioned *Claire-Solange, âme africaine,* or Oruno Lara's pedantic 1923 novel *Question de couleurs (blanches et noirs).*

Lara's book opens with a double dedication "to colored women from all countries and all colonies, *in a hopeful homage*" and "to white women who frequent Negroes [*qui fréquentent les noirs*], *in a homage of gratitude and respect.*"[109] It is mainly structured as a Socratic dialogue between René Frault and Nelly Guérin, two Guadeloupean civil servants who meet in Paris after having known each other as teenagers in the Caribbean. In a series of humorous exchanges, René convinces his old acquaintance to recognize that she is a *négresse.* As he puts it, when one is called a *nègre,*

> the best thing was to face up to idiotic color prejudice. . . . One shouldn't lower one's head, declare oneself "half-white," cowardly turning one's back to the epithet. . . . And besides, to what good? You'd be scorned anyway. Ah! Let them come, those who say such prejudices don't exist in France, let them come! . . . [I]t was better to show oneself as one was, to call oneself Negro [*noir*] because one was, to claim the word *nègre* and work to instruct oneself, to better oneself, in order to make it respected, both the word and the thing, in acquired rights.[110]

In the course of their debates about the race problem, René also seduces Nelly. Yet *Question de couleurs* is no simple story of "native" love discovered in the metropole. In a version of the feminism espoused in Marcelle Besson's articles in *La Dépêche africaine,* René instructs Nelly that she has a historic duty as an Antillean woman to "uplift" and "influence" her race through moral education. In an extraordinary twist, he is assisted in this pedagogic undertaking by a number of white Frenchwomen who tell Nelly about woman's proper influence. One white feminist explains that if she spends time with Negroes, it is "not a preference, but a generous tendency to love those who are misunderstood [*méconnus*]. Those who do so brave prejudice and open the paths unto the future. The white women who frequent Negroes [*les noirs*] are the true messengers of Progress."[111] By the conclusion of the novel, a convinced Nelly returns to Guadeloupe, writing to René that he has made her conscious "of a nobler duty, the uplift of our race; of a better and sweet virtue, the collaboration of the woman in the man's bold dream." "I'm yours," she proclaims in the letter, but adds that "it's over, I'll never get married." Nelly has decided to "consecrate" herself to the "task" of being a teacher in Guadeloupe in order to educate "a generation that will follow in your footsteps."[112] She leaves "without a glance behind her," asking René to help her by composing an instruction book *(un livre d'enseignement)* she can use in "popular education."[113] And René remains in the metropole to write and study. Lara's short novel is largely forgotten, but noteworthy as an unprecedented attempt at renovating the image and self-conception of the Antillean woman—even if the book ends up a bizarrely reactionary vision of a gendered division of labor in the service of racial nationalism.

In her biography of Josephine Baker, Phyllis Rose notes that a major difference between French colonialism and British colonialism is manifested culturally, visible in the "fantasy productions" of the Paris music halls:

> The French were publicly willing to imagine themselves making love with colonial women. . . . An important colonial administrator put it tellingly in his book about governing West Africa: "The territory is not just raw material for finance, commerce, army and administration to work with; nor is it something to be made an idol of. It is a living body, and we must enter into relations with it if we are to govern it with full knowledge of what we are doing."[114]

Still, after World War I, the *vogue nègre* brings about a ground shift in the feminization of the colonial relationship, particularly due to contact in Paris between French artists and colonial "natives" (former soldiers, laborers, servants, students, performers). Between the world wars, the construction of the "colonial woman" becomes inherently *metonymic:* it is no longer simply that French Caribbean islands are "feminized," but moreover that metropolitan popular culture elaborates and commercializes a broader "colonial grammar book" that represents "exotic" women throughout the empire. What changes drastically is that this discourse of the "native" sexual other becomes increasingly indiscriminate, paying less attention than ever to detail and projecting a vision of a nearly continuous feminized object of desire across *la France d'outre-mer.* It is not by chance that this development neatly coincides with the evolution in political discourse of the notion of the "greater" French Empire as a single unifying entity.

Expatriate African American performers played an important role in this extension, and none was as successful and instrumental in this regard as Josephine Baker. In 1931, at the height of her popularity, Baker was even asked to serve as the "Queen" of the Exposition Coloniale, an honor which was quickly rescinded due to a chorus of loud objections that Baker was a U.S. citizen, not an *indigène* (she had never even been to the French colonies). But in a complex dynamic between the craze for jazz and the desire for a feminized exoticism, shows were constructed around Baker precisely to make the point that she *could* represent a kind of universal feminine colonial other. She opened in the fall of 1930 at the Casino de Paris with a show called "Paris qui remue" (Paris When It Sizzles), "a series of colonialist fantasy skits, in which Baker generally played a young native girl from somewhere in the French Empire in love with a dashing Frenchman."[115] "Paris qui remue" was hugely successful, running through the year for 481 performances, and in it Baker's body was the consummate "ideological artifact," as James Clifford has put it. In her shows, "archaic Africa (which came to Paris by way of the future—that is, America) was sexed, gendered, and invested with 'magic' in specific ways."[116] But her performances not only enabled an exotic Africanist detour, but also served as the locus of a metonymic operation: black, brown, and yellow bodies were all incarnated in the writhing limbs and "sculptural" gestures of Baker as interchangeable objects of colonial desire. In "Paris qui remue," she not only danced the Charleston, but also sang in one skit, "Voulez-vous de la canne à sucre?" ("Would you like some sugar cane?"), as the sexually teasing Martinican *doudou;* in another, she was "La Petite Tonkinoise," a little Vietnamese girl singing about her French lover.[117] The revue also introduced what became Baker's signature song, "J'ai deux amours": "J'ai deux amours, / Mon pays et Paris. / Par eux toujours / Mon coeur est ravi" ("I have two loves, / My country and Paris. / By them my heart / Is always delighted"). In later years, Baker would sometimes add a new line at the end of the song, proclaiming her cosmopolitan autonomy: instead of "Mon pays et Paris," she would sing "Mon pays *c'est* Paris" ("My country *is* Paris"). But as Rose points out, the song, which had been originally written by Vincent Scotto in 1905 for another music hall star, was not the sugary nostalgia of an American in Paris, but yet another colonial metonym:

> "J'ai deux amours" was not the song of an American girl who has made it in Paris and yearns for home. It was part of an elaborate sketch called "Ounawa," for which the leopard Chiquita had been purchased, set in the equatorial jungle. It is the song of an African girl in love with a French colonist. He invited her to return with him to Paris and she wants to go, but the people of her tribe won't allow this betrayal. She is torn: "J'ai deux amours." On the one hand racial and national identity, on the other romance, sex, and swinging Paris.[118]

Indeed, much of the pleasure of Baker's performance seems to have come precisely from its metonymic structure: that here on the Parisian stage of the Casino, the modern and the primitive *coexisted* in an eroticized female body—at once the light-skinned black American performer from Harlem, with her jazzy dance steps and pronounced American accent, *and* the "archaic" colonial others from so far away. Unlike most women from the colonies, however, Josephine Baker herself was in the end able to transcend many of the stereotypes of this troubling grammar book, for as the greatest star of the music hall era she "was able to mock the role of the exotic primitive even as she played it to the hilt."[119]

Black Magic

With regard to the African diaspora, the most pernicious example of this metonymic extension of the *doudou* may be the 1928 best-selling collection of short stories by Paul Morand called *Magie noire* ("black magic"), which was translated the next year in a widely read English edition illustrated by Aaron Douglas.[120] The stories featured locales across the Atlantic basin, from Haiti to the Ivory Coast, from Brussels to Charleston, from Liberia to the Côte d'Azur, from Baton Rouge to Paris. Animated by Morand's sophomoric but sensational writing style, the tales all strove to bring together caricatures of familiar black modern figures (Baker, Du Bois, A'Lelia Walker) with overdetermined references and primitivist stereotypes of the Jazz Age (lynching, "passing," "voodoo," the Pan-Africanist and Garvey movements, the U.S. occupation of Haiti, international communism) to portray a unified black world ultimately determined by its *atavism*—the susceptibility of even the most seemingly civilized and modern black subject to revert at any moment to his or her "essential" primitive nature. The order of the stories followed the route of Morand's travels through the Americas and then Africa in 1927 and 1928, when he was on honeymoon with his wife Hélène, reading the racist theories of Gobineau.[121] *Magie noire* shares with much colonial literature a pretension to a social scientific "verisimilitude," enumerating in a chronological preface the "30,000 miles, 28 Negro countries" that Morand claimed to have traversed during the book's composition (481–482/v–vi).

W. E. B. Du Bois must have been especially incensed by "Syracuse ou l'homme panthère," the story that featured a Renaissance man who closely resembles him: Dr. Lincoln Vamp, founder and leader of a "House of the New Negro" of educational and social uplift, to which he had given a grandiose classical name: "Syracuse" (one thinks of Du Bois's evocations of "Atalanta" in *The Souls of Black Folk*). The story is set during the Brussels session of the 1921 Pan-African Congress, where Vamp takes a break from the grueling debates to visit the Congo Museum. Wandering alone through the building, the doctor undergoes a strange and irresistible transformation: first, he recognizes himself as having the same seductive eyes as a "fetish-conjurer" depicted in an exhibit, and then he starts hearing the "calls" of the magical objects collected around him, the "plain, harmonious expression of happiness, the happiness of the man whom nothing has reft from his soil or his setting, who continues to live just where God placed him" (566/87). The "spirits" inhabiting the old fetishes, calabashes, amulets, and death shrouds speak to Dr. Vamp, resuscitating his "true" nature (with a mocking pun on his name):

> "Flee!" they were saying, "flee! Leave the land that is your dwelling-place; her fertility is but a show, and ruin broods over her. Her progress is an illusion. She makes you a vampire, no more. Come back to the land where stones and trees speak in the name of the Spirit." (566/87–88, modified)

Vamp ends up hallucinating that he has turned into a panther, being hunted deep in the jungle, and when his colleagues come to search for him the next day when he is absent at the Pan-African Congress, he has vanished without a trace: the museum guard recalls seeing only "un grand nègre fou, qui rougissait" ("a tall Negro . . . mad—and bellowing") (568/ 89) running out of the museum.

Du Bois held himself above this kind of preposterous pulp, writing in a supercilious review of the translation simply that *Black Magic* "is mainly nonsense. It is built around the thesis that all persons of Negro descent have atavistic urges to 'go native' on the slightest provocation."[122] The more central objects of the atavism thesis in Morand's collection, however, are black women, and the stories go to great lengths—picking up on the metonymic culture of the Parisian stage and dance hall and on the older literary tradition of the *doudou*—to make the argument that black women, as the "mothers of the race," have an especially pronounced susceptibility to "go native." In "Good-Bye, New York!" for example, the reader is presented with Pamela Freedman-Orfei, a young "light-skinned" American woman, who takes a transatlantic cruise to see the coast of Africa. Pamela is the daughter of a woman who invented a well-known hair straightener (the portrait is loosely based on A'Lelia Walker). She grew up in Paris and is "passing" for white on the cruise ship. There is a man on the ship who knows Pamela's mother—as often in the tales, black atavism passes through the maternal line—and eventually her secret is the main course of gossip among the scandalized and disgusted white passengers. Partly due to their machinations, the ocean liner (named the "Mammoth") leaves her in Africa by mistake, after a day at anchor along the shore. Pamela is panicked at first, lost in the jungle, but after she finds a French colonial administrator, she quickly adapts to the situation and becomes his obliging mistress. The narration switches to present tense as "son atavique manque de mémoire, l'ardeur à vivre qui est dans son sang" ("her atavistic shortness of memory and the ardor for life that runs in her blood") (587/164) make Pamela forget the day before and enable her to live in the bliss of an eternal present. One day she goes into the jungle with one of the administrator's servants, Mamadu, who eagerly leads her to his village to witness a ritual ceremony. In a startling passage, yet another metonymic mix of modern jazz and "primitive" percussion, Pamela succumbs:

> The terrible musky smell of the *nègre* was overwhelming her, but she could not withhold it from her nostrils. She felt herself entering into the black world [*le monde noir*]; she was drowning in it. Ritually, the moon had risen. . . . Pamela remembered Irving Berlin's latest success:

> *Niggers are only really niggers in the moonlight [Les nègres ne sont*
> *vraiment des nègres que sous la lune] . . .*

In that dull thudding of the tom-toms she felt once more the same numbness, the same ecstasy, that she sought in Montmartre jazz at the hour of the full blast of intoxication. . . . She was sick of being a fake White woman! Why should she take pride in a progress borrowed from others? Her own progress was to return, in an astounding, harmonious union, to the land of her ancestors. . . . O the femininity, the vast maternity of this continent! The *négresses* are the queens of the black world. (591–593/172–173, modified)

It is the perfect image of atavism—embodied in the reversion of a thoroughly modern black American woman with only a fraction of "black blood," which is still powerful enough to call her back to "the vast maternity of this continent." Pamela Freedman finally yields to Mamadu's advances in an orgiastic sex ritual and goes "back into the womb of Africa" where she rightfully belongs:

Good-bye, New York! Pamela Freedman was going back into the womb of Africa. No longer was she worth three million dollars: she was worth three oxen, like the other women. There she was, clapping her palms, bent double at every cadence, her feet together and legs tightly pressed, her loins held stiff like all the Negro women. She was one of them now. (593/173)

Many of the African and Antillean students and intellectuals in Paris at the end of the 1920s wrote reviews of Morand's collection.[123] Perhaps the most extraordinary perspective is offered in Léon-Gontran Damas's 1939 essay "Misère noire," which reads *Magie noire* as an example of the "irritation" caused by the cultural conquest of Europe by black art and music. He retells the story of "Good-Bye, New York!" slightly changing the details: as Damas recalls it, the tale is the story of a perfectly civilized colored American woman who "during the course of a cruise in Africa, seeing a coconut tree, rejects all the customs of civilization as useless garments, and climbs back up the ancestral coconut tree." Damas writes, "This 'story' vexed considerably the better French Negro society [*la bonne société noire française*], which believes that the apex of human dignity consists in going back to the cave era via the paths offered by Mr. Paul Morand's civilization." He goes on:

> We are of a certain number, on the contrary, to consider the act of Paul Morand's heroine with a great deal of sympathy. . . .
>
> Nevertheless, what is most interesting is that on the one hand Paul Morand kindly sends back to the coconut trees a Minister of Justice, a Vice-President of the Legislative Chamber, a good half-dozen generals, etc. . . . , of *his* country, while at the same time, in the salons that M. Paul Morand haunts, the sisters of M. Paul Morand are dancing the tango, the fox-trot, the blues, the rumba, the conga, the son. . . .
>
> The Romans showed more propriety. When they offered sacrifices to the gods of those they colonized, they at least refrained from offering them in their own homes.[124]

As rudely humorous as the passage is—reminding a French readership that assimilation is a double-edged sword—Damas relies throughout on a racialist vision of "civilizations" competing through the exchange of women. Thus his critique matches Morand's atavistic banishment of Pamela Freedman up the coconut tree with its own images of "Paul Morand's sisters" shaking their hips to the sounds of black rhythms.

In *La Dépêche africaine,* Jane Nardal wrote another review of *Magie noire* specifically in a manner not just to challenge the atavism thesis as an extension of earlier figures such as the *doudou,* but also to critique the gendered construction of "civilization" that Damas takes for granted. In an essay titled "Pantins exotiques" (Exotic puppets), she focuses on the images of black Francophone women that comprise "illusions profondément ancrées dans l'esprit français et tombées de la littérature dans le domaine public" ("illusions profoundly anchored in the French mind and fallen out from literature into the public domain").[125] She writes: "De la puissance d'évocation de certains mots, le créole qui a séjourné en France peut facilement se rendre compte. Vient-on à savoir ou à s'apercevoir que vous êtes 'exotique,' vous suscitez un vif intérêt, des questions saugrenues, les rêves et les regrets de ceux qui n'ont jamais voyagé: 'Ah! les Isles d'or! les pays merveilleux! aux heureux, aux naïfs, aux insouciants habitants!'" ("The creole who has visited France can easily attest to the evocative power of certain words. As soon as people learn or perceive that you are 'exotic,' you elicit lively interest, ludicrous questions, the dreams and regrets of those who have never traveled: 'Ah! The Golden Isles! The wonderful country-side! The happy, naive, carefree inhabitants!'"). In false innocence, Nardal queries:

> Aurions-nous le courage de nous dépouiller du prestige que nous confère la littérature exotique et de détonner, modernes, sur le décor passé, rococo des hamacs, palmiers, forêts vierges etc.
>
> Quelle déception pour celui qui évoque en votre honneur des princesses exotiques, si vous alliez lui dire que, tout comme une petite bourgeoise française, vous poursuivez à Paris des études commencées là-bas, sous les tropiques, au Lycée?

> Will we have the courage to shed the prestige that exotic literature confers upon us, and to clash, as modern women, with the decor of the past, the rococo of hammocks, palm trees, virgin forests, etc.
>
> What a disappointment it would be for he who evokes exotic princesses in your honor, if you were to tell him that—just like any French petit bourgeois girl—you were here in Paris to pursue studies you'd started over there, in the tropics, in high school?

In the face of these persistent stereotypes and assumptions, she jokes, the only question left is "à quelle sauce voulons-nous être mangés: à la sauce idéaliste ou à la sauce réaliste?" ("in which sauce would we like to be eaten: the idealist sauce or the realist sauce?"). She sketches a brief survey of the literary figurations of black women, from the early exoticism of Bernardin de Saint-Pierre, to the humanitarian or abolitionist romanticism of Victor Hugo, Alphonse de Lamartine, and Jules Michelet in France and Harriet Beecher Stowe in the United States, up through the more naturalistic portraits of Marius-Ary Leblond's *Ulysse nègre* or Joseph Conrad's *The Nigger of the Narcissus* around the turn of the century, and concluding with the current violent urban primitivism of Philippe Soupault's 1927 novel *Le Nègre* and Carl Van Vechten's 1926 *Nigger Heaven*.

But Nardal suggests that the grammar book of such metaphors has shifted in recent years away from the romanticism of exotic literature. Of late, "la boîte aux accessoires exotiques soit boulversée" ("the box of exotic accessories has been shaken up"). This shift, Nardal argues, is thanks to the metonymic whirlwinds of the *vogue nègre* and black popular culture in the

Parisian metropole. It is especially Josephine Baker who has "shaken up" the standards of nineteenth-century *doudouisme:*

> Voilà que bondit en scène une femme de couleur, aux cheveux laqués, à l'étincelant sourire; elle est bien encore vêtue de plumes ou de feuilles de bananes, mais elle apporte aux Parisiens les derniers produits de Broadway (Charleston, jazz, etc.). La transition entre le passé et le présent, la soudure entre la forêt vierge et le modernisme, ce sont les noirs américains qui l'accomplissent, et la rendent tangible.

> Then onto the stage leaps a colored woman with lacquered hair and a sparkling smile; she is still clothed in feathers or banana leaves, but she brings the latest Broadway products (the Charleston, jazz, etc.) to the Parisians. The transition between the past and the present, the fusing of virgin forest and modernism—it is American Negroes who are carrying it out and rendering it tangible.

French artists—"blasé snobs," in Nardal's estimation—have discovered in figures such as Baker and Ada "Bricktop" Smith a means to renovate and extend the *doudou* image. Like James Clifford, Nardal describes this metonymic field in terms of eroticized collage and alluring juxtaposition: "le contraste savoureux, pimenté, d'êtres primitifs dans un cadre ultra-moderne de la frénésie africaine se déployant dans le décor cubiste d'une boîte de nuit" ("the flavorful, spicy contrast of primitive beings in an ultra-môdern frame of African frenzy, situated in the cubist decor of a night club").

Nardal reads Paul Morand's collection as no more than an exploitation and sensationalization of this development. She offers a few conjectures about his sources: besides popular culture, there is the apparent influence of Lucien Lévy-Bruhl's *La Mentalité primitive,* and for the U.S. sections, per-haps Alain Locke's *The New Negro.* As for the Caribbean sections of the book, there are the literary models of the *doudou* and the "dangerous mu-latto," to supplement Morand's brief "stop-overs" *(escales)* in the islands. She also notes that Morand was known to "haunt" the Bal Nègre on the rue Blomet, the Antillean dance hall featuring beguine that in the late 1920s became an attraction to Parisian society as fashionable as the Cotton Club in Harlem. In fact, Nardal blames the *vogue nègre* and clubs such as the Bal

Nègre for instilling images of blacks as *only* entertainers for white metropolitan amusement, for the "artistic or sensual pleasure of the white man." She complains that "lorsqu'il s'agit de qualités intellectuelles, ou morales, lorsqu'il s'agit de ne plus être leur bouffon, mais leur égal par l'intelligence, cela dérange le plan de la nature et les vues de la providence" ("when it has to do with intellectual or moral qualities, when it has to do with no longer serving as the whites' buffoon, but instead their equal in intelligence—that disturbs the natural order and the plans of fortune"). The black woman is left in a conundrum: for the "aesthetic pleasure of Paul Morand and company," she is a "puppet" *(pantin)* consumed in a sauce putatively *both* idealist ("the vast maternity of the African continent") *and* realist (her essential atavism).

Nardal is not so concerned with countering each and every stereotype deployed in *Magie noire;* instead, she looks for the ways such a text is received in the social context of the *vogue nègre.* Morand's position, she contends, amounts to an ultimately unsurprising brand of paternalism, involving, on the one hand, a lament for a "pure" or "authentic" black primitive culture that is disappearing as colonized black populations come into contact with Western civilization and, on the other hand, an infatuation with the "magic" of African diasporic religious practice, ritual, and music. Morand's entire stance on black modern culture is shaped through such assumptions: the *nègres* "nous modifient, mais nous les déformons" ("modify us, but we deform them"), as he puts it in a contemporaneous article.[126] In the end, Nardal recognizes that Morand's construction of a gendered and atavistic set of black images is self-reflexive—more about "the representation of the French to the French" than any kind of sociological claim about black modern life. Encountering a key passage in "Good-Bye, New York!" that basically concedes this point, Nardal expresses relief. One of the characters on the ocean liner announces that

> our age is a *nègre* age. Just think of the general slackness, the distaste of the young for hard work, the nudity on the Lido or on Palm Beach, equality, fraternity, clay houses that last three years, public lovemaking, divorce, advertising. . . . The charlatans, the soap-box orators, the fortune-tellers, the petters, the fake jewellery . . . All in all, the *nègre* is just our own shadow! [*En somme, le nègre, c'est notre ombre!*] (577/150, modified)

The atavistic *nègre* is exposed as a function of the French imagination, a way of coming to terms with the threats of modernity. In *Magie noire,* Nardal comments, one ultimately encounters not the "portrait du nègre, mais celui de l'Européen d'après-guerre, assimilé au nègre, pour qu'il en éprouve de la honte" ("portrait of the black man, but that of the European after the war, assimilated to the *nègre,* who therein expresses his shame over that assimilation"). Thinking back to the racist reception of a book such as *Batouala,* Nardal concludes by expressing hope that one day a European critic will attribute to *la race nègre* not just the physical and performative prowess of a Josephine Baker, but also the intellectual and moral qualities of a René Maran.

Begin the Beguine

In their writings, Jane and Paulette Nardal both evidence an interest in those instances of black modern culture in the Parisian metropole, like Baker's performances, where "the box of exotic accessories has been shaken up." It is to this end that they turn especially to considerations of black music in the interwar period. A number of historians have written of the "international style" of Parisian popular musical activity between the wars, the quickly changing and highly syncretic mix of black U.S. jazz and fox-trot, European *artistes* such as Jean Cocteau and the avant-garde composers known as *Les Six* jamming their versions of *le jazz hot* at the club Le Boeuf sur le Toit, Martinican beguine and Cuban *son* and *rumba,* and the French popular *chanson* in the music halls and casinos.[127] Like Kojo Tovalou Houénou and *Les Continents* in 1924, the Nardal circle and *La Dépêche africaine* sponsored a number of musical performances toward the close of the decade, both in the salon and in theaters. Programming included "Grandes Fêtes Coloniales," which featured a wide range of black musicians in the spirit of the "international style": for example, one featured Ernest Léardée's Orchestre Antillais de la rue Blomet, the Noble Sissle jazz orchestra, the dancer Jeanne Longrais performing demonstrations of the beguine, Fernande Dorade and Félix Ardinet dancing the "black bottom," and the African American singer Ethel Oughton Clarke offering a short classical recital of arias by Mozart and Rossini.[128]

The critical work of the Nardals shows a particular interest in the *beguine* [*biguine*], which had emerged in the first decades of the twentieth century at the same time as jazz in the United States, *paseo* in Trinidad, tango in Argentina, and *son* and *danzon* in Cuba. The form had been developed during the last half of the nineteenth century in Saint-Pierre, Martinique. In one of the great traumas of Antillean history, Saint-Pierre was obliterated by the eruption of the Mt. Pelée volcano on May 8, 1902 (which claimed at least 30,000 victims), but until that tragedy the city was one of the most important cultural crossroads of the Antilles, with a lively theater and music scene featuring popular dance tunes with lyrics in creole, which were performed in a range of musical forms such as the beguine, the polka, the *valse créole,* the mazurka, the *quadrille,* and the Central American *valse pasillo.*

In the late 1920s, after Fort-de-France had been established as the new artistic and political capital of the island, a number of musicians from Martinique brought the music to France. The most famous was Alexandre Stellio, the Martinican clarinetist in whose playing some heard echoes of the great jazz reedman Johnny Dodds. Stellio would go on to record at least 130 sides in the boom of interest in Caribbean music in the next decade. He became a recognizable figure in black Francophone circles in Paris and, according to Paulette Nardal, was a spectacular performer on the bandstand:

> Don't assume that he exerts himself like a black jazz musician [*un noir de jazz band*], acrobat and juggler. Stellio's moves are entirely different. He doesn't just use his mouth to propagate that unique cadence, it is his whole body, his eyes, his head, which he turns from right to left, his neck, his shoulders, his right foot marking time, everything in him drawing out such intensity, such driving power, that you can only let yourself get carried away by the spirited rhythm of the beguine. And meanwhile, this remarkable man [*ce diable d'homme*] is still able to retain his gentlemanly airs.[129]

Stellio brought a traditional beguine dance band with him to Paris, including Ernest Léardée on violin, Archange St. Hilaire on trombone, Victor Colas on cello, and Crémas Orphélien on percussion, and they played Antillean dance halls around Paris until Léardée left to form his own band at the Bal Nègre on the rue Blomet in 1930.

Once in Paris, though, beguine underwent a transformation through the influence of the black transnational music scene. Fascinating derivatives began to develop in the cauldron of metropolitan popular culture. In particular, there were a number of musicians who crossed over between forms such as black American jazz and black Caribbean beguine during this period, cross-fertilizing and reconceptualizing each in the process. For example, Bertin Depestre Salnave, a Haitian who had come to Paris in October 1913 to study classical music, ended up playing with Will Marion Cook's orchestra in London in 1919 and then pursued a career playing jazz in Europe with black U.S. musicians such as Sidney Bechet, Arthur Briggs, and Crickett Smith. There was the Cuban guitarist Don Barreto, in Paris after 1925, who was active in both Cuban and jazz circles and whose band featured musicians from the States, Cuba, and the French Caribbean, as well as gypsies such as the clarinetist Edouard Pajaniandy. Trumpeter Arthur Briggs played with the drummer Robert Monmarché, an Antillean who went on to work with U.S. saxophonist and orchestra leader Benny Carter. And Antillean musicians such as the reed players Félix Valvert and Robert Mavounzy commonly recorded with both jazz musicians and beguine groups and introduced jazz instruments (the trap set, the banjo, the saxophone) and swing rhythms into beguine performances.[130]

The beguine remained a dance music, however, and no dance hall was more famous than the Bal Nègre located at 33 rue Blomet in the Fifteenth Arrondisement. It was open on Saturday, Sunday, Tuesday, and Thursday nights, and at the height of its popularity it was easily attracting crowds of four or five hundred dancers each night.[131] In the New York *Amsterdam News,* J. A. Rogers described the Bal for black U.S. readers: "Paris now has a miniature Harlem and all within the space of three months. It is the Bal Nègre on the Rue Blomet."[132] He compares the increasing hordes of white French gawkers and hangers-on to Manhattanites slumming uptown in Harlem. "The majority of the Negroes," Rogers writes, "are very dark, and come from the French West Indies or parts of Africa. The visitor who speaks only English had better take his interpreter with him. And as to the racial composition of the hall, the scientist who said that there were only five varieties of the human race must have been buried in some hole at the time, for here there are at least twenty-five: among them are Chinese, Japanese, Egyptians, Russians, Hungarians, Germans. One is faced with the fact that the human race, if it is anything at all, is certainly mixed." Rogers notes the differences between beguine and U.S. jazz in terms of the music itself as well as the styles of dancing and patterns of dress. He is especially fascinated by the *chacha,* the percussion instrument that sets the basic rolling rhythmic foundation of the beguine and propels the dancers, writing that "the tempo is set by a shiny tin container filled with pebbles. This container resembles a cocktail shaker pierced with many holes; the leader shakes it in a manner as if he were continually throwing it away from him." But the dancing was the point of the Bal Nègre, of course, and the unique and easy grace of the beguine mesmerized European and American commentators alike. Andrée Nardal, another of the sisters, described the dance in an article published in *La Revue du monde noir:*

> In the real biguine, as it is danced by the Creoles themselves, the performers do not embrace; they mimic the everlasting pursuit of woman by man. The former advances and withdraws to the accompaniment of a thousand enticing gestures while her partner artfully approaches and feigns a haughty indifference which he drops quickly in order to catch up to his flippant companion who is running away, borne along by her swishing skirts.[133]

Nonetheless, as we might expect, the feature of the Antillean dances that always attracted the most interest was the black women: their hairstyles, their dress, their accessories, such as the "bright-colored" bandanna described by Rogers ("worn outward like the horns of a snail"), and above all their "everlasting pursuit . . . by man." In the many descriptions of the beguine, it is as though those "thousand enticing gestures" are mobilized for the composition of that new modern and metropolitan grammar book, updating the *doudou.* In one frivolous article, journalist George Paul spends paragraphs simply cataloging the "dark women that give the real verve and color to this melange," with intense, almost clinical attention. One, he effuses, is dancing

> with a very little black man with a Charlie Chaplin mustache, whose head comes only level with her vast bosom. . . . She dances with her head flung back, and her great brown eyes from their burning, melting depths actually cast sparks upward to meet the glances of the row of hanging heads that gaze down from the balcony railings. The little black man with his fingers moving up and down over his partner's hips plays some strange tune, with all the care and precision and apparent foreknowledge as a musician lovingly fingering the keys of a piano.[134]

In this account, a great deal of work goes into imagining erotic "sparks" between the writer and the female dancers, whose burning glances are depicted in communication with and in supplication of the "row of hanging heads" in the balcony (at the Bal Nègre, journalists and wallflowers watched the dancing masses from the balcony). The women are silent instruments beckoning to be used, and the writer's own "frank" desire is to join that melange, "one jungle melody of motion, to which is added the technique of the piano, played by men's hands, black, white and yellow, upon the heaving backs of women."

The African American poet Countee Cullen also visited the Bal Nègre in the summer of 1928. That April he had married W. E. B. Du Bois's daughter, Yolande, in what was considered the "Harlem social event of the decade."[135] But in a sign of the state of their relationship (and possibly his own predilections), two months later Cullen left her in the States, kicking off his year-long Guggenheim Fellowship by voyaging to France with his friend Harold Jackman. He sampled the dance scene without his new wife, who joined him in Paris at the end of the summer. In his "Dark Tower" column in *Opportunity,* he described the Bal Nègre as "probably the most cosmopolitan and democratic dance hall in Paris, which may mean in the world." The beguine "is a weird sort of playing, a melange or cross between modern jazz and the residue of old West Indian folk pieces."[136] Like Rogers, Cullen comments on the mixed crowd, but instead of hanging out in the balcony with the tourists, he heads to the dance floor where "all the fun is being had." Even though the music reminds him of jazz, Cullen immediately recognizes that this isn't an easy black transnational space to navigate. The dashing young poet finds himself a tongue-tied "alien": "As an American Negro we are somewhat startled to find that our dark complexion avails us nought among these kindredly tinted people. Language must be the open sesame here, and it must be French. The Martiniquan lady whom we have had the temerity to ask to dance with us seems to sense an alien tongue in us, for she glides along amiably enough, but allows our painful attempts at conversation to languish gently" (272).

Cullen's description of the dancing is somewhat patronizing, but he takes the time to note differences even within the Martinican community, singling out one older couple in traditional dress who are "perhaps the remnants of what the Bal Colonial was before the tourists discovered it." He comments:

The dancing for the most part is hard and slightly reprehensible, faintly suggestive of the antics of some of the New York night clubs. In the midst of it all, however, one couple, as if disdaining such modern contortions, glides slowly along in an old Martiniquan step. Perhaps it is not strange that the woman is the only one who has not doffed her homeland costume, a one piece dress with a tightly fastened waist and a long flowing skirt, the whole brilliantly colored. And perched like a blazing star on her head she wears the old homeland turban. Her partner is dressed modern fashion, but there is a derisive curve to his lips and a mocking light in his eyes as he glides along, one hand upon his hip, the other gently supporting his companion. These two are like strong trees in a storm; they do not bend. (272)

The beguine in Paris dance halls often draws out language like Cullen's: claims of authenticity, testimonies to rapid cultural transformation dramatized among the diversity of dancers and parasitic onlookers in a single dance hall, all in addition to the familiar straining to describe this "dance of love" while invoking all the old deep-set desires, all the familiar "exotic accessories," all the echoes of the literary *doudou* suddenly staged among a modern and cosmopolitan crowd. Paulette Nardal's essays on the dances are especially concerned with the implications of this rhetoric. In the 1930 "Musique nègre: antilles et aframérique," she sketches the differences between the "two genres of *nègre* music" then confronting one another in Paris: Antillean music such as the beguine, which she describes as "essentially choreographic," and U.S. black music such as jazz and the spirituals.[137] Here, Nardal is interested in protecting what she sees as the "true beguine" from its metropolitan appropriation; but that desire is expressed less out of a prudish sensibility (and much less out of any disapproval of Antillean folk culture) than out of a critical stance against the commercializing and exoticizing appropriation of yet another element of black popular expression in the quicksand of *les années folles* in Paris.

Nardal is also critical of the ways that appropriation hinges on a depiction of the black Francophone woman, on a pernicious extension of the *doudou* into the metonymic space of the metropole. With such concerns in mind, she wrote an article on the new, second Bal Nègre that opened in 1929 in a large union meeting hall located in the industrial and popular neighborhood of La Glacière. It was mainly a means for the Antillean community to evade the throngs of European spectators who were overwhelming the first Bal Nègre on the rue Blomet. (This was a losing battle: as J. A. Rogers put it, describing the insane thirst for black bodies in motion in Paris in the 1920s, "[t]he American Negro was brought from over 3,000 miles away, and were he taken 'back' to Africa, it is sad to say that an equal number of boats would have to be provided for the white people who would want to go along.")[138] Unlike the first Bal Nègre, violinist Ernest Léardée explains, the Bal Nègre de la Glacière was explicitly "reserved for natives [*originaires*] of Overseas France, and it was necessary to have the blue card of the 'Foyer Colonial' in order to get in. Not once was there ever a brawl, unlike a number of Antillean bals that I had the occasion to frequent later."[139]

Nardal visited the new Bal a few months after publishing her short story "En Exil," and part of what emerges in her impressions is her own nostalgic fondness for Martinican music. But most important, she focuses on the Bal as an attempt to find room for black cultural expression unsusceptible to appropriation in the metropole—a desire for what Georgia Douglas Johnson once called a "clearing space, elbow room in which to think and write and live beyond the reach of the Wolf's fingers."[140] Not surprisingly, Nardal is also one of the only commentators on the Bals to evidence a related desire to establish critical space for the Antillean women dancing there to express themselves without immediately falling prey to the same *doudouisme*, as still more exotic puppets in an eternally revised colonial grammar book. Nardal's description of a woman dancing alone is subtly effective:

> Here is a woman who does not seem to have found a partner "up to her speed" [*de cavalier "à la hauteur"*], for she has launched herself all alone into the dance, arms lifted, hips rolling, in a sort of rhythmic gallop, reminiscent of the progression of the crowd of an Antillean *masque* coming wearily down the streets of Fort-de-France with music in their heads on a Carnival Sunday.[141]

Looking back to Fort-de-France, this passage is clearly a response to "exile," but it is neither backward-looking nor utopian: it evidences a determination above all to recuperate—and if necessary, to invent—such "clearing spaces" of cultural expression and memory for the female Antillean migrant in the metropole.

L'Etudiant noir 1 (March 1935). Centre des Archives d'Outre-Mer, Aix-en-Provence, Archives Nationales, France. SLOTFOM V, Box 21.

I will close by returning to Paulette Nardal's short fiction in tracing this determination to discover spaces of autonomy in the metropole. She contributed a brief *récit* called "Guignol Ouolof" ("Wolof clown") to the single issue of *L'Etudiant noir*, the journal of the Association des Etudiants Martiniquais en France.[142] Published in March 1935, *L'Etudiant noir* is the journal that is generally considered to mark the inception of the Négritude movement, bringing Aimé Césaire and Léopold Senghor together in a unified "black" student movement for the first time. In her groundbreaking book on the Négritude generation, Lilyan Kesteloot devotes ten pages to the importance of *L'Etudiant noir* while admitting that she had never even seen a copy of the journal. She cites an unpublished essay by Léon-Gontran Damas (who, though active in student circles at the time, was not even a contributor), which calls *L'Etudiant noir* a "corporative journal of combat with the objective of ending tribalization, the clannish system in force in the Latin Quarter. One ceased to be an essentially Martinican, Guade-loupean, Guyanese, African, Malagasy student, in order to be only one sole and same black student [*étudiant noir*]. It was the end of life in isolation [*la vie en vase clos*].[143]

As Edward Ako and Martin Steins have more recently shown, the eleva-tion of *L'Etudiant noir* as the periodical of the incipience of Négritude is a misrepresentation of the journal's contents and significance.[144] In reality, Senghor was the only African contributor, and the publication was still very much centered on the Martinican student group. Moreover, as in *La Dépêche africaine,* there is in fact a great deal of ideological divergence among the pieces in this legendary eight-page document rather than any sort of collective claim of a unifying "black" identity. There are a number of straightforward articles in the first section of the journal, which is titled "Questions Corporatives": these include Aristide Maugée's "La question des bourses" (The question of scholarships), André Charpentier's "Puisse-t-on nous entendre! . . ." (Let us be heard!), and André Midas's "A propos de l'Association" (About the Association), that are simply accounts of the concerns of the Association, especially around the issue of government scholarships.

There is an especially sharp contrast between the contributions of Senghor and Césaire in the second section of the journal, "Les idées et les livres." Senghor's essay, "L'humanisme et nous: René Maran" (Humanism and us: René Maran), reads the Francophone precursor's work to construct a notion of "black humanism" *(l'humanisme noir),* defined as "a cultural movement which has as its goal the black man, with Western reason and the black soul [*l'âme nègre*] as the instruments of its research; for both rea-son and intuition are necessary" (4). In defining the term, Senghor writes that he "will not cross the Atlantic today," arguing that "Negro humanism" is evident "right beside us" *(tout près de nous)* in Maran's Francophone met-ropolitan oeuvre. The essay espouses Maran's "objectivity" as the proper perspective in investigations of black culture, a means to unite rationality— a quality of Western civilization imparted in education—with intuition—a quality that allows the "black soul" *(l'âme nègre)* to sense the "âme de la

Brousse, dont l'homme noir est, en quelque sorte, l'émanation" ("soul of
the jungle, of which the Negro is in some sense the emanation") (4). If
Batouala "tries a little too much to strike a blow [*frapper*]," Maran's humanism emerges in later works, including *Djouma, chien de la brousse* (1927)
and especially *Le Livre de la brousse* (1934). For Senghor, Maran's recent
work relies both on *l'âme nègre* (as the Martinican author "follows with interest the slow intellectual ascension of his race, to which he contributes so
effectively" [4]) and on "Western reason" (as Maran continues to find expressive resources in his reading of classical Greek and French literature).

The holistic humanism of Senghor's essay appears tepid in contrast to
the essay that precedes it in the journal, Aimé Césaire's "Nègreries: jeunesse
noire et assimilation" (3). Césaire calls for a sharp and complete break with
Western civilization and with the assimilation espoused by the "elders" *(la
tribu des Vieux)*.[145] The essay hypothesizes three stages or "episodes" in the
maturation of a people: servitude, assimilation, and emancipation. At the
same time, it relies on a gendered rhetoric of emancipation that implies
that servitude and assimilation, both "passive," are both implicitly
gendered: "'Men,' they will call us, for only a man walks without a tutor on
the great paths of thought. Servitude and assimilation resemble one another; they are two forms of passivity." The strident tone of "Nègreries" recalls Langston Hughes's 1926 essay "The Negro Artist and the Racial
Mountain" with its emphasis on self-definition and "Negro youth." Césaire
writes:

> Negro youth [*La Jeunesse Noire*] wants to act and to create. It wants to
> have its poets, its novelists, who will tell it of its own failings, of its
> own greatnesses; it wants to contribute to universal life, to the hu-
> manization of humanity; and for that, once again, it is necessary to
> preserve or to rediscover the primacy of the self [*le primat du soi*].
>
> But to be oneself [*pour être soi*], it is necessary to struggle; first of all
> against those lost brothers who are afraid to be themselves. This is the
> senile mob of the assimilated. (3)

Still, even with this loud critique, Césaire is vague at best in suggesting
where that "primacy of the self" might be located: he does not call for
the end of colonialism, and he never uses the word he would invent four
years later, *négritude*. As we have seen, the single piece that takes an anti-
imperialist and Marxist stance in the journal is by far the longest piece in

L'Etudiant noir, Gilbert Gratiant's essay, "Mulâtres . . . pour le bien et le mal" (5–7). In contrast, Césaire's essay concludes with a somewhat opaque call to "be oneself" not just by rejecting servitude and assimilation but also by "struggling against oneself [*lutter contre soi*]: it is necessary to destroy indifference, to eradicate obscurantism, to cut off sentimentalism at its root" (3).

In the midst of such hue and cry, it is easy to overlook the single piece in the journal that might fall under the heading of literature. Precisely because there is no other fiction or poetry, Paulette Nardal's "Guignol Ouolof" (4) raises a question of genre, as it is a short narrative written in the first person of an Antillean woman in the metropole. Its deliberate tone and its generic wavering toward autobiography is a striking departure from the company of the criticism in the journal (including Césaire's youthful soapbox ire, Senghor's lofty universalism, Gratiant's impassioned creolity, as well as Henry Eboué's "Langage et musique chez les Nègres du Congo" and Léonard Sainville's article on "Littérature antillaise" praising the work of Lafcadio Hearn as a model for French Caribbean literature). Placed back in the wider trajectory of Nardal's writing, "Guignol Ouolof" is another attempt to find the space in which the black woman in the metropole can speak—here, specifically, an attempt to find the space for the practice of black interaction across national, class, and gender difference in the midst of the exploitation and overdetermination of the *vogue nègre.* I reproduce the story in full:

Huit heures du soir. Avant le théâtre, "quick lunch" dans un café du Quartier Latin, qu'illumine le bariolage barbare des tubes de néon.

Tout à coup, entre la lumière et moi s'interpose la silhouette d'un Noir immense. Costume de général d'opérette. Drap noir sur lequel éclatent des brandebourgs imposants, épaulettes, casquette plate d'officier allemand, galonnée d'or et de rouge, et détail encore plus inattendu, monocle à cordonnet noir, encastré dans l'arcade courtilière gauche. Ce détail incongru, dans ce costume absurde n'arrive pas à donner au long visage ouolof, l'effet de grotesque recherché. Pris en lui-même, il me rappelle curieusement certain visage blanc, au sourire grave et à l'air infiniment noble . . .

Mais l'ensemble est indéniablement comique, et quand passe à coté de notre chasseur noir, vendeur de cacahouètes, son collège métropolitain, éphèbe blond à la sobre livrée marron, et qui vend, lui, des cigarettes, le contraste est simplement révoltant.

Révoltant? Du point de vue d'une Noire antillaise trop occidentalisée, peut-être. Mais ce Noir caricatural est là pour la plus grande joie des consommateurs blancs; et quelle magnifique réclame il représente pour l'établissement en question!

Il s'approche de notre table. Il va nous parler. Tous les yeux sont braqués sur nous. Allons-nous contribuer nous aussi, à amuser un moment les Blancs désœuvrés? Ou allons-nous, comme telle mulâtresse antillaise, nous enfuir à la vue de ce Noir grotesque, le coeur plein de ressentiment contre ce congénère sans dignité et son employeur Blanc? Ou encore, prendrons-nous des airs pincés et affecterons-nous de ne pas le voir?

Car enfin, en acceptant de porter cette livrée ridicule, qu'il n'a pas composée, il contribue à ancrer chez les Blancs, le préjugé du Noir amoureux du grotesque, histrion, baladin, non perfectible, toutes choses fort désagréables aux Noirs assimilés qui se prennent au sérieux . . .

Il y a cependant, entre nous et lui, à défaut de solidarité réelle, celle apparente de la couleur.

Et puis, rejetant cette mauvaise gêne, pour ne penser qu'à la fraternité réelle qui nous unit aussi bien à ce Noir qu'à ces Blancs pleins d'illusions, nous répondons gentiment au vendeur de cacahouètes.

Poussée par la curiosité professionnelle, je n'hésite pas à lui poser une question dénuée de tact: "Ne trouve-t-il pas pénible de porter ce costume ridicule, et de faire rire les gens?" La voix éraillée et un peu assourdie, il me répond avec beaucoup de bon sens: "Pas plus qu'un acteur comique au théâtre. J'ai d'ailleurs été acteur. J'aime autant faire ce métier ridicule que d'être chômeur ou de vivre des femmes . . ." Et puis, avec un sourire d'une inimitable finesse: "Les Blancs veulent qu'on les fasse rire; moi, je veux bien . . . au moins, je peux manger . . .".

Eight o'clock in the evening. Before the theater, a "quick lunch" in a Latin Quarter café, illuminated by a barbarous motley of neon lights.

Suddenly, the silhouette of an immense Negro is interposed between me and the light. A general's costume from the operetta. Black cape on which imposing brandenburgs glitter, epaulettes, the flat cap of a German officer, trimmed with braid of gold and red, and an even more unexpected detail, a monocle attached to a black cord, set in courtly arch to the left. This incongruous detail in the absurd costume does not succeed in giving the long Wolof face the desired grotesque effect. Taken by himself, he reminds me curiously of certain white faces, with grave smiles and an infinitely noble air . . .

But the ensemble is undeniably comic, and when next to our black bellhop, the peanut vendor, there passes his metropolitan colleague, a blond ephebe in a sober brown livery, selling cigarettes, the contrast is simply revolting.

Revolting? From the point of view of an overly Westernized Antillean Negro woman, perhaps. But this caricatural Negro is there for the greater pleasure of the white customers; and what a wonderful advertisement he is for the restaurant!

He comes toward our table. He is going to speak. All eyes are fixed on us. Are we too going to contribute to the amusement of these idle whites? Or are we going to flee, like some Antillean mulatress, at the sight of this grotesque Negro, heart full of resentment against this fellow Negro without dignity and his white employer? Or else, will we put on airs, tight-lipped, and pretend not to see him?

For finally, in accepting to wear this ridiculous outfit that he did not arrange himself, he helps to anchor the whites' prejudice against the Negro, grotesque, histrionic, showman, unperfectible, all those things so displeasing to assimilated Negroes who take themselves seriously . . .

Meanwhile, there is between us, in the absence of real solidarity, the apparent solidarity of color.

And then, rejecting this discomfort, thinking only of the real fraternity which unites us as much to this Negro as to these whites, full of their illusions, we reply kindly to the peanut vendor.

Pushed by professional curiosity, I do not hesitate to ask him a question devoid of tact: "Doesn't he find it hard to wear that ridiculous costume, and to make people laugh?" His voice hoarse and slightly lowered, he replies with a great deal of sense: "No more than a comic actor in the theater. Besides, I used to be an actor. I like do-

ing this ridiculous job as much as being unemployed, or living off
women . . ." And then, with a smile of an inimitable finesse: "The
Whites want us to make them laugh; me, I really want . . . at least, I
can eat . . .".

There are a number of finely honed, sometimes surprising turns in the
short tale. We are informed that the narrator is a woman of African descent
(apparently, an "overly Westernized Antillean Negro woman [*Noire*]"), but
only after being given certain other markers: she is relatively privileged, in
that she has the leisure to attend the theater, and educated—perhaps bilingual, since she preciously terms her pre-curtain snack a "quick lunch" in
English. Her reaction to the *Noir* in the "general's costume" is complex and
multilayered. Note that she first sees his "silhouette," his shadow rather
than his face—that is, the way he is framed by the optics and play of illumi-
nation in the café. From the first, she refers to him with the term *Noir* (the
same term she uses to refer to herself) rather than the derogatory *nègre*.
Hers is not at all a knee-jerk reaction of disgust or shame. On the contrary
she notes that the elaborate "absurd costume" in fact "does not succeed in
giving the long Wolof face the desired grotesque effect"; in fact, the African
peanut vendor attains a certain gravity and nobility that reminds her of certain white faces. The narrator is "revolted" instead by the *contrast* between
the vendor and his European ("blond ephebe") colleague, selling cigarettes
in a "sober brown livery." That response is both announced and immediately distanced with a phrase that underlines the ironies of the speaker's
own position in the third person: it is revolting "from the point of view
of an overly Westernized Antillean Negro woman," who is disturbed by
the way the contrast strives to frame or "silhouette" a racialized grotesque
(or "caricature") in the service of commercial spectacle (a "wonderful advertisement").

In anxious hesitation and reflection, the narrator considers what to do as
the African vendor approaches the table. Her consternation in the face of
having to *perform* herself as a gendered Other before a metropolitan audience is palpable—as though she were leafing through that grammar book of
doudous and "evil mulattas," every page a more hideous image of the self
that that audience demands she assume. (Of course, the power of this moment is heightened by the fact that she is on her way to the theater.) She
considers three possibilities. The first would be to participate in the

racialized spectacle ("contribute to the amusement of these idle whites"). Or else, she can "flee like some Antillean mulatress" from the *Noir immense* and the atavistic racial "truth" he represents. Or, as an "overly Westernized" *Noire antillaise,* she can "put on airs" and ignore the African vendor, since his willingness to wear the grotesque costume only serves to "anchor the whites' prejudice." In another sarcastic aside, she pulls away from this last possibility, the reaction of "assimilated Negroes who take themselves seriously."

There is an echo of what Jessie Fauset describes as the self-imposed "restraints" on the "refined colored woman," here, but the narrator is determined to find a way out. What follows is a one-sentence paragraph: "Meanwhile, there is between us, in the absence of real solidarity, the apparent solidarity of color." There is no grounds for "real" solidarity here, no way to forge and naturalize an alliance across the many differences that separate them. She rejects the "discomfort" of the "apparent solidarity of color" because for her it only undergirds the spectacle: the white customers are looking at them to watch the fireworks between differently placed Francophone individuals with dark skins (citizen and subject, *évoluée* and *indigène*). Interestingly, the specific phrase is the seemingly redundant "bad discomfort" *(mauvaise gène),* as though—in a different context, in another *cercle*—the discomfort and irritation of that difference might be "good," might be useful or acceptable or negotiable.

Their short, open-ended conversation finds a bond not exactly on the basis of race or skin color, but instead through what I would term a mutual recognition of *coevalness,* the cohabitation of this particular metropolitan space in all its contradictions. The phrase "real fraternity" is obviously an allusion first of all to the rhetoric of French national identity, the Rights of Man and the putatively abstract citizen-subject. But it is also an allusion to the very circuslike exploitation that has put the two of them on this kind of public stage in the first place: thus, the "real" racist metropolitan culture that "unites" the narrator, the African vendor, and the "whites, full of their illusions." It is a feminist gesture in the sense that it exposes the "symptoms" of the "constitutive contradictions" of imperial "fraternity," the ways it is predicated on certain gendered and racial exclusions.[146]

Then, in an extraordinary nuance, the narrator (speaking, it should be added, in "professional curiosity," although we are not told what profession—a journalist?) asks the African vendor not directly about himself, but

instead about his white colleague: "Doesn't *he* find it hard to wear that ridiculous costume, and to make people laugh? [italics added]." This is a
stunning shift, but there is no other way to read the direct address to the
peanut vendor; she pointedly does not say "you," but asks about the cigarette seller. (The reader's resistance to this grammatical positioning—the reaction that she *must* mean the African vendor with the pronoun "he," that
it *must* be a "slip," that it *must* be a faulty use of quotes indicating direct address—might best be considered a "symptom" of the reader's own implication in this narrative staging of colonial spectacle.) We have already been
informed that the African's costume does not render him "grotesque"; here
she reiterates this point by implying that it is precisely the white vendor's
uniform (his "sober brown livery") that is "ridiculous." The story closes
with the "inimitable finesse" of the African's smile and his awareness of the
ways his situation is overdetermined. He cannot express what he "wants,"
but at least the role does not involve some other exploitation ("living off
women"), at least it allows subsistence ("at least, I can eat . . .").

The work of this small tale is to propel us from the impositions of a "box
of exotic accessories" to the moment when an Antillean female intellectual
can speak to an Senegalese would-be actor attempting to work his way
through hard times. Another indicator of that moment's vulnerability is the
subtlety of its first person plurals. "The whites want us to make them
laugh" *(les Blancs veulent qu'on les fasse rire),* the peanut vendor says; and the
possibility of a shared positionality between these two *Noirs* hangs in the
ambiguity of the French pronoun *"on,"* which can suggest the abstract third
person ("one"), the second person ("you"), the passive, or the first person
plural. So the point of contact—the hint of a "we"—is quiet and vulnerable, "hoarse and slightly lowered," endlessly imperiled in a racist metropolitan context of spectacle. That subtlety is also an insistence that
l'internationalisme noir is not predetermined "solidarity" but a hard-won
project only practiced across difference, only spoken in ephemeral spaces.

CHAPTER 4

VAGABOND INTERNATIONALISM:
CLAUDE MCKAY'S *BANJO*

Aside from Alain Locke's 1925 collection *The New Negro,* the book that had the most profound influence on black intellectuals in Paris between the world wars was Claude McKay's 1929 *Banjo,* written while the great Jamaican writer was living in Marseilles and then finished in Barcelona, Casablanca, and Rabat.[1] Early in 1924, McKay had met Franco-phone figures including the Nardal sisters and Kojo Tovalou Houénou in Paris; that April, he published a fascinating portrait of Tovalou Houénou in the *Crisis.*[2] McKay dropped from view in Francophone circles when he left the capital at the end of the year to live in the south of France. But his work remained influential, especially when a translation of *Banjo* was published in 1931.[3] McKay's poetry was translated in *La Revue du monde noir,* and the following year, *Banjo* itself was excerpted in the explosive single issue of the journal *Légitime Défense,* assembled by the young radical students of the Martinican Surrealist Group, a planned offshoot of the Association des Etudiants Martiniquais en France.[4] The journal openly expressed the hope that, in the words of Etienne Léro, "the wind rising from black America will quickly cleanse our Antilles of the aborted fruits of an obsolete cul-ture." In particular, Léro pointed to the work of "deux poètes noirs révolu-tionnaires," McKay and Langston Hughes, whose writing ("soaked in red alcohol") offered "the African love of life, the African joy of love, the Afri-can dream of death."[5]

Banjo was just as indispensable for the students who would go on to found the Négritude movement a few years later. Aimé Césaire considered *Banjo* "truly one of the first works in which one saw an author speaking of the *nègre* and giving the *nègre* a certain literary dignity."[6] Léon-Gontran Damas, whose well-known 1937 poem "Hoquet" unravels the racist stereo-types around the banjo, would call McKay's book a "fountain of youth." Damas claimed that he, Césaire, and Léopold Sédar Senghor "contributed

Claude McKay in Paris in
the 1920s. Beinecke Rare
Book and Manuscript Li-
brary, Yale University.

to its success, to the measure of our means," passing *Banjo* to their fellow
black students "whose eyes were opening up to reality."[7] In 1937, Senghor
closed his first speech in Africa, at the Foyer France-Sénégal in Dakar, with
a famous quote from the section of McKay's novel printed in *Légitime
Défense:* "Plonger jusqu'aux racines de notre race et bâtir sur notre profond
fond, ce n'est pas retourner à l'état sauvage: c'est la culture même" ("Diving
down to the roots of our race and building on our deep reserves is not returning to a savage state: it is culture itself").[8] Senghor may have quoted
from memory, as his version differs both from the published French translation and from McKay's original: "Getting down to our native roots and
building up from our own people . . . is not savagery. It is culture" (200). In
the 1937 novel *Mirages de Paris,* another Senegalese student of the Négritude generation, Ousmane Socé, placed McKay's *Banjo* on the bookshelf

of one of his characters, a black Francophone intellectual living in the metropole, along with the poetry of Langston Hughes and an eccentric assortment of European-language works: René Maran's *Le Livre de la brousse,* Maurice Delafosse's *Les Nègres,* Albert Londres' *Terre d'ébène,* Durkheim's *Du suicide,* and Hitler's *Mein Kampf.*[9] *Banjo*'s influence even reached black Britain, where Paul Robeson starred in a mediocre 1936 film version called *Big Fella,* which attempts—with ludicrous results—to revise the book into a tale of upstanding racial heroism in which the Banjo character helps the Marseilles police find a boy missing from an ocean liner in the port.[10]

Banjo's portrait of the Vieux Port section of Marseilles, especially *La Fosse* (the Ditch), a popular red-light district just off the harbor of that Mediterranean city, has been widely celebrated as well, especially after the quarter became a center of French resistance activity in World War II and was completely leveled by the Germans in February 1943. *Banjo* is often cited next to other key *reportages* on the "lost quarter" of Marseilles by writers and journalists such as André Suarès, Albert Londres, Pierre MacOrlan, and Walter Benjamin.[11] As McKay biographer Wayne Cooper writes, "Because [*La Fosse*] no longer exists, McKay's description of its congested alleyways, dark habitations, seedy bars, and sinister denizens has become for some French a classic evocation of the quarter as it was between the wars."[12] Indeed, as we shall see, it is possible to read *Banjo* as a *roman à clef* portraying friends and acquaintances from McKay's time living in Marseilles, particularly in the summer of 1926 and the spring of 1928. McKay would later comment that he "may have sinned" in *Banjo* "by being too photographic, too much under the fetid atmosphere of the bottoms of Marseilles," and at least one of the French critics who reviewed the book claimed in extravagant detail to have met the owner of the Café Africain as well as the man who provided the inspiration for the title character.[13]

Banjo is subtitled with a striking phrase: "A Story without a Plot." The book immediately raises a question of literary form, in other words—a question of the relation between its apparent "plotlessness" and its portrait of a transnational community of black drifters and dockers in Marseilles. The loose-knit group includes Lincoln Agrippa Daily, better known as "Banjo," a generous and uninhibited musician from the American South; Ray, the Haitian intellectual and writer (who first appeared in McKay's *Home to Harlem*) who befriends Banjo in the second section of the book; the ill-fated Bugsy, the militant black nationalist and dark-skinned West Indian; Malty, the cocky West Indian guitarist and drummer; Taloufa, the Nigerian guitar man who had worked in Cardiff and who is an ardent Garveyite; Goosey, the "high yellow" American flute player who grew up middle-class in New Jersey, but is at least as much a "race man" as Bugsy (Goosey insists that he will never go back to what he calls the "United Snakes") (117); Dengel, the fun-loving Senegalese, "always in a state of heavenly inebriety" (33); and Latnah, the big-hearted and financially sensible "Oriental"[14] prostitute who is the sole woman to befriend the gang. In three faintly distinguished sections, these characters come into various fleeting configurations: talking, debating the "race problem" around the world, telling tall tales, drinking cheap wine, working for food sporadically as dockers or loaders or errand boys, swimming off the breakwater, playing music now and then, and wandering through the Ditch, from bars and dives (the Café Africain, the Cairo Café, the British-American Bar, the Antilles Restaurant, the Monkey Bar) past the prostitutes on narrow streets such as rue de la Bouterie (which they call "Booty Lane") over to the Place Victor Gélu (or "Bum Square") along the Vieux Port.

Nearly all the contemporary reviews of *Banjo* comment on the subtitle, often in order to claim the book is not a novel at all. Even if its language is "dense and variegated," according to French critic André Levinson (who reviewed the English original in 1929), *Banjo* in the end is "an invertebrate tale [*récit*] with the inconsistency of a mollusk." The book is not a novel, he continues, but "a suite of episodes aligned at random, of detached chapters that one by one crumble away into an anecdotal dust."[15] Likewise, Georges Friedmann, who wrote the preface to the French edition, describes Banjo as a "suite de vagabondages." It is perhaps not coincidental that so many critics turn to musical metaphors in attempting to describe the formal qualities of the work. Gwendolyn Bennett, for example, writing in *Opportunity,* lauds it as "a symphony of vagabondry."[16] The trope has something to do with the slippery nature of the work—critics turning to another expressive medium in an attempt to describe the structure of a "story without a plot," a tale without a scheme in which the qualities of the narrative would seem geared to parallel the wandering of the characters through the bars and along the breakwater of Marseilles. But it also bespeaks a realization that— even if the book does not aim directly to imitate musical form—in *Banjo,* a black transnational community is defined more than anything else by a certain relation to music.

Légitime Défense: Translating *Banjo*

The glowing reception of *Banjo* in metropolitan Francophone circles was cemented by the publication of a section of the novel in the journal *Légitime Défense* in June 1932. The first and only issue of *Légitime Défense* is a telling document of the time not because it led directly to any lasting project—in fact, the planned Martinican Surrealist Group never came into being—but because of the violence of its break with traditions of reformist and assimilationist Caribbean intellectualism. The young students, including Etienne Léro, René Ménil, Jules-Marcel Monnerot, and Pierre Yoyotte, announced a kind of class suicide, railing against the decrepitude of the bourgeoisie in Martinique and the *misère* of Caribbean literature in French and allying themselves explicitly with both international communism and surrealism. As the opening "Declaration" proclaimed:

> We insist on being completely committed. We are certain that there exist other young people besides ourselves who are prepared to sign what we have written and who . . . refuse to become part of the surrounding ignominy. . . . We rise up against all those who are not suffocated by this capitalist, Christian, bourgeois world, to which, denying our bodies, we reluctantly belong. . . . [W]e adhere to Marx's dialectical materialism freed of all tendentious interpretation and victoriously put to the test of events by Lenin. In this respect, we are ready to accept the discipline such convictions demand. In the concrete realm of figurative modes of human expression, we equally unreservedly accept surrealism to which—in 1932—we bind our destiny.[17]

Much of the prestige of this journal, roundly condemned in the conservative press of the Antilles as a pernicious revolutionary influence,[18] was established by the first major study of the roots of Négritude, Lilyan Kesteloot's 1963 *Les Écrivains noirs de langue française,* which many critics now consider to have overemphasized the importance of *Légitime Défense* at the expense of the wide range of black intellectual work in the 1920s and 1930s.[19] In this broader sphere of material (almost all of which was unavailable to Kesteloot), *Légitime Défense* looks much less like a radical break and much more like the loud but rather hasty student journal that it was.

The main accomplishment of the journal was its attempt to propel

Antillean literature away from an insipid and bourgeois acceptance of the stereotypes of colonial literature, by mercilessly assailing the assimilationist "Antillais de couleur" (colored Antillean) who denies "his race, his body, his fundamental and particular passions, his particular way of reacting to love and death, and finally comes to live in an unreal domain determined by the abstract ideas and the ideal of another people."[20] Ménil and Léro castigate Martinican literature, which too often passively accepts French exoticism, *doudouisme,* and Eurocentrism as the only possible models for Antillean writing. This results, they contend, in a debased and sycophantic literature in which

> expression is given neither to strange bursts from afar, nor to mille-narian revolts, nor to fundamental needs, all of which are condemned for the sole reason that they are not encountered in European litera-ture. The feelings of the cane cutter in front of the implacable factory, the lonely feeling of the *noir* throughout the world, the revolt against the injustices he often suffers, especially in his own country, the love of love, the love of alcohol dreams, the love of inspired dances, the love of life and of joy, the refusal of power and the acceptance of life, etc., etc.: here are the things our distinguished writers never speak about, things that would affect black, yellow and white people [*noirs, jaunes et blancs*] just as the poems of the American *nègres* affect the whole world.[21]

Although some have connected *Légitime Défense* to subsequent revolution-ary political work in the Antilles, it is in fact more appropriate to note that the young students tend to undermine their own radicalism by explicitly conceptualizing their audience as the small circle of their peers, rather than even considering the labor organizing of black Communists such as Lamine Senghor and Tiemoko Garan Kouyaté. The students of *Légitime Défense* claim a poor excuse for this abdication, placing the burden of communica-tion on the proletariat rather than assuming it themselves: "For the lack of the Negro proletariat [*à défaut du prolétariat noir*], from which interna-tional capitalism has withheld the means of understanding us, we address ourselves to the children of the Negro bourgeoisie."[22]

Scholars who celebrate *Légitime Défense* as "unprecedented" in its radi-calism tend also to overemphasize the influence of André Breton's surrealist movement on circles of young Francophone intellectuals in Paris. In the presentation of *Légitime Défense* in the promising 1996 collection *Refusal of the Shadow: Surrealism and the Caribbean,* for example, editor Michael Richardson shapes the selections from *Légitime Défense* and Aimé Césaire's journal *Tropiques* (published in Martinique between 1941 and 1945) largely in the aim of reflecting the influence of Breton's surrealism. Tellingly, *Refusal of the Shadow* disregards the excerpt from McKay's *Banjo* published in *Légitime Défense*—without even noting its absence—as well as essays from *Tropiques* such as Aimé Césaire's July 1941 essay on the poetry of the Harlem Renaissance, which offered translations of James Weldon Johnson and Jean Toomer. By all appearances, the collection has been deliberately framed and edited to emphasize surrealist models at the expense of African American influences. Richardson's introduction underlines this polemical construction:

> Surrealism was instrumental in providing the students [of *Légitime Défense*] with a point of departure for their critique of colonial society for, in breaking with the ethics of European culture, it offered them a sort of Trojan Horse in which to enter the previously impregnable white citadel. In surrealism they heard white masters with new voices, voices that renounced that mastery.[23]

The implication that Breton's surrealism is a "white master" (even one that "renounces mastery") at the origin of all radical Caribbean intellectual work is strange enough; the introduction reinforces it with a wrong-minded quote from critic Jacqueline Leiner ("Reinvented by the Other, the Black could no longer deny himself")[24] as though the great and pure accomplishments of surrealism single-handedly broke through the alienation of the group of Caribbean students. The characterization of surrealism as a "Trojan Horse" is just as bizarre—Richardson seems to forget that these are scholarship students, children of the bourgeoisie of Martinique, firmly in the channels of establishment power before they conceive their rebellion. If *Légitime Défense* discovers anything in surrealism, it is a way to break *out* of the prison house of assimilation. Indeed this is the reason the journal was so controversial to the bourgeoisie in Martinique, which did not take lightly the revolt of its scions.

This skewed emphasis ends up flattening out to some degree what is actually a complex field of influence and debate, in which surrealism is only one term, and a hotly contested one at that. In fact, for instance, the debt of Césaire's *Tropiques* (published in the Caribbean during World War II) to *Légitime Défense* (published in Paris between the wars) has long been in question—they are not simply linked by a trajectory of influence originating with Breton's surrealism. In April 1967, Césaire told biographer Georges Ngal that he "found [*Légitime Défense*] to be quite penetrated by assimilationism. These angry young men were surrealists like the French surrealists; communists like young French communists. They weren't *nègre* enough [*Ils n'étaient pas assez nègres*]."[25] For Césaire, *Légitime Défense* "knew how to critique" but not how to "construct." Ménil and Léro castigate earlier generations of Caribbean poets with a standard of "racial" authenticity, but their own poems are equally flaccid and ironically even less "racially" informed.[26] Similarly, though they offer grand pronouncements about surrealism and communism, the students have no idea how to negotiate the tensions between the two movements, and no means to articulate their potential function in the environment of the Caribbean.

The most lucid and unsparing critique of *Légitime Défense* may be René Ménil's own preface to the 1978 reissue. Ménil first distinguishes the work in the journal from the Négritude movement, dispelling any illusion that it was simply a precursor for the postwar efforts of Césaire and Senghor: "Whereas négritude affirms the priority of 'black values' [*valeurs nègres*] with regard to social contradictions—*Légitime Défense,* on the contrary, concerned principally with the anti-imperialist struggle that pits the colonized peoples both against the western bourgeoisies and against their own bourgeoisie, situates political action in the marxist frame of social transformations and only conceives of the development of 'black values' within this political combat." For Ménil, the journal was closer to the perspective of Frantz Fanon *avant la lettre* than Senghorian or even Césairist. At the same time, Ménil writes, "it must be acknowledged that *Légitime Défense,* practicing a kind of naive and spontaneous—thus false—psychology, started (with the best of intentions) to sketch the features [*traits*] of a general *nègre* mentality [*une mentalité nègre en général*], which can be found, amplified and pushed to the extreme, in the incredible caricature of the '*négro-africain*' of which Senghor has made himself the humorless theoretician." Even though these "features" held a largely "polemic" importance in *Légitime Défense*—analyzing the "result of a concrete and transitory historical situation" of colonialism in the Antilles—they were ultimately susceptible to appropriation for the purposes of an "alienating mythology." Ménil concludes by criticizing the poetry in the journal as well: "In *Légitime Défense,* we accepted a disjunction that would be shocking to us later. On the one hand, we took Antillean colonial society into account, and we offered a realist critique and description of it. But on the other hand, we were producing poems that were without roots in that society, poems of nowhere, poems of nobody."[27] With the last phrases *(poèmes de nulle part, poèmes de personne),* Ménil alludes to one of his own contributions to the verses in the journal, the rather indistinct "Nulle part," which runs in part: "L'été tournant autour de son noyau / déplie l'écharpe d'inconscience / Les paroles oscillent leur mâture / Lançons à la tête du ciel / à la dérive / l'étourdissement lappé au bord de midi" ("The summer turning around its core / unfolds the scarf of unconsciousness / Words waver their masts / Let us throw the dizziness lapped up at the edge of midday / to the top of the sky / adrift").[28]

Légitime Défense demands to be read in a complex field of debate among black periodicals of the period, especially in its conjunction with *La Revue du monde noir. Légitime Défense* was founded one month after the demise of the *Revue* by Etienne Léro (who, like Monnerot and Ménil, had contributed to Nardal's journal), and *Légitime Défense* is explicitly designed to combat some of what the young students considered to be the frailties of the predecessor journal. In fact, however, as critic Régis Antoine has pointed out, *Légitime Défense,* its virulent rhetoric notwithstanding, actually takes some steps backward from the achievements of *La Revue du monde noir.*[29] Most significantly, the younger journal relinquishes the ethnographic interest of the *Revue,* replacing the analyses of black cultural forms (by Jean Price-Mars, Louis-Thomas Achille, Andrée Nardal, and Leo Frobenius, among others) with pseudo-surrealist platitudes about "alcohol" and "the African love of life, the African joy of love." It also gives up the breadth of the *Revue's* project, concentrating only on Martinique, but failing even to offer an articulate call for a Martinican nationalism in the place of the *Revue's* ambitious pan-Africanism. In this light, it is difficult to argue either that *Légitime Défense* marks the single definitive break in the genesis of the Négritude movement or that it initiates the period of revolutionary communist activity in Martinique itself. The latter is more properly rooted in Jules Monnerot's "Jean Jaurès" group, which published the journal *Justice* beginning in 1920, as well as the "Front commun" alliance of young intellectuals linked to the Popular Front in 1933–34, and individual radicals including André Aliker and Stéphane Rosso, who worked throughout the 1920s with Parisian black radical groups such as Lamine Senghor's Ligue de Défense de la Race Nègre.[30]

Let us look in more detail at the section from McKay's *Banjo* included in *Légitime Défense,* in the journal's most significant gesture toward diasporic concerns. The passage reproduced in *Légitime Défense* comes from the beginning of chapter 16, "The 'Blue Cinema,'" where the main character, Ray, encounters a Martinican student:

> Ray had met a Negro student from Martinique, to whom the greatest glory of the island was that the Empress Josephine was born there. That event placed Martinique above all the other islands of the Antilles in importance.
>
> "I don't see anything in that for *you* to be so proud about," said Ray. "She was not colored."
>
> "Oh no, but she was a Créole, and in Martinique we are rather Créole than Negro. We are proud of the Empress in Martinique. Down there the best people are very distinguished and speak a pure French, not anything like this vulgar Marseilles French." (199)

Ray spends the next two pages putting the *aliéné* Martinican student in his place, telling him: "You're a lost crowd, you educated Negroes, and you will only find yourself in the roots of your own people" (201). In *Légitime Défense,* then, the excerpt seems to serve a clear didactic purpose, preaching respect for black folk culture, praising the beauty of "native African dialects," and advocating a nationalism modeled on "the Irish cultural and social movement," as well as Gandhi and the Indian anticolonial struggle. According to Ray, Negroes are "merely beginners" in the "modern race of life." Cultural achievement and "racial advancement" *must* involve a racial consciousness that does not simply reproduce the class hierarchies and prejudices of the "white race." "If this renaissance we're talking about is going to be more than a sporadic and scabby thing," Ray contends, "we'll have to get down to our racial roots to create it" (200).

Banjo was translated by Ida Treat and Paul Vaillant-Couturier, the Communist legislator from Paris who also served as an editor at the French Communist Party newspaper, *L'Humanité,* and held close ties to the Communist-affiliated black pressure groups in Paris in the 1920s including the Union Intercoloniale and the Ligue de Défense de la Race Nègre. As critic

Martin Steins has pointed out, their French version of *Banjo* plays a direct role in a subtle but crucial misapprehension of the "Harlem Renaissance" in *Légitime Défense.* I have retranslated some of the passages back into English for the discussion that follows. It might seem redundant at first glance to retranslate a French translation of a passage originally in English. But the selection provides a number of nuances that prove crucial to any understanding of the politics of *Légitime Défense.* The journal places the passage from chapter 16 of *Banjo* under the title "L'étudiant antillais vu par un noir américain" (The Antillean student seen by an American Negro) in a manner to elide the specifics of that Americanness: McKay, of course, is Jamaican, and his character Ray is—as is often forgotten—Haitian.[31] In *Légitime Défense,* the passage is framed as the "étudiant antillais" in the metropole learning blackness Socratically from the U.S. Negro, from an exemplary text of the Harlem Renaissance, in a narrative of vanguardism and "influence" that is too often taken for granted. But when one considers this encounter as an *intra-Caribbean* dialogue in the metropole, as a dialogue between an exiled Haitian writer and an assimilated Martinican bourgeois snob, the contestatory exchange takes on quite different contours. Take the central passage of Ray's speech:

> We educated Negroes are talking a lot about a racial renaissance. And I wonder how we're going to get it. On one side we're up against the world's arrogance—a mighty cold hard white stone thing. On the other the great sweating army—our race. It's the common people, you know, who furnish the bone and sinew and salt of any race or nation. (200)

The last two sentences are translated into French as:

> De l'autre, l'immense armée des travailleurs: notre race. C'est le prolétariat qui fournit, savez-vous, l'os, le muscle et le sel de toute race ou de toute nation. (Fr 257)

> On the other the great army of workers: our race. It's the proletariat, you know, who furnish the bone, muscle and salt of any race or nation.

Steins enumerates a number of examples of this kind of dogma-adding (mis)translation as contributing directly to the abortive project of the black

Martinican surrealist group, which in *Légitime Défense* never comes close to espousing the racial consciousness associated with later forms of Negritude and which—buttressed in part by this passage—positions itself rhetorically in terms of a "black proletariat" that it does not know how to grasp conceptually, much less approach organizationally.[32]

I depart from Steins, though, when he sets up an easy opposition between the communist-inflected surrealism of the *Légitime Défense* group and the "ethnic renaissance of the race" that he reads in McKay's work.[33] For Steins, McKay's "ambition" in *Banjo* is to bring about neither a class revolution nor a racial nationalism, but instead "to promote in each of the different black populations of the world the consciousness that they formed peoples, ethnicities."[34] It seems to me on the contrary that what one might term the "vagabond internationalism" elaborated in *Banjo,* with its dizzying portrayal of the great idiosyncratic variety of ideological and group commitment among shifting black male communities in Marseilles, is shaped by an extreme skepticism about any such "promotion" of consciousness.

Vagabond Internationalism

The book is marked by radical "doubt," to use McKay's word, that blacks can "fit" into the logics of modern civilization. For Ray:

> . . . with the growth of international feelings and ideas he had dreamed of the association of his race with the social movements of the masses of civilization milling through the civilized machine.
>
> But traveling away from America and visiting many countries, observing and appreciating the differences of human groups, making contact with earthy blacks of tropical Africa, where the great body of his race existed, had stirred in him the fine intellectual prerogative of doubt. (324)

Such "international feelings and ideas" are at least twofold. On the one hand, Ray's race does not fit into the "international idea" of capitalist development. The vagabond "boys" in *Banjo,* part of what McKay would later describe in his autobiography as a transnational flotsam community of "beachcombers, guides, procurers, prostitutes of both sexes and bistro bandits—all of motley-making Marseilles, swarming, scrambling and scraping sustenance from the bodies of ships and crews,"[35] work when they have to, play music when they can, generally roam and range the teeming port.

Banjo is a "barbarous international romance" (69) of men without a country, aliens drifting along the edge of the Mediterranean "as if all the derelicts of all the seas had drifted up here to sprawl out the days in the sun" (18). While the encounters and episodes are freely stitched together around the seam of Banjo, Ray, and their "black gang" of friends and hangers-on, the novel presents a broader swathe of modern existence, even a global community of the dispossessed: "white men, brown men, black men. Finns, Poles, Italians, Slavs, Maltese, Indians, Negroids, African Negroes, West Indian Negroes—deportees from America for violation of the United States immigration laws—afraid and ashamed to go back to their own lands, all dumped down in the great Provençal port, bumming a day's work, a meal, a drink, existing from hand to mouth, anyhow any way, between box car, tramp ship, bistro, and bordel" (6). Marseilles is attractive because it is loose, because the city doesn't tie the refugees and drifters down: it is a "fine big wide-open hole" (68), giving out into the "gorgeous bowl of blue water unrestingly agitated by the great commerce of all the continents" (66).

In contrast to what historian Winston James rightly describes as McKay's "Bolshevist" period in the early 1920s, when McKay wrote (during his trip to Moscow) that the duty of the Negro Communist was to "spread revolutionary ideas among the ignorant masses of his own race,"[36] *Banjo* would appear to mark a shift in McKay's political focus away from the proletariat, traditionally conceived, and toward such cosmopolitan, fleeting communities of men. The book's fascination with Marseilles's transient denizens points less to an interest in the expansion and unionizing of the port city's industrial maritime base than to the margins of that development. Though some of them serve on ships to get to Marseilles, the black boys of *Banjo* are not even the short-term ship workers, the stokers and mess help, who are at the bottom rung of the labor pool. Every now and then, they find day work as dockers or loaders. But this is hardly steady employment. Albert Londres, describing the men on the edges of the Place de la Joliette (near the Marseilles seaport) in his classic description of the city written in the same period, argues that being a docker is not even a true profession *(métier)*. "What is a docker?" he asks.

They'll tell you: It's a man who loads and unloads the ships in ports. . . . Obviously, a docker is a man who lugs bundles around the docks. But what kind of man becomes a docker? One learns to be a mechanic, a coppersmith, or a mason. One becomes a docker. Being a miner, a blacksmith, a carpenter is a profession. Docker isn't one. Being a docker, one isn't a worker. If circumstances demanded it, I would require time to be a watchmaker, a roofer or a glazier. I'd be a docker the next morning at seven o'clock. One meets workers among dockers; they are precisely workers without work. A docker is a man who works hard for the sole reason that he has nothing to do. . . . But one has to eat.[37]

Banjo, Ray, Bugsy, and Taloufa are men who would rather beg for food from sympathetic black crews on Mediterranean coal freighters than work under the racist capitalism that is the only available mode of labor relations.

The book earned the wrath of a number of critics precisely because of the space it gave to black "laziness" and "bumming." In the *Chicago Defender,* Dewey Jones titled his review with one word: "Dirt."[38] He reads *Banjo* as a catalog of vices, proclaiming that one might be "enthusiastic" about it only "if you like filth, obscenity, vagabondage, pimpery, prostitution, panhandlery, and more filth." Part of the problem is that the book veers toward autobiography and documentary: McKay (whom Jones describes as "poet and vagabond") has obviously "done some independent studying of the subject he chooses to discuss." Still, no one can "rave over the photography of a dung heap." Jones considers *Banjo,* even more than McKay's first novel *Home to Harlem,* a direct assault on the upward mobility and bourgeois respectability (the "air of decency," as he puts it) preached by organs such as the *Defender* and is particularly appalled by the characters' disdain for labor: the book features "a group of tramp sailors who prefer loafing and bumming to working and earning an honest dime." It is a critique that *Banjo* itself anticipates. One "Negro steward" on a ship yells at them when they ask him for food: "I wouldn't even give you all a bone to chew on. Instead a gwine along back to work, you lay down on the beach a bumming mens who am trying to make a raspactable living. You think if you-all lay down sweet and lazy in you' skin while we others am wrastling with salt water, wese gwine to fatten you moh in you' laziness?" (28). In the French press, André Levinson sneered more sarcastically that even though the author of *Banjo* did not manifest much "indulgence" toward France, his "*lazzaroni noirs,* the scum of two continents" were living quite a "benign poverty" *(misère bénigne)* that would only be possible there, in the "land of plenty" *(pays de cocagne)*.[39]

With the Italian word *lazzaroni,* this critique alludes to a familiar European catalog of epithets for those outside the labor pool. Indeed, it is difficult not to hear, in McKay's extended enumerations of this "bawdy" population at Europe's "best back door" (69), an echo of Karl Marx's own catalogs in his dismissive descriptions of the *lumpenproletariat*—the marginal, the drifters, eking out an existence, sometimes parasitically, on the edges of modern industrialized society. The most often-cited definition of the *lumpenproletariat* appears in *The Eighteenth Brumaire,* in a passage where Marx is lambasting Louis Bonaparte's strategy of marshalling influence through a political group he formed in Paris in 1849, called the Society of 10 December:

> Alongside decayed roués of doubtful origin and uncertain means of subsistence, alongside ruined and adventurous scions of the bourgeoisie, there were vagabonds, discharged soldiers, discharged criminals, escaped galley slaves, swindlers, confidence tricksters, *lazzaroni,* pickpockets, slight-of-hand experts, gamblers, *maquereaux,* brothel-keepers, porters, pen-pushers, organ-grinders, rag-and-bone merchants, knife-grinders, tinkers, and beggars: in short, the whole indeterminate mass, tossed backwards and forwards, which the French call *la bohème.*[40]

Marx excoriates this self-professed "charitable organization" as being charitable only in the way that "all its members, like Bonaparte, felt the need to provide themselves with charity at the expense of the nation's workers." Marx's unforgiving characterization of those who do not fit, or who reject, the logic of the class struggle as defined in the mid-nineteenth century— what he terms "the scum, the leavings, the refuse of all classes"—has always represented a problem area in Marxist theory, for the few intellectuals who have not chosen simply to toss *lumpen* around as a broad term of sectarian denigration.

The recent work of historians such as Peter Linebaugh and Marcus Rediker has in part attempted to rethink and to problematize this wholecloth, albeit vivid, classification, through explorations of the role of what Linebaugh calls "proletarian internationalism"[41] in the period of expansion of British mercantile capital. As Linebaugh writes: "just as the accumulation of international capital depends on the exploitation of Atlantic labour, so 'pauses' or 'arrests' in the process of accumulation are the results of the many-sided oppositions of living labour brewing within and among the modes of production" (92). Linebaugh's aim is to sketch the rich "anti-nomian tradition" represented in the mobile and vulnerable communities of "sturdy rogues and beggars," sailors, itinerant workers, and vagrant wanderers throughout ports in the greater Atlantic Ocean. Marx's critique of political economy, he argues, functions only within the limits of that tradition and thus is bound by the conventional "ideological fetters of political economy that chain the understanding of living labour to the wall of capitalist development." He continues,

> thus, the pauper or "surplus population" is understood either as the passive recipient of alms . . . or as compromising, to quote C. H. George, the "swollen streams of human misery." In the sixteenth century, however, there is a powerful history of proletarian self-activity that cannot be understood within the limits of these largely passive notions. (96)

Linebaugh emphasizes the juridical construction of a malleable labor force in the sixteenth and seventeenth centuries, through criminalization codes and press gangs throughout the port cities of the Atlantic and Mediterranean (100).

In *Banjo,* there is a twentieth-century version of this argument, with regard to the "the scum, the leavings, the refuse" of European colonialism and global commerce: port city communities of color, likewise characterized by their "mobility, their freedom, and their footlooseness" (95), and equally resistant to the passive frame that political economy would have them fit. Early circum-Atlantic abstention from the expansion of the industrial age does not disappear in the modern age, in other words: the "pauses" or "arrests" in the process of accumulation are closely woven into the fabric of colonial development. It is not as though capitalist accumulation develops and then is infected "later" by race and gender: on the contrary, accumulation proceeds only through the institutions of capitalism and slavery.[42] So it will not be surprising to discover in the high colonialism of the early twentieth century new mixes of that same rhythm, new "brews" of those same "many-sided oppositions of living labour" in teeming cosmopolitan ports such as Marseilles. In this regard, it is crucial to recall that the word "vaga-

bond" first appears in *Banjo* not in a proclamation of irresponsibility or bohemian excess, but as a term imposed by the authorities in an attempt to
deport the black drifter with the "long-term record of existence on the
beach." Ginger, McKay writes, "had lost his seaman's papers. He had been
in prison for vagabondage and served with a writ of expulsion. But he had
destroyed the writ and swiped the papers of another seaman" (5).

A number of scholars considering black structural underemployment
in the twentieth century have extended a rehabilitation of the *lumpen* to
note the ways resistance to racist wage labor conditions can occasion quite
creative modes of expression, an entire range of what Robin D. G. Kelley
calls "dissident political culture."[43] One particularly apropos example is the
concluding chapter of *Policing the Crisis,* the brilliant 1978 study of the
black "settler colony" in Britain written collectively by Stuart Hall, Chas
Critcher, Tony Jefferson, John Clarke, and Brian Roberts. There, in a thorough reconsideration of the applicability of the term *lumpenproletariat* to
the question of black joblessness in the 1970s, the authors contend that a
range of activities that fall under the popular term "hustling" should be
conceived not at all as the taint of black pathology and behavioral back-
wardness, but instead as "modes of survival," and even as the potential
ground of black consciousness and community resistance.[44] One might see
the sketch of black music making and "vagabondage" in *Banjo* in the same
light—not simply as evidence of cultural transmission and "survival," but
moreover as the sign of such a culture of opposition. So when, in seedy bars
around the quarter such as the Café Africain and the Cairo Café, the "black
boys" sing lyrics such as "Dry land will nevah be my land,/ Gimme a wet
wide-open land for mine" (48), it is expressive in exactly this rebellious,
"vagabond" spirit.

The black vagabonds in *Banjo* cannot be understood simply as an emergent proletariat, however. Certainly they float among "proletarians from far
waters" (67) in the Ditch, and initially Ray's ambition is to find a "haven"
where he can "exist *en pension* proletarian of a sort and try to create around
him the necessary solitude" to write (66). But there are significant tensions
between the black drifters and the regularly employed sailors who descend
on the port—tensions that sometimes erupt in racial violence. Indeed, the
organized proletariat, especially the white ethnic unions, view the black
groups drifting along the docks with condescension: at best as a "swollen
stream of human misery" to be registered in the ranks of the class struggle,

and at worst as parasites feeding off life in the Vieux Port, worthless and lazy "bums" to be violently stamped out of existence. The novel recounts an incident when a gang of white laborers come *en masse* into the quarter, indiscriminately beating and kicking any "Senegalese" they see (71–72). Aware of this charged imbrication of class and race, Ray espouses "proletarian politics" as a strategic stance, but one that in no way softens the bitterness of his distaste for traditional union organizing. He tells Crosby, a "sentimental radical," white American poet whom he befriends briefly, that

> I hate the proletarian spawn of civilization. They are ugly, stupid, unthinking, degraded, full of vicious prejudices, which any demagogue can play upon to turn them into a hell-raising mob at any time. As a black man I have always been up against them, and I became a revolutionist because I have not only suffered with them, but have been victimized by them—like my race. . . .
>
> I've never confused faith with politics. I should like to see the indecent horde get its chance at the privileged things of life, so that decency might find some place among them. (270–271)

Ray's politics are the hard politics of a vagabond in the face of the "ideological fetters" on all sides, which forcibly strive to define his gang's "vagabond existence" only as a surplus labor population needing to be either pressed into service or absolved into organized labor.

In *Banjo,* ultimately the "vagabond existence" does not fit—it lives its own logic and will not be passive in the face of such forces. Ray regards it neither as a lifestyle choice nor as a passing fancy, but as the most crucial tool of survival in the modern world: "He had associated too closely with the beach boys not to realize that their loose, instinctive way of living was more deeply related to his own self-preservation than all the principles, or social-morality lessons with which he had been inculcated by the wiseacres of the civilized machine" (319). Vagabonding is not the irresponsible evasion of a proletarian normalcy, but a necessary recourse for those like Banjo, Ray, and Taloufa who do not possess the "instinct of civilization," as Ray puts it (289). They reject what they consider to be the hypocrisy and cynicism of modernity; even college-educated Ray, with his supposed "social advantages" and "better breeding," ultimately cannot bring himself to "scramble out of the proletarian world into that solid respectable life, whence he could look down on the Ditch and all such places with the mean, evil, and cynical eyes of a respectable person" (288). It is in this sense that the black boys, like the sixteenth- and seventeenth-century rogues and vagabonds described by Linebaugh, represent what *Banjo* terms a "challenge of civilization":

> When the police inspector said to Ray that the strong arm of the law was against Negroes because they were all criminals, he really did not mean just that. For he knew that the big and terror-striking criminals were not Negroes. What he unconsciously meant was that the police were strong-armed against the happy irresponsibility of the Negro in the face of civilization.
>
> For civilization had gone out among these native, earthy people, had despoiled them of their primitive soil, had uprooted, enchained, transported, and transformed them to labor under its laws, and yet lacked the spirit to tolerate them within its walls. . . .
>
> Thus [the Negro] became a challenge to the clubbers of helpless vagabonds—to the despised, underpaid protectors of property and its high personages. He was a challenge of civilization itself. (313–314)

In rejecting the principle of wage labor, they challenge the very logic of civilization itself and, moreover, expose its underbelly, its elusive escape hatch—precisely by proving with "happy irresponsibility" that civilization can be defied.

What should be noted is that this stance represents a shift in Ray. In McKay's earlier novel, *Home to Harlem,* Ray adopts the position of an exile, with the pronounced sense of deprivation and uprooting that characterizes the state of forced departure from one's home country. He is bitterly critical of the U.S. occupation of Haiti and remembers his pride "to be the son of a free nation." This sentiment is closely related to Ray's sense of injustice at his life in Harlem: whereas he used to feel sorry for U.S. blacks, these "ten millions of suppressed Yankee 'coons,'" suddenly "he was just one of them and he hated them for being one of them." In New York, Ray ultimately consoles himself not with some new-found sentiment of black internationalism, but with the nationalist certainty that "he was not entirely one of them. . . . He possessed another language and literature that they know not of. And some day Uncle Sam might let go of his island and he would escape from the clutches of that magnificent monster of civilization and retire behind the natural defenses of his island, where the steam-roller of progress could not reach him."[45]

Though we find a similar critique of civilization in *Banjo*, Ray's sense of nationalist privilege has vanished: now, in Marseilles, "the vagabond lover of life finds individuals and things to love in many places and not in any one nation." Indeed, nationalism has been linked, for Ray, to the perniciousness of modern civilization: "Man loves places and no one place, for the earth, like a beautiful wanton, puts on a new dress to fascinate him wherever he may go. A patriot loves not his nation, but the spiritual meannesses of life of which he has created a frontier wall to hide the beauty of other horizons" (136). This sense of footlooseness and mobility (gendered, as is characteristic in McKay's writing: the earth dresses "like a beautiful wanton" to fascinate "him"), this extreme antinationalism, gives Ray a purpose that is in many ways reminiscent of McKay's own adoption of the term "vagabond" in his 1937 autobiography, *A Long Way from Home*. There, McKay writes:

> I became a vagabond—but a vagabond with a purpose. I was determined to find expression in writing. . . . I looked for the work that was easy to my hand while my head was thinking hard: porter, fireman, waiter, bar-boy, houseman. I waded through the muck and the scum with one objective dominating my mind. I took my menial tasks like a student who is working his way through a university. My leisure was divided between the experiment of daily living and the experiment of essays in writing.[46]

The recurrent use of the word "vagabond" in *Banjo* must be understood in this light: not as what Ray dismisses as "mere unexciting drifting, a purposeless, live-for-the-moment, negative" mode of existence in some of the inhabitants of the Ditch (138), but instead the vibrant resistance of the black boys to the forces that would contain them, to the civilization that Ray knows would "take the love of color, joy, beauty, vitality, and nobility out of *his* life and make him like one of the poor mass of its pale creatures" (164).

Ray, who is regularly reading newspapers—including the *New York Herald Tribune* and the mainstream French *Le Journal* (264, 274), the Communist Party weekly *L'Humanité* (269), the London *Daily Mail* (136), and even rabidly imperialist, "obscene" French papers such as *L'Action française*

(273–274)—and ruminating over the social position of his little gang of friends, is particularly attuned to the ways both French state authorities and broader transnational commercial forces relentlessly control and reshape the lives of men of color in the Vieux Port. Some of the other characters such as Goosey and Banjo recognize change—they notice that it is more difficult to find black ship crews who will feed them, that the police and colonial authorities are becoming "more brutal and strict" (23)—without quite understanding the historical significance of this development. At times the narrative steps back and offers such a perspective, noting at one point that the black boys

> did not know that the Radical government had fallen, that a National-Union government had come into power, and that the franc had been arrested in its spectacular fall and was being stabilized. They knew very little about governments, and cared less. But they knew that suddenly francs were getting scarce in their world, meals were dearer in the eating-sheds and bistros. . . . (222–223)

Toward the end of *Banjo,* the drifters, dockers, and seamen are discussing a shift in British colonial policy that repatriates all undocumented migrants, giving them fresh papers stamped with an official phrase, "Nationality Doubtful" (312). When his Nigerian friend Taloufa is denied entry to England, Ray considers this new restriction of mobility:

> West Africans, East Indians, South Africans, West Indians, Arabs, and Indians—they were all mixed up together. . . . This was the way of civilization with the colored man, especially the black. The happenings of the past few weeks from the beating up of the beach boys by the police to the story of Taloufa's experiences, were, to Ray, all of a piece. A clear and eloquent exhibition of the universal attitude, which, though the method varied, was little different anywhere. (312–313)

Ray sees a consistency to the "way of civilization" as evidenced in the state's treatment of colored men, the "universal" refusal of their civil rights. Just as a gratuitous and "merciless beating" one afternoon at the hands of the Marseilles police demonstrates a capricious state control of their bodies (261–262), papers stamped with the phrase "Nationality Doubtful" by a state immigration office denies any claim to national identity and citizenship.

Both are means of herding the black drifters, giving them "no place to go" (313) at the margins of the transnational wage labor system and in a limbo of undocumented, officially "doubtful" status.

In a chapter called "Everybody Doing It," the lyrics of an old popular American song, an insipid invitation to "Turkey Trot" ("Everybody's doing it, / Everybody's doing it"), ridiculously but stubbornly stick in Ray's head like a refrain to this realization. The phrase alludes to the universal scheming on the quayside: the denizens "peddling" or "plugging" to get by, all "massed pell-mell together in a great gorgeous bowl" (141). But it also describes the ubiquity of oppression. As Ray tells one Englishman in a café at the corner of the rue de la République and the Quai du Port, it is always "we, the poor, the vagabonds, the bums of life" who pay heaviest "for banditry in high places" (142). We are told later that "as a Negro," Ray is particularly sensitive to the fact that "many of the titled and ennobled and fashionable and snobbish gentry of this age have the roots of their fortunes in the selling of black bodies" (288). The most complex point in *Banjo* may be this suggestive double entendre ("Everybody's Doing It") that points both to sexuality and desire and to bodily exploitation in the modern capitalist system. "Selling black bodies" here has to do with gender and sexuality, not just race. This is suggested both in particular encounters—love affairs gone wrong, disputes over money—and in the broader claims of the narrative: "Commerce! Of all words the most magical. The timbre, color, form, the strength and grandeur of it. Triumphant over all human and natural obstacles, sublime yet forever going hand in hand with the bitch, Bawdy. In all relationships, between nations, between individuals, between little peoples and big peoples, progressive and primitive, the two lovers spread and flourish together as if one were the inevitable complement of the other" (307). At the same time, this point is given additional nuance by the gender politics of the nearly all-male community portrayed in the novel,[47] where casual talk refers to ships in the port as "broads," and Marseilles itself as a "bum hussy" (168). One thinks in particular of Ray's hypothesis that "society is feminine," as he tells Goosey:

> Property controls sex. . . . When you understand that, Goosey, you'll
> understand the meaning of the struggle between class and class, nation and nation, race and race. You'll understand that society chases
> after power just as a woman chases after property, because society is

feminine. And you'll see that the white races today are ahead of the colored because their women are emancipated, and that there is greater material advancement among those white nations whose women have the most freedom. (205–206)

This proposition is a peculiar mix of feminism (a call for the emancipation of women) and the claim that if "woman chases after property," that pursuit has an essentially "feminine" quality that can be extended by analogy into social analysis. For Ray, "woman is woman all over the world," and that identity is defined by two characteristics: "she is cast in a passive rôle and she worships the active success of man and rewards it with her body" (206). In other words, a cogent feminist critique is combined with a problematic insistence about the "nature" of woman.

With regard to Latnah, the one significant female character in *Banjo,* there is something like this uneven approach. Among the black boys, there is on the one hand an understanding of her position as a prostitute: "Whatever personal art she might use as a woman to increase her chances was her own affair" (32). At the same time, there are disturbing elements to the portrait of Latnah in the book, especially after she becomes Banjo's lover, as in one scene when she thinks that Banjo has abandoned her for a white woman and is left "seething with that deep-rooted sexual resentment that the women of the colored and white races nourish against one another—a resentment perhaps even more profound among the women than among the men of the species, because it is passive, having no outlet for brutal expression" (169). And when *Banjo* ends with the title character and Ray leaving Marseilles together to "go vagabonding," Ray mentions that it would have been nice to take Latnah along, but Banjo tells him he should never "get soft ovah any one wimmins." Indeed, the book concludes with his dismissal: "Tha's you' big weakness. A woman is a conjunction. Gawd fixed her different from us in moh ways than one. And theah's things we can git away with all the time and she just kain't. Come on, pardner. Wese got enough between us to beat it a long ways from here" (326).

Diaspora and the "Passable Word"

The second part of *Banjo*'s critique of the logic of internationalism is more complicated and more surprising, given the reception of the novel. Just after the passage quoted in *Légitime Défense,* in which Ray would appear to preach racial consciousness and self-sufficiency, the vehemence of the argument with the Martinican student is drastically pulled back: "It was no superior condescension, no feeling of race solidarity or Back-to-Africa demonstration—no patriotic effort whatsoever—that made Ray love the environment of the common black drifters. He loved it with the poetical enthusiasm of the vagabond black that he himself was" (202). What is somewhat unexpected about *Banjo* is that the depiction of the community of "black boys" along the Marseilles docks evidences a resistance to the modern idea of black internationalism as well. Thus the novel concludes with the group scattering and Ray professing reluctance to make easy gestures of racial consciousness as he leaves the city. In the end, *Banjo,* the most emphatically transnational black novel of the interwar period, is paradoxically also a radical critique of black internationalism.

Time and time again, the book emphasizes the pronounced diversity of the community of black boys and elaborates their heated arguments about the "race question." In a 1929 letter to his agent William Aspenwall Bradley, McKay writes similarly about the beach boys' conceptions of France: "Goosey loves France and wants to stay. Banjo is not in the least disturbed about loving or hating any country. The Senegalese opts for America. Ray is cynical about it all. He is intelligent enough to know that all human beings suffer and enjoy life in varying degrees in every country under the sun, although he is not unaware that the colored man has especial handicaps to meet with under the world-wide domination of occidental civilization."[48] This critique is furthermore worked out on the grounds of translation, the slippery babel of tongues and dialects clashing in color on the waterfront. W. E. B. Du Bois's review of *Banjo* called it "on the one hand, the description of a series of episodes on the docks of Marseilles, and on the other hand a sort of international philosophy of the Negro race."[49] But finally the episodes *are* the philosophy, and it is not an internationalism of coordinated social movement, but an internationalism of debate, miscommunication, and light-hearted and hot-headed accusation—the Dozens writ large, with Ananse, Frère Lapin, and the Signifying Monkey soused and clamoring for the soapbox.

Encounters begin and end over disputes. Recall that Ray first meets Banjo by offering to translate in an argument over prices with a bistro owner who has overcharged him. As the angry discussion of the *prix fixe* menu outdoes the black American musician's slim mastery of the native language,

> Banjo's tongue turned loose a rich assortment of Yankee swear words. . . . "God-damned frog robbers. I eat *prix fixe.* I pay moh'n enough. *Moi paye rien plus.* Hey! Ain't anybody in this tripe-stinking dump can help a man with this dawggone lingo?"
>
> A black young man who had been sitting quietly in the back went over to Banjo and asked what he could help about.
>
> "Can you get a meaning, boh, out of this musical racket?" Banjo asked.
>
> "I guess I can." (63)

Ray's success at interceding and negotiating with the woman cements his friendship with Banjo, who proclaims: "Le's blow this heah two francs to good friendship beginning. . . . My twinkling stars, but this Marcelles is a most wonderful place for meeting-up" (64).

As Michel Fabre has noted, the French language is positioned in *Banjo* as "a barrier, or an open sesame. Language and culture appear as important as color or nationality in creating cleavages in group consciousness."[50] This point is only emphasized all the more when one reads the novel in English next to the 1931 French translation read by Senghor and Césaire. What I have termed a basic grammar of blackness is often fully dislodged, lost in translation, as it becomes impossible to trace the putative links between "Negro," "black," "darky," "man of color," on the one hand, and "noir," "nègre," "bon nèg," "homme de couleur," on the other. Take this exchange:

> "Did he say *niggers?*" cried Goosey.
>
> "I should say not. He said 'colored people.'"
>
> "Well, I wish you would all learn to say 'colored' and 'Negroes' and drop 'darky' and 'niggers,'" said Goosey. "If we don't respect ourselves as a race we can't expect white people to respect us." (128)

> "Il disait *nègre?*" s'écria l'Oison.
>
> —Jamais d'la vie! Il disait 'peuple de couleur.'

—Ben moi, je voudrais que vous disiez 'de couleur' ou encore 'noir'
et que vous laissiez tomber 'nègre' et 'négro'. (Fr 177)

Here "nègre" is used at first to translate "nigger" and then to translate
"darky" (another term, "négro"—even more derogatory, but less common
—is also used for "nigger"). At another point, when Goosey again takes of-
fense at Ray's use of derogatory terms, the French version uses still another
word, "bon nèg," to translate "niggah," and the word "raton" (rat) to translate Ray's dismissal of Goosey as a "coon—a stage thing, a made-up thing
. . . half baked, half educated, full of false ideas about Negroes" (183).
"Raton" is perhaps the best choice, but in French it is an epithet more commonly directed at North Africans, and the translators put it in quotes to indicate they are stretching its application: "toi tu es bien un 'raton,'" Ray
says, "quelque chose d'artificiel, de théâtral" (Fr 239).

But this isn't solely a point about the French translation: what is evident
in *Banjo* is the degree to which characters such as Ray and Goosey do not
share an understanding of the basic terms of racial identification in English
alone. Thus their arguments over the ideological accentuation of "Negro"
or "nigger" turn caustic precisely because they are arguments about the contours of racial politics in a transnational sphere. More than any other interwar work, *Banjo* relentlessly underlines the inescapable, nearly mundane,
gaps in comprehension: the impossibility of translating a racial consciousness through some foolproof or stable system. We are left with the vertigo
of intradiasporic communication, the small and crucial work of carrying
words over, one by one, often only to have them thrown back or miscon-
strued.

Banjo makes this point most emphatically in a startling passage that utterly loses its texture in French translation. At one point, Ray is mulling
over the common myth that France offers a civilized "paradise" for colored
people, annoyed, for he knows so intimately the persistence of colonial
prejudice in the country. Ray "looked deeper than the noise for the truth,
and what he really found was a fundamental contempt for black people
quite as pronounced as in the Anglo-Saxon lands." Indeed, the French difference, if there is one, could hardly be called a heavenly bounty: "There
was, if anything, an unveiled condescension in it that was gall to a Negro
who wanted to live his life free of the demoralizing effect of being pitied

and patronized." The question for Ray is the proper response in the face of such hypocrisy:

> Here, like anywhere . . . one black villain made all black villains as one black tout made all black touts, one black nigger made all black niggers, and one black failure made all black failures. . . .
>
> Supposing he were to react to French or any other civilization solely from the *faits divers* columns of the newspapers. For one crazy month of the past summer he had read of nothing but crazy crimes . . . all the sordid *crimes d'amour et de la passion* that were really *crimes d'argent.* (275–276)

Ray is particularly amused by one newspaper article recounting a "terrible crime" committed by an African soldier. The unnamed journalist, apparently writing in one of the conservative pro-imperialist French papers, extrapolates from the singular horror to hale the entire black race "before the bar of public opinion." What is startling for the English-language reader is that *Banjo* goes on to quote the entire editorial (nearly a page and a half in the original edition) in French, with no translation or summary:

> Un tirailleur sénégalais, pris d'on ne sait quel vertigo, a fait, à Toulon, un affreux carnage.
>
> On s'évertue maintenant à savoir par quelle suite de circonstances ce noir a pu fracturer un coffre et s'emparer des cartouches avec lesquelles il a accompli le massacre.
>
> Qu'on le sache, soit. Mais la question me semble ailleurs. Il faudrait peut-être se mettre la main sur le cœur et se demander s'il est bien prudent d'apprendre à des primitifs à se servir d'un fusil.
>
> Je n'ignore pas qu'il y a de belles exceptions; qu'il y a des "nègres" députés, avocats, professeurs et que l'un d'eux a même obtenu le prix Goncourt. Mais la majorité de ces "indigènes" à peau noire sont de grands enfants auxquels les subtilités de notre morale échappent autant que les subtilités de notre langue. La plus dangereuse de ces subtilités est celle-ci:
>
> Tu tueras des êtres humains en certaines circonstances que nous appelons guerre.
>
> Mais tu seras châtié si tu tues en dehors de ces circonstances.

Le Sénégalais Yssima appartient à une catégorie humaine où il est
d'usage, paraît-il, quand on doit mourir de ne pas mourir seul. Le
point d'honneur consiste à en "expédier" le plus possible avant d'être
soi-même expédié.

Si cela est vrai, on voit oú [*sic*] peuvent conduire certaines blagues
de chambrées. Pour tout dire franchement, il n'est pas prudent de
faire des soldats avec des hommes dont l'âme contient encore des
replis inexplorés et pour qui notre civilisation est un vin trop fort.
Sous les bananiers originels, Yssima était sans doute un brave noir, en
parfaite harmonie avec la morale de sa race et les lois de la nature.
Transplanté, déraciné, il est devenue un fou sanguinaire.

Je ne veux tirer de cet horrible fait divers aucune conclusion. Je
dis que de semblables aventures (qui ne sont d'ailleurs pas isolées)
devraient nous faire réfléchir sérieusement. . . . (278)[51]

An African soldier, seized by who knows what kind of vertigo, has
caused a terrible carnage in Toulon.

The authorities are doing their utmost to find out by what se-
quence of events this *noir* was able to break into a chest and seize the
ammunition with which he enacted the massacre.

If they find an answer, so be it. But it seems to me that the question
lies elsewhere. It might be necessary to put one's hand on one's heart
and ask oneself if it is really prudent to teach primitives how to use a
gun.

I am not unaware that there are some fine exceptions; that there are
"nègre" legislators, lawyers, professors, and that one of them even won
the Prix Goncourt. But the majority of these black-skinned "natives"
are big children, for whom the subtleties of our ethics are as evasive as
the subtleties of our language. The most dangerous of these subtleties
is the following:

You will kill human beings in certain circumstances that we call
war.

But you will be punished if you kill outside of these circumstances.

The Senegalese Yssima belongs to a human category for whom it is
a custom, apparently, not to die alone, when one has to die. The
point of honor consists in "sending off" as many others as possible
before being killed oneself.

If this is true, one sees how far certain barrack-room jokes can lead. To put it frankly, it is not prudent to make soldiers out of men whose souls still contain unexplored corners, and for whom our civilization is too strong a wine. Originally, under his banana trees, Yssima was doubtlessly a good black man, in perfect harmony with the ethics of his race and the laws of nature. Transplanted, deracinated, he has become a bloodthirsty madman.

I do not want to draw any conclusion from this horrible news item. I say that such adventures (which moreover are by no means isolated) should make us reflect seriously. . . . [my translation]

The silliness Ray reads in this patronizingly magnanimous exercise (its measured call to "reflect" on whether it is a good idea to conscript Africans, "for whom our civilization is too strong a wine") is obvious—if one can read it. The abrupt page and a half in French can appear only as a confrontation to the English-speaking reader who stops short, challenged to find a way to continue, but unable to navigate a thicket of unfamiliar words. Indeed, for a bilingual reader the joke of the passage becomes the editorial's lament that ethics don't carry over from one linguistic context to another: the claim that for the *indigènes*, "the subtleties of our ethics are as evasive as the subtleties of our language."

The passage thus functions as *Banjo*'s stark performance of linguistic difference. Not just for the black vagabonds themselves, but for some readers too, French is "barrier and open sesame": moving through the narrative, the reader is forced to negotiate a disjuncture between a strongly worded introduction and its inaccessible example. The article is framed with the aside that Ray had saved it as an "amusing revelation of civilized logic" particularly because "he was in tacit agreement with the thesis while loathing the manner of its presentation" (277). If one cannot follow the French, this sentence is bewildering: what would Ray find to agree with in an article that extrapolates a *fait divers* into a racist generalization? The answer would seem to reside in the editorial's claim that the norms of Western civilization are incomprehensible to the transplanted African. Presumably Ray would accentuate the argument somewhat differently, though: in other words, what the editorial calls "subtlety" ("You will kill human beings in certain circumstances that we call war. But you will be punished if you kill outside of these circumstances") Ray would term perversion and illogic. As the nar-

rative explains, the newspaper in question supports the colonial regime under which Africans during World War I had been "torn out of their native
soil, wrenched away from their families and shipped to Europe to get acquainted with the arts of war and the disease of syphilis" (276–277). The
argument takes on a different resonance if it is "presented" with such a critique of "civilized logic." Still, the primary lesson of the passage for the majority of English readers must be the jarring inaccessibility of its French.
And it is precisely this effect (a linguistic disjuncture in the reading process
itself) that cannot be reproduced in the French translation of *Banjo,* where
the quoted passage does not stand out at all. In this sense, the subtleties do
not carry over.

In the modern transnational context depicted in *Banjo,* if terms such as
nègre and *noir*—each hotly contested and "multi-accentuated" in French—
can be understood only in their diachronic relation of tension and divergence, then equally contested uses of the term *Negro* must be read as a
name for the synchronic failure of that tension to carry over into English.
With the limited lens of translation in the strict sense (translation between
languages), *Banjo* suggests that this is the only way to read a diaspora. This
state of affairs should not be understood to be solely negative, an impassable wall, however: *Banjo* also makes it clear that the walls are continually
vaulted—those incommensurabilities, the gaps, the points of *décalage,* are
the reservoir of communication across which diaspora is practiced. So the
constant arguments in the novel do not come across as frustrating dead
ends, but instead as precisely the most vibrant and creative moments. It is
in an awareness of this creativity in a hostile linguistic context and across
difference—this recognition that the workable translation, the "passable"
word, is *always* discovered—that Ray admires

> the black boys' unconscious artistic capacity for eliminating the rot-
> ten-dead stock words of the proletariat and replacing them with star-
> tling new ones. There were no dots or dashes in their conversations—
> nothing that could not be frankly said and therefore decently—no act
> or fact of life for which they could not find a simple passable word.
> He gained from them finer nuances of the necromancy of language
> and the wisdom that any word may be right and magical in its proper
> setting. (321)

We are still left with the consequences of that "crossing over," of course—exemplified most starkly in the ideological mutation from McKay's "common people" to the French *Banjo*'s "le prolétariat," misrecognitions that appear unavoidable in any effort to translate among diasporic settings.

We are still confronted with difference, in other words. With those inextricable gaps and discrepancies, stitched up provisionally in the "necromantic" fabric of communication. In the passage from *Banjo* reprinted in *Légitime Défense,* on the one hand, the French translation of "common people" as "le prolétariat" is simply incorrect, an imposition of an explicit Marxist vocabulary onto a text that in English is nothing if not reluctant to assent to such institutional forms of radicalism. But on the other hand, the translation raises the necessary question of just how one might translate in this period a phrase such as "common people" (or "folk"), which resonates in English with U.S. populist discourse and the history of African American lives in the rural South, to a French metropolitan context molded by a very different set of forces, including labor migrancy and imperial notions of a "backward" native populace in the overseas colonies. Even if the translation fails, then, it remains true to *Banjo*'s overall aim of indicating the ways that black internationalism is necessarily haunted by difference.

The Boys in the Band

If part of the work of *Banjo* is to imagine the "passing word," the means of translation, it should be apparent that more often than not the successful connections in the book hinge on black expressive production. This includes oral culture in the famous chapter 10, "Story-Telling," where Ray, "trying to get some of the Senegalese to tell stories like the Brer Rabbit kind or the African animal fables of the West Indies" (114), is only successful when he himself tells a folk tale from his own home—then, "nearly all the Senegalese wanted to tell a native story" (121). But *Banjo* finds its links especially in music. Most of the men in the group play one kind of instrument or another, and on a number of occasions they get together to jam in one of the many cafés and bars around the squalid Vieux Port.

They play a varied repertoire that includes both lesser-known or made-up lyrics ("Stay, Carolina, Stay"; "Everybody's Doing It"; "Hallelujah Jig") and a number of popular hits from the 1920s such as "Shake That Thing," which was recorded by Ethel Waters, among others, in 1925 (49, 280);

"Yes, Sir, That's My Baby" (7, 14); "Then I'll Be Happy," a mid-decade hit for the Fletcher Henderson orchestra (35); and Jelly Roll Morton's 1915 composition "Jelly Roll Blues" (46). At one point, Malty sings a bit of "West Indies Blues" (81), a lyric written by J. Edgar Dowell, Spencer Williams, and Clarence Williams that is of interest not only because it was one of the top-selling "race records" of 1924 (with versions by at least eleven groups) but also because it is one of the socially conscious popular songs of the period. The refrain expresses a Jamaican's desire to return to the Caribbean: "Gwine home, won't be long / Gwine home, sure's you born, / I'm gwine home, won't be long / 'Cause I've got no time to lose. / . . . I'm gwine home, I can't wait / 'Cause I've got the West Indies Blues." And one verse mentions Marcus Garvey by name: "I'm gonna be a great big 'Mon' / Like my frien' Marcus Garvey."[52] Malty doesn't sing the lyrics to "West Indies Blues" in *Banjo;* still, the allusion would be clear to any reader familiar with black musical culture in the 1920s.

It is only at these brief dance-driven encounters that the language of *Banjo* turns exalted and inclusive. At the Martinican-owned Antilles Restaurant, one night, the group unites spontaneously to play through an unlikely mix of black musical forms, squeezed into unity by the force of the prose:

> They played the "beguin," which was just a Martinique variant of the "jelly-roll" or the Jamaican "burru" or the Senegalese "bombé." . . . It was an eye-filling ensemble of delicious jazzing, and the rhythm of it went tickling through the warm blood of Taloufa, who was still smacking his lips over his sausage-and-rice, tempered with a bottle of old Bordeaux.
>
> "Beguin," "jelly-roll," "burru," "bombé," no matter what the name may be, Negroes are never so beautiful and magical as when they do that gorgeous sublimation of the primitive African sex feeling. In its thousand varied patterns, depending so much on individual rhythm, so little on formal movement, this dance is the key to the African rhythm of life. (105)

Such ecstatic writing about the unifying qualities (and common roots) of the variety of black music in Marseilles—from the United States, the Caribbean, and Africa itself—is almost entirely unique in descriptions of the "lost quarter" of the city. Much more common are the words of André

Suarès, in his well-known 1933 *Marsiho,* describing black music as an ab-
horrent savage soundtrack overwhelming the thin streets. Suarès, writing
about rue de la Bouterie, complains that "infernal black music [*musique
noire*] sets the rhythm for all sounds. Without a doubt, this racket is the
voice of hell. Is there a *nègre* orchestra hidden on every floor? The phono-
graphs are *nègres* too, omnipresent and invisible. . . . The whole quarter is
no more than a monstrous saucepan being beaten in measure by a thousand
pairs of feet."[53]

Banjo is above all else a book about a boy who wants to start a band.
"Banjo dreamed constantly," we are told early on, "of forming an orchestra,
and the boys listened incredulously when he talked about it. He had many
ideas of beginning" (19). Often under the influence of wine stolen along
the docks, Banjo waxes rhapsodic about this dream at every opportunity,
in spite of the boys' skepticism and his own lack of organizational and
conductorial skills. "It would need an orchestry to fix them right," he
thinks. "The American darky is the performing fool of the world today.
He's demanded everywhere. If I c'n only git some a these heah panhandling
fellahs together, we'll show them some real nigger music. Then I'd be setting pretty in this heah sweet dump without worrying ovah mah wants"
(14). Ever the proper nationalist, Goosey tells him in no uncertain terms
that the banjo is an inappropriate instrument for "race music": "Banjo
is bondage. It's the instrument of slavery. Banjo is Dixie" (90). But for
Banjo it is "preëminently the musical instrument of the American Negro"
and his "loud music of life—an affirmation of his hardy existence in the
midst of the biggest, the most tumultuous civilization of modern life" (49).
Banjo tells Goosey that he doesn't want to play minstrel music, but instead
wants to play what he calls "the money stuff today" in the craze for black
U.S. performance sweeping France: "that saxophone-jazzing" and "them
blues" (91).

The dream expressed in the word "orchestra" is of course bigger than
simply playing music: more than anything, Banjo wants to find in the
music a model of the social, a way to institutionalize the black boys' easy
good-time interaction. This word, and the sporadic, ephemeral attempts to
achieve it, are the closest the book comes to espousing any form of black internationalism, any means for a relatively permanent structure that would
articulate a black transnational community into a singular albeit shifting
expression of the "African rhythm of life." Although there is no suggestion

that musical performance would evade the economic exploitation around them, this dream of a black band is the only exit offered in *Banjo,* imaginary or otherwise, into some form of stability that the men can accept in the "capitalist machine." Banjo seems to have no trouble seeing himself bound in a stereotype, as the "the performing fool of the world today." In a broader sense, an orchestra expresses a dream to formalize in musical performance the "spirit of solidarity" (158) among the black drifters, their ways of supporting each other with food, drink, shelter, and commiseration. Music seems for Banjo equally to provide an *aesthetic* model of the "vagabond existence." In one early scene, he tells Bugsy: "When I turn mahsalf loose for a big wild joyful jazz a life, you can bet you' sweet life I ain't gwine neveh regretting it" (24). Here "jazz" comes to describe a vision of life, "loose" and joyous and without regret. So if the dream to form an orchestra is the dream to institutionalize a vision of black internationalism, it is inherently an open and wandering, performative representation of the links between men of African descent, a vision of "vagabond internationalism."

And yet Banjo can't even remember to pass a hat to collect money from bar customers after they play, much less produce some kind of regular date for a performance or organize rehearsals (40). In fact, it is Latnah, with "all her instincts of acquisitiveness and envious rivalry" (25), who insists that he should be making money for his performances:

> [W]hen he played in any of the bistros of the quarter and she was there, she always took up a collection. . . . That was the way the white itinerants did it, she said. *They* never played for fun as Banjo was prone to do. They played in a hard, unsmiling, funereal way and only for sous. Which was doubtless why their playing in general was so execrable. When Banjo turned himself loose and wild playing, he never remembered sous. (40)

The implication of this arrangement is that there is something in Banjo's approach to music that makes the vision of an orchestra a mirage or a delusion. It seems that a vagabond approach to the music ("loose and wild") never remembers to collect—and indeed, this obliviousness to wage and profit seems to be not just absentmindedness but actually inherent in the aesthetic. This is a contradiction that neither Banjo nor Latnah can resolve with any permanence.

The nearest that Banjo, "quite unconscious of it," comes to the "aesthetic realization of his orchestra" (97) is just another of these informal jam sessions at a no-name café that the boys simply refer to as "Banjo's hang out":

> Taloufa had taught them a rollicking West African song, whose music was altogether more insinuating than that of "Shake That Thing."
>
> > "Stay, Carolina, stay,
> > Oh, stay, Carolina, stay!"
>
> That was the refrain, and all the verses were a repetition, with very slight variations, of the first verse. Taloufa had a voluptuous voice, richly colored like the sound of water lapping against a bank. And he chanted as he strummed the guitar:
>
> > "Stay, Carolina, stay. . . ."
>
> The whole song—the words of it, the lilt, the pattern, the color of it—seemed to be built up from that one word, Stay! (95–96)

It is as though, in this recurring chorus, in the tune of the Nigerian coast calling out to the American Carolinas like a distant lover with an endless complaint, black music itself is the figure that would keep the band together, the forlorn voice that would have them "stay." On the one hand there is a gendered representation of desire, which is also an exilic desire for a home that is ever-receding, ever-elusive, always slightly beyond the reach and capacities of the speaker: "I took her on a swim and she swim more than me, / Stay, Carolina, stay" (96). But the song "built up from that one word, Stay!" might also be heard as an expression of desire for the music itself, a desire to continue and even to perpetuate the state of collaboration and communion it orchestrates.

For Ray, the music becomes a sign both of the ways community is performed and of a particularly "African rhythm of life." It is almost exclusively in these passages that one encounters what is usually the only feature emphasized in readings of *Banjo*—that is, its supposed evocation of the "primitivism" of black culture. "Close association with the Jakes [the protagonist of *Home to Harlem* who shows up briefly in *Banjo* (292)] and Banjoes," Ray thinks, "had been like participating in a common primitive birthright" (321). It is as near as Ray comes to expressing a racial consciousness. Given the linguistic vertigo that the novel foregrounds, it is not insignificant that Ray's sentiment is rooted especially in hearing African languages:

> Ray was not of the humble tribe of humanity. But he always felt humble when he heard the Senegalese and other West African tribes speaking their own languages with native warmth and feeling.
>
> The Africans gave him a positive feeling of wholesome contact with racial roots. They made him feel that he was not an unfortunate accident of birth, but that he belonged definitely to a race weighed, tested, and poised in the universal scheme. (320)

It is crucial to notice that Ray's "feeling" of "wholesome contact with racial roots" is based in a "humbling" experience of difference. "Belonging," here, is predicated on privation, on Ray hearing languages he can't speak or understand. Not surprisingly, he feels no such confidence about African-derived populations in the Americas, "who, long-deracinated, were still rootless among phantoms and pale shadows and enfeebled by self-effacement before condescending patronage, social negativism, and miscegenation" (320). In such passages there is both the "primitivism" that many critics expect from McKay and a more critical pragmatism that the boys "buttress" Ray with a "rough strength and sureness that gave him spiritual passion and pride to be his human self in an inhumanly alien world." In fact, for Ray the drifters have "more potential power for racial salvation than the Negro *literati*, whose poverty of mind and purpose showed never any signs of enrichment, even though inflated above the common level and given an appearance of superiority" (322). Still, it is this kind of language in the novel that has attracted an apparently endless critical litany about McKay's portraits of "primitive Negroes, untouched by the decay of Occidental civilization," and the "lower-class Negro's stubborn resistance to assimilation."[54]

It is risky, however, to accept blindly a discourse of "primitivism" without noting the ways that McKay's book twists it and wrenches it out of shape. The word "primitive" is always used with a certain sarcasm, as an imposed vocabulary. It is seldom noticed, for instance, that in *Banjo* the discourse cuts both ways: McKay invokes the "jungles of civilization" (194) as much as the "African rhythm of life." And "black primitivism" is not all about instinct and intuition, but is sometimes positioned as the basis of the most rational—albeit unruly—social critique. When Crosby wants Ray to lodge a formal complaint about police brutality and demand "justice," Ray thinks to himself that he doesn't believe in that word, "that prostitute lady who is courted and caressed by every civilized tout" (265). He tells Crosby that "for me there is no such animal as a civilized nation" (274). In his musing over the *fait divers* columns in the daily papers, it becomes clear that "primitive" is most of all a method of reading the pretensions and hypocrisies of "civilization." A "primitive sense of comparative values" is precisely what keeps Ray from jumping to conclusions, from condemning Western modernity with overarching and prejudiced generalizations. Ray considers the innumerable articles about violence and crime he reads every day in the papers:

> It could have been easy for him, a black spectator of the drama, to seize upon and gloat over these things as evidences of the true nature of this civilization if he had allowed them to warp and rob him of his primitive sense of comparative values and his instinct to see through superficial appearances to the strange and profound variations of human life. (275–276)

This is much less the atavistic primitivism, the primitivism that hinges around some "racial" essence, that we have been taught to consider the dominant theme of *Home to Harlem* and *Banjo,* and much more a position that understands "primitive" as the basis of another ethical system, one *exterior* to the crushing logic of "civilization"—as the foundation for a fine-tuned insistence that "the most precious thing about human life is difference" (208).

It may not be helpful to think about primitivism in *Banjo* simply in *opposition* to civilization, in other words. Indeed, the word "primitive" in *Banjo* is trying to do something very different, to open a very different kind of space from what we might expect in the context of black modernist debates about culture as propaganda, and "high class" or "low class" literary themes. It is possible to suggest, in fact, that in thinking through the complex specificity of this usage, it might be more instructive to read *Banjo* next to some of the other works opening up similar issues in the same period, rather than next to works such as Carl Van Vechten's *Nigger Heaven* and Paul Morand's *Magie noire.* Elsewhere I have suggested that *Banjo* and the later work of black surrealists such as Aimé Césaire might be not unrelated to the work of Georges Bataille and the journal *Documents* in 1929 and

1930.[55] *Documents,* like the work of McKay and Césaire, was a journal geared to rethinking the term "primitive" at the very moment when European exoticism reigned supreme, when the 1931 Exposition Coloniale was just around the corner. Bataille, rather like McKay, considers black expression less as atavistic or savage, and more as the "excretion" or waste produced by the Western "civilizing machine" during the process of assimilation to the standard of capitalist accumulation. This is to suggest an unfamiliar "back door," to unearth one of the unsuspected links that traverse and reconfigure the seemingly neat cartography of Western modernism.

Banjo attempts to locate what eludes or exceeds the logic of capitalist civilization. It is for this purpose, as much as any mystification of African roots, that *Banjo* falls into passages suggesting for instance that "a black man, even though educated, was in closer biological kinship to the swell of primitive earth life. And maybe his apparent failing under the organization of the modern world was the real strength that preserved him from becoming the thing that was the common white creature of it" (323). If this language flirts with "racial" essentialism, it also announces a fascination with the flotsam and jetsam of life, the goings-on at the margins, the pungent and busy "wide-open dumps" of whatever any system must reject and extrude in order to function. Ray often expresses a characteristically modern admiration for waste in the world, in precisely the spirit of what Bataille a few years later would term *heterology:* "There was something sublime about waste. It was the grand gesture that made life awesome and wonderful. There was a magical intelligence in it that stirred his poetic mind. Perhaps more waste would diminish stupidity, which was to him the most intolerable thing about human existence" (260).

In *Banjo,* then, black culture ends up being portrayed not in juxtaposition to modern civilization, but as resistive expression that evades the "civilizing machine." That elusiveness in turn must be denigrated by the civilizing system with words such as "primitive," as the system attempts to preserve its own integrity through what Bataille calls "the excretion of unassimilable elements."[56] It is thus not surprising that those denigrated, those violently pushed out, such as the beach boys and Ditch-dwellers in *Banjo,* would claim such terms as their own, as the clearest proof of that resistance and resiliency. Toward the end of the novel, this relationship between black culture, the "composite voice of the Negro," and the "civilizing machine" is expressed with a memorable metaphor:

> Looking down in a bull ring, you are fascinated by the gay rag. You may even forget the man watching the bull go after the elusive color that makes him mad. The rag seems more than the man. If the bull wins it, he horns it, tramples it, sniffs it, paws it—baffled.
>
> As the rag is to the bull, so is the composite voice of the Negro—speech, song, and laughter—to a bawdy world. More exasperating, indeed, than a Negro's being himself is his primitive color in a world where everything is being reduced to a familiar formula, this remains strange and elusive. (314)

The "rag" is not the man who holds it, obviously: so-called primitive black culture is not the sign of some essential black identity. But it is the colorful expression of resistance and evasion in the face of an onslaught of trampling force. The use of "elusive" here is reminiscent of James Weldon Johnson's use of the term in his prefaces to the *Book of American Negro Spirituals*.[57] The passage evokes an autonomous system, a "composite voice," at the fringes of modernity: irrepressible, goading, infuriating the civilization that would crush it—and yet elusive, somehow of a different order, of a different logic, one that civilization wants desperately to reject and obliterate as a social possibility.

Black Radicalism and the Politics of Form

I would like to return to the questions of form and genre raised by this "story without a plot." Does *Banjo*'s ambition to portray a cosmopolite group of black vagabonds, arguing about internationalism on the docks, have something to do with what McKay himself described as its documentary, even "photographic" characteristics? *Banjo* is first of all the depiction of a group of men McKay knew while he was living in Marseilles, working on a collection of short stories and then on *Home to Harlem*. In McKay's papers conserved at the Beinecke Library at Yale University, there is even a somewhat mysterious photo that may be a snapshot of the group that inspired the black boys in the book: ten men, smiling, gathered outdoors around a French café table. There is no banjo, but one is casually cradling a guitar. Affixed to the bottom of the photo is a faint handwritten card with a

A group of men in Marseilles (c. 1927). Claude McKay Papers, Beinecke Rare Book and Manuscript Library, Yale University.

phrase in *petit nègre* ("Y'a bon," with a connotation something like the U.S. Southern "Sho' nuff good"), as though to headline the complex good times McKay enjoyed in the city with that phrase, associated with advertisements featuring popular stereotypes of the "smiling African."[58] Aside from *Banjo* itself, this unannotated, unidentified photo may be the only documentation of a group that assembled and dissipated around the port while McKay was there in the summer of 1926. When he returned the next spring, the men were mostly gone. He wrote to William Aspenwall Bradley that "their number was diminished by about one-half. Two had died in hospital and three others, after being very ill in hospital were sent home by the American Consul. The guitar and banjo players were hired by some kind of traveling show, but a few remain rather sad, dirty and scantily-clothed, but hanging on the beach all the same and having no desire to leave it."[59]

Banjo is also a historical record that touches on some of the most important black intellectuals and activists in the metropole during the period. In
the conversations and debates, René Maran's *Batouala* is mentioned (199),
and one character even recounts the story of Kojo Tovalou Houénou being
thrown out of a Montmartre bar in 1923 at the insistence of a racist American tourist (194). But Lamine Senghor and Pierre M'Baye are featured
more prominently. Although their original encounter may have been earlier, Lamine Senghor probably met McKay in Marseilles during the spring
of 1927, when Senghor was making regular trips to the south in an effort to
organize black dock workers, who were largely ignored by traditional Communist and Socialist unions. Senghor's main contact in Marseilles was Pierre M'Baye, the Senegalese bar owner who had lived in the United States
and made enough money to buy a café along the Vieux Port waterfront.
Called the Comptoir Marseillais, the café (located at number 42 on the
Quai du Port) was the center of radical activity in the port, and M'Baye
would later serve an official role as secretary of the regional (Bouches-du-
Rhône) section of the Ligue de Défense de la Race Nègre.[60] M'Baye not
only distributed copies of journals such as the Ligue's *La Race nègre* to black
sailors traveling around the world, but also fostered links between West African sailors and their Vietnamese and North African counterparts—gar-
nering a significant amount of surveillance from the colonial authorities in
Marseilles in the process.[61] In the subsequent years, M'Baye took out an advertisement in *La Race nègre* that highlights the Comptoir's crossroads cre-
dentials ("English Spoken, Se Habla Español"); in fact, the main text is
written in an English that wouldn't have been out of place in the *Amsterdam News:* "IF YOU WANT A GOOD TIME / COME AND TRY OUR PLACE / DANC-
ING SALOON OPEN ALL / NIGHT."[62]

Banjo's Café Africain is patterned after M'Baye's bar. McKay's description of M'Baye in *A Long Way from Home* is worth quoting here. "One Senegalese had a big café on the quay," he writes,

> and all the Negroes ganged there with their friends and girls. The
> Senegalese was a remarkable type, quiet, level-headed, shrewd. He
> had served in France during the World War and had been a sergeant.
> He went to the United States as soon as he could after the armistice.
> He got a job such as the average Negro works at and at the same time

he ran a rooming house for Africans and Negroid Moslems in New York. He amassed a tidy sum of money, returned to France after six years, and bought the bar in the Vieux Port. His family in Goree was old, large and important.[63]

In one extended scene in *Banjo,* the unnamed *patron,* described as "small and eager," wearing glasses and a "melancholy aspect," tells a Senegalese seaman that racism exists in France and that it is "no better than America. In fact, America is better every time for a colored man." He goes on to lavish praise on U.S. "industry, business, houses, theaters, popular music, and progress and opportunity for everybody—even Negroes" and says that "the Negroes knew how they stood among the Americans, but the French were hypocrites" (73). He brings out an issue of *La Race nègre,* which is "displayed conspicuously for sale in the café, although some colored visitors had told the proprietor they did not think it was good for his business to sell it there" (74). When the Senegalese sailor continues to insist that he's wrong, the bar owner starts reading a list of complaints about the abuses of the French colonial system in *La Race nègre,* to the "murmurs of approval" of a growing crowd, until "the protesting seaman appeared crushed under the printed accounts" (75–77). When the owner extends his anticolonial declamation into praise for Marcus Garvey's Back-to-Africa movement, Banjo himself butts in, exclaiming that Garvey was "nothing but a fool, big-mouf nigger" (77). He "had a white man's chance" to succeed and to help other blacks, but "he done nigger it away" (76). The owner replies that U.S. Negroes have wasted the "biggest chance that black people ever had in the world" because most of them are "just trifling and no-'count like you," and Banjo storms out of the Café Africain. He asks Ray why he didn't say anything, and Ray replies, "I always prefer to listen. . . . You know when he was reading that paper it was just as if I was hearing about Texas and Georgia in French" (77). It is his only comment about the scene: beneath the bluster and grandstanding, Ray hears a kind of translation, a consonance to racist oppression that extends from the U.S. South to the French colonies.

Lamine Senghor, the original editor of *La Race nègre,* is also discussed in McKay's autobiography. One day McKay is introduced by M'Baye to "one of his countrymen named Senghor. This Senghor was also a war veteran and a Negro leader among the Communists. He was a tall, lean intelligent Senegalese and his ideas were a mixture of African nationalism and international Communism."[64] McKay records a "strange scene" between M'Baye and Senghor about the latter's white French wife: the café owner tells his friend that as a race leader, he should not be married to a white woman, and Senghor responds that he considers that "as Communism was international, it was an international gesture for him to be married to a white woman, especially since white chauvinists objected to intermarriage."[65] (The two men abruptly stop discussing the question when M'Baye's lover, also a white French woman, comes into the bar.) Senghor takes McKay to the Communist International Seaman's Building in Marseilles and instructs him about the special difficulties faced by black dock workers and stokers.[66]

Lamine Senghor is mentioned by name in *Banjo* as well, although only briefly and elliptically. It is clear that Ray knows him, but no details are provided. When the black boys are discussing intermarriage, Ray says that he cannot understand an "intelligent race-conscious" black man marrying a white woman: "Take Senghor and his comrades in propaganda for example. They are the bitterest and most humorless of propagandists and they are all married to white women. It is as if the experience has oversoured them. As if they thought it would bring them close to the white race, only to realize too late that it couldn't" (207). Later, when he is arguing with Crosby about police brutality in Marseilles, Ray says that the French "imagine that the Negroes like them. But Senghor, the Senegalese, told me that the French were the most calculatingly cruel of all the Europeans in Africa" (267). But intriguingly, Lamine Senghor is portrayed in *A Long Way from Home* as one of the only people pushing McKay to write not just about Harlem, but about Marseilles, while he is in France. "Senghor was interested in my writing," McKay recalls, "and said he wished I would write the truth about the Negroes in Marseilles. I promised him that I would some day." Later, McKay is having a drink with a man called Le Corse who wishes him success in his writing, and "right then I remembered Senghor, the Senegalese, begging me to write the truth. I settled down to work and began *Banjo*."[67]

Before his premature death later in 1927, Senghor himself found time to write his own fiction, a short book published by a French Communist Party printing house titled *La Violation d'un pays* (The violation of a country).[68] In *A Long Way from Home*, McKay writes that Senghor handed him "a little pamphlet he had written about the European conquest of Africa. The sentiment was quaint and naïve, like the human figures stamped on old-fashioned plates."[69] *La Violation d'un pays* is a didactic text, sketching the history of French colonialism in Africa. Illustrated with the drawings McKay mentions, the book opens by describing a "perfect harmony" *(une parfaite entente)* among a family deep in the jungle that reigns until the arrival of a strange "pale man" who comes down the river to trade his alcohol and leather for the animal hides, cattle, fruit, jewels, and gold of the people. The "pale man," whose name is Bourgeois, convinces one of the natives— who are described either as "ebony" *(à couleur d'ébène)* or as "tan" *(les bronzés)*—named Dégou Diagne that if he delivers one of his own brothers in captivity to the "pale man," the man will give him a powerful "fetish."[70] When Diagne (a rather obvious caricature of Blaise Diagne, the Senegalese legislator who was in charge of African "recruitment" for France during World War I) delivers one of his brothers, Bourgeois shows him how to use his "fetish" (a rifle, as it turns out). Bourgeois returns later as a representative of "King Colonialism" *(le roi Colonialisme)* to claim the country and enlist the people in the war between the king's sister, "La reine République," and one of her brothers named "Germain Bourgeois." The Queen promises to end the people's slavery if they fight in her war, but she instead doubles their taxes and increases their workload. Throughout the world, the different peoples suffering under her rule *(les bronzés,* but also *les jaunes* [the yellow men] and finally even the "pale citizens" of the Queen as well) revolt and overthrow the Queen and King, forming a "fraternal alliance of free countries" *(l'alliance fraternelle des pays libres).* "VIVE LA REVOLU-TION!!!" the book concludes.

Critic Christopher Miller has evaluated the goals of this text, which he summarizes drawing on the preface. (The preface was written by none other than Paul Vaillant-Couturier, the translator of *Banjo*.) For Miller, "the idea of breaking through the bounds of francophone literacy and touching the African masses" is explicit in *La Violation,* where in the preface Vaillant-Couturier proclaims that "one must read it, and have it read [*Il faut le lire, le faire lire*]. . . . It must return to the countries from which it departed like a plant from hot lands, and it must grow there. . . . This tale [*récit*] must fly from mouth to mouth, and the old men, at the thresholds of their huts, must tell it in the evening to the women and the young people."[71] Miller argues that Senghor's text "must be seen as an early experiment along these lines" and compares it to another early Francophone African fiction, the "equally propagandistic" but ideologically "diametrically opposed," pro-

French *Les Trois Volontés de Malic* published in 1920 by Ahmadou Mapaté Diagne. As Miller explains, "The procolonial text describes French letters as miraculous and powerful tools; the anticolonial text tries to transcend its own francophone medium."[72] In fact, there is at least one record of the dissemination of *La Violation d'un pays* in Africa in the files of the colonial authorities from the period. As historian J. S. Spiegler recounts it:

> In late July, the ship *Nil* called at Dakar and reportedly, cards with a hammer and sickle emblem were passed out to dockers unloading the boat. Police suspected that a stoker on the *Nil* had brought a package of *Race Nègre,* but they couldn't identify him in time and the ship proceeded to other coastal ports. Moreover, a Senegalese foreman had previously given the Rufisque-born headwaiter on the *Nil* a photograph for enlargement in France. On the ship's return, the latter handed him the enlargement together with a pamphlet, reportedly saying with apparent nonchalance "look here, take this book. It doesn't interest me. Seems that it's been written by a Negro. Read it and pass it along." The pamphlet in question was Lamine Senghor's *Violation d'un pays.*[73]

Nevertheless, for Miller the text is ultimately an interesting "failed attempt" that dramatizes "the gap between, on the one hand, active and organized resistance to colonialism in France and, on the other, the effective suppression of dissent within the colonized territories during this period."[74] Considering the five "crude" drawings (Miller terms them "cartoons") that accompany *La Violation d'un pays,* he analyzes the "impoverished production values available to anticolonial resistance" and characterizes the "aesthetic quality" of the illustrations as "roughly equivalent to the literary quality of the novella itself: this is a work of propaganda, with no attempt at subtlety or finesse." Its main value is that despite its "artlessness," it is the "first fictional text from francophone Africa to oppose colonialism."[75]

But just what kind of fiction is *La Violation d'un pays?* Miller terms it a "novella,"[76] although he cites Papa Samba Diop's description of the work as a "fable" (Diop more specifically reads the book in the Wolof tradition of a *léeb* or a didactic, coded parable). The book opens with the lines: "Il y avait une fois, dans un pays perdu aux fins fonds des brousses . . . ("Once upon a time, in a country lost deep in the jungle").[77] Diop also claims that Senghor's text adheres to "norms established between African authors be-

La Race nègre 1 (June 1927). Centre des Archives d'Outre-Mer, Aix-en-Provence, Archives Nationales, France. SLOTFOM V, Box 3. All rights reserved.

tween 1915 and 1946: short texts, aimed at a public of schoolchildren, and illustrated if possible." In 1968, the first historian to write on the text in English, J. S. Spiegler, calls *La Violation d'un pays* "a vigorous pamphlet attacking the European colonization of Africa."[78] More recently, the French historian Philippe de Witte has described it as a "symbolic story" *(conte symbolique)* and "a little brochure" *(une petite brochure),* following *La Race nègre* itself, which in its June 1927 inaugural issue announced the publication of a work by its director, *La Violation d'un pays,* "une brochure" whose price of two francs would benefit the Ligue.[79] Even Vaillaint-Couturier's preface vacillates as to the text's genre, characterizing it as a "tale" *(récit)* that would seem to have some historiographic elements, since it contains in "simple and striking" form "the whole history of colonialism" *(toute l'histoire du colonialisme).* Vaillant-Couturier adds that the book "possesses, along with discrete doctrinal qualities, the lively and seductive colors of popular imagery," and even says that he read it in one sitting "like a marvelous legend [*une légende merveilleuse*], as cruel as the children's stories [*contes*] that make up the foundation of the folklore of all peoples."[80] In addition to this range of characterization, I would also note that with its descriptions of "Bourgeois" and "King Colonialism," *La Violation d'un pays* clearly aims at a sort of allegory as well.

It is crucial, I would argue, to attempt to account for such complexity, which raises first of all a question of the formal parameters of radical writing in the interwar period. The only way to achieve this is to recognize the specific aims and accomplishments of works such as *La Violation d'un pays* and *Banjo,* neither of which is simply an extension or an evocation of some sphere of "pure" politics of labor activism and historical context. As I have attempted to attend to the singularity of McKay's "story without a plot," I would also like to hold onto the experimental form—albeit uncertain and polemic, perhaps hurried and perhaps "impoverished"—of *La Violation d'un pays,* which should not be dismissed too quickly. Indeed, what are the (apparently quite pressing) reasons that a peripatetic and extremely devoted black labor organizer, suffering from severe lung ailments that would kill him only months later, would take the time to write a fictional text? Certainly, Senghor was trying to support the Ligue with the profits of *La Violation,* but the illustrated, generically uncertain form he chooses would appear to evidence an imperative based on the conviction that writing a *fiction* (even one that tells "the whole history of colonialism") does a kind of work that labor organizing and more straightforward history are unable to do.[81] This is an issue that is not limited to the texts of Senghor and McKay, but one that affects much of the black writing in this period, which is characterized so often by generic searching and mixture—particularly in the texts that aim to express a certain vision of black radicalism and revolution.

This is equally a question for another book I will consider briefly, a kind of contemporary to the transnational themes of McKay's *Banjo:* W. E. B. Du Bois's extraordinary 1928 novel *Dark Princess: A Romance.* The book is a spectacular fantasy of an underground organization of "the darker races of the world," which is racially consummated in a love affair between the African American intellectual Matthew Towns and the Indian Princess Kautilya.[82] Here I am not going to take up recent critiques of Du Bois's exoticism (an "Afro-Orientialism") in his depiction of Kautilya, nor the question of Du Bois's supposed feminism or his "All-Mother Vision"[83] as articulated in the novel. I want to focus on the peculiar generic status of the book, which Arnold Rampersad has termed a "queer combination of outright propaganda and Arabian tale, of social realism and quaint romance."[84] The novel is often read as proposing an internationalism, an anti-imperial movement culminating in the union of Matthew and Kautilya—and, as Alys Weinbaum has pointed out, literally *incarnated* in their royal "golden brown" baby, born at the end of the novel into his role as the "Messenger and Messiah of the Darker Worlds."[85] In this sense it heals through "romance" what Du Bois had elsewhere diagnosed as the "vast gulf between the red-black South and the yellow-brown East,"[86] forming a common globalist consciousness.

The novel's structure, its "queer combination" of forms, is not incidental to this larger project, however. It should be no surprise that an intellectual so taken with the edges of his texts—the "Forethoughts," prologues, postscripts, "Afterthoughts," and epigraphs that formally limn the "veils" into which the reader enters—would so carefully frame *Dark Princess,* his own professed "favorite" among his works.[87] The book is dedicated to "Her High Loveliness" Titania XXVII,

BY HER OWN GRACE

QUEEN OF FAIRIE,

Commander of the Bath; Grand Medallion of

Merit; Litterarum Humanarum Doctor; Fidei

Extensor; etc., etc.

OF WHOSE FAITH AND FOND AFFECTION

THIS ROMANCE

WAS SURELY BORN

Why this deliberate—and oddly whimsical, for a novel so politically ambitious—allusion to Shakespeare? (At least one commentator on the novel, Mary White Ovington, recalled the Indian Princess whom Du Bois met at the 1911 Universal Races Congress in London, who is often considered to be the model for Kautilya, and connected that encounter precisely to this framing of the book: "Did this Indian Princess remain in the American Negro's memory to becomes the Titania of his Midsummer Night's Dream?")[88]

We should recall first that Shakespeare's *A Midsummer Night's Dream* is nothing if not a play about "combining totally disparate worlds." It places the artisan Nick Bottom next to the trickster fairy Puck. Titania, Queen of Fairie, falls in love with a man far below her "station," like Kautilya in *Dark Princess*—but Titania is tricked: her jealous husband Oberon gives her "magic juice," which makes her fall for the first face she sees upon waking (who happens to be Bottom, given the head of a donkey by a mischievous Puck). Recall also that King Oberon is jealous because Titania has taken into her train of servants "a lovely boy, stolen from an Indian king," a "sweet changeling" who Oberon wants for himself. What is the relationship between this hinted reference to a desired youth from India, on the one hand, and the explicit royalist vision of "India" in *Dark Princess*'s portrait of Kautilya, on the other?

The chapters of *Dark Princess* are framed by dates: the novel unfolds between August 1923 and May 1927. Interestingly, the dates are not without resonance in Du Bois's own life; the first chapters of the novel, for instance, up to the point Matthew is sentenced to prison for revolutionary conspiracy, are set in the fall of 1923, the period not only of the Third Pan-African Congress in Lisbon in November, but also of Du Bois's momentous first trip to Africa, to Liberia and Sierra Leone. In his 1940 autobiography *Dusk of Dawn,* Du Bois comments that his trip to Africa was "in a way the culmination of this Congress."[89] Du Bois claims in *Dusk of Dawn* that the greatest day in his memory was the first of January 1924, in Liberia:

> Liberia had been resting under the shock of world war into which the Allies forced her. . . . Liberia stood naked, not only well-nigh bankrupt, but peculiarly defenseless amid scowling and unbelieving powers.
>
> It was then that the United States made a gesture of courtesy, a little thing, and merely a gesture, but one so unusual that it was epochal. President Coolidge . . . named me, an American Negro traveler, Envoy Extraordinary and Minister Plenipotentiary to Liberia . . . the special representative of the President of the United States to the President of Liberia, on the occasion of his inauguration.[90]

I wonder how much of an echo we might hear between Du Bois's pompous title in Liberia and the ridiculous epithet he confers on the Queen of Fairie in the dedication to *Dark Princess.* Of course, to ask this is to ask about the status of humor in the novel—to ask whether Du Bois might not be attempting to escort the reader into a narrative laced with parody (indeed, *self*-parody) rather than solely portentous social importance.

Likewise, the blow-out "pageant" of Negro spirituals and Hindu pomp that crowns the baby of Matthew and Kautilya "Messenger and Messiah" is intriguingly set on May 1, which is International Labor Day (and thus an appropriate day to culminate a revolution), but also the same date as the wedding ceremony in *A Midsummer Night's Dream*. (Of course, too, part of what moves Du Bois greatly during his stay in Liberia is a "Christmas masque" in Kru-town, a performance of the Christ story: "the little black mother of Christ crossing with her baby, in figured blue, with Joseph in Mandingan fez and multi-colored cloak and beside them on her worshipping knees the white wreathed figure of a solemn dark angel.")[91] In other words, Du Bois would appear to turn to Shakespeare's play in attempting to posit a concordance between his romance of the "darker peoples of the world" and a radical internationalist politics. But this glue may be humor, a bit of melodramatic farce and sly self-parody, as much as it is the weight of coincidence. *Dark Princess,* thus, ends with a "play inside the play" that both brings the framing action to a culmination (the realization of a project of anti-imperialist international organization) and exposes its artifice (the pretensions of its globalism, its reliance on a heterosexist consummation and a brown "Messiah" to incarnate that alliance).

This attempted light touch frames the book, in fact, returning in the novel's "quaint postscript,"[92] which is called—perhaps not coincidentally echoing Du Bois's designation as special ambassador on his Liberia trip—the "Envoy":

> The tale is done and night is come. Now may all the sprites who, with curled wing and starry eyes, have clustered around my hands and helped me weave this story, lift with deft delicacy from out the crevice where it lines my heavy flesh of fact, that rich and colored gossamer of dream which the Queen of Faërie lent to me for a season.[93]

This single paragraph send-off goes on to ask the Queen's elves to return the "rich and colored gossamer of dream" to her "Mauve Majesty" and to "beg her, sometime, somewhere . . . to tell to us hard humans: Which is really Truth—Fact or Fancy? the Dream of the Spirit or the Pain of the Bone?" Even if this gesture is often overlooked, the concluding frame of *Dark Princess* forces us to question the relation between the historical "facts" of imperialism and exploitation and the exoticist "dreams" of an underground revolutionary internationalism.

This is *not* just a "utopian exercise," however, as some critics would have it. It is a structuring that strives to force the reader to consider the possibilities of fiction itself—as a means to line the "heavy flesh of fact" with imagined correspondences and "dreamt" connections. They may be potential links, usable strategies in the world, or they may not. As Bottom comments in Shakespeare's play upon awakening: "I have had a dream, past the wit of man to say what dream it was. Man is but an ass, if he go about to expound this dream. . . . It shall be called 'Bottom's Dream,' because it hath no bottom" (4.2.218–22). In other words, it is precisely the generic ambivalence of this framed historical "Romance" that undoes readerly expectations and creates space to think across the boundaries of nation and language. The complexly articulated imagination of black internationalism, in other words, is what "pulls the bottom" out from under the color line and *dreams* it toward a radical articulation of diaspora.

If *Dark Princess* thus posits the imaginary as a necessary supplement to any "political" radicalism of labor organization and propaganda, then similarly *La Violation d'un pays* wants to find "toute l'histoire du colonialisme" in a fable or allegory, and *Banjo* strives to imagine the music that would allow a radical, "wandering" black internationalism to coalesce. This is not to say, of course, that the three works' experiments in fiction result in anything like similar articulations of diaspora. In *La Violation d'un pays,* Senghor remains committed to a Leninist vision of revolutionary internationalism as a "fraternal alliance of free countries" under the banner of socialism. This vision bears more than a passing resemblance to the internationalism developed by the pressure group Senghor belonged to in the early 1920s with Nguyen Ai Quoc (Ho Chi Minh) and Hadj Ali: the Union Intercoloniale, an affiliation of activists from various French colonies (Algeria, Indochina, Senegal, Madagascar, Martinique) under the aegis and tutelage of the French Communist Party. *La Violation d'un pays,* describing only a single *pays des bronzés,* does not even broach the issue of Pan-Africanism. Moreover, Senghor's fiction holds to a vanguardist Party conception of the dissemination of revolutionary consciousness, in which the metropolitan left makes the colonial subjects "comprehend" their exploitation. Patronizingly, the metropolitan left "would give back" the freedom of self-determination to the colonial subjects:

The anger increased . . . and increased . . . and increased until one day, the pale citizens, wanting to revolt against their queen, thought that if they did not bring along [*s'ils n'entrainaient pas*] the other slaves, then the defenders of the "crown" . . . would indoctrinate them and make them counter-revolutionaries.

They sent qualified emissaries to all the enslaved countries to organize their revolt, making them comprehend how they had been tricked and despoiled. . . .

You see! They said . . . your brothers in poverty [*vos frères de misère*] would give you back [*rendraient*] the freedom of self-determination; everyone who recognizes the truth of their speeches understands their duty.[94]

Du Bois's *Dark Princess* concludes quite differently, not with a successful revolution, but with the incarnation of the requisite internationalist alliance to bring about a revolution. If it is framed as fantasy, the "dream" that lines the "heavy flesh of fact" in *Dark Princess* is no less a flirtation with a doctrinal elitism, most egregiously in its depiction of Matthew and Kautilya, the would-be royal couple of antiracist global radicalism. Here, experimentation in fiction may function finally as a kind of alibi for Du Bois's tendencies toward "oligarchy," toward visions of "mass" organizations led by enlightened elites. As Kenneth Warren phrases it, *Dark Princess* in this way serves Du Bois as a "tool with which to eroticize, spiritualize, and thus revitalize his technocratic rationalism so that it could continue to play a role in his political and aesthetic interventions over the next decade."[95]

Banjo goes yet another route. In 1928, as he was concluding revisions on the book manuscript, McKay was living in Morocco. McKay describes an encounter in his autobiography *A Long Way from Home:*

A *chaoush* (native doorman and messenger) from the British Consulate had accosted me in a *souk* one day and asked whether I was American. I said I was born in the West Indies and lived in the United States and that I was an American, even though I was a British subject, but preferred to think of myself as an internationalist. The *chaoush* said he didn't understand what was an internationalist. I laughed and said that an internationalist was a bad nationalist. He replied gravely: "All the Moors call you an American, and if you are British, you should come and register at the Consulate."[96]

McKay comments that he dropped this line "by way of a joke without thinking of its radical implications." But it is tempting to take those implications seriously and consider whether "bad nationalism" might indeed be a decent phrase to describe *Banjo,* where for Ray "the vagabond lover of life finds individuals and things to love in many places and not in any one nation" (136). A "bad nationalist" is not exactly a "cosmopolitan," nor is it a "flexible citizen."[97] It would seem to describe a subject that is mobile and loosely transnational ("I was born in the West Indies and lived in the United States and . . . was American, even though I was a British subject"); but more pointedly, it indicates a subject who doesn't *perform* nationalism, who doesn't follow the protocol, who doesn't register. A "bad nationalist" is a subject defective for nationalism. What's intriguing here is the seeming conundrum that an "internationalist" is defined as defective for nationalism—stubbornly, McKay insists on locating internationalism against the grain of nationalism without grounding it in any alternate universalism (an internationalism of the "human" or an internationalism of the "proletariat," for instance). This is an internationalism of the defective: the unregistered, the undocumented, the untracked—an ab-nationalism, as it were, of all the "Doubtful."

The consulate worker in *A Long Way from Home* is disturbed by McKay's self-description precisely because it laughs at the logic of consulates. Though his papers are in order, McKay writes, he does not register his presence because "I have always relied on my personality as the best passport." But in his joke and smile, the "grave" Moroccan hears a threat. A week later, McKay is confronted by a French police inspector, who escorts him to the British Consulate, where he is accused of "sleeping in native houses" and of being a "radical propagandist." The officials cannot find any proof to deport him, but McKay's "native holiday" is spoiled because the experience makes him recall "miserable" times in Europe: "now even in Africa I was confronted by the specter, the white terror always pursuing the black. There was no escape anywhere from the white hound of Civilization."[98]

McKay's experiment in fiction strives to articulate a culture of "bad nationalism," and more, to imagine an institution for that culture in the music of black drifters at Europe's back door. As *Banjo* would have it, the Negro is the "one significant and challenging aspect of the human life of the world as a whole" (272) because black expressive culture—and music in particular—represents an active threat, the "rag" constantly mocking and deforming the pretensions of a civilization that "had uprooted, enchained, transported, and transformed" peoples of African descent "to labor under its laws, and yet lacked the spirit to tolerate them within its walls" (313–314). The colored rogues and vagabonds along the Marseilles docks in *Banjo* are struggling irritants to the "normal" cycles of life around them—above all refusing to fit into the grooves of the machines that would work them, above all traveling, elusive, moving on. To return to the double metaphor in the novel's subtitle ("A Story without a Plot"): music is the only place the black boys stand—there is no other "plot," no other ground or foundation, whether nation or narrative, engine or economy, that contains them. The music's "composite voice" is itself still ephemeral (and still unsalaried), but in *Banjo* it is all that riffs across difference: only the music sings "Stay, Stay."

CHAPTER 5

INVENTING THE BLACK INTERNATIONAL:
GEORGE PADMORE
AND TIEMOKO GARAN KOUYATÉ

In his 1973 memoir, *Pan-Africanism from Within,* T. Ras Makonnen poses a provocative formulation about the emergence of anticolonialism among intellectuals of African descent during the period between the two world wars. For him, shifts in consciousness among the interwar generation were rooted above all in their experience of migration to Europe, in their exposure to the centers of imperial dominance. "But when you look at the results of those Africans who had been to England," he observes with characteristic irreverence, "you wouldn't be far wrong in saying that England had been the executioner of its own colonial empire. In the sense that she had allowed these blacks to feel the contrast between freedom in the metropolis and slavery in the colonies. Hence it became the old retort: 'What are you going to do with these boys back on the farm, once they have seen Paree (Paris)?'"[1]

Born under the name Thomas Griffiths in British Guyana, Makonnen was one of the key collaborators in the anticolonial organizations that sprung up around George Padmore and C. L. R. James in London in the mid-1930s. But even taking into account Makonnen's tireless work as an organizer, propagandist, and tenacious fund-raiser in the period leading up to the 1945 Pan-African Congress in Manchester, it is hard not to be troubled by Makonnen's rather glib suggestion that England was the main catalyst in black anticolonialism, the "executioner of its own colonial empire." Cedric Robinson has noted a tone of "near-reckless admiration" in Makonnen's book for England and all things English, an uncritical metropolitan enthrallment that can only be read as "delusion."[2] What is intriguing about the passage, though, is its shift between metropolitan contexts, from England to France ("Paree")—a shift that can slip by quickly in the lightness of the rhetoric.

It should be evident to any student of the complex interactions of intellectuals of African descent with organized Marxism that "the socialist traditions to which Blacks of Africa and the Caribbean were exposed in the British metropole differed decidedly from those of their Francophone and American counterparts."[3] But I would like to hold on to this conjuncture, this possibly careless shift in contexts. Makonnen does have a point to make, clarified in his next paragraph: "Africans were not only compelled to think out the position of their own people, but were forced by the pressures of the times into making alliances across boundaries that would have been unthinkable back home" (155). For Makonnen, in other words, the interwar historical context was above all else multiple and heterogeneous—fostering alliances among "natives" that broke the hold of the metropole-colony dichotomy. The metropolitan situation allowed contacts and collaborations that would have been "unthinkable" in the colonial world, so dominated by that dichotomy, so overwhelmed by the special relation to an imperial *Mère-Patrie*. In this sense, these many moves "across boundaries" (from colony to metropole, from one colonial system to another) were the real threat to colonialism, which is a discourse articulated first of all as singular and inescapable. This chapter considers one instance of this kind of collusive, boundary-crossing work, a Caribbean-African, Anglophone-Francophone alliance in Paris.

My example is the collaboration during the 1930s between George Padmore, the intellectual and agitator who was born in Trinidad but best known for his work in the Pan-African movement first in Britain and then in Ghana, and Tiemoko Garan Kouyaté, the West African labor organizer and propagandist who led the Ligue de Défense de la Race Nègre and then the Union des Travailleurs Nègres. Kouyaté is one of the many Francophone figures whose story has only partly been told, and part of my aim is to resuscitate his role and the role of the French context in interwar black anticolonialism. Histories of blacks and organized communism and histories of Pan-Africanism both tend to focus on Anglophone intellectuals such as Padmore and C. L. R. James, neglecting their Francophone counterparts and sometime collaborators such as Kouyaté, Lamine Senghor, and Emile Faure.[4] James himself, commissioned to write an essay on "Black Intellectuals in Britain," used the occasion to comment that he found the title to be inherently problematic ("I doubt if there are many black men who have made the impact on England that Paul Robeson has made") and insisted on

"a few words about similar activities in France," sketching the work of
Alexandre Dumas, René Maran, Aimé Césaire, and Frantz Fanon.[5] As
James says, "Once the complexity of definition has been established we can
go ahead cheerfully, knowing that many who are in ought to be out and
quite a few who are out ought to be in." With regard to Kouyaté, part of
my intention is to reintroduce a figure who "ought to be in" a genealogy of
the Pan-African movement.

But I also want to use this approach, this reading of a collaboration, to
make a larger point about black intellectuals in this period. It is not only
that Padmore and Kouyaté travel. More important, my argument is that
their radicalism is forged first and foremost by the very way they are "forced
by the pressure of the times" to cross boundaries, to move through and beyond the "decided differences" of their Francophone and Anglophone colonial contexts. I am suggesting, in other words, that black internationalism
is not a supplement to revolutionary nationalism, the "next level" of anticolonial agitation. On the contrary, black radicalism necessarily emerges
through boundary crossing—black radicalism *is* an internationalization.

Such a conjuncture does not commence with Padmore and Kouyaté. Indeed, it characterizes black activism throughout the interwar period, going
back to the intellectuals prominent during and directly after World War I,
who were equally keen to work internationally, even when they did not
travel to the European metropoles. In the United States, for instance, the
initial demands for a "Black International," an explicitly anticapitalist alliance of peoples of African descent from different countries around the
world, were quite deliberate attempts to respond to and intervene in the
discourses of policy and institution building that arose after World War I in
the Communist International and the League of Nations. Hubert Harrison, the legendary street speaker and black nationalist born in St. Croix in
the Virgin Islands, who influenced the entire generation of 1920s radical
intellectuals in New York, was one of the first to call for such an alliance.
Writing in Marcus Garvey's *Negro World* in May 1920, Harrison commented bitterly that internationalism appeared to be something "of varying
value" to the "overlords" who ran the postwar world. Harrison writes:
"When Mr. Morgan wants to float a French or British loan in the United
States; when Messrs. Wilson, Clemenceau, Lloyd George and Orlando
want to stabilize their joint credit and commerce; when areas like the Belgian Congo are to be handed over to certain rulers without the consent of

their inhabitants—then the paeans of praise go up to the god of 'internationalism' in the temple of 'civilization.'" But when the world's oppressed peoples, the world's "disinherited," decide to come together in their common interest, those same Western leaders denounce the very idea of internationalism as "anarchy, sedition, Bolshevism and disruptive propaganda." The reason is that "the international linking up of peoples is a source of strength to those who are linked up. . . . Today the great world-majority, made up of black, brown and yellow peoples, are stretching out their hands to each other and developing a 'consciousness of kind'. . . . They are seeking to establish their own centers of diffusion for their own internationalism, and this fact is giving nightmares for Downing Street, the Quai d'Orsay and other centers of white capitalist internationalism."[6] Nevertheless, Harrison's attempts at what he would come to call a "Colored International" (particularly in the group he founded in 1924, the International Colored Unity League) never succeeded in establishing a lasting organization with the transnational reach of Du Bois's Pan-African Congress or especially Marcus Garvey's Universal Negro Improvement Association.[7]

The institution building pursued by Padmore and Kouyaté in the subsequent decade diverges from the model of the International Colored Unity League in a number of ways, most important, in its relationship to international communism. Harrison's calls emphasize mainly the ways that African Americans' "enforced participation in the first World War brought us into contact with the wider world of color."[8] But the war also introduced peoples of African descent to the revolutionary discourse incarnated in communism, which for many intellectuals of African descent implied both anticapitalism and anticolonialism: both the Communist International's critique of economic exploitation, and Lenin's 1920 call for national self-determination in the colonial world.[9] Unlike Harrison, Padmore and Kouyaté—both working in uneasy, shifting affiliations with the Comintern—strove in the early 1930s to find a way to "develop racial solidarity" and to institutionalize an autonomous "center of diffusion" for black internationalism *within* the structures of communism.

Describing the emergence of a black intelligentsia between the wars, Cedric Robinson contends that "the social cauldron of black radicalism is western society. Western society, however, has been its location and its objective conditions but not—except in a most perverse fashion—its specific inspiration. Black radicalism is a negation of western civilisation, but not in the direct sense of a simple dialectical negation." Somewhat confusingly, at the same time Robinson writes of a black intelligentsia emerging through the "dialectic of imperialism."[10] Is it correct to theorize the interaction of black radicalism and Western society as a "dialectic," and if so, how would one describe its particular form? Since figures such as Padmore and Kouyaté are mobile not just in their own colonial spheres, but moreover *among* metropolitan "centers," within each other's circuits of activity (Padmore moving from a British colony in the Caribbean to the United States, and then not just to London but to Moscow, Hamburg, and Paris; Kouyaté moving from one French colony to another and then to Paris and to Moscow), would it make more sense to think of this emergence as something more like what Edward Kamau Brathwaite—in a spirit of serious play—calls a "tidalectic": a counterlogic, a more unruly pattern of flows and alliances, a structure interweaving at least three points?[11] Although I will take up the issue Robinson raises (considering black radicalism as a special sort of "negation" of Western civilization), I will not retain the term "dialectic" in what follows, as I remain unconvinced that it will suffice to describe the complex dynamics of this emergence. With Kouyaté and Padmore, we encounter a collaboration, a nascent discourse of black internationalism, that is at once inside communism, fiercely engaged with its ideological debates and funneled through its institutions, and at the same time aimed at a race-specific formation that rejects the Comintern's universalism, adamantly insisting that racial oppression involves factors and forces that cannot be summed up or submerged in a critique of class exploitation. Here, black radicalism as internationalization is a special sort of "negation" because Padmore and Kouyaté do not entirely relinquish a communist class analysis. Most striking, black internationalism takes shape in detour, in dialogue, as one intellectual from the Caribbean and another from Africa attempt to find common ground in Paris.

The Negro Worker

James Hooker's biography of George Padmore is especially thin around the early 1930s. He tells us for example that 1933 "was a lean year and not much of Padmore appears on the record."[12] This is unfortunate, for the period in the mid-1930s may be the most important in understanding Padmore's evolution toward Pan-Africanism in that decade. In 1933, Padmore leaves his position as head of the International Trade Union Committee of Negro Workers (ITUC-NW), the unit created by the Communist International to organize workers of African descent around the world, and by 1935 he ends up in London with C. L. R. James's International African Friends of Ethiopia. How do we explain this striking shift from the institutions of international communism to a nonaligned effort at "international African" work? Hooker does include one tantalizing letter to W. E. B. Du Bois, written in February 1934. Intriguingly, Padmore types this missive on letterhead from the Union des Travailleurs Nègres in Paris, a group headed by Tiemoko Garan Kouyaté between 1931 and 1933. Padmore had apparently corresponded with Du Bois before, because he thanks Du Bois for "the acknowledgment of my article," adding that he is "glad it came in useful." Publication of the *Negro Worker* (the journal Padmore edited for the ITUC-NW) has been suspended, but "we are trying to re-organize our forces." He continues:

> The French Negroes recently held a conference under the leadership of a young Sudanese whom you no doubt have heard about, Mr. Garan Kouyaté, the editor of *La Race Nègre.* The Negro problem was discussed relative to the present economic and social crisis the world over, and the fascist danger which threatens our racial extermination. It was the most serious political discussion which I have ever listened to among Negroes. The Conference decided to take the initiative to convene a Negro World Unity Congress, for the purpose of hammering out a common program of action around which world unity among the blacks can be achieved. The Negro students in Europe are demanding action. I also found this attitude very evident among the West African students when I was recently over in London.
>
> I took the opportunity of informing the French Negroes about the work of the N.A.C.P. [*sic*] and your work in connection with the Pan African movement. They decided to invite your organization to participate in the Congress which has been fixed for the summer of 1935—providing the war-makers give us so much time. This is another question which is agitating the minds of French Negroes very much. For they have not forgotten how Diagne and other so-called leaders inveigled them into the last one, but this time they will have a wideawake youth to deal with.

Will you help us in trying to create a basis for unity among Negroes of Africa, America, the West Indies, and other lands?[13]

Padmore asks Du Bois to put his Negro World Unity Congress effort in
contact with Negro student groups at Atlanta University and elsewhere,
specifying that his "personal correspondence" should be sent to Kouyaté's
address on rue Mouton-Duvernet in the Fourteenth Arrondissement of
Paris. It is an odd request, since by the spring of 1934 Kouyaté no longer
had a connection to the Union des Travailleurs Nègres, and he had not edited *La Race nègre* since 1931. Still, the letter represents the inception of a
relationship between Padmore and Du Bois, opening the door to mutual
respect and finally to collaboration in the Fifth Pan-African Congress organized after World War II. Not long before, in the *Negro Worker,* Padmore
had habitually referred to Du Bois and a list of nationalist and civil rights
leaders as a "wing of misleaders," the "black agents of international capitalism," the "petty-bourgeois reformists" who were "merely office-seekers
and demagogues paid by the ruling class to befuddle the Negro masses."[14]

C. L. R. James has famously described the 1945 Pan-African Congress in
Manchester as incarnated in this alliance between Du Bois and Padmore.[15]
What is suggestive is that the impetus of Padmore's gesture to Du Bois originates not in London, but in Paris; not around the international crisis when
Italy invaded Ethiopia, but around a meeting of Francophone blacks, "the
most serious political discussion" Padmore "had ever listened to among Negroes"; not even in the Union des Travailleurs Nègres, as the stationery
would imply, but in a different, fleeting organizational impulse to create a
"Negro World Unity Congress" planned for the summer of 1935. Significantly, such a congress is conceived at the very moment when both
Padmore and Kouyaté are each officially expelled from the Communist International. It is a signal period in the history of black internationalism:
two formerly Communist black radicals groping toward a new institution
for their work.

One might be tempted to say that Padmore and Kouyaté are "uprooted,"
here, even desperate. Still, I will suggest that it is possible to read this period
as enabling in certain ways, not simply in terms of the "boundary-crossing"
alliance between the two men, but for more practical reasons as well. For
Padmore leaves the Comintern already established as an "institution all by

George Padmore. From *Afrika:
Unter den Joch der Weissen*
(Erlenbach-Zurich/Leipzig: Rotapfel
Verlag, 1937).

himself," taking with him his carefully fostered "net" of more than 4,000
connections "throughout the colonial world."[16] Born in Trinidad in 1904,
Padmore had been educated in the United States (at Fisk University in
Nashville and at Howard University in Washington, D.C.), studying law
before joining the Communist Party in the late 1920s. Between 1929 and
1933, he was vaulted into a position of great power and influence as the
highest black representative in the Comintern at a moment when Moscow
was keenly interested in the "Negro question," and his work attempted to
"organize and educate the black masses on a world scale in the theory and
practice of modern political parties and modern trade unionism."[17] His ex-
ploits in these years are legendary. There are whispers that he led "a gun-
running expedition into the Belgian Congo to help a native revolt there"
and that he personally recruited a "bumper crop" of sixty or more African
radicals to study in Moscow, smuggling them into Europe. Supposedly he

was a master of disguises, a "first class conspirator, a specialist in decoys, codes, and stratagems."[18] He told one reporter that he had arranged passage on one of his recruiting trips to Africa by pretending to be an "anthropologist" embarking on field work to "study the life and customs of primitive peoples." When he went to South Africa, he entered posing as a "chauffeur" for the white junior officer who was actually his assistant.[19]

In May 1930, the French Consulate in Bathurst (in Gambia) wrote to the gouverneur général of French West Africa to report that Padmore had attempted to travel from that port to Dakar. The British authorities intercepted him and forced him to board a ship (named the "Henry Stanley," of all things) traveling instead to Sierra Leone. Referring to Padmore under his birth name, Malcolm Nurse, the letter comments somewhat confusedly that "without being a convinced Bolshevist, [he] seeks to win the support of the Negroes [*noirs*] in Africa for the cause of the blacks [*nègres*] in America." The note adds that Padmore had undertaken suspicious activities in Gambia and links him to trade union activism and to a publication called the *Gambia Outlook*.[20] It is an interesting document, given that in November 1929, one of the first trade unions in West Africa, the Bathurst Trade Union in Gambia—led by E. F. Small, the editor of the *Outlook* and later a correspondent for the *Negro Worker* under Padmore's editorship—brought about a general strike that led to armed clashes between African workers and the British colonial authorities, in an uprising that succeeded in disrupting economic activity in all of Gambia for nearly three weeks.[21]

Kouyaté was never as peripatetic as Padmore, but he also might be described as an "institution" of Francophone anticolonial activity. He had his own extensive set of contacts in West Africa, and indeed, when he was ousted from the Union des Travailleurs Nègres and the journal *Le Cri des Nègres,* one of his main transgressions had been a refusal to turn over his address lists—rumored to run to 2,800 names in Africa and the Caribbean.[22] In this specific sense, the initial pan-African coalition represented by the "Negro World Unity Congress" is rooted transnationally—grounded in a global black radical circuit that is literally wrenched out of the Communist International by two of the preeminent black organizers of the time. Even if their "Negro World Unity Congress" ends up an abortive collaboration, these origins have a great deal to tell us about the complex ways Pan-Africanism emerges out of and against Communism. In this collaboration, we find the roots of the network that Padmore took with him to England in

1935, and on which later organizations such as the International African Service Bureau were constructed. As C. L. R. James would later describe it: "The basis of that work [in the International African Service Bureau] and the development of ideas was Padmore's encyclopedic knowledge of Africa, of African politics and African personalities, his tireless correspondence with Africans in all parts of the continent, the unceasing stream of Africans who made the Bureau and its chairman their political headquarters when in London. Revolutionaries and bourgeois nationalists all came."[23]

Kouyaté was born April 27, 1902, in Segu in the French Sudan. He studied at the celebrated Ecole William Ponty on the Ile de Gorée in Senegal and then worked as a schoolteacher in the Ivory Coast from 1921 to 1923. That year, he was sent to Aix-en-Provence in France for further studies, but in 1926 was reportedly thrown out of school for circulating "communist propaganda" among the students. He moved to Paris, audited courses at the Sorbonne, and fell in with the group of French African and Caribbean communists affiliated with Lamine Senghor that became the Comité de Défense de la Race Nègre in 1926. After the schism of that group, he followed its more radical section into the Ligue de Défense de la Race Nègre (LDRN) in 1927, playing a central role in the publication of the newspaper *La Race nègre,* and upon Senghor's death later that year, became the general secretary of the LDRN. In 1931, the LDRN split as well: Emile Faure and his black nationalist supporters kept the name and the publication, while Kouyaté left with a group of left-leaning radicals and labor organizers to form a new group, the Union des Travailleurs Nègres, founding a new paper called *Le Cri des Nègres.* In 1933, the hard-line members of the group loyal to the Parti Communiste Français ousted Kouyaté, in part due to the history of tension between him and the French Communist hierarchy, and in part for his collaboration with outside figures including Padmore. By the middle of the decade, Kouyaté was affiliated with Messali Hadj's Algerian independence group, the Etoile Nord-Africaine and, with its support, founded another more moderate journal called *Africa.* Increasingly beleaguered and isolated as the war approached, he became a supporter of the Popular Front, eventually accepting financial support from it and apparently even from the French Ministère des Colonies. Little is known about Kouyaté's activities after about 1938, but it is generally accepted that in 1942 he was executed by the Germans at the Fort de Montluçon in central France.[24]

Tiemoko Garan Kouyaté. From the *Negro Worker* 2, no. 6 (June 1932). General Research Division, Schomburg Center for Research in Black Culture, Astor, Lenox and Tilden Foundations.

Padmore and Kouyaté apparently first met at the July 1929 Second Congress of the League Against Imperialism in Frankfurt.[25] The African American communist James W. Ford brought Padmore from the United States to serve on a Provisional Executive Committee on "the Negro Question" formed directly after the Frankfurt Congress to organize a long-term strategy for an international conference of Negro workers. Kouyaté was also named to the Provisional Committee.

The year 1929 brought a number of shifts in the organization Kouyaté led, the Ligue de Défense de la Race Nègre. The group had been in difficult financial straits, and in late January, the Guadeloupean militant Stéphane Rosso (who would later become a paid Communist functionary) came to Kouyaté with an offer for a possible monthly subvention from the French Communist Party, one that the Ligue decided it had to accept. On February 2, 1929, the LDRN received 800 francs, a sum that increased to 1000 francs per month. This was enough to fund part of the publication costs of the Ligue's monthly newspaper *La Race nègre,* allowing it to appear regularly for the first time (in 1927, the paper appeared only four times, while in 1928, it was even more sporadic, with issues only for May and October).[26] Even as he granted the necessity of an alliance with the Party, Kouyaté resisted full Communist control of the Ligue and of *La Race nègre.* The fluctuation in his viewpoints and ideological positions were a source of constant concern for the Party.

The ideological shifts in *La Race nègre,* even in this period of Party support, are pronounced and sometimes bewildering. Kouyaté's reluctance to relinquish control of the periodical is also an insistence that the Ligue maintain an independent (even if Party-funded) venue for debate and experimentation with the very language of radicalism. Indeed, what is most striking in the journal is its internal variance, the constant sense of searching, the sometimes convoluted attempts at innovative theorization, the disparate realms of knowledge thrown together, all in a quest to discover the most efficacious modes of black anticolonialism. In the March 1929 issue, Kouyaté published a long front-page essay called "Vox Africae" that called for the extension of the Ligue into permanent African and Caribbean sections, relying on the already-existing structures of society:

> Businessmen, planters, harvesters, workers, forestry developers, bureaucrats, students, schoolchildren, Negroes and mulattos [*noirs et mulâtres*], in a word all the blacks [*nègres*] who are conscious of the vital interests of the race, must join the Ligue and subscribe to *La Race Nègre.* . . . Take care, compatriots! The minor colonists [*petits colons*], small businessmen and white workers are also suffering economically. They must not be neglected. In sum, a racial problem on the one hand, an economic and social problem on the other.[27]

Here Kouyaté seems to call for an organization based primarily on racial lines ("the interests of the race") rather than class. At the same time, he goes so far as to argue that, if the situation calls for unity among *nègres,* some Europeans implicated in colonialism (the "petits colons") are "also suffering" from the "economic and social problems" of that system and that they shouldn't be forgotten *(il ne faut pas les négliger).*

In the same issue, also on the front page, *La Race nègre* published an unsigned editorial called "Vers l'élaboration d'un programme" (Toward the elaboration of a program), which shuttles between a global anti-imperialism, an "African Zionism," and a more traditional communist analysis:[28]

"Destruction and reconstruction," building national institutions on the ruins of those imposed by the conqueror: this is a program which responds to the urgent needs of all oppressed peoples, especially colonized peoples. The Vietnamese, the North Africans, and the *nègres* should be in accord on this essential point in order to coordinate their efforts. . . .

But what is our program, we *nègres?* A complex and varied problem! For the Negro problem [*le problème nègre*], ever global, is aggravated more and more by the social question. The Ligue de Défense de la Race Nègre, attentive to this evolution of difficulties, is presently elaborating a program which will be published after its discussion in general assembly. . . .

To realize this program as quickly as possible, *nègres* must understand each other, join the Ligue en masse, take support from other oppressed peoples, whether in Europe, Asia or America, and take support from the intellectual and manual workers of France. Race prejudice will have lived out its life the day that a great Negro State [*un grand Etat nègre*] is established on modern foundations: African Zionism.

On the one hand, this language recalls the anticolonial alliance among radicals throughout the French colonies pursued in the early 1920s in the Union Intercoloniale, which united Caribbeans, West Africans, North Africans, and Vietnamese militants under the aegis of the French Communist Party. Some of the language here even echoes the cadences of Lamine Senghor's *La Violation d'un pays,* as when the editorial claims that "the peoples will love one another because they will live with national liberty and international equality." But the editorial also reverberates with the ideas of Marcus Garvey—whose poetry and articles had been translated in *La Race nègre* as early as November 1927.[29] Black nationalism here seems to be articulated as a vanguardist version of what would later come to be called "continental Pan-Africanism"—a "Zionist" call for return to an Africa united into a "grand Etat nègre." The shifts and contrasts within and between "Vox Africae" and "Vers l'élaboration d'un programme" are fairly representative of the dizzying fluctuation of opinion that characterized *La Race nègre* in the late 1920s.

By the summer of 1929 and the Frankfurt Congress, Kouyaté apparently decided to hew more closely to the Comintern line. In his address to the League Against Imperialism, he opened by invoking the memory of the legendary speech by his predecessor in the LDRN, Lamine Senghor, at the League's first congress in Brussels in 1927. Kouyaté gave a detailed critique of colonial exploitation in the French Congo and in the Antilles. Then, recounting a long list of rebellions against colonialism, Kouyaté called these uprisings the "prelude" to "the true struggle for national independence, the struggle without useless sacrifices, the struggle organized against imperialism and its agents [*succédanés*]. We will do everything to coordinate, centralize, unify the national emancipation movements of the Negroes of black Africa [*les Nègres de l'Afrique noire*]. We will continue to demand the absolute independence of Liberia and Ethiopia. The national emancipation movement of the Negroes of Africa and the Negro movement for political and social emancipation in America will mutually support each other."[30]

It should be noted that even here, Kouyaté turns to an explicit pan-Africanism—"mutual support" among Africans and African Americans, not necessarily under the aegis of the worldwide Communist revolutionary movement. His particular gift as an organizer was an ability to foster just these kinds of transnational links. After the congress in Frankfurt, Kouyaté traveled through Eastern Europe, visiting Poland and the Soviet Union. In Berlin, he helped assemble a section of the LDRN (called the Liga zur Verteidigung der Negerrasse), led by an architect from Cameroon named Joseph Bile, that was reported to involve as many as two hundred members.[31] From Paris, Kouyaté was an energetic letter writer, keeping in touch with correspondents in the Americas and in Africa itself, especially among the *évolués* of the small West African bourgeoisie in many of the categories he enumerated in "Vox Africae": small businessmen, schoolteachers, bureaucrats. (The lists of Kouyaté's contacts, meticulously gathered by French surveillance, contain a number of surprises, showing for instance that he was in touch with Léon M'Ba, the future president of independent Gabon.)[32] To the dismay of the colonial authorities, the LDRN succeeded in establishing sections in Senegal and along the railway between Dakar and Bamako, and attempted to found units in Dahomey and French Cameroon. Most of these were fleeting efforts, but in 1929 the LDRN reportedly sent militants to the French Congo in the midst of a series of violent revolts, calling for "absolute and immediate independence." In the summer of that year, the French gouverneur générale contended that the Ligue's "clearly communist" propaganda and activism were behind uprisings in the Upper Sangha Province (in what is now the Central African Republic), which briefly liberated the area from French control. In 1931, the LDRN was even rumored to be planning an armed rebellion in Cameroon.[33]

In 1930 on his return from Moscow, Kouyaté devoted himself to labor organizing, especially among the African and Antillean dock workers and sailors in Marseilles, Bordeaux, and Le Havre. At the end of January, he sent a telegram to Pierre M'Baye (the café owner portrayed in McKay's *Banjo*), announcing his arrival in Marseilles and scheduling a meeting at the International Seaman's Club. At the subsequent gathering (involving a few hundred West Africans, a number of Malagasies, a dozen Central Africans, a handful of North Africans and Antilleans, and a few Europeans), Kouyaté spoke both in French and Bambara, urging the workers to join a branch of the Ligue. Perhaps inspired by his visit to the Lenin Institute in Russia, he added that he wanted to found an educational institute "that would receive children sent from the colonies in large numbers—two thousand in the beginning—in order to prepare them to spread in the future the idea of independence in their countries."[34] Others spoke out in favor of the Ligue in other West African languages (Saracolé and Tukolor) and in Arabic, and Kouyaté distributed the January 1930 issue of *La Race nègre*. He also passed out a flyer titled "Appel aux Nègres" (A call to Negroes), which called not just for union organizing, but specifically for *independent* black unions attentive to the special concerns of black workers in French port cities:

> Considering that black sailors [*navigateurs nègres*] must be conscious of their interests, of those of the working class, without becoming the instrument of syndicalist politics elaborated outside of their direct collaboration. . . .
>
> Considering that, taking everything into account, the situation of the black sailors remains frustratingly particular and that in order to ameliorate it, the black sailors must first of all count on themselves in forming a single union for all the black sailors in the port of Marseilles. . . .
>
> The goal of the union is to protect and to support the corporative

claims of the black sailors in all categories . . . regarding questions of hiring, salaries, unemployment, food, sleeping arrangements, security and hygiene on board, etc.[35]

Not surprisingly, the French Communist Party reacted quickly and negatively to these efforts at race-based labor organizing, the construction of unions that would refuse to become "the instruments of syndicalist politics elaborated outside of their direct collaboration." An unsigned Party statement published in May mentioned that "for some time, we have been aware of attempts to organize black port workers [des travailleurs nègres des ports] on the basis of autonomy. . . . This is a danger to the unity of the working class. The CGTU [the Confédération Générale du Travail Unitaire of the French Communist Party] and its colonial office cannot remain indifferent in the face of this movement, and they denounce it as counterrevolutionary."[36] Kouyaté pulled back from his language of "autonomy," but this exchange represents a pattern of disagreement over strategy that would characterize his interactions with the Party over the next three years.

As early as July 1928, the Comintern had published a bulletin called the *International Negro Workers' Review* under the editorship of James Ford and a group called the "International Negro Workers Information Bureau."[37] The Provisional Executive Committee created at the 1929 Frankfurt Congress was charged with making the Bureau a permanent one, seeking ways to spread its influence not just in Moscow but throughout the colonial world. Toward this end, Padmore was instrumental in putting together the World Conference of Negro Workers in Hamburg, held in July 1930. The Red International of Labor Unions (RILU), also known as the Profintern, named Padmore the head of the newly created ITUC-NW and the editor of the *Negro Worker,* which was to coordinate a "syndicalist approach" to black workers throughout the globe.[38] The Committee included the Africans E. F. Small (Gambia), Albert Nzula (South Africa), Herbert Macauley (Nigeria), and Kouyaté; Ford and Padmore (representing U.S. black workers); and G. Reid (representing the West Indies).[39] Even though Kouyaté was involved in the planning of the Hamburg conference, he was unable to attend the meeting, and it is possible that the French Communist Party, furious over his race-based organizing in Marseilles, refused him funds for his journey. But forgiveness came quickly, for the next month, Kouyaté was again sent to Moscow for the initial meetings of the ITUC-NW.

The importance of the *Negro Worker* under Padmore's editorship should not be underestimated. Padmore announced the aims of the journal in the first issue he assembled, in January 1931:

> This journal is the official organ of the International Trade Union Committee of Negro Workers. But it is our aim not to make this a sort of "theoretical" journal to discuss resolutions, "opinions" etc. . . . It is our aim to discuss and analyse the day to day problems of the Negro toilers and connect these up with the international struggles and problems of the workers. It is therefore necessary that we receive the fullest cooperation of Negro workers. This means that articles, letters, points of view and pictures of your daily life must be sent to us. It is only in this way that we can build a much needed popular journal, taking up the broad international problems of Negro workers.[40]

In other words, even if the journal emanates from the highest echelons of the Profintern, Padmore intends its orientation to be driven by the needs and concerns of the workers themselves: their "day to day problems." The *Negro Worker* has propagandistic aims as well, as the editorial goes on to outline: first, to "raise the international outlook of the Negro workers" (mainly by providing news of the international labor movement) and, second, to "enlighten" black workers against the forces of "Negro bourgeois nationalism" (Garvey) and "trade union reformism" (Kadalie in South Africa, A. Philip Randolph in the United States). But what stands out most of all is Padmore's determination to make the *Negro Worker* a space for the "points of view" and "daily life" of workers of African descent, rather than a place for the Communist hierarchy to debate the "Negro question."

One sees just how much of a shift this is when one compares Padmore's mode of address ("*your* daily life") with the editorial Losovsky wrote for the old *International Negro Workers' Review* in 1928, which seemed to envision an entirely different readership and an entirely different program, in which black labor is the object of inquiry rather than a participating audience. "The Negro workers must be drawn into the political and trade union movement," Losovsky prescribed, adding that it was important to publish the journal directed at black workers because "their potential force must be turned into an active force, into an instrument that will free the exploited masses from the capitalist yoke."[41] In contrast to this familiar tone, Padmore's call for "a much needed popular journal, taking up the broad international problems of Negro workers" is a notable departure not just in its unprecedented internationalism but also in its aspirations as a "popular" publication driven by the "fullest cooperation" of black workers around the world.

Edward Wilson has argued that the content of the *Negro Worker* was to a large extent controlled by Moscow even when Padmore was nominally the editor, and certainly the periodical emphasizes the themes one might expect: that black workers in Africa should emulate the great example of the Soviet Union (there was a regular feature on life "in the Land of Socialism"); that the Soviet political model offered the best solutions and strategies for the struggle for national independence and rights; that there was no racial prejudice in Soviet society; that international affairs and colonialism were best understood through a communist lens.[42] At the same time, the journal contains an unprecedented wealth of information on contemporary politics in Africa, with contributions not only from the redoubtable Padmore himself and from Kouyaté, but also from correspondents in East Africa (Jomo Kenyatta), South Africa (Nzula), and West Africa (Small and I. T. A. Wallace-Johnson) reporting on local scenes. C. L. R. James has made the most forceful argument for the journal's significance, claiming that "tens of thousands of black workers in various parts of the world received their first political education" from the *Negro Worker*. According to James,

> [i]t gave information, advice, guidance, ideas about black struggles on every continent. All movements need an ideology, a body of ideas and information to which effort can be related and which has significance beyond that which is immediately visible. This *The Negro Worker* gave to hundreds of thousands of active blacks; and while the educated in Trinidad, for example, were sunk in the acceptance of ideas inculcated through British imperialism, Uriah Butler and the workers of the oil-fields were nourishing themselves on illicit copies of Padmore's paper and preparing for the outburst which was to launch the West Indies on the paths of nationalism and democracy. It developed too, the consciousness among blacks that they were part of an international movement.[43]

Perhaps the most convincing proof of its significance is the extraordinary lengths taken by both British and French colonial authorities to squelch the paper's circulation in Africa. As Wilson concedes, "beyond its immediate utility to the Comintern as an instrument for spreading propaganda and revolutionary advice, *The Negro Worker* provided one of the first channels for political communication" and "cross-pollination" among Africans.[44]

Kouyaté was given special responsibility in the ITUC-NW for organizing black port workers and sailors in the International of Seamen and Harbor Workers that was established in 1931, and he regularly covered this activity in articles for the *Negro Worker.*[45] That summer, Kouyaté was arrested and jailed for a few weeks after he led a protest of African sailors along the Canebière in Marseilles.[46] On his release, he worked with Padmore to organize the Conference of the International of Seamen and Harbor Workers in Hamburg that took place in May 1932, drawing a large audience from around the world and featuring a visit from Ada Wright, the mother of two of the African American teenagers falsely accused of rape in Scottsboro, Alabama. Kouyaté was in charge of the entire French delegation and presented the "colonial report" at the conference.[47]

Starting in 1930, Padmore also wrote for *La Race nègre,* and the French journal began to reflect his editorial influence and Anglophone connections.[48] But the Ligue de Défense de la Race Nègre was torn apart by dissension that autumn, when the group's other primary leader, the Senegalese engineer Emile Faure, grew increasingly impatient with Kouyaté's extended absences and loose managerial style. Throughout 1930, the LDRN was also destabilized by a series of articles by a Parisian editor named François Coty, a reactionary who ran a far-right newspaper called *L'Ami du Peuple.* Written in a tone of apocalyptic breathlessness, Coty's articles (under the title "Contre le communisme") relied on information gathered by the spies of the French Ministère des Colonies—including the names and home addresses of a number of black students and militants—to charge that all the groups of Africans and Antilleans in Paris (including not only the political pressure groups, but also the moderate student and cultural groups) were "taking orders" directly from the Communist International.[49] Coty's vitriol caused confusion and squabbling in the LDRN, where members began to suspect each other of being the infiltrators who had provided the information to the colonial administration. In this climate, the "personal conflict between Kouyaté (pre-eminently an organizer—impatient, pragmatic, and at best rather careless in money matters) and Faure (deliberate, more scru-

Masthead of the *Negro Worker* 1, no. 6 (June 1931).

pulous and more pre-occupied with consistency in the initiatives and thinking of the Ligue)" was incendiary, and the Ligue fractured.[50]

With the Ligue in disarray, *La Race nègre* fell silent after its November–December 1930 issue. The next April, there appeared competing versions of the newspaper, one printed by Faure's faction and another printed by Kouyaté's. By the middle of 1931, Kouyaté and a group of committed black Communists founded the Union des Travailleurs Nègres (UTN). The new group's organ, *Le Cri des Nègres,* opened publication with an illustration on its masthead similar to the image adopted a few months earlier for the *Negro Worker:* a bare-chested black worker "breaking the chains of enslavement that bind the Negro masses in the main Negro centers of the world—United States, West Indies and Africa."[51] The single worker symbolizes the "power and strength that lies in the organization of the great masses of Negro toilers," but is at the same time an articulation of diaspora,

Masthead of *Le Cri des Nègres* 3 (October 1931). Centre des Archives d'Outre-Mer, Aix-en-Provence, Archives Nationales, France. SLOTFOM V, Box 23.

a great revolutionary body straddling the Atlantic. (Kouyaté's paper emphasizes this point by revising the image: whereas on the *Negro Worker* cover, the figure simply reaches across the United States, Cuba, Haiti, and Africa, in *Le Cri* the worker stands with one foot on the United States—identified only by its Caribbean appendix: "Floride"—and one foot on Africa, while a bright star rises behind him in the Soviet East.) *Le Cri des Nègres* was much more frankly Communist than *La Race nègre,* although the paper continued to feature articles on African American life in the United States and found space for "cultural" questions, particularly in a flood of articles condemning the Paris International Colonial Exposition, the ostentatious celebration of worldwide colonialism (featuring life-size replicas of West African villages, North African mosques, and even Angkor Wat), which attracted tens of thousands of visitors to the Bois de Vincennes in the summer of 1931.[52] Kouyaté also kept up his ties with a remarkable number of African contacts and with Padmore, who contributed to the new journal.[53]

Black Collaboration, Black Deviation

How should one consider the exceptional activity of this period, as Kouyaté and especially Padmore were increasingly ensconced in communist institutions, increasingly committed to the Comintern's effort to theorize and organize a revolutionary black proletariat in the port cities of Europe and in Africa itself? A number of scholars tend to characterize Padmore's position as ultimately ineffectual, a kind of sideshow in the midst of the temporary diversion when Moscow deigned to throw its energies toward revolution in the African colonies. When the ITUC-NW was established, Padmore was given an office in the Kremlin and the privileges of a high member of the

Comintern bureaucracy. But to what extent was his position itself a facade, directed at an entirely different audience? According to Edward Wilson, "the elevated status he was accorded in the Kremlin was itself a propaganda device" geared to demonstrate the Soviet Union's "benevolent treatment of Negroes," in contradistinction to capitalist racism in the West. This involved a certain kind of staging: "when the occasion arose for May Day parades in Red Square, he was duly displayed on the sacrosanct balcony of the Lenin Mausoleum—a black figure of the Soviet socialist utopia."[54] C. L. R. James recalled later that Padmore told him about the spectacular fiction of his "election" to the Moscow Soviet during this period. A Party functionary had pressed him to run, and although Padmore argued that he didn't know anything about Moscow politics or even speak Russian, he finally relented. He was duly elected along with Stalin and Kaganovich, but was never given any responsibilities and promptly forgot about the matter. Its utility became apparent only some time later, when a group of "distinguished" British figures (including George Bernard Shaw) visited Russia. The same Party functionary made a point of introducing the visitors to Padmore, noting that he was a member of the Soviet and adding, "Now look at you all. You have the British empire there for so many years. You never had a Negro as a Member of Parliament. Look at us. He is not even a Russian. He is a member of the Moscow Soviet. You see the difference between our system and yours." The visiting group was visibly impressed, staring at Padmore in silence. It was the last he ever heard of his membership on the Soviet.[55]

Kouyaté was in a somewhat different situation, given access through the ITUC-NW to high circles in the Profintern, but wrestling mainly with the French Communist Party and the lumbering, veiled racism of its organizing efforts in France. In a different sense, though, he found himself in something like Padmore's position. Kouyaté lived during this time at 43 rue des Ecoles in the Fifth Arrondissement of Paris, and like many of his colleagues in the Ligue, he survived by passing through a series of temporary jobs. He worked in the 1920s in the accounting department at the Hachette department store, but he also regularly found part-time work as a *figurant* (an extra or walk-on in music theater productions) at the Casino de Paris.[56] It is not difficult to imagine precisely the kind of humiliating spear-shaking stereotypes he would have been asked to embody in the theater. In this sense Padmore and Kouyaté, both striving tirelessly to radicalize black labor, found themselves on different versions of the same European stage of racialized spectacle.

But is this characterization accurate? Is it possible to make the more nuanced argument that the institutions of international communism actually proved enabling to both Padmore and Kouyaté? Certainly, the two militants were brought together in the corridors of the Comintern. But more broadly, one might argue that especially Padmore was able to find political leverage, even in the moments when his position appeared to have more to do with spectacle than with policy. As with *La Race nègre* in 1930, the French Communist Party strove in 1933 to ensure that their funding of *Le Cri des Nègres* would mean complete Party control over its contents. What is remarkable is that in both cases an alliance developed between Padmore and Kouyaté in which the latter would go over the heads of the French Party, turning directly to Padmore at the Comintern for financial assistance. In 1931, for instance, Padmore responded with a stern letter regarding *La Race nègre,* reminding the French Party of the need to prioritize any channels to organizing the black dock workers in crucial port cities such as Marseilles and Bordeaux:

> There is no need to stress the importance of work among the *Nègres* and your obligations concerning the application of the colonial resolution of the Fifth Congress. . . . We must consider our central task to be the integration of the *nègre* dockers and sailors of French ports (Marseilles, Bordeaux, Le Havre) into revolutionary unions.
>
> To this end, we suggest that you use the services of comrade Kouyaté as broadly as possible. . . . However, this is not to say that the comrade should be placed under the general control of the Colonial Commission of the CGTU. . . . Previously, one of the great difficulties you encountered in this union work among the *Nègres* was the absence of a special propaganda organ. The newspaper *La Race Nègre* did not sufficiently reflect the economic situation of the Negro workers [*travailleurs noirs*] in France and in the Colonies. In view of remedying this state of affairs, we have decided to assist comrade Kouyaté in the regular publication of this journal in conformity with the resolution.[57]

On at least one other occasion when the French Communist Party proved troublesome, in October 1932, Kouyaté received funds for *Le Cri des Nègres* directly from Padmore.[58]

In this extraordinary arrangement, a transnational alliance between two black militants "cries" through the Comintern—speaks the language of international communism—in order to trump the limitations of a particular national communist party. The structures of authority of international communism are used as a lever to influence and reshape national communism in the context of the French Empire. There are at least two versions of black internationalism here. The Padmore-Kouyaté collaboration is on the one hand a function of the Comintern policy envisioning an "international trade union" approach to black labor. But their circumventing of the French national party points toward another internationalism as well, one not wholly subsumed in a Comintern agenda, one that emphasizes race-based organizing and anticolonial alliances among differently positioned revolutionaries of African descent.

Another way to make this point is to note that it is precisely the discourse of the Communist International that opens the possibility of a Black International—even if the Comintern insists that race-specific movements are ultimately antithetical to (and even a threat to) worldwide proletarian revolution. As Philippe de Witte has suggested, even to discuss the "Negro question," the term of choice in the Comintern, is to theorize a black internationalism. Moscow "itself legitimizes the idea of a worldwide black identity [*identité nègre*]" in founding a "Negro Worker" division, because that institution frames the issue precisely as universally "Negro"—implying that black labor raises a set of concerns that are unique and consistent internationally and then formulating an approach to those concerns through race, above and beyond particular national contexts.[59] Working in and against the French Party, Kouyaté came to consider "the Third International as not only a natural ally, but as in itself a *means* toward international Negro unity, a Negro International *through* the Worker's International."[60] If we are to believe C. L. R. James, Padmore comes to arrive at such a pragmatic position as well: "But nevertheless [Padmore] called them 'those people' and it became clear to me afterwards . . . that he had never been completely swept away by the Stalinist conception of Marxism. He said: 'I lived there; I saw what was going on. . . . I stayed there because there was a means of doing work for the black emancipation and there was no other place that I could think of.'"[61] It should be underlined that the "means toward" a Black International is primarily a trio of periodical publications: the *Negro Worker, La Race nègre,* and *Le Cri des Nègres.* Print culture is the ground of the collaboration because these periodicals are the ground of a nascent discourse of black internationalism—spaces of independent thinking, alternative modes of expression and dissemination, articulating transnational groupings of black intellectuals into collectives and conversations.

The collaboration ran into an unexpected problem in 1933. Not surprisingly, when the French Party again withheld funds for *Le Cri des Nègres* after the January–February 1933 issue, Kouyaté tried to approach Padmore once more.[62] But at the beginning of the year, Nazi terror had descended on Hamburg, where Padmore was editing the *Negro Worker.* In its April issue (printed exceptionally in Copenhagen), the *Negro Worker* announced that Padmore had been "dragged from his bed by Nazi police and imprisoned for about two weeks, during which time the Nazi[s] raided the offices of the Negro workers' Union and destroyed all their property."[63] Padmore was deported from Germany on his British passport. Although he traveled a great deal over the following months, after July 1933 his main base of operations was established in Paris, where he lived with Kouyaté and with another UTN member, the Haitian Camille Saint-Jacques. But until midsummer, Padmore was largely out of contact and unable to intervene in Kouyaté's dispute with the French Party. This time the Party started internal proceedings to remove *Le Cri des Nègres* from Kouyaté's control and prevented him from publishing it independently.

By April 1933, Kouyaté had lost all hope of prevailing in the proceedings against him. In the face of defeat and what he considered betrayal at the hands of the Party's colonial section, he turned again to concentrate on race-based work. On June 22, at the restaurant of La Samaritaine on the Right Bank of Paris, he convened a planning meeting for an old dream of his: to found a West African student *foyer* in Paris, a "Maison des Nègres"—envisioned as something akin to the hostel established by the West African Students' Union and the League of Coloured Peoples in England.[64] The meeting attracted a fascinating collection of young scholars who would be active in the 1935 journal *L'Etudiant noir* and later in the Négritude movement: Léonard Sainville of the Association des Etudiants Guadeloupeans, a student named Megrone of Association des Etudiants Martiniquais, and—most intriguingly—an aspiring poet named Léopold

Sédar Senghor, the leader of the Association des Etudiants Ouest-Africains.[65]

It was not the first time Kouyaté had pursued ties with the moderate and student elements of African and Caribbean society in Paris: the LDRN had attempted to form a "student section" in the late 1920s, and a number of the young Africans and Antilleans in the metropole in the next decade, including Senghor, Aimé Césaire, René Ménil, and Bernard Dadié, would later recall the influence of Kouyaté and especially *Le Cri des Nègres*.[66] Aside from his ties to Léo Sajous of *La Revue du monde noir*, Kouyaté was reported to be in "close contact" *(relations étroites)* with Etienne Léro, the young poet and editor of *Légitime Défense*, whose ideas the colonial authorities considered "revolutionary and anti-French."[67] According to one surveillance report, Kouyaté told Sainville, Megrone, and Senghor that the UTN's goals were "material, moral, and cultural assistance" and that he wanted to create a sanctuary *(une maison de refuge)* for *nègres* in Paris, as well as a library and a university. The students asked how they would raise money for the project—and indeed, how the UTN funded *Le Cri des Nègres*—and Kouyaté explained evasively that the group asked for help from individuals who were "favorable to Negro causes."[68]

The students wanted time to consider an alliance, which of course would have been a remarkable ideological stretch. None of the groups was particularly critical of the French Empire—for instance, when Léopold Senghor wrote an article about the Association des Etudiants Ouest-Africains a year later in the student journal *L'Etudiant martiniquais*, he specified that its "precise cultural goal" was a "common ideal" born out of the "agreement [*accord*] between [its members'] indigenous civilizations and the demands of the modern world." It could be summed up, Senghor wrote, with a "slogan": "assimiler la culture européenne en restant près de son peuple" ("assimilate European culture while remaining close to one's people"). According to Senghor, this slogan was in no way "anti-European" or "anti-French," even though the "riches of French culture" were above all an inspiration to develop "a critical spirit and originality, rather than mechanized and bleached [*oxygénée*] imitation."[69] Still, at least Senghor kept up his ties with the UTN even after Kouyaté's departure and went on to publish a modest announcement about his association in *Le Cri des Nègres* more than a year later, in August 1934.[70] But the initial meeting between Kouyaté and the students led nowhere. A follow-up was scheduled with the students for July 8, but it never came about: on July 3, the Control Commission of the French Communist Party suspended Kouyaté from his duties in the UTN and demanded he appear to explain his activities.

When Padmore, released from jail in Germany, arrived in Paris in the middle of the summer and met with members of the UTN (Kouyaté, of course, not among them), he was shocked to learn that *Le Cri des Nègres* had not been appearing. Padmore had been planning to send facsimiles of the most recent *Negro Worker* bundled with copies of *Le Cri des Nègres* out to contacts in the colonies. According to the French surveillance files, he said, "It's the first time that I've seen a Negro [Communist Party] section holding everything in hand, and yet doing nothing."[71]

Kouyaté's official expulsion from the Party was not published in *L'Humanité* until October 1933. It was reprinted in the *Negro Worker* (by then no longer under Padmore's editorship), which announced his expulsion from the ITUC-NW and from the editorial board of the paper. The statement provides four "reasons" for the "exclusion," all quite vague:

1. Kouyaté deceived the revolutionary movement, he never wanted to give an account of the administration in the responsible posts that were entrusted to him.
2. He tempted [*sic*] to disrupt the organization of the Union of Negro Workers.
3. He entertains connections with expelled members and enemies of the revolutionary Trade Union Movement.
4. Called twice to explain his actions he did not respond.[72]

In *Le Cri des Nègres,* the list was slightly different: an article a few weeks later charged that Kouyaté refused to hand over the UTN's accounting books; that he refused to discuss the conflict, except to say that he "had decided to resign"; that his "attitude" toward the Union was "plainly hostile"; and that he "entertains relations with suspect elements, the same elements who provoked the scission in the old Ligue de Défense de la Race Nègre."[73] A follow-up article added the complaint that Kouyaté never turned over the membership cards, subscription lists, and official seal of the Union.[74] The charge that Kouyaté "entertains connections with expelled members and enemies" of the movement is the most interesting in terms of Kouyaté's later activities. The "suspect elements" may be an allusion to the students in the June meeting, as well as to the wide range of figures that Kouyaté began to contact in September as he began to plan the Negro World Unity Congress, including former adversaries such as René Maran, Maurice Satineau (the publisher of *La Dépêche africaine*), and even Emile Faure.

One of the most peculiar and persistent rumors concerning this period, apparently originating in James Hooker's biography of Padmore, is that Kouyaté was expelled from the Communist Party for some form of "embezzlement."[75] There were numerous accusations on both sides of the Union des Travailleurs Nègres conflict, but the only ones that come close to this rumor are Emile Faure's assertion that Kouyaté was "wasteful" in the use of funds at his discretion and that he did not have the "elementary delicacy" of returning the books and membership lists of the UTN after his expulsion. Nevertheless, as reflected in the expulsion notices, embezzlement was never charged. As Spiegler has pointed out, Hooker's patronizing professions of incomprehension about the friendship between the two men ("Padmore's attachment to the man remains unexplained, for Padmore was scrupulous about money matters and thoroughly law-abiding") originates with this error.[76]

In the middle of August 1933, just as Kouyaté was being expelled from the UTN and the Party, Padmore apparently learned of a drastic about-face in Comintern policy: the ITUC-NW would be abandoned, and the International's long-standing efforts in the African colonies would be relinquished in a strategic decision to concentrate on events in Europe. The Soviets had decided to align themselves with the so-called democratic imperialist countries against fascism, even if it meant ignoring the abuses of European colonialism. Padmore immediately resigned from the International. He would later discuss his decision in some detail. In one essay published a few years later, he writes that the Comintern

> was called upon . . . to put a brake upon the anti-imperialist work of its affiliate sections and thereby sacrifice the young national liberation movements in Asia and Africa. This I considered to be a betrayal of the fundamental interests of my people, with which I could not identify myself. I therefore had no choice but to sever my connection with the Communist International. I formulated my position quite clearly in a political statement which I submitted to the Comintern Executive, and which was subsequently published by the Negro Press, so that my case would be put before my own people.[77]

In any case, he all but announced his resignation publicly in an editorial—written in Paris and called "Au Revoir"—in the August–September issue of the *Negro Worker,* which indeed ceased publication for almost a year.[78] There, Padmore says nothing about policy debates or personal dissatisfaction and offers the vague explanation that the paper is having a "difficult time in trying to make ends meet," even finding itself "faced with bankruptcy." Nevertheless, when the *Negro Worker* was finally revived under new direction in May 1934, the Communist International kept up the usual tradition of announcing expulsions by publishing the "Expulsion of George Padmore from the Revolutionary Movement" (in a note dated February 23, 1934).[79] The newspaper published a series of denunciations of Padmore as a "betrayer of the Negro struggle," reserving special disdain for the "dim prospects" of "his proposed 'Negro Congress.'"[80] Likewise *Le Cri des Nègres* called Kouyaté an individual with *grands appétits,* willing to taint himself with "fat bourgeois *nègres*" as he "nourished the speculative dream of organizing" a "Congrès Mondial Nègre."[81] Of course, if Padmore indeed stepped down as early as August 1933, then the charge that Kouyaté "entertains connections with expelled members and enemies" may refer to the collaboration between the two and their first efforts to plan the congress.

The crisis between Kouyaté and the Union des Travailleurs Nègres culminated in November 1933, when he scheduled a meeting of the planning committee for the "Congrès Mondial Nègre" (Negro World Unity Congress) on the same day and hour as the UTN meeting at which he was supposed to explain his conduct. Kouyaté was reluctant to meet the hard-liners, but he sent the UTN an effusive letter on November 4.[82] Fiercely assertive and at the same time almost anguished in tone, it is a vivid articulation of Kouyaté's position at the time and, as such, is worth quoting at some length:

> J'espère que les diviseurs de nègres, instruments de blancs qui tiennent les ficelles dans les coulisses politiques parleront avec mesure, impartialité et loyauté. Ils doivent se rappeler qu'il n'est pas aisé de salir un militant qui en quinze ans de lutte à la direction des nègres pour la libération de notre race [*sic*]. On doit vous dire pourquoi je ne veux plus militer dans l'Union ce qu'est devenu le Cri des Nègres. . . . On a transféré dans notre association mon conflit avec le Parti communiste français au mépris de tout intérêt du mouvement nègre.

I hope that the dividers of blacks, instruments of the white men who hold the political purse strings, will speak with restraint, impartiality, and loyalty. They should remember that it is not easy to tarnish a militant who has fought for fifteen years to lead blacks in the liberation of our race. They should tell you why I no longer want to be a militant in this Union that *Le Cri des Nègres* has become. . . . They have transferred into our association my conflict with the French Communist Party, disregarding the interests of the black movement.

For Kouyaté, the issue is not the Negro World Unity Congress, but his earlier personal power squabbles with the French Communist Party, now being used as an excuse to undermine the work of the UTN.

Ma réponse paraîtra dans un livre "Je demande la parole" afin de me donner une audience mondiale nègre. On y trouvera des documents, chiffres, photos, fac-similés etc. . . . mettant à nu les graves maladies qui rongent le mouvement nègre. On y verra défiler des figures plus ou moins étranges, plus ou moins hypocrites, ou sincères, comment notre mouvement est freiné, saboté, désagrégé sous le couvert des grandes phrases de solidarité de races, de travailleurs, comment la provocation policière et la délation sont organisées, comment on élimine les meilleurs d'entre nous, pour mieux opprimer les autres avec l'inévitable mentalité impérialiste. Le problème maladroitement soulevé à l'occasion de mon cas dépasse les cadres français. Ce sont les mêmes maux en Angleterre, Afrique du Sud, États-Unis, partout la même attitude de domination du dernier des blancs envers le nègre. Il se trouve malheureusement que ces blancs découvrent des instruments dévoués et serviles comme l'esclave parmi les éléments de notre race. Les impérialistes eux-mêmes n'ont pas d'autre doctrine séculaire: diviser pour régner, éliminer les résistants pour avili[r] les autres dans la soumission honteuse et l'humiliation de race ou de peuple. Or, les traditions nationales et familiales de la grande Afrique m'ont inculqué l'amour inné de la liberté dans la discipline[,] une indépendance de caractère et une fierté de race que j'aime à chérir et à conserver, sinon je ne serais plus Africain.

My response will appear in a book called "I Demand the Floor" in order to reach a worldwide Negro audience. In it there will be documents, figures, photos, reproductions, etc. . . . bringing to light the grave maladies that are gnawing at the black movement. One will see a parade of figures, more or less strange, more or less hypocritical, or sincere; how our movement is halted, sabotaged, divided under the cover of grand phrases of racial solidarity, worker solidarity; how police provocation and denouncement are organized; how the best among us are eliminated, so as to better oppress the others with the inevitable imperialist mentality. The problem awkwardly raised by my own case goes beyond the French frame. There are the same wrongs in England, South Africa, the United States, everywhere the same attitude of domination of every last white man with regard to the black. Unfortunately, it so happens that the whites discover instruments among our race who are devoted and servile like slaves. The imperialists themselves have no other secular doctrine: divide and conquer, eliminate those who resist, in order to degrade the others in shameful submission and in the humiliation of a race or a people. But the national and familial traditions of great Africa have inculcated in me an innate love of freedom in discipline, an independence of character, and a racial pride that I would like to cherish and preserve—otherwise I would no longer be African.

In announcing his "true" audience to be a worldwide black one, Kouyaté prefigures Padmore's explanation of his own resignation, in which he claims that the African American press is a "medium" that makes it possible to bring "the real facts of the situation" to his "own people." Padmore proclaims similarly that even if the Comintern would not dare to give him a hearing, "I intend nonetheless to take my day in court. The Negroes of America, of Africa, of the West Indies, of the world, will be my judges. They will know who are the liars."[83] In one of the articles Padmore published in the *Amsterdam News,* he complains that "the international Negro work is being sacrificed at a time when we cannot afford to weaken the Negro liberation struggles, especially in the black colonies where there are no Communist parties."[84] Here the shift in priorities is explicit: African independence movements, and more broadly "the international Negro work," deserve support whether or not communism takes root in Africa—indeed, the "liberation struggles" need immediate assistance "especially" in those colonies where there are no communist parties.

Kouyaté's proposed exposé is envisioned not as an autobiographical document but as a larger project, a kind of counterhistory of the encounter of the black radical intelligentsia with the globe-straddling and ultimately restrictive discourse of international Communism. (In this light, one might read Padmore's 1956 book *Pan-Africanism or Communism?* in part as something like his own belated version of Kouyaté's project for "Je demande la parole.") Kouyaté rejects the divide-and-conquer mentality that he considers common among imperialists and Communists alike, writing defiantly in his letter to the UTN that it is precisely the "friends" who speak against his transnational black connections and his work for African liberation who are the ultimate betrayers:

> Un dicton vous enseigne que nul n'est plus dangereux qu'un ami qui déclare nous aimer mieux que nous-mêmes, et il nous embrasse pour nous étrangler et nous donner le baiser de Judas. Rien ne m'empêchera de procéder au travail urgent de redressement nègre avec l'appui des dirigeants et masses nègres du monde entier surtout et principalement de la grande Afrique dont la libération par les Africains eux-mêmes conditionnent [*sic*] l'émancipation de notre race et la pratique vraie de l'égalité des races.

> There is a saying that teaches that nothing is more dangerous than a friend who claims to love us better than ourselves, and embraces us to strangle us and give us the Judas kiss. Nothing prevents me from proceeding with the urgent work of black retribution with the support of black leaders and masses worldwide, especially and principally in great Africa, whose liberation by the Africans themselves is a condition of the emancipation of our race and the true practice of the equality of the races.

At this point, Kouyaté seems much more willing than Padmore to speak in racial terms, going so far as to uphold the necessity of what he calls "racisme nègre." In one fascinating passage, he comments on his own upbringing and on the metropolitan black intellectual's responsibilities to "home":

> Je concéderais peut-être que ma tendance soit imprégnée de racisme nègre dû à l'éducation familiale, si exalter [*sic*] les possibilités de développement, encourager ses capacités d'expansion sans haïr au-

cune autre race, créer une psychose de confiance illimitée en elle-même, afin de lui permettre un réveil national salutaire pour briser les chaînes d'esclavage, son corset séculaire, à ce racisme nègre là, j'aurais adhéré avec enthousiasme puisque beaucoup de dirigeants révolutionnaires blancs ont toujours l'esprit farci de la prétendue supériorité de leur race. Ils ont raison quand on bénéficie de la domination impérialiste de son pays, on "contribue" à sa consolidation sous une forme que la masse ignore.

I would perhaps concede that my tendency is impregnated with black racism, due to familial education, if [such racism means] to celebrate possibilities of development, to encourage capacities of expansion without hating any other race, to create a psychosis of unlimited confidence, in order to permit a salutary national awakening, to break the chains of slavery and the corset of secularity. To that black racism, I would adhere with enthusiasm, because so many white revolutionary leaders have always had their minds stuffed with the pretended superiority of their race. They are right: when one profits from the imperialist domination of one's country, one "contributes" to the consolidation of that domination, in a form of which the masses remain unaware.

Especially striking in this formulation is Kouyaté's espousal of a *racisme nègre* that would mean creating a "psychosis of unlimited confidence" culminating in nationalism. In clinical psychiatry, the term "psychosis" fluctuated in application in the early part of the twentieth century and was used in reference to a whole range of mental illnesses. But it is nonetheless intriguing that Kouyaté suggests that racism be understood as a kind of illness in the human psyche that is "salutary" when it leads to "national awakening." Decades later, Frantz Fanon would analyze examples of what he termed "reactionary psychoses" engendered in the Algerian "native" by the violence of colonialism, but in general Fanon's idiosyncratic vocabulary (drawn both from clinical psychiatry and from an unsystematic reading in psychoanalysis) describes the "colonial situation" primarily as one of *neurosis* in the "native," not psychosis.[85] In this informal, impassioned passage, Kouyaté flirts with an argument that anticolonialism necessitates—"celebrates"—a kind of deliberate derangement, a madness of "pretended superiority" in the fight for independence and "expansion." Although Fanon does not use the clinical term, Kouyaté's application of "psychosis" here is somewhat anticipatory of the argument in Fanon's *Les Damnés de la terre* that the "native intellectual," in rejecting the old claim of colonialism that there was no culture in Africa, must "break away" *(s'arracher)* from Europe in an "ardent, despairing return to anything." This breaking away often ends up as a boundless exaltation of "race" and "unknown roots" *(racines ignorés),* precisely a kind of "unlimited confidence" that permits a nationalism to emerge.[86]

If the fall of 1933 had seen a flurry of collaboration and coincidences, February 1934 was a cataclysm. There were violent demonstrations in the streets of Paris: on February 6, a revolt of French fascist mobs "tried to fight their way from the Place de la Concorde across the Seine bridge to the Chambre des Députés" and were met in the streets by leftist and labor groups throughout the city—with the Parisian police protecting the fascists and shooting at counterdemonstrators.[87] The battles culminated in a general strike on February 9. Many of the radical black French intellectuals participated. One Senegalese member of the Ligue de Défense de la Race Nègre, Aldolphe Mathurin (a cousin of Alioune Diop, the founder of *Présence africaine* after World War II), would later recall that "the parties of the Left had appealed to us to come out on the streets. . . . On Feb. 6th and afterwards we were there, along with Communists, Socialists and Radicals against the supporters of [François] Coty and the Croix de Feu, who carried poles set with razor blades, and used to single us out."[88] Mathurin added that in the street battles, they had "a score to settle" in particular with Coty, whose inflammatory articles had been an important factor in the split in the LDRN in 1930.

The next two weeks saw a tumult of activity. On February 15, 1934, Nancy Cunard, the feisty English shipping heiress—a friend of both Padmore and Kouyaté—finally published her monumental collection *Negro: An Anthology* after years of work. On February 17, Padmore composed his aforementioned letter to W. E. B. Du Bois, on stationery Kouyaté still had from the Union des Travailleurs Nègres. And on February 23, the Control Commission of the Comintern finally published Padmore's "official" expulsion from the Party that he had quit six months before. Just as the French Communist Party appeared to use Padmore as an excuse to exclude Kouyaté, the Communist International used Kouyaté as an excuse to oust Padmore:

Padmore, a member of the Communist Party, despite repeated warnings did not break off his connections with the exposed provocateur Kouyaté and lived in the apartment of the provocateur [Camille Saint] Jacques. In order to deceive the Party organs, Padmore repeatedly stated that he had already broken with Jacques. . . .

Padmore carried on work which undermined the class unity of the toiling Negro masses, and under the pretense of advocating the necessity for the unity of all Negroes on a racial basis, he tried to lay the path for unity with the Negro bourgeois exploiters and with their agents, the national-reformists.[89]

After the whirlwind of early 1934, the Negro World Unity Congress effort crumbled. There was a meeting at Kouyaté's home on February 2, and Padmore agreed to try to raise money to print up copies of a subscription notice for the Congress, but apparently was not able to do so.[90] (One assumes that it was at least partly with such a task in mind that Padmore wrote to ask Du Bois for assistance two weeks later.) Kouyaté fell seriously ill during the spring of 1934 and spent an extended period in the hospital.[91] Padmore, for his part, turned to other work, sending his "Open Letter" to contacts in the Negro press in the United States and working on a book that was published two years later as *How Britain Rules Africa*. In June 1934 Padmore was staying with Nancy Cunard in her home in Normandy, where Cunard said that he "spent all the day and half the night writing . . . and most of the hours of the day I typed for him, from his rather difficult handwriting. . . . His capacity for sheer, lengthy hard work was very great, and his knowledge seemed to me immense."[92] It is unclear how much contact there was between Padmore and Kouyaté during the remainder of 1934, and Padmore left for England early the next year, even though his bylines in the press in England and the United States reported that he was living in Paris as late as May 1935.[93] C. L. R. James recalls that "George came to London to live some time in the spring or summer of 1935."[94]

Although it is commonly assumed that Padmore and Kouyaté were no longer in touch after the middle of the decade, there is a wealth of evidence to the contrary.[95] As we shall see, Kouyaté was quite active in the organizations and pressure groups that sprung up in Paris during the crisis around Italy's invasion of Ethiopia in 1935, and it seems likely that the two kept in contact around that effort, since James's International African Friends of

Ethiopia in London was linked to sibling groups in Paris such as the Comité de Défense d'Ethiopie.[96] Describing the London organization, Makonnen names Kouyaté among the group's "closest associates in the pan-African movement."[97] Padmore and Kouyaté were definitely in touch during the second half of the decade. When the African American intellectual Ralph Bunche visited Paris in the summer of 1937, Padmore sent him Kouyaté's address on rue Cité de Paradis in the Tenth Arrondissement and wrote, "Do look him up. I shall soon be writing to him."[98] Likewise, Padmore was adamant that C. L. R. James meet Kouyaté while James was researching *The Black Jacobins* in the Bibliothèque Nationale in Paris, probably in 1936.[99] James comments that "George kept up that acquaintance with Kouyaté although Kouyaté remained in the CP and George had left and would have nothing to do with them."[100] Evidently James was unaware of the history of Kouyaté's own break, but the statement remains important for the purposes of chronology. In a later interview, James recounted an exchange with Kouyaté that had amused him: "I knew one man who was very friendly with Padmore—that was Garan Kouyaté. When I went to Paris, Padmore insisted I see him. I discussed the Trotskyist movement with him and he commented that he could agree with me about everything except that one thing would be needed. I asked what that was. 'That Trotsky was a black man, that's all.'"[101]

Black Marxism in Translation

The files of the French National Archives hold a smattering of materials relevant to the plans for the Congrès Mondial Nègre (Negro World Unity Congress): surveillance reports, minutes from the meetings, the organization's statutes, and a call for participation written in French by Kouyaté and translated and expanded in English by Padmore. Generally the Italo-Ethiopian crisis is considered to represent the first impetus toward worldwide networks of black organizations, laying the ground for what J. S. Spiegler calls a "Negro Popular Front" and for the Fifth Pan-African Congress in 1945.[102] I will suggest that the Negro World Unity Congress, as proposed by Padmore and Kouyaté for 1935, represents an earlier effort to think in such international terms, extending the impulses of Du Bois's Pan-Africanism and Garvey's Back-to-Africa movement in the 1920s. As we have seen, calls for a Black International were not uncommon even earlier: Kouyaté himself, writing to American Civil Liberties Union lawyer Roger

Baldwin in the spring of 1929, had insisted on the necessity for an international approach to the "Negro question":

> The black leaders [*leaders nègres*] in the United States are mistaken not to comprehend the necessity of broad mutual support within the race. The world situation of blacks [*situation mondiale des nègres*] is such that no action can lead anywhere if its results are only partial and momentary, responding to the needs of only a small group of blacks—in a word, satisfactions without future and without extension, rock of Sisyphus.[103]

Such an approach is carried to its logical extreme in the Congrès Mondial Nègre effort in the fall of 1933. After assembling his contacts in Paris, Kouyaté convened a meeting in early December to design and ratify some initial organizational decisions about the shape the Congress would assume.

The Congress was to be held in July 1935 in Paris, London, or Geneva, depending on the political circumstances in Europe at the time, "particular reasons not permitting the Congress to meet in Ethiopia, in Liberia, or in another Negro country, in spite of the Assembly's desire." The broad goal of the Congress was summarized as follows:

> Le Congrès mondial aura pour but de faire le bilan de la situation morale, économique, intellectuelle, sociale et politique de la race nègre, de réaliser son unité, de lui créer une charte et de constituer une organisation universelle destinée à diriger à l'avenir le mouvement nègre de tous pays.

> The world Congress will have as its goal to take stock of the moral, economic, intellectual, social and political situation of the Negro race, to unify it, to create a charter for it, and to establish a universal organization destined to direct the future of the Negro movement in all countries.

The members of the planning committee included a striking and politically diverse collection of the black intellectual luminaries on the Paris scene at the time: Kouyaté, Padmore, André Beton, Camille Saint-Jacques, Emile Faure, René Maran, Joseph Ebele, Jules Alcandre, Ibrahim Sow, Rita Diallo, and even one member from Cuba, Medina Perez, and one from

Portugal, Joan Segure. (Documentation from the Congress and a permanent journal that was to emerge out of the event, titled *Le Monde nègre*—in a deliberate evocation of Garvey's *Negro World?*—were to be translated into Spanish and Portuguese.) The committee was divided into the following sections: politics and propaganda; workers and peasants; economics and financial; press and news; cultural and artistic; women and children *(section féminine et de l'enfance);* and ethnology and sociology. National committees were to be established worldwide, both in colonies and in independent states. The documentation shows an especial interest in reaching South America and also a particular concern with the three historically independent black nations: Haiti, Ethiopia, and Liberia.[104]

The "Manifesto" is the most significant surviving document available. It is undated, but apparently was written some time around December 1933.[105] It is, in effect, two documents: a typescript of Kouyaté's original draft, and a translation into English, which Padmore extensively revised and expanded. In his portrait of Padmore, C. L. R. James noted that "despite his wide contacts" Padmore knew "no foreign languages," and so his interaction with Kouyaté would have involved constant cobbled interpretation of the latter's makeshift English as much as Padmore's poor French.[106] One surveillance report from the fall of 1932 records that Padmore arrived at a UTN meeting with a translator *(un nègre interprète)* from Sierra Leone named Touret; at another meeting in Paris the next year, he arrived with a female translator named Jeanne who apparently was employed by the French Communist Party.[107] Nothing more is recorded about these figures, but they indicate the degree to which the friendship and collaboration between Padmore and Kouyaté was a confrontation with linguistic difference, a conversation across boundaries that made their interaction a continual series of revisions and re-accentuations. Whatever the particular process with the "Manifesto," the result is that the draft in English is not simply a translation of the draft in French. From the beginning, Padmore's version rewrites and rethinks Kouyaté's, talks back to it, edits it, and repositions it ideologically. In French, the "Manifesto" opens: "Depuis plus de cinq siècles, les nations blanches du monde ont opprimé l'Afrique et les Noirs" ("For more than five centuries, the white nations of the world have oppressed Africa and the Blacks"). The English tweaks this proposition into cynicism: "For more than five centuries the so-called white 'civilizing nations' have been oppressing Africa and the Blacks." So we are left with two takes, two slightly aberrant visions of the Congress's call.

I will simply outline a few of the divergences here. The English draft excises a number of Kouyaté's references to Hitler and German fascism, placing the emphasis much more directly on a crisis around the abuses of world *imperialism* rather than on a single culpable European regime. Thus, Kouyaté writes:

> Partout, les forces de la réaction sont mobilisées contre nous. Partout ceux qui nous oppressent et nous dénient tous "droits humains" preparent fièvreusement une nouvelle guerre sans égale dans les Annales de l'Histoire et pour laquelle ils s'apprêtent, une fois de plus, à se servir de nous comme chair à canon—précipitant ainsi l'extermination de notre race pour compléter l'œuvre criminelle de stérilisation de masse proposée par HITLER.

> Everywhere, the forces of reaction are mobilized against us. Everywhere those who oppress us and deny us all "human rights" are feverishly preparing a new war, without equal in the annals of history, and for which they are preparing, once more, to use us as cannon fodder—thus bringing about the extermination of our race so as to complete the criminal project of mass sterilization proposed by HITLER.

Compare this to Padmore:

> We can see from these manoeuvres that the forces of reaction are everywhere mobilized against us. In Africa, in America, in the West Indies, in South and Central America—to be Black, is to be a slave. Despised, humiliated, denied justice and human rights in every walk of life. Everywhere the ruling powers which oppress us and deny us those universal principles embodied in the "Rights of Men," are today preparing a new world slaughter unparalleled in the annals of history, in which they are planning to use us once more as cannon fodder to all the quicker hasten our racial extermination.

The specific announcement of the Congress also diverges: where Kouyaté writes of a kind of vanguard based in the metropole, Padmore elaborates a much more pointed vision of solidarity and the politics of intellectual labor. Kouyaté writes:

> En présence de ces dangers imminents, nous, vos compatriotes d'Europe, avons pris l'initiative salutaire d'organiser un Congrès Mondial de la Race Nègre, en juillet 1935, afin de les combattre et de hâter l'amélioration de vos conditions de vie en Afrique et dans les autres pays.
>
> Africains, Frères, sœurs nègres, et surtout ardente jeunesse Nègre du monde entier!

> Facing these imminent dangers, we, your European compatriots, have taken the salutary initiative of organizing a World Congress of the Negro Race, in July 1935, in order to combat these dangers, and in order to hasten the amelioration of your living conditions in Africa and in other countries.
>
> Africans, Negro brothers and sisters, and above all, ardent Negro youth of the world!

And here is Padmore's more incisive version:

> Because these forces of oppression and reaction seek to devour us and the old men who posed as our leaders have deserted the camp at the moment when 250 million of your people are crying for leadership, we, the African youths—workers, students and intellectuals—have taken the initiative to organize a Congress of the Negro Peoples of the World for the purpose of establishing unity in our ranks and adopting a platform of struggle for the Africans and people of African descent the world over. This is the historic task of the toiling masses, revolutionary intellectuals, and youth of our race!

In the final paragraph, Kouyaté closes with an almost desperate appeal to "brotherhood" that seems to bespeak his personal fatigue at the time:

> Frères, ne perdons pas d'espoir! Ne devenons pas des victimes de pessimisme et de défaitisme. Quoique le présent soit sombre, l'avenir de l'Afrique et les destinées de notre race sont entre nos propres mains. Si nous restons faibles, nous continuerons d'être méprisés par amis et ennemis. C'est pourquoi nous devrons nous rassembler en

compacts bataillons d'acier, pour faire de notre Congrès la démonstration la plus forte qu'on ait jamais vue au monde.

Brothers, let us not lose hope! Let us not become victims of pessimism and defeatism. Though the present may be dark, the future of Africa and the destinies of our race are in our own hands. If we remain weak, we will continue to be despised by friends and enemies. This is why we will have to come together in compact battalions of steel, to make our Congress the strongest demonstration the world has ever seen.

Padmore adjusts this to form more of an admonition toward unity of understanding among various groups of African descent:

West Indians, stop hating American Negroes! American Negroes, stop despising West Indians! Negroes of the Western World stop considering Africans as savages and "cannibals." Africans, cease reproaching your American and West Indian brothers to be the children of slaves! Mulattos and Blacks—cease flying at each others' throats!— For, while we squabble and fight each other, the whites are getting away with the spoils!

What interests me in this translated and doubled document, finally, is the possibility of reading a structure—more, a mode—of black radicalism as situated somewhere *between* the two texts. Although it is likely that the French version preceded the English, they stand not quite in a hierarchy of (infallible) original and (inadequate) translation. Due to Padmore's revisions, they read obliquely as two texts that speak to and sometimes against one another. To a certain extent, the effect is reminiscent of the famous theory of translation elaborated by Walter Benjamin a decade earlier, in the introduction to his 1923 translation of Baudelaire's *Tableaux parisiens*. Benjamin suggests that just as a tangent "touches a circle lightly [*flüchtig*] and at but one point, with this touch rather than with the point setting the law according to which it is to continue on its straight path to infinity, a translation touches the original lightly and only at the infinitely small point of the sense, thereupon pursuing its own course according to the laws of fidelity in the freedom of linguistic flux."[108] Benjamin's introduction contends that in this approach, the translation cannot carry over the particular relationship between signifier and signified in the original; instead, it supplements the original language's "mode of intention" in signification. For Benjamin, "the language of a translation can—in fact, must—let itself go, so that it gives voice to the *intentio* of the original not as reproduction but as harmony, as a supplement [*Ergänzung*] to the language in which it expresses itself." Ultimately this effect expresses a yearning for what Benjamin terms "pure language" *(reine Sprache),* a "language of truth" that reconciles and fulfills all the "intentions" of particular languages in a "predestined, hitherto inaccessible realm."[109]

Notwithstanding the complex implications of Benjamin's argument, which has garnered a great deal of critical attention in translation studies, it should be evident that if the French and English versions of the "Manifesto" supplement each other in such a manner, their differences are by no means simply a matter of signification and syntax. Padmore's English may touch Kouyaté's French fleetingly, but it does not proceed simply "in the freedom of linguistic flux." The shifts in the English are specifically ideological departures and revisions, rephrasings of the political "language" of black internationalism. In this light the tangential relation between two versions reveals the linguistic sign to be what Volosinov a few years later called an "arena" of ideological struggle. The *décalage* between the two "Manifestos" highlights the "multiaccentuality" of the sign—language as the vital and mutable "intersecting of accents"—as a particularly *social* dynamic (as Volosinov writes, "accent, as such, is interindividual").[110] In other words, Kouyaté's French and Padmore's English versions, together, point at an ideological "language" of black internationalism that inheres in the ways their "modes of intention" diverge from and supplement each other. In the tangential relation between the two texts, what is "concealed and fragmentary," to use Benjamin's phrase, is not just a "higher" realm of language *(reine Sprache)* but also a "harmony" of ideology: black internationalism.

Toward a Francophone Internationalism

I hope that the connections and collaborations sketched here will ultimately lead to a rethinking of the possibilities and impossibilities of the advent of the 1945 Manchester Pan-African Congress. Indeed, it should remind us that the Congress was originally scheduled to take place in Paris, planned to coincide with the World Trade Union Conference in September 1945. Under Padmore's initiative, a "provisional committee" (including members from Africa, the West Indies, British Guyana, and Great Britain) drafted a "Manifesto to the United Nations" as a Pan-African "call to action" in preparation for the revival of the movement Du Bois had initiated decades earlier. Just as the black organizations that emerged in the 1920s appropriated the discourse of Wilson's Fourteen Points and the League of Nations, the provisional committee's manifesto is expressly written in the wake of the Atlantic Charter and the United Nations, the new "International Organization" established to provide "the framework of future world security and prosperity." The manifesto included six demands to the international community: the demand for the "rapid development of the economic, social and cultural life of the African peoples"; the demand that Africans must have the opportunity to participate "at all level[s] of administration of the International Organization"; the demand that the "present system of exploitation" in Africa, in which the majority of the continent's wealth goes to enrich "foreign monopoly firms and individuals," must be replaced with "systematic planning and development whereby in the first place the Africans themselves shall be the principal beneficiaries of the wealth produced"; and perhaps most provocatively, the demand for independence, that "steps should be taken to associate Africans with the management of their own affairs with a view towards the achievement of a full self-government within a definite time-limit." Padmore published an article in the *Chicago Defender* in March 1945 outlining the manifesto and calling for a gathering in France later that year, and Du Bois quickly offered his services in the effort.[111]

Various complications made it unworkable to organize the Congress in postwar Paris, and the meeting was held in Manchester in October. But the initial plans, and Padmore's previous work in Paris, prompt the question of the almost complete absence of Francophone participation in the gathering. Ras Makonnen is one of the few commentators to take up this issue:

There was very little French African participation in the conference, partly because of language differences, but mainly stemming from the structure of black association with metropolitan politics in France which was very different from English-speaking blacks. . . .

It made one reflect with thanks that the British system was not the same as the French; if it had been, many of these fellows would have been caught by it, and remained in London as deputies representing their various constituencies. They would have become possibly like some of the French blacks with their houses in Paris, and the occasional visit back to their constituency in Martinique or wherever. Here, therefore, in the British world was a historic process of decentralization, moving out from London to declare war on the empire; no longer worried about the stamp of approval in London, but determined to show that the system at the outpost of that empire was shady. [112]

This explanation is unacceptable. Certainly, if one looks at Algeria, Vietnam, or even parts of West Africa, the "move out" from Paris "to declare war on the empire" is equally evident. Makonnen's fierce anticommunism seems to cloud his vision: certainly black labor organizers and propagandists such as Lamine Senghor, Emile Faure, and Kouyaté are no "deputies" lounging in Paris! Makonnen disingenuously reduces the complex history of Francophone intellectuals in the metropole to the story of the few conservative black legislators in the French assembly (Blaise Diagne and Gratien Candace, for instance) whom the LDRN and UTN battled bitterly both in Paris and in Africa.

An explanation becomes apparent if instead one simply examines the situation of Francophone intellectuals in 1945, after the destruction of World War II. By the conclusion of hostilities, the Francophone internationalist and radical movements are simply "defunct," as J. Ayodele Langley puts it. With the exception of René Maran (who stayed in Paris but suffered greatly during the German occupation), the central interwar figures are almost all deceased, imprisoned, or no longer in France. Kouyaté, Lamine Senghor, Etienne Léro, and Kojo Tovalou Houénou are dead; Emile Faure is in forced exile; Paulette Nardal, Aimé Césaire, and René Ménil are back in Martinique; Léo Sajous is a diplomat in Liberia; Léopold Sédar Senghor is back in Senegal after the summer of 1945, having served time in a Nazi prison camp.[113] Moreover, the main thread in the history of black Francophone intellectual activity is not abstention or ideological timidity—much less a rush to "assimilation" in any overarching sense—but instead the French colonial authorities' persistent and ruthless suppression of black intellectuals. Even the most innocuous cultural efforts were crushed. The moderate *La Dépêche africaine,* which habitually supported the "civilizing mission" of French colonization, was described in 1928 intelligence reports as "a disguised communist enterprise."[114] Repeated efforts to found a center or residence for African immigrants in Paris, including Kouyaté's Maison des Nègres and a 1930 effort at an Institut Nègre, all met resistance from the Paris police.[115] In a 1927 article sardonically titled "French Generosity under the Third Republic," *La Race nègre* commented on the "still medieval conception of generosity" that had led the French ministry of the colonies to attempt to ban its circulation in Africa. "We will always remember that a Mahatma Gandhi would never have the right to live freely in a French colony," the article notes. Referring to the West African National Congress in the 1920s, it continues:

> [I]n the English colonies of Africa, the Africans hold congresses, have outspoken [*hardi*] and active newspapers, are in intellectual relations with the outside world. In French Africa, it is entirely different. If we were ill-advised enough to hold congresses for example in Dakar, Bamako, Grand Bassam, Porto-Novo or Libreville, we know what would lie in store for us. . . . In French West Africa, it is forbidden for us to receive the papers of our race brothers of the United States, Brazil, Argentina, etc. Without a doubt, we are living under the three colors that have protected the Principles of 1789 with a sublime heroism.[116]

Having spent significant time in France, Padmore himself harbored no illusions about the state of affairs in the empire, either in the colonies or in Paris. In an essay written for the *Crisis* in 1940, he remarks that

> most non-French Negroes, especially Americans, visiting Paris, with its relative absence of color prejudice, its gaiety and charming cultured atmosphere, invariably adduce that France is the most liberal imperialist nation in the world. There is no greater illusion. It is quite true that the French, as compared with the Anglo-Saxon peoples, manifest less racial antipathy toward people of color. But the same can be said of . . . other Latin races, regardless of their political ideology. . . . [W]hile I personally consider the French in many ways a charming people and Paris a delightful city, this in no way blinds me to the fact that French colonial policy is as reactionary, and in many respects more repressive than that of the British.[117]

Makonnen at least implies that he is cognizant of this repression. When he encounters a number of Francophone intellectuals (including Kouyaté,

Félix Houphouët-Boigny, Lamine Gueye, Aimé Césaire, and Léon-Gontran Damas) a conference in Paris in 1938, he comments that "what one noticed in contrast to Britain was a lack of freedom of expression. The French blacks gave the impression of being pursued."[118] Still, Makonnen does not think through the implications of this state of affairs (not to mention the effects of the German occupation during the war) for French participation in the 1945 Pan-African Congress.

What would it mean to resuscitate this unrecognized French chapter as crucial to the development of Manchester Pan-Africanism and the postwar drive toward independence? Most important, it would be necessary to consider the impact of living in Paris, and collaborating with figures in the Francophone world (Kouyaté in particular), on Padmore's subsequent career. For instance, there is little question that Padmore's notion of knowledge production changes drastically during the early 1930s. Much of Padmore's writing up to this point—whether in the *Negro Worker* or in informational and propaganda pamphlets such as *The Life and Struggles of the Negro Toilers*—is, as James Hooker has noted, "pragmatic and unsentimental . . . and it assumed an identity of interest, *though not of culture,* among all blacks wherever they might be."[119] C. L. R. James concurs that Padmore's writing "was not noticeable for style; it was usually a remorseless compilation of the facts of tyranny and oppression and the struggle against them. He was at his best as a journalist, knocking off at short notice an article on a remote African problem with a clear orientation and bristling with detail."[120] One of the striking propositions in Padmore's opening editorial statement for the *Negro Worker* is his goal to rebuild it as "a much needed popular journal." By the end of his tenure in 1933, Padmore is starting to achieve a definition of "popular": the *Negro Worker* expands its purview, printing poetry by Langston Hughes and Nancy Cunard as well as extensive coverage of the Scottsboro trial, and Padmore himself begins to write differently and to conceive differently of his intended readership, thinking in particular about the uses of the "medium" of the black press. Of course, one of the complaints of the Comintern in ousting Padmore was that—while still in Paris—he had begun publishing articles in "Negro bourgeois newspapers" such as the *Pittsburgh Courier* and the *Amsterdam News,* periodicals (along with the *Chicago Defender* and the *Crisis*) that he would remain committed to during the rest of his lifetime.[121]

In the spring of 1934, Padmore even flirted with the French popular press, publishing an article called "Un Noir Accuse" under the pseudonym "Africanus" in the "special colonization issue" of *Vu,* a large-format, glossy Parisian weekly.[122] In an editorial statement, the magazine describes "Africanus" as a "Negro [*noir*] from a foreign colony" and distances itself from his "violent indictment against the white race," arguing that any opinion is valuable "when, as is the case here, it gives the sound of authenticity and translates a widespread state of mind." Padmore pulls no punches, opening with "[f]or more than four centuries, Europe has made Africa its prey, and it is only due to the extraordinary vitality of the Negroes [*Noirs*] that they have avoided, so far, complete extermination." The article, which the magazine illustrated with sensationalist photos (a "fetishist" in the Congo; women suffering under forced labor; *tirailleurs sénégalais* in Niger), comments specifically on the French colonial system, citing critiques such as André Gide's *Voyage au Congo* (1927) and Albert Londres's *Terre d'ebène* (1929). "The French have a lower degree of racial prejudice than all the Anglo-Saxon peoples," Padmore concludes, "but where colonial questions are concerned, they are no different from other propagandists of 'the white man's mission.'"

Even with examples such as the *Vu* article, it is difficult to gauge the precise effect of Padmore's Paris sojourn on his writings. But it seems reasonable to assume that he was exposed to a wider variety of contacts and black popular culture there than he had encountered in Moscow or Hamburg. In the spring of 1933, the Union des Travailleurs Nègres—like Tovalou Houénou's *Les Continents* and Satineau's *La Dépêche africaine* in the 1920s—decided to throw a benefit, in the Maison de la Mutualité on rue Saint Victor in the Fifth Arrondissement. They called it a *fête nègre,* perhaps inadvertently echoing the primitivist gala the Comte de Beaumont concocted for the Parisian avant garde in 1919.[123] With a five-franc entrance fee, the party drew a mixed audience of about four hundred, who watched a boxing exhibition and danced to a jazz band (organized by Léo Sajous, who had tried unsuccessfully to hire Josephine Baker). The UTN apparently lost money on the event, but Kouyaté considered it "good for propaganda." Even in June 1933, as Kouyaté's conflict with the Party was unraveling the organization, the UTN was considering throwing another benefit to raise money for the defense in the Scottsboro trial.[124] These efforts were part and parcel of a broader line of thinking in the LDRN and UTN, which even as they attempted to organize dock workers and foster anti-

colonial consciousness, remained committed to what as early as the fall of
1927 was being referred to as a necessary "affirmation of the black personality" *(la personnalité nègre)* in their efforts.[125]

I am suggesting, in other words, that under Kouyaté's leadership, the
LDRN and UTN in Paris pursued a vision of black cultural politics that—
perhaps more forcefully than any other black group of the late 1920s and
early 1930s, whether the NAACP or the Urban League in New York, or
formations in London including Garvey's UNIA, the West African Students' Union, and Harold Moody's League of Coloured Peoples—conjoined anticolonialism with a rich attention to black expressive culture.
This was not the principal theme articulated in either *La Race nègre* and *Le
Cri des Nègres,* but a great deal of the work in the periodicals is written under the assumption that (to rephrase James Hooker) peoples of African descent shared not only political concerns, but a complex cultural heritage as
well. Moreover, these newspapers were not content simply to celebrate
black art, but contended that it was necessary to theorize a politics of black
expressive culture at the height of European colonialism. Thus, although
some of the debates recapitulate earlier work in the United States, such as
mid-1920s exchanges among African American writers in *Opportunity,* the
Nation, and the *Messenger,* the issue of cultural politics is posed in *La Race
nègre* and *Le Cri des Nègres* not so much in the familiar Harlem context—
civil rights, class concerns, American cultural nationalism, skin color tensions—as under the particular pressures of French imperialism: surveillance
and harassment in Paris; censorship, brutality, and exploitation in Africa.

One of the best examples of the Francophone radical take on black cultural politics is Kouyaté's review of Paul Morand's *Magie Noire* in the fall
of 1928.[126] J. S. Spiegler remarks that "on no other occasion did an article
of similar orientation and tone appear, and this one seems rather a display of Kouyaté's versatility than an indication of his main concerns."[127]
Certainly the essay, as a work of literary criticism, is exceptional both
among Kouyaté's contributions and in the overall scope of the articles in *La
Race nègre.* (It would be incorrect, though, to claim that the paper generally
neglected literature: on other occasions, for example, it published excerpts
from books by Lucie Cousturier and André Gide, a poem by Jeanne
Marqués, and a reprinted review of Philippe Soupault's 1927 novel *Le
Nègre.*)[128] At the same time, the essay hews to the periodical's consistent investment in a notion of "la personnalité nègre" and insists on situating its

reading of Morand's fiction within the contemporary context of French colonialism. The subject of the article is not haphazard, of course: just as *La
Race nègre*'s publication of poems by Marcus Garvey in 1927 had forcefully
marked a departure from the common representation of African American
literature in the moderate "cultural" periodicals in Paris such as *La Dépêche
africaine,* Kouyaté's review amounts to a contention that the "political"
Ligue de Défense de la Race Nègre had a position with regard to the literary representation of peoples of African descent. Kouyaté's reading is at
least as eloquent and passionate as the reviews by Jane Nardal, Léon-
Gontran Damas, and W. E. B. Du Bois mentioned earlier, but his inflec-
tion of the issues raised by Morand's book diverges in significant ways from
other black critiques.

Kouyaté's review essay is called "La trahison du clerc Paul Morand" (The
treason of the clerk Paul Morand). The title alludes to another work that
had appeared in 1928, philosopher Julien Benda's *La Trahison des clercs*
(translated into English as *The Treason of the Intellectuals*).[129] Kouyaté
commences by invoking Benda, the "restless philosopher" *(le philosophe
inquiet),* and then asks a pointed rhetorical question: "When is it that the
intellectual betrays?" Since his "social role" is "to illuminate the people, to
guide the masses towards an ideal of existence," the intellectual commits
"treason"

> when he preaches an aggressive patriotism instead of the love of one's
> country, when he cultivates race hatred, which leads to national or in-
> ternational insecurity; in a word, when he places his spiritual author-
> ity in the service of an unjust collective cause. (2)

Kouyaté charges that "M. Morand has betrayed his intellectual mission [*sa
mission de clerc*] in writing *Black Magic*" since the book is nothing more
than a "plea in favor of color prejudice." Although five years later, the notion of a Black International would be quite concrete for Kouyaté, here (a
year before he first met Padmore) he lists it as one among the fanciful cal-
umnies that Morand imposes in his catalog of the rising tide of color:

> In it, the author has deliberately piled all the sins of Israel on the head
> of the poor *race nègre*. The approaching formation of a "Negro Inter-
> national" [*Internationale noire*] annexed to the Third International,
> the inexistence of a national language permitting the *nègres* to under-

stand each other, the impossibility for our American race brothers to live in Africa because of their stage of evolution, the imperfectibility of the *nègre,* his overflowing sexual vitality, such are the principal themes treated with disconcerting verve and imagination. (2)

Of all of Morand's hallucinated "heresies," Kouyaté writes, the most offensive is the supposed "imperfectibility of the *nègre.*" In contrast to Nardal's feminist complaint and Damas's biting sarcasm, Kouyaté's critique draws its force from its measured tone and astonishing erudition. The review makes reference to an overwhelming barrage of contemporary French intellectuals (including Pierre Mille, Maurice Delafosse, Paul Souday, René Maran, André Gide, and Lucie Cousturier), as well as quoting from classical sources (Epicurus, Herodotus, Horace). Interestingly, rather than dismiss *Black Magic* as racist fantasy, Kouyaté attacks Morand's credibility as an anthropological observer and self-professed scholar of the black world. To contend that the black man was incapable of civilization, one would have to ignore the "beautiful history of Africa, which for so long has been evolving alone, without the aid of any other continent, and which has had its centuries of thought and reflection, for example in the Sudan from the fourteenth to the eighteenth century." Although Morand claims to have traveled more than "30,000 miles, [in] 28 Negro countries" while writing the book, Kouyaté comments that "his descriptions of the countries are pale, to the point that one cannot tell whether he is speaking of the savannas of the Sudanese plains, the mountains of the Fouta-Djallon, the clearings in the woods of the Sudan, or the hundred-year-old virgin forest of the Ivory Coast" (2).

Above all, Morand the "voyager" should have told us "something new" about black music, Kouyaté complains. For black music *(la musique nègre)* is "infinitely richer in varied notes than European music." In Africa, he continues,

> where the least resonance makes the atmosphere divine and quivering, where exuberant nature, still untouched by certain profanations of men, whispers with musical vibrations whose beauty equals the very solemnity of the surrounding silence, the voyager heard nothing. He stayed on the beaten paths, in search of something picturesque, out of fashion, and ridiculous. One hoped to see M. Morand, the artist, be stirred by real African music, mother of jazz. (3)

Kouyaté's profession of disappointment shifts into a fulsome appreciation of music in Africa. The songs of African warriors *(les chants guerriers),* for Kouyaté, contain "something distant, something nostalgic." For Kouyaté, they "evoke the grandeur of heroic and sublime times," and when one

> understands their historical and traditional signification, they drive you [*ils vous conduisent*] from Orphic elation to ecstasy, to the inebriation of the Dionysian dream. The soul of the subject [*l'âme du sujet*] is annihilated for a time in immanent logos [*le logos immanent*]. Psychological reactions thus follow from the imperious need to seek a field of energy [*rechercher un champ d'énergie*]. This explains the dynamism of our dances, the mimed scenes of war. (3)

It is an extraordinary attempt to explicate the function of "possession" in African performance traditions without recourse to the then widespread notions such as Lévy-Bruhl's "primitive mentality." Kouyaté attempts to develop a different theoretical vocabulary for what he calls one of the "mystères d'Afrique": the effect of black music in performance. What music brings about is not oblivion or the abolition of functions of signification or an atavistic return to nature, but on the contrary a condition of absolute intimacy (to the point of the temporary "annihilation" of the subject) with what Kouyaté terms "immanent logos," the materiality of the linguistic sign.

Subtly countering the old Western contentions about Africa, Kouyaté theorizes the "psychological" effects of African music as an eminently *historical* sensibility. The music is "dynamic" and effectual due to the listener's "understanding" of history and tradition; indeed, the quest for a "field of energy" appears to depend on (or even be rooted in) the listener's sense of the past. Even if it can involve affective "ecstasy" and "inebriation," the quest is not blind or wild, but an action marked by a certain "research" *(rechercher)* that the songs "drive" *(conduisent)* in the listener who knows their significance. Surprisingly, the article closes almost graciously—or to use Kouyaté's own word, with a certain "indulgence" *(usons d'un trésor d'indulgence envers notre contempleur M. Paul Morand)*—lightly discarding Morand's offenses rather than obsessing over them, in order to focus instead on the richness of African culture. In order to "penetrate the psychic atmosphere of our countries," Kouyaté concludes, "one would need more of a visit than M. Morand gave, more sympathy than he can give. . . . Africa, whose geographic form is that of the heart, encloses in its sad destiny the beginning, the goals and the end of human civilization [*enferme dans sa triste destinée le commencement, les buts et la fin de la civilisation humaine*]" (3). In another shift of register, a trope of sentimentality allows Kouyaté to position continental Africa as the origin and ultimate object of a universal humanism.

I have already argued that to a remarkable extent, the impetus for transnational communication and exchange among intellectuals of African descent in the interwar period arises from the Francophone side. Like René Maran opening a dialogue with Alain Locke, Kojo Tovalou Houénou pursuing ties with Marcus Garvey and W. E. B. Du Bois, or the Nardal sisters questioning Locke about translating *The New Negro,* Kouyaté was keen to engage black U.S. and Caribbean figures in correspondence. In fact, Kouyaté was the most prolific letter writer among Francophone intellectuals during the interwar period—a pursuit that may have had some influence on Padmore during the years leading up to his own missive to Du Bois from Paris in February 1934. Even as the Congrès Mondial Nègre effort was collapsing, Kouyaté was thinking about transnational connections: the same week Padmore wrote Du Bois, Kouyaté arranged a meeting with a black journalist from the United States who wanted to write an article about their plans.[130]

As early as September 1927, an unsigned article in *La Race nègre* instructed that "our American brothers offer us a living example of the way we must struggle. It is in their school that we will learn how to emancipate ourselves, bringing some originality to the expression of our personality [*l'expression de notre personnalité*], in harmony with the catalyzing milieu."[131] This injunction first of all led to the paper's concerted interest in the African American press over the next few years, as in its translations of writings by Garvey and other items from the United States. In the spring of 1929, for instance, the paper translated an article from the *Pittsburgh Courier* that itself was a review of a previous issue of *La Race nègre.*[132] In other words, the translations functioned not just in the service of an ideology of vanguardist "instruction" from the Harlem Renaissance, but also to confirm the transnational audience of *La Race nègre*—as though the fact that the French periodical had garnered a readership among U.S. blacks (and specifically the African American press) was itself evidence that the black

French struggle was viable and "original," a vital part of a broader dialogue on black liberation and modernity.

But whether penned by Kouyaté himself or not, the 1927 article is also consonant with his many attempts during the period to contact black intellectuals directly. In one case, the exchange seems to have commenced with a note from London. That same September, one of the surveillance agents for the French government charged with tracking the LDRN reported that Kouyaté had "received a letter from London from Mme Marcus Garvey, congratulating him and urging him to persevere in the struggle undertaken by French Blacks [*Nègres de France*] for the emancipation of the race. At the same time she [sent] him an English-language pamphlet, suggesting that he translate it and give her his opinion."[133] Amy Jacques Garvey, Garvey's former secretary and second wife, by the fall of 1927 was a central force and a key feminist voice in the UNIA. She had developed into a leader of the movement after Garvey was indicted for mail fraud in 1923, even serving for a time as associate editor of the *Negro World*.[134] This contact apparently led to other Anglophone ties as well. In August 1927, the Nigerian Lapido Solanke of the West African Students' Union in London had written in English to Kouyaté, addressing him as "brother," and noted that Amy Jacques Garvey had suggested he contact Kouyaté to request a copy of *La Race nègre*. Solanke included a copy of the latest issue of his own organization's periodical, *Wasu,* and in the next two years *La Race nègre* would translate material not only from Garvey's *Negro World* but also from *Wasu*.[135]

Marcus Garvey may have had links to Kouyaté and the LDRN even earlier, since one list of subscribers to *La Race nègre* in August 1927, compiled by the French colonial authorities, recorded one "Marcus Garvey, P.O. Box 1913, Atlanta, Georgia" (Garvey served his sentence for mail fraud in the Atlanta Federal Penitentiary from February 1925 until his deportation from the United States in December 1927).[136] The UNIA leader was definitely in touch with Kouyaté by the beginning of 1928, when the French Colonial Ministry intercepted a letter in which Garvey wrote that he regretted that he could not send a financial contribution to the LDRN, but that he hoped to work together in the future "for the good of the blacks [*nègres*] of French Africa."[137] In Amy Jacques Garvey's autobiographical history of the movement, she offers the tantalizing but vague information that she and Garvey met with members of the "Comte [*sic*] de la Race Nègre" when they visited Paris in August 1928. Some historians have even claimed that Garvey actually became a member of the Comité de Defense de la Race Nègre around this time.[138] (Given the timing of the visit, it seems more likely that it would have been the LDRN, the Comité's successor— unless Garvey had joined before his visit to France and before the schism of the Comité in April 1927.) Just before that visit, in July, Kouyaté had written to Garvey himself, sending a letter in French that is familiar to the point of being chatty, including some details (a reference to a previous telegram and other letters) that imply a more voluminous correspondence between the two men. "For a number of months, we haven't had any news from you, and we assume that all is well," the letter opens. "If we haven't written you again, it is because we thought that you would be here during the spring, and that our letter would find neither you nor Mme Amy Jacques Garvey in Jamaica. We can only hope to see you in the summer."[139]

Even in the midst of his ongoing squabbles with the French Communist Party, Kouyaté sought connections with black intellectuals across the political spectrum, just as Kojo Tovalou Houénou had in 1924. He corresponded with the Garveys, but also was in contact with the NAACP. In October 1927, the French surveillance reported that Kouyaté received a brochure about the activities of the civil rights organization, as well as a number of press releases.[140] Nearly a year later, he wrote to James Weldon Johnson, asking if Johnson could provide some sort of directory or address listing of African America, in which one could find the addresses of all the "important establishments" under black ownership: "universities, newspapers, industrial enterprises, banks, churches and temples, businesses, etc." Such a direct resource, Kouyaté explained, "would permit us if the need arose to make connections between black American businesses [*les entreprises nègres d'Amérique*] and those in Africa and the French Antilles." Kouyaté also thanked Johnson for the assistance of the "Press Service" (apparently referring to the Associated Negro Press, one possible source for the previously mentioned article from the *Pittsburgh Courier* that *La Race nègre* published in the spring of 1929) in providing articles from U.S. periodicals and added that the NAACP would be receiving a regular subscription to *La Race nègre*.[141]

In the summer of 1929, Kouyaté apparently used an address list provided by the NAACP, sending a circular to a wide variety of individuals and organizations in the United States (including W. E. B. Du Bois at the

NAACP and administrators at a number of historically black colleges and universities) to announce that the LDRN was forming a "Student Group" *(Groupe des Etudiants).* "Young Negro intellectuals" *(la jeunesse intellectuelle noire)* must count on each other," he writes, "cooperating across national and linguistic borders towards the development of quality systems of instruction in Africa, Europe, and the Americas." As Tovalou Houénou had argued in 1924, Kouyaté writes that even if there had been great strides in black education in the United States, the center of the common effort should be located in Paris, which "in the future will be the place of rendez-vous of all the black [*nègres*] intellectuals passing through France."[142] This letter followed up on two articles in *La Race nègre* in the spring of 1929, calling for a student section in the Ligue. Black intellectual youth "stagnates" *(végète)* since it develops without aid, "without a national flag, without existing governments who are concerned for its full education [*éducation intégrale*]."[143] So the initiative was an attempt to come to terms with the condition of diaspora: an attempt to conceive an institution fostering intellectual exchange and development by providing support and dissemination networks that might have otherwise been the responsibility of a nation-state or states.

It was not the first time he had written to W. E. B. Du Bois. At the end of 1928, Kouyaté and a delegation from the LDRN had been received by Roger Baldwin, the American Civil Liberties Union lawyer, who apparently suggested they contact the great scholar and *Crisis* editor.[144] In April 1929, Kouyaté followed up by posting an effusive description in French of the work of the Ligue, dropping Baldwin's name and asking for the "moral and financial solidarity" of the NAACP. "The goal of our Ligue," Kouyaté explained,

> is the political, economic, moral and intellectual emancipation of the whole of the black race [*la race nègre*]. It is a matter of winning back, by all honorable means, the national independence of black peoples in the colonial territories of France, England, Belgium, Italy, Spain, Portugal, etc. . . . and of setting up in black Africa a great Negro State [*un grand Etat nègre*]. . . . On the other hand, we desire to co-ordinate our actions with your efforts. . . . [I]t is for the American Negroes [*Nègres américains*] to tell us what they wish, and how they intend to fulfill their aspirations. The cardinal point lies in the elaboration of a

common and precise program, in the unification of the world Negro movement [*mouvement nègre mondial*], without ever losing sight of the details of difference.[145]

Du Bois may have been amenable to the letter's focus on emancipation and even anticolonial nationalism. Nevertheless, the patrician statesman would have taken Kouyaté's call for "un grand Etat nègre" as wishful thinking at best—and at worst, as an echo of Marcus Garvey's imperialist fantasies. But the letter also expresses Kouyaté's keen interest in pan-African initiatives of any sort, as well as his conviction that the "Negro race" suffers above all from "internecine divisions" and a "lack of a spirit of solidarity" (an argument Kouyaté made in many venues in this period, such as the previously cited "Vox Africae" from *La Race nègre* and his speech to the League Against Imperialism in Frankfurt). In closing, Kouyaté requests "financial help," a "temporary" assistance for the "fortification of [the Ligue's] liaison with the black [*nègres*] masses of Africa and the Antilles." In a significant aside, he adds that "the regularity [*périodicité*] of our newspaper would especially benefit" from the NAACP's aid.

In these varied instances, it is possible to glean a sense of what the institutionalization of a particularly Francophone black internationalist practice—at least in Kouyaté's vision—might have involved, had it found the necessary resources and response: the possibility of educational exchanges and financial support for students of African descent around the world; the pursuit of transnational black business cooperatives and economic alliances; the fostering of channels of information sharing and strategizing among differently placed civil rights organizations, periodicals, and anticolonial pressure groups; and an understanding of cultural politics that insisted on combining critiques of racial representation in literature and music with critiques of colonial exploitation. But for the most part, the promise of such initiatives, and more broadly the promise of a Francophone internationalism, remain only conjecture, only shadows in the archive, only traces and hints. Du Bois never answered Kouyaté's letter.

International African

The high point of black transnational organizing between the wars arose in response to the Italian invasion of Ethiopia in the middle of the decade. The travesty of the fascist incursion into one of the three independent sovereign black nation-states, and the feeble response of both the international community generally and the League of Nations in particular, triggered an explosion of outrage and concern among communities of African descent around the world, punctuated by large public protest demonstrations throughout the period.[146] A number of commentators considered the invasion not just an outrage but more ominously the initial gambit in a coming "race war," a new tentacle of European colonialism. "The real dimensions," Makonnen explains, "can only be gathered by estimating the kind of vast support that Ethiopia enjoyed amongst blacks everywhere. . . . It was clear that imperialism was a force to be reckoned with, because here it was attacking the black man's last citadel."[147] The efforts around the crisis, which began with the initial Italo-Ethiopian disputes in late 1934 and escalated with the invasion ordered by Mussolini in the autumn of 1935 and the fall of Addis Ababa in May 1936, might also be said to mark the high point of Francophone participation in black transnational organizing in the first half of the twentieth century—and as such (particularly due to the decimation of the Francophone intellectual and activist community in Paris during World War II) they are crucial to a reconsideration of the emergence of postwar Manchester Pan-Africanism.

It should come as no surprise that even compared to those in London, the protest organizations that sprang up in Paris were characterized by an astounding degree of boundary crossing and "intercolonial" projects, drawing together not just peoples of African descent but a much broader coalition of colonial peoples and oppressed minorities around the globe. In 1936, there was held in Paris an International Conference of Arabs and Negroes, which "attracted representatives from African organizations throughout Europe and Africa. The gathering was apparently concerned with wider issues than simply Ethiopian independence and harbored ambitions of becoming a permanent political organization uniting Arabs and Negroes."[148] The longest lasting and most significant of these efforts was the Rassemblement Coloniale, organized in 1937 by Algerian nationalist Messali Hadj, which brought together activists from North Africa, the French Caribbean (Raoul Cénac-Thaly), Africa (Kouyaté, Ramananjato, Faure), and Asia (Nguyen The Truyen).[149] T. Ras Makonnen and a group of black Anglophone figures attended at least one meeting of the Rassemblement, which brought together trade union activists and anticolonial intellectuals.[150]

Almost all the major interwar figures still living in the metropole were involved in organizing around the Ethiopian crisis. René Maran published a number of articles calling for France to intervene against fascist Italy.[151] Kouyaté, while publishing a stream of essays mainly in the Algerian nationalist newspaper *El Ouma,* went on a speaking tour in the capital region ("Paris, Boulogne-Billancourt, Livry-Gargan, Chatou, Croissy, etc.") with none other than Professor Marcel Griaule, the great French ethnologist and scholar of Ethiopia who had led the government-sponsored Mission Dakar-Djibouti from 1931 to 1933. One Saturday afternoon in October 1935, they appeared together at the Club du Faubourg, debating the politics of the "war in Ethiopia" with conservative speakers from the Front National.[152]

Paulette Nardal played a key role in the effort due to her fluent English. She served as the secretary of the "Comité de Défense d'Ethiopie" (Ethiopian Defense Committee) founded by Kouyaté that year. The Comité served as an umbrella organization in Paris that united a host of "colonial" groups in protest and educational activities in order to "call for, centralize, harmonize and stimulate their efforts towards a solidarity acting in favor of Ethiopia."[153] The groups brought together included Emile Faure's LDRN, Messali Hadj's Etoile Nord Africaine, the UTN (now headed mainly by Stéphane Rosso), the League Against Imperialism, the Comité Schœlcher (run by a Guadeloupean, Léon Hanna-Charley), the Tunisian Parti Destourien, and a Catholic group called "Aide-toi, le Ciel d'aidera." In *Le Cri des Nègres,* Nardal published a short article including a telegram sent to the League of Nations protesting the invasion in the name of "the colored peoples [*les groupements de couleur*] of the entire world, without distinction of nationality, party or class."[154] She was one of the rare black intellectuals in Paris to publish on the Ethiopian crisis in Africa itself, penning a moderate article on the upswing of black internationalist consciousness for *Le Périscope africain,* a bi-monthly newspaper edited in Dakar by Galandou Diouf and Ibrahim Sow.[155]

Nardal was the primary relay between the Comité de Défense d'Ethiopie in France and a parallel group formed in England by C. L. R. James called the International African Friends of Ethiopia (IAFE), which George Padmore joined when he moved to London in 1935.[156] I will close by commenting briefly on the group that emerged out of this formation: the International African Service Bureau (IASB), which was assembled by Padmore in March 1937. Its executive committee included Padmore, James, Makonnen, Jomo Kenyatta, I. T. A. Wallace Johnson, Peter Milliard (Guyana), William Harrison (Jamaica), Chris Jones (Barbados), Laminah Sankoh (Sierra Leone), and Babalola Wilkey (Nigeria).[157] The IASB "devoted itself to the study of the colonial question and the spread of propaganda and agitation all over Britain, in Africa and in the territories inhabited by people of African descent."[158] It also would provide the most direct connection between interwar black anticolonialism and the movements after World War II, since the IASB was at the center of a number of smaller groups that merged in 1943 to form the Pan-African Federation, which would revive Du Bois's movement over the next two years.[159]

The origins of this small but crucial organization are usually located in the Italo-Ethiopian protests, for as Makonnen puts it, the "whole movement towards the IASB derived directly from the Ethiopian crisis, and although our interests now became broader, a link was maintained with Ethiopia right through the period in London."[160] But I am concluding with the IASB in order to suggest some of the ways this formation points further back, at the internationalist projects Kouyaté and Padmore pursued in Paris. Like the earlier formations, the IASB was especially concerned with knowledge production and the politics of print culture. Its members spoke at numerous leftist gatherings in London, but concentrated their efforts on a remarkable series of publications over the next four years: books (including James's *The Black Jacobins* and *A History of Negro Revolt,* as well as his play *Toussaint l'Ouverture,* in which Paul Robeson acted the lead role in a 1936 London production; Padmore's *How Britain Rules Africa* and *Africa and World Peace*), periodicals (*African Sentinel* and *International African Opinion*), and pamphlets (including titles such as *The West Indies To-day, Hands Off the Protectorates, Kenya, Land of Conflict, African Empires and Civilization, The Negro in the Caribbean,* and the quixotic Socratic dialogue between Nancy Cunard and Padmore published as *The White Man's Duty*).

From July until October 1938 (when he departed for the United States), C. L. R. James served as the editor of *International African Opinion,* the monthly journal of the Bureau. The "Editorial" to the first issue in July— unsigned, but most likely written largely by James—is perhaps the most emphatic statement of the aims of the group. The two-page piece is both a position paper on "black political consciousness" in the period of the apotheosis of European imperialism and a call to internationalization. It explicitly addresses a transnational audience, avowing its Anglophone origin but grounding its appeal in what Aimé Césaire a year later would term the "compass of suffering" among black populations throughout the world, "scattered" by imperialism and by language: "Although our position in London makes us more immediately familiar with the problems of Negroes in the British colonies, yet our appeal for collaboration is to Negroes wherever they are, in French and Belgian colonies, in the United States and in South America. Problems differ from country to country, but there is a common bond of oppression, and as the Ethiopian struggle has shown, all Negroes everywhere are beginning to see the necessity for international organization and the unification of their scattered efforts."[161]

The editorial is forcefully antivanguardist, basing its conception of revolutionary change in what James would come to call "the self-activity of the masses." In this regard it recalls earlier work such as Kouyaté's "Vox Africae" and Padmore's editorial stance in the *Negro Worker* in its effort at a theoretical articulation of the complex relations between radical intellectual work in the metropole and black mass resistance in the colonies themselves: "We base ourselves upon the great masses of the people. The individual achievements of a few black men do not and cannot solve the problems of the blacks." The black intelligentsia and the black middle classes must learn that "in the present state of world affairs there is no way out for them by seeking crumbs from the tables of their imperialist masters" (2). But this does not mean that the highly educated, the upwardly mobile, the *évolués* hold a privileged position in the ongoing struggle against colonialism. On the contrary,

[w]e know our limitations. We know that we cannot liberate the millions of Africans and people of African descent from their servitude and oppression. That task no one can do but the black people themselves. But we can help to stimulate the growing consciousness of the blacks, to give them the benefit of our daily contact with the European movement, to learn from the black masses the lessons of the profound experiences that they accumulate in their daily toil, to point out certain pitfalls that may be avoided, to co-ordinate information and organization, to do an incessant propaganda in every quarter of

Masthead of *International African Opinion* (July 1938).

Britain, exposing evils, pressing for such remedies as are possible, and mobilising whatever assistance there is to be found in Europe for the cause of African emancipation. (2–3)

Here the editorial is attempting, in other words, to theorize the precise valence of the term "service" in the phrase "International African Service." What can a journal accomplish? For *International African Opinion,* the answer involves education (the "study" of colonial questions) and consciousness raising, links between colony and metropole through exchange and dialogue in its pages, debates over political strategy and coordination, financial assistance for anticolonial struggles in Africa, and propaganda in Europe. Reminiscent of the *Negro Worker* and *Le Cri des Nègres,* the masthead prints the phrase "International African Service" under an image of an

African woman holding up a torch, superimposed on a map that highlights points in the diaspora, naming the "West Indies," "Brazil, etc.," "Africa," and—interestingly—"Malaysia" and "Borneo, etc." The "service" designation is to some degree itself strategic, in a milieu when any organization not affiliated with the Popular Front was being designated as "fascist." As Makonnen recalls, as early as 1937 "we had naturally considered the possibility of reviving DuBois's pan-African movement, but it seemed safer to operate under the umbrella of service rather than risk a frontal attack by taking a bolder pan-African title."[162]

Aside from a lengthy description of a speech by Emile Faure criticizing the colonial policy of the Popular Front government in France, there is almost no Francophone coverage or participation in *International African Opinion,* and Kouyaté's name never appears.[163] Nevertheless, as I mentioned earlier, Padmore was still in contact with Kouyaté at this point and was definitely aware of Kouyaté's journal *Africa,* founded in December 1935 with the help of the Etoile Nord Africaine and the LDRN.[164] There are intriguing parallels in the ideological positioning of the two journals, although overall Kouyaté's *Africa* evidences his "passage from far to centre Left"[165] during the period, moving away from any kind of overt critique of French colonialism and eventually accepting an affiliation with (and financial support from) the Popular Front, which had come into power in the legislative elections in May 1936 just prior to the fall of Addis Ababa. But the editorial statement in the first issue of *Africa* announces its project as one of education and propaganda in a tone that presages the appeal in *International African Opinion:* Kouyaté writes that his journal "has the ambition of contributing to informing, enlightening, and educating the public opinion of France and its Colonies about all problems relating to Africa, about the vital interests of its peoples, and about the interests of peoples of African origin."[166]

The editorial in *International African Opinion* announces that it will be "no literary journal or giver of advice from the mountain-tops. It will be a journal of action." As with *La Race nègre,* the refusal of a high literary elitism in *International African Opinion* does not mean the journal ignores the politics of literary representation. On the contrary, alongside Padmore's "Labour Unrest in Jamaica" and Makonnen's "A Plea for Negro Self-Government," the reader also encounters detailed reviews of Zora Neale Hurston's *Their Eyes Were Watching God* and Kenyatta's *Facing Mount*

Kenya, as well as shorter notes on the death of James Weldon Johnson and the publication of Richard Wright's *Uncle Tom's Children,* and poems by Langston Hughes, Paul Potts, J. R. Ralph Casimir, and Claude McKay (a reprint of the militant "If We Must Die").[167] The larger issue involves the definition of the phrase "journal of action"—a periodical geared to "serve," as the editorial puts it, as "a living weapon in the struggle" (3).

What makes *International African Opinion* a "journal of action" is not only the space it creates for political dialogue and cultural criticism in the interest of a black internationalist project, but also the particular version of diaspora it articulates: the way it speaks across *décalage,* an avowedly uneven and "scattered" transnational context of "unco-ordinated struggle." It is important to recognize that this articulation is not just symbolic (the masthead) and ideological (the variety of opinions and sites represented), but perhaps most pointedly discursive, lodged first and foremost in the very proposition stated in the journal's title: "International African." The IASB "styles itself African," the editorial specifies (2). In one of the IASB's publicity statements, the group claims to be "primarily an African organisation, run solely by Africans."[168] But what exactly is an "international African," especially as a description in a periodical run primarily by Caribbean intellectuals? "African" here indicates not some mystification of "roots" or "common blood," but instead an expressly antiracialist stance (rejecting any "racial chauvinism," the editors "repudiate the idea of substituting a black racial arrogance for a white") (2). In other words, the term "African" is above all a claimed identity, an identity clutched and guarded and celebrated, in something approaching the way Ralph Ellison would later describe "Negro American" identity as a *"willed* (who wills to be a Negro? *I* do!) affirmation of self as against all outside pressures."[169]

At the same time, "African" marks a particular take on internationalism: as a project of "service" rather than elitist directives; as a space for exchange and argument that prioritizes—rather than ignores or mentions in passing—the "African struggle" (2); as an insistence on self-reliance and self-emancipation instead of any "forced dependence" on patronage and aid (2); as a populist dialogue and open collaboration similar to that which Padmore had announced in the *Negro Worker* ("We . . . ask our black brothers to look upon this journal as their own, to see with us that it is through their co-operation that we can make it effective") (3). Moreover, the "styling" of the journal and of the IASB more generally as "African" positions black internationalism in a broad array of contemporary antifascist and anticolonial fights. "We take no isolated view of our task," the editorial notes. "With the struggle of the Spanish Revolution, with China's fight against Japan, with India's struggle for independence, and with the struggle of the workers everywhere against Fascism in all its aspects, we unite ourselves not only in words but in action, and shall strive to arouse in our people a consciousness of the common destiny of all the oppressed of whatever nationality or race" (3).

The journal, in the end, recalls the Congrès Mondial in that it attempts to institutionalize a space not for some predetermined or hierarchized interaction but precisely for the *practice* of black internationalism. The editorial argues that

> international organization of all forms of struggle is a necessity and the aim of all thinking persons today, but this will not be achieved by abstract repetition of forms of words, which cover a half-conscious denial of African aspirations and needs, it will be accomplished only by mutual confidence and respect on a basis of complete equality, learnt in discussion, struggle and danger honestly shared and reciprocal assistance generously given. (3)

This call echoing what a decade earlier René Maran termed "reciprocity" does not set the scope of "action," the particular strategic contours, or the ultimate prospects of an anticolonial project pursued through a transnational organization. It aims to install a structure of interaction among various actors—the many meanings of "international African"—that is both just and efficacious: a practice where equality is "learnt in discussion, struggle and danger honestly shared." As with the Congrès Mondial, its main ideological imperative is ideological autonomy—as Makonnen puts it, the establishment of an "international African" movement "free from any entanglement."[170] This imperative, that the "international African" also and above all means the *independent* African, is part of what Cedric Robinson means when he writes that the experience of slavery and Western imperialism is "merely the condition for black radicalism—its immediate reason for and object of being—but not the foundation for its nature or character. Black radicalism, consequently, cannot be understood within the particular context of its genesis. It is not a variant of western radicalism whose proponents happen to be black."[171]

It is at first glance a perplexing claim: is it possible to divorce the emergence of black radicalism from the history of Western radicalism, especially when so many of its key activists and intellectuals (including Padmore, Kouyaté, and James) were formed through contact with international communism? Interestingly, this is an assertion that appears in Padmore's own work in the 1930s, in his claims that "black civilisation was heterogeneous to the civilisation of Europe."[172] Later C. L. R. James, looking back at the interwar period, wrote in a similar vein that "whatever the future of tropical Africa will be, one thing is certain, that it will not be what the colonial powers are trying to make of it. It will be violent and strange, with the most abrupt and unpredictable changes in economic relations, race relations, territorial boundaries and everything else."[173] The prevalence of such language demands the recognition that the unfinished, groping nature of projects such as the Congrès Mondial Nègre and the International African Service Bureau marks the work of constructing something radically new, framing a space in the midst of worldwide turmoil and unrest for a radically new kind of collaboration and political practice: an other epistemology of blackness, "heterogeneous," "unpredictable," "violent and strange." If one result—one celebrated practice of the "international African"—is the 1945 Manchester version of Pan-Africanism, then the embattled, aborted, eclipsed Paris collaboration between Padmore and Kouyaté is one of its lesser-known blueprints.

CODA:
THE LAST ANTHOLOGY

One might approach T. Ras Makonnen's provocative paean to the European metropole from an entirely different angle. "What are you going to do with these boys back on the farm, once they have seen Paree?"—this phrase isn't an "old retort" at all, and it doesn't originate in the context of the British Empire either. In fact, it is an allusion to U.S. popular culture. The boundaries are crossed in yet another sense. In 1919, one of the greatest hits among American audiences was a tune called "How 'Ya Gonna Keep 'Em Down on the Farm (after They've Seen Paree?)." The song was a collaboration of the lyricists Sam M. Lewis and Joe Young and the composer Walter Donaldson (later the source of hits including "Yes Sir, That's My Baby," "Love Me or Leave Me," and "What Can I Say after I Say I'm Sorry"). In facetiously countrified verbiage, the lyrics enunciate the worry of a rural couple that their son will come back from the war so utterly enthralled by the French metropolis and the excesses of modern life that it will be impossible for him to stand the simple life on the family farm. The song culminates in the chorus:

> How 'ya gonna keep 'em down on the farm
> After they've seen Paree?
> How 'ya gonna keep 'em away from Broadway,
> Jazzin' aroun' and paintin' the town?
> How 'ya gonna keep 'em away from harm?
> That's a mystery;
> They'll never want to see a rake or a plow,
> And who the deuce can parley vous a cow?[1]

(In the second verse, the last two lines were replaced by another couplet: "Imagine Reuben when he meets his pa, / He'll kiss his cheek and holler 'oo-la-la!'") The song was popularized in versions by Nora Bayes and Arthur Fields. But it had a special resonance for African Americans, too, especially in recordings by Ford Dabney and James Reese Europe. Nearly sixty years later, the scabrous Harlem critic George Schuyler recalled in an interview the ways the lyric touched on issues crucial to the lives of African Americans during the Great Migration, when in the space of three decades, tens of thousands moved from the U.S. South to the urban centers of the North, seeking employment and opportunity. It meant something slightly different for a black audience, as Schuyler points out, to raise the risk of "jazzin' around," to wonder what happens when commerce and modernity "bring the boys into town."[2]

To note the source of Makonnen's phrase in a popular song lyric is also to suggest a point about the ways that, after World War I, discourses of black internationalism—and modes of imagining transnational migrancy—were not necessarily limited by class in the ways one might expect. They were not confined to the corridors of elitism, to conversations among the Talented Tenth in rarefied venues such as the sparsely attended Pan-African Congresses or Paulette Nardal's salon, where a dozen or two sipped tea. Nor, inversely, were they limited to the vagabond dreams of the men who attempted to evade or resist class interpellation, improvising transnational bands at Europe's best back door.

Coming back from the war, James Reese Europe's 369th U.S. Infantry Band, known as the "Hell Fighters," were renowned not just for their concerts in the United States but also because they had been received so warmly in France as one of the first "exporters" of jazz.[3] Both in their concerts and in their March 1919 recordings for Pathé, Europe's group popularized a black version of the war experience for broad African American audiences with songs such as "How 'Ya Gonna Keep 'Em Down on the Farm?" (with the vocals sung by Noble Sissle), "All of No Man's Land is Ours," and "My Choc'late Soldier Sammy Boy."[4] During their ten-week U.S. tour in the spring of 1919, the Hell Fighters' "variety format" shows for black audiences included "straight (or 'High Brow' as the program sometimes explained) renditions of classical or operatic selections, medleys of popular Broadway and Tin Pan Alley tunes, familiar 'plantation' or Southern melodies, short recent compositions by black composers (like William Tyers' 'Panama'), and their own jazz specialties." Just before the finale (a "rousing march"), Europe played the piano accompanying Sissle singing "On Patrol in No Man's Land," which featured a battery of light and sound effects in an imitation of cannons and guns.[5]

It is possible to track the cultures of black internationalism in a number of popular forms. John J. Niles, a white pilot who came to Paris in the U.S. army at the end of 1917, published a book ten years later called *Singing Soldiers* that attempted to document the music of African American soldiers, which he considered to be "something original—a kind of folk music, brought up to date and adapted to the war situations—at the same time savoring of the haunting melodic value found in the negro music I had known as a boy in Kentucky."[6] In a remarkably detailed, illustrated narrative, he transcribes dozens of songs sung in camps and on battlefields by the black soldiers, including prototypical blues ("Deep Sea Blues") and—not surprisingly, since the majority of African Americans who served in the war were put on service details—work songs: "Motor trucks and caissons / Cut a mighty trench, / have to pile de metal on / Fur dese poor damn French / Diggin, diggin, diggin in Kentucky, / Diggin in Tennessee; diggin in North Carolina—Diggin in France" (30–32). There are call and response songs, prideful boasts, and more salacious songs about sexuality and desire across the waters, such as the two-faced choruses Niles heard from soldiers in the 367th Infantry Regiment nicknamed the "Buffaloes":

> Mademoiselle from Armentiers, parlez-vous,
> Mademoiselle from Armentiers, parlez-vous,
> I'd like to git myself a sip
> O' what you got restin' on your hip—
> Inky Dinky, parlez-vous.
>
> Mademoiselle from Armentiers, parlez-vous,
> Mademoiselle from Armentiers, parlez-vous,
> I wouldn't give my high-brown belle,
> For every mademoiselle dis side o' hell—
> Inky Dinky, parlez-vous. (61–62)

And the soldiers adapted a number of spirituals to their situation, including "I'm a Soldier in the Army of the Lord" (42), "I Don't Want to Go" (44), "De Old Ark's a Moverin' an I'm Goin' Home" (80–81), and "Roll, Jordan, Roll":

Roll, Jordan, roll—roll, Jordan, roll—
Soldier, you'll be called on,
To shake that thing you're settin' on,
Dey's a battle bein' fought in de Argonne,
Roll, Jordan, roll. (151)

When a tune was appropriated from the white soldiers, "the colored fellows made up their own verses," sometimes with extraordinary results: "When I came over I was mama's pride and joy— / Now I'm just one of the Hoy-Poloy. . . . / I don't want any more France. . . . / Jesus, I want to go home" (69–71). These inventions and improvisations shaped more of black popular culture in the United States after the war than is sometimes recognized: the issues they raise echoed in the weekly concerts sponsored by Garvey's UNIA at Liberty Hall in New York and were discussed at length in periodicals such as Cyril Briggs's the *Crusader* (where the Malagasy composer Andy Razaf was a regular contributor of poems).[7] They filtered even into blues lyrics in the South, where Sonny Boy sang: "When you go to heaven, gonna stop by France / When you go to heaven, gonna stop by France / Gonna stop by there just to give these girls a chance."[8] Ras Makonnen's allusion to popular culture should serve as a reminder, in other words, that black internationalism is elaborated not just at the podium and in the classroom, but in the barbershop and in the blues:

Hey, when Uncle Sam call you, leave by one, two and three
Yes, when Uncle Sam call you, be by one, two and three
There's no use you a worryin'—just leave all your women back
    here with me.[9]

Although James Weldon Johnson goes "afield" to consider black popular culture and Aframerican expression in the preface to *The Book of American Negro Poetry,* there is only one anthology in the interwar period that attempts to document discourses of black internationalism in a manner that would combine the political—and more particularly, the communist—with the poetic, the musical, the vernacular, the historical, the sculptural, and the ethnological. The only work that dares such a constellation is the 1934 *Negro: An Anthology,* the monumental work compiled over the space of four years by Nancy Cunard.[10]

Raised in an upper-class family in England, Cunard moved to Paris in

1920 and was quickly ensconced in the swirling whirlpools of metropolitan modernist culture. Her salons and parties attracted all the literary lights, and the small publishing house she ran, the Hours Press, published a storm of controversial literature by Ezra Pound, Robert Graves, Louis Aragon, Laura Riding, and Samuel Beckett. Cunard was by all accounts an extraordinary personage, tall and rail-thin, adorned in African bracelets and trinkets up to her elbows. She was voracious and volcanic in appetites and interests, working in the 1920s as "a poet, essayist, editor, journalist, war correspondent, memoirist, translator, avant-garde publisher, African art collector, and political activist."[11] She was also a woman notorious for her sexual relationships with black men, and her efforts at collecting works for her anthology reverberate with some of the same dynamics that infuse black vernacular lyrics such as "Mademoiselle from Armentiers": a shifting erotics of black transnational culture, a complex politics of seduction and danger-laden flirtation across the color line and across the sea.

In this sense *Negro* is also one record of the ways "the arc of desire" can "intersect with the arc of intellectual activity," as Jane Marcus phrases it.[12] The anthology attempts to "record" black internationalism as a sort of dialectal materialism precisely by producing blackness as an inescapable presence (Cunard writes that "the growing volume of the Communist consciousness among the black workers, and in some of the Negro intellectuals" is "something new, *more and more tangible*") (74). This materialist desire is made manifest above all in the document-gathering materiality of the book itself. At one point, frankly discussing the "desire to get close to the other race" among white visitors to Harlem, Cunard writes that "whites are unreal in America; they are *dim*. But the Negro is very real; he is *there*" (69). *Negro's* relentless acquisitiveness and its mind-boggling breadth thus enact an eroticized consumption of blackness that is part and parcel of what the foreword announces to be the necessary "recording of the struggles and achievements, the persecutions and the revolts against them, of the Negro peoples" (iii).

This is also to suggest that *Negro* is the recording or embodying of Cunard herself as a remarkable "living network" of black internationalist connections and alliances in the early 1930s.[13] If George Padmore and Tiemoko Garan Kouyaté strive to *institutionalize* a new International, a working organization channeling and linking the networks of activists and information they represented, Cunard's practice of the anthology strives to *archive* her own related International—to torque and cajole her worldwide contacts into a collaborative articulation of diaspora, into what one contributor called a "collective book" *(livre collectif)*.[14] It is an archive in the sense that Jacques Derrida envisions when he describes a *mal* (both "fever" and "trouble") constitutive to any project of documentation—Cunard's big book betrays a compulsive desire for the archive in its excess, in its overwhelming weight, a condition where the drive to collect and assemble seems "never to rest, interminably, from searching for the archive right where it slips away."[15]

Arlette Farge has argued that the archive is inherently "difficult in its materiality," and perhaps it should not be surprising that every consideration of *Negro: An Anthology* opens by marveling at its sheer unwieldy size.[16] The original edition weighs eight pounds and runs to 855 pages, including 385 illustrations. The book involves approximately 150 contributors, around two-thirds of whom were of African descent.[17] (It was an extremely expensive book to produce, and in fact Cunard—who had been disinherited by her family—was able to pay the London printing house Wishart only when she successfully sued a number of English newspapers for libel after they published salacious reports of her interracial love affairs.) *Negro* is composed of seven sections, a hodgepodge of regional, thematic, and generic designations. "America" includes poetry (Langston Hughes's "I, Too" opens the volume [3]); historical coverage on slavery, abolition, and lynching; memoirs (varying from personal narratives of racial prejudice to William Carlos Williams's "The Colored Girls of Passenack," a disturbingly lurid account of spying on his family's maid in her bath [93–96]); U.S. journalism on the "Negro question"; Cunard's review of her visit to Harlem; a glossary of Negro slang; literary criticism (by V. F. Calverton, John F. Matheus, and Alain Locke); sociology (by E. Franklin Frazier and James W. Ivy, among others); W. E. B. Du Bois's overview of "Black America" (which, in an inflammatory gesture, Cunard preceded with her own unsparing denunciation of the NAACP's insufficient radicalism, a piece titled "A Reactionary Negro Organisation: A Short Review of Dr. Du Bois, *The Crisis,* and the NAACP in 1932" [142–152]); essays on African Americans and communism by Will Herberg, Michael Gold, Eugene Gordon, and James Ford; Cunard's consideration of the Scottsboro case; and the first publication of some of Zora Neale Hurston's most important ethnographic work (including the incomparable "Characteristics of Negro Expression" [39–46]).

The second section, "Negro Stars," includes essays and poems on jazz, surveys of black theater and film, and memoirs by the boxers Bob Scanlon and Jack Taylor. Next "Music," assembled with the help of the composer George Antheil, covers the United States, the Caribbean, and Africa, reproducing a number of scores. It has not been previously noticed that the article on Martinican music ("The Biguine of the French Antilles," signed only with the pseudonym "Madiana") (401–402) is actually the article Andrée Nardal wrote for *La Revue du monde noir* in 1931, reprinted with a somewhat different and longer opening.[18] (It is unclear whether Nardal herself contributed the piece to *Negro* or whether Cunard reprinted it without crediting the original source.) "Poetry" assembles "white poets on Negro themes" as well as Aframerican poets in James Weldon Johnson's expanded sense of the term (Langston Hughes, Arna Bontemps, Sterling Brown, Countee Cullen, Nicolás Guillén, Regino Pedroso, Jacques Roumain, among others), with the Spanish and French works translated by Hughes. The fifth section, "West Indies and South America," contains historical essays, folklore, and sociological analyses, while "Europe" documents racism in England and on the Continent with articles and illustrations (including an inflammatory poster for François Coty's book *Le Péril rouge en pays noir*, a publicity poster from the 1931 Exposition Coloniale in Paris, and a Banania advertisement). This section includes the screed against colonialism called "Murderous Humanitarianism" (574–575) by the Paris Surrealist Group (including André Breton, Roger Callois, Paul Eluard, Yves Tanguy, and the Martinicans Jules-Marcel Monnerot and Pierre Yoyotte), which was translated by a young Samuel Beckett (Beckett in fact translated the majority of the French-language prose in *Negro*).[19] The last quarter of the book is devoted to "Africa" and includes maps, historical portraits, Arthur Schomburg's consideration of African explorers, Ezra Pound's "A Note on Leo Frobenius" (623), anthropological studies by Melville Herskovits and others, dozens of reproductions of African art, and essays on colonialism and contemporary African politics in Ethiopia, Liberia, and elsewhere.

After page 580 in the "Europe" section, there is a hole in *Negro*. The pagination halts, and there is inserted an essay that doesn't appear in the table of contents: René Crevel's "The Negress in the Brothel" (paginated I–III), a hard-hitting and sarcastic take on the ways race and gender are implicated in the dynamics of imperialism, spectacle, and sex in the metropole. It is another critique of the endless variations on the *doudou*. "When for one reason or another" the Frenchman "is obliged to remain at home he demands to be entertained and debauched by the exotic curiosity that lifts him clear of the national fact into an illusion of renewal. Hence the popularity of Martinique jazz, Cuban melodies, Harlem bands and the entire tam-tam of the Colonial Exhibition. . . . Then again the average Frenchman . . . , who is merely seeking the picturesque, can go to the brothel and meet a thoroughbred Negress" (III). Evidently the piece is hidden because of its incendiary content, in a strategy to evade the censors. But more pointedly, "The Negress in the Brothel" rips a hole in the very fabric of the anthology's "Europe" section: its framing is itself part of the critique, for it parallels on the level of the book itself the central (if obfuscated and unavowed) economics of sexual exoticism that lurk at the heart of the metropole.

Negro's acknowledgments thank Raymond Michelet, who lived and worked with Cunard for two years to edit the volume. It is sometimes forgotten that aside from Michelet and Beckett, two of Cunard's most important collaborators were Padmore and Kouyaté. Padmore was instrumental in helping find African contributors, and his own participation is impressive: "Ethiopia Today" (612–618), an excerpt from *The Life and Struggles of Negro Toilers* (807–809), "How Britain Governs the Blacks" (809–813), and "White Man's Justice in Africa" (813–816). On a number of occasions *Negro* also reprints material Padmore had edited for the *Negro Worker*.[20] For his part, Kouyaté most likely provided the 1930 excerpt from *La Race nègre* ("American Attempt to Plant Race-Poison in France") that appears in the section of *Negro* called "From the European Press" (559). The long concluding essay by Michelet, "The White Man Is Killing Africa: Colonisation in Africa," draws from a wide range of sources including Du Bois, André Gide, and Albert Londres, as well as periodicals such as *Le Temps, Le Courrier de l'Afrique,* the *Missionary Year,* and *Le Cri des Nègres* (from 1931 when the paper was under Kouyaté's editorship).

In fact, Cunard was a subscriber to *Le Cri des Nègres* in the early 1930s. After Padmore later recruited her to be the British organizer of funds for the Scottsboro defense effort, Kouyaté's UTN organized at least one fundraising fête in Paris for the case, taking similar events Cunard had hosted in London as a model.[21] In her brilliant indictment of the events in Scottsboro, an essay that reads the case not as a singular instance of extraordinary injustice but as one particularly publicized example of the "world-issue" of "capitalist oppression and brutality" against black workers, Cunard surveys the broad international outcry over the case and adds:

> A sidelight on the official American mentality, regarding the intellectual status of the Negro, is given by Comrade Garan Kouyaté (a Bambara African) after going with a delegation to the American Embassy in Paris at the time of the U.S. Supreme Court appeal in November 1932: "When we got there we were told the ambassador was out. The chargé d'affaires who received us admitted that deputations had been coming all day with the same object. His whole manner showed the utmost surprise at Negroes talking correct French. His astonishment turned to anger and mortification when we told him in plain terms that we held [Ambassador] Miller and the President of America responsible for the lives and fate of the boys." (260)

French surveillance reported that Cunard received frequent visits around this time not just from Kouyaté but also from Léo Sajous, who passed on copies of *Le Cri des Nègres* along with his own journal, *La Revue du monde noir*.[22] Cunard was in touch with Kouyaté even as World War II broke out, since she moved through France and Spain in the late 1930s working as a correspondent for the Associated Negro Press, the *Manchester Guardian,* and Sylvia Pankhurst's newspaper *New Times and Ethiopia News.* In the fall of 1939, she devoted an article in *New Times* to Kouyaté, calling him "a writer of merit, long considered one of the principal leaders of his race in France, a man whom I know very well."[23]

Two months after *Negro*'s publication, Alain Locke wrote Cunard to congratulate her on what he calls "the finest anthology in every sense of the word ever compiled on the Negro." He had "feared a scrapbook," he admits, but the anthology's "miracle of arrangement" brings about a "unity of effect and a subtle accumulative force of enlightenment that is beyond all contradiction and evasion."[24] But the majority of the few critics who have considered the anthology since then have stressed its disparity and its odd incongruities. For instance, Michael North writes that "what is most remarkable about *Negro* is how little connection there is between the outrage about the Scottsboro Boys and the relish expressed for black popular art. The episodic nature of the anthology form has a weirdly dissociative effect that is nonetheless quite distinct." Even taking into account *Negro*'s attention to "responsible black commentary," North avers, "the anthology still tended to present African Americans as objects of pity or comedy."[25] In North's view, all language for Cunard is either "instrumental" or "decorative," and so the anthology ends up split between its sectarian pronouncements about racist oppression (not to mention Cunard's "hectoring" about glories of the Soviet Union) and its lush, exoticist praise-songs to the glories of black art and music. *Negro* "succeeds in defining political action in an exceedingly narrow way," North contends.[26] He contrasts the collection with Zora Neale Hurston's "The Eatonville Anthology," a short and suggestive hybrid suite of fragments published in the *Messenger* in 1926, and with Hurston's essays in *Negro* such as "Characteristics of Negro Expression," in order to claim that *Negro's* framing strategies serve ironically to divide "what Hurston's contribution did so much to connect, political action and performance."[27]

One might note first of all that the group anthologized in *Negro* is not "African Americans." The book's many sections, its astounding reach, and its concluding long section on Africa make it clear that we must read the title itself as a particular kind of intervention, one that tries to take the term "Negro" and revise the significance of that vocable in something like the spirit of "International African." It would seem crucial to ask furthermore whether, in an effect reminiscent of Hughes's *Fine Clothes to the Jew*, the achievement of *Negro* is precisely to highlight the discontinuity among its pieces—a discrepancy that, when one reads through the volume, seems much more various than any simple binary between the instrumental and the decorative. That is, one might read the preface as a sort of gambit that above all produces its own failure. The stern ideological frame of Cunard's two-page foreword ("The Communist world-order is the solution of the race problem for the Negro," it proclaims summarily; "to-day in Russia alone is the Negro a free man, a 100 per cent. equal" [iii]) by no stretch of the imagination can contain or appropriate the interpretive power of Hurston's prose, much less the more disparate texts that populate the anthology. If *Negro* attempts to frame its 850 pages of contents, it is a framing that is defied over and over again, a framing that fails.

The effect has something to do with Cunard's observation in her review of Harlem that any "appreciation of the race" necessarily demonstrates—with the very excess of its materiality, its unmanageable variety—that "the different types are uncountable" (74). If one of the main functions of an anthology is to determine "who counts in the cultural whole," then

Cunard's collection signifies the difficulty of that project with regard to that revised, outer-national vocable *Negro*.[28]

Certainly, one could simply call this the effect of an editorial naiveté or overambitiousness. Cunard herself said much later that "my making of it was, I suppose, much of it, going out into the blind."[29] Hugh Ford muses that "despite efforts to bring some order to *Negro,* it continued to push out in all directions. Contributions often defied classification. No clear thesis emerged from the articles that had arrived, and the situation worsened as contributors failed to send Nancy the essays they had promised. Little by little it was decided that *Negro* would have to be published with gaps."[30] But in the end it may be more useful to come to terms with the text we have, and with its constitutive "gaps," whether "decided" or not. And any attempt to read the sprawling, messy text of the anthology necessitates coming to terms with the ways that it exhibits "an internal limit to formalization."[31] It is "the last anthology" neither in the sense that it is canonical or definitive, nor in the sense that it somehow closes a historical period. *Negro* is "last" in the sense that it demonstrates—it attempts to *practice*—the impossibility of anthologizing blackness.

In a 1932 letter to Claude McKay, Cunard explains that the book she is working on is "not a *literary* anthology" but instead what she terms "a very large symposium."[32] A symposium would seem to imply a gathering or dialogue that is at once more various and more documentary than a "literary anthology" of Negro creative writing. At the same time a symposium connotes an assembly that is relatively informal—or deforming—in relation to the framing pretensions of the modernist anthology. In another early plan for the book, a 1931 circular, Cunard emphasizes not only that the book will be "entirely documentary," but also that she wants "contributions from Negroes" in particular:

> I want outspoken criticism, comment and comparison from the Negro on the present-day civilisations of Europe, America, South America, the West Indies, African Colonies, etc.—where conditions are best for Colored people—individual documents, letters, photographs from those that have travelled and can judge of [*sic*] the attitude of diverse countries and races.

This is the first time such a book has been compiled in this man-

ner. It is primarily for the Colored people and it is dedicated to one
of them.[33]

In other words, North's critique may be misleading in suggesting that the
aim of *Negro* is to "present African Americans as objects" not just because
the book constellates blackness beyond the U.S. nation, but also because
the book has quite specific notions about the *audience* of its symposium. "It
is primarily for the Colored people"—one has to reconsider the complex
framing of the book in view of its goal of "recording" a symposium of the
self-representation of this "new" international Negro.

In this regard, the project of *Negro* has a more intriguing relation to the
claims Hurston makes in "Characteristics of Negro Expression" about an-
gularity and asymmetry being two paradigmatically Negro qualities. "The
presence of rhythm and the lack of symmetry are paradoxical," Hurston
comments. "There is always rhythm, but it is the rhythm of segments. Each
unit has a rhythm of its own, but when the whole is assembled it is lacking
in symmetry. But easily workable to a Negro who is accustomed to the
break in going from one part to another, so that he adjusts himself to the
new tempo" (41). Like the anthology as a whole, this passage figures its
privileged reader as a Negro able to navigate the "break" that necessarily interrupts any moving—a Negro able to negotiate the condition of diaspora,
in other words. Thus *Negro* has a way of defining "political action" that is
more subtle and more suggestive than a simple reading of the more hard-
boiled communist contributions might imply. Political action in the sphere
of black internationalism is modeled in the book by the kind of reading it
demands, in the book's very difficulty and discontinuities. Unlike Hurston's
"The Eatonville Anthology," which as North argues convincingly is woven
together by a careful calibration of a vernacular narrative voice, *Negro: An
Anthology* demands that the reader articulate the discrepant relation between its documents—"adjusting," say, to the "break" between Hurston's
"Characteristics" and the horrific photo of a Maryland lynching that faces
its first page.[34]

Over and over again, *Negro* attempts to find the link between politics
and performance through figurations of black musical practices. Cunard
closes her foreword with the explanation that Michelet's "The White Man
Is Killing Africa" is the last piece in the book: "I have ended the book with

this—I cannot say: I have ended it on this *note,* for the chord of oppression, struggle and protest rings, trumpet-like or muffled, but always insistent throughout" (iv). In this metaphor, "oppression, struggle and protest" are not a single "note" but a shifting harmonic principle, the "insistent" if not consistently audible characteristic that links the disparate documents. Even George Antheil's peculiar and sometimes sensationalist contribution to the music section, "The Negro on the Spiral, or A Method of Negro Music," strives to define the ways that black music is "so intricate in rhythmic pattern, so delicately balanced in contra-rhythms and proportions" (346–347). One might hear these passages in counterpoint with Hurston's well-known description of what she terms "jagged harmony" in another essay in *Negro,* "Spirituals and Neo-Spirituals," where she describes the performance style in the spirituals as one that in harmonizing, undoes the principle of harmony—a style of "harmony and disharmony," "shifting keys and broken time." Hurston instructs that "each singing of the piece is a new creation. The congregation is bound by no rules. No two times singing is alike, so that we must consider the rendition of a song not as a final thing, but as a mood" (360). What if the anthology enables the articulation of a *mood* rather than conducting a census, drawing a map, or founding a museum?[35] Neither "a final thing" (a framing of the past) nor a "prophecy" (a prediction of the future), but a space of "new creation" in the performance of reading that takes place in the subjunctive, in a condition of probability. As Cunard writes elsewhere, probability "links conviction with instinct, is almost instinct itself, is the feeling of coming things."[36] Here what is hinted in the breaks, what must be continually recreated and debated, what must be translated "from one part to another," is the symposium that is black internationalism in practice. Reading the *Negro* anthology, then, offers a model for that practice, in which diaspora can be articulated only in forms that are provisional, negotiated, asymmetrical. Black internationalism, the book suggests, is less like a sturdy edifice or a definitive program than like the uncertain harmony of a new song.

NOTES   ACKNOWLEDGMENTS   INDEX

NOTES

Prologue

1. W. E. B. Du Bois, "To the Nations of the World," in *W. E. B. Du Bois: A Reader*, ed. David Levering Lewis (New York: Henry Holt, 1995), 639. See also Lewis, *W. E. B. Du Bois: Biography of a Race, 1868–1919* (New York: Henry Holt, 1993), 246–251.

2. Du Bois, "The Forethought," *The Souls of Black Folk* (1903), in *Writings* (New York: Library of America, 1986), 359.

3. Du Bois, "The Color Line Belts the World," *Collier's Weekly* (October 20, 1906): 30, collected in *W. E. B. Du Bois: A Reader*, 42.

4. Du Bois, "The Negro Mind Reaches Out," *Foreign Affairs* 3, no. 3 (1924), collected in *The New Negro* (1925; reprint, New York: Atheneum, 1989), 385.

5. Nathan Huggins, *Harlem Renaissance* (New York: Oxford University Press, 1971), 41.

6. Alain Locke, "The New Negro," in *The New Negro*, 13, 14. I should note that the characteristically modernist gesture that announces this internationalism as "new" does not preclude the fact that—even if World War I marks a certain different historical conjuncture in ways I will emphasize here—black internationalist discourses do not begin only in the twentieth century. African Americans have long made recourse, of course, to a two-pronged strategy of national civil rights work and international appeal, and it would be possible to track the history of this strategy back to abolitionism (the European appeals against U.S. slavery by Frederick Douglass, William Wells Brown, and Mary Prince) and forward to movements such as the *Chicago Defender*'s "Double V" (victory against fascism abroad, victory against racism at home) in World War II. Nikhil Pal Singh has recently termed this persistence "black worldliness," a useful phrase in that it encapsulates both the considered breadth (the move beyond the level of the nation-state) and the explicit political ambition (the universalism) of such a strategy. Indeed, Singh argues that this imperative "is perhaps this country's only consistent universalism." See

Singh, "Culture/Wars: Recoding Empire in an Age of Democracy," *American Quarterly* 50 (September 1998): 514.

7. Hubert Harrison, "Our International Consciousness," *When Africa Awakes* (1920; reprint, Baltimore: Black Classic Press, 1997), 100–101, 103.

8. I will use the term "Harlem Renaissance" at times in this book, despite my dissatisfaction with it, partly as a means to approach critically the scholarship that has accepted it. I would echo the concerns of dissenters such as Sterling Brown, who comments that "the New Negro is not to me a group of writers centered in Harlem during the second half of the twenties. Most of the writers were not Harlemites; much of the best writing was not about Harlem, which was the show-window, the cashier's till. . . ." Brown, "The New Negro in Literature (1925–1955)," in *A Son's Return: Selected Essays of Sterling A. Brown,* ed. Mark A. Sanders (Boston: Northeastern University Press, 1996), 185. See also Gerald Early, "Introduction," in *My Soul's High Song: The Collected Writings of Countee Cullen, Voice of the Harlem Renaissance* (New York: Doubleday, 1991), 24–25. Conversely, George Hutchinson has recently made a convincing argument that "Renaissance" is in fact an appropriate moniker, at least for Locke's anthology *The New Negro.* See Hutchinson, *The Harlem Renaissance in Black and White* (Cambridge: Harvard University Press, 1995), 424–428.

9. Robert B. Stepto, "Sterling A. Brown: Outsider in the Harlem Renaissance?" in *The Harlem Renaissance: Reevaluations,* ed. Amritjit Singh, William S. Shiver, and Stanley Brodwin (New York: Garland, 1989), 73. See also Melvin Dixon, "Rivers Remembering Their Source: Comparative Studies in Black Literary History—Langston Hughes, Jacques Roumain, and Negritude," in *Afro-American Literature: The Reconstruction of Instruction,* ed. Dexter Fisher and Stepto (New York: MLA, 1979), 25–43; Melvin Dixon, "Toward a World Black Literature and Community," in *Chant of Saints: A Gathering of Afro-American Literature, Art, and Scholarship,* ed. Michael S. Harper and Stepto (Urbana: University of Illinois Press, 1979), 175–194.

10. Du Bois, "My Mission," *Crisis* 19 (May 1919): 9.

11. French policy during the war envisioned Africans mainly as soldiers, not as workers, and the numbers reflect this: in 1918, the projections were for 85,000 soldiers from Africa (70,000 from French West Africa, and 15,000 from French Equatorial Africa), but only 10,000 workers; this in comparison to 10,000 soldiers and 15,000 workers from Madagascar, and 80,000 soldiers and 100,000 workers from Indochina. See Jean Vidalenc, "La main d'œuvre étrangère en France et la Première Guerre Mondiale (1901–1926)," *Francia* 2 (1974): 524–550; Tyler Stovall, "Colour-Blind France? Colonial Workers during the First World War," *Race and Class* 35 (1993): 35–55; *The Marcus*

Garvey and Universal Negro Improvement Association Papers, vol. 1: 1826–August 1919, ed. Robert A. Hill (Berkeley: University of California Press, 1986), 292n1; Philippe de Witte, "Le Paris noir de l'entre-deux-guerres," in *Le Paris des étrangers: depuis un siècle,* ed. A. Kaspi and A. Marès (Paris: Imprimérie Nationale, 1989), 157–169. As de Witte points out, it should be noted that French Caribbeans were considered citizens and thus not counted as immigrants.

12. Reid Badger, *A Life in Ragtime: A Biography of James Reese Europe* (New York: Oxford University Press, 1919); Chris Goddard, *Jazz Away from Home* (New York: Paddington Press, 1979); Michael Haggerty, "Transes Atlantiques," *Jazz Magazine* 325 (January 1984): 30–31.

13. Raymond Williams, *The Politics of Modernism: Against the New Conformists* (London: Verso, 1989), 45.

14. Tyler Stovall, *Paris Noir: African Americans in the City of Light* (Boston: Houghton Mifflin, 1996), 90.

15. Claude McKay, *The Negro in America,* translated from the Russian by Robert Winter, ed. Alan McLeod (Port Washington, N.Y.: Kennikat Press, 1979), 49. The celebration in the U.S. black press of the "apparent absence of racism in Europe" is also discussed usefully in Kenneth R. Janken, "African American and Francophone Black Intellectuals during the Harlem Renaissance," *Historian* 60 (1998): 490–491, 503–504.

16. Kenneth W. Warren, "Appeals for (Mis)recognition: Theorizing the Diaspora," in *Cultures of United States Imperialism,* ed. Amy Kaplan and Donald E. Pease (Durham, N.C.: Duke University Press, 1993), 404–405.

17. Locke, "The New Negro," 14.

18. Edward Said, "Third World Intellectuals and Metropolitan Culture," *Raritan* 9 (Winter 1990): 31.

19. David Scott, "Preface," in "The Archeology of Black Memory: An Interview with Robert A. Hill," *Small Axe* 5 (March 1999): 82. See also Michel Foucault, *The Archeology of Knowledge,* trans. A. M. Sheridan Smith (New York: Pantheon, 1972), 129.

20. Hill, "The Archeology of Black Memory," 120.

21. Walter Benjamin, "One-Way Street" (1928), in *Selected Writings, vol. 1: 1913–1926,* trans. Edmund Jephcott, ed. Marcus Bullock and Michael W. Jennings (Cambridge: Harvard University Press, 1996), 444 (modified). The original is Benjamin, *Einbahnstrasse* (1928; reprint, Frankfurt am Main: Suhrkamp Verlag, 1955), 8.

22. More than a bit hyperbolically (yet in a tone that is by no means extraordinary in such missives), the letter goes on to warn of "potential repercussions of a propaganda whose goals and means may seem normal to metropolitan

mentalities, but whose results can be singularly disappointing within turbulent minorities, still in a state of ambiguous fermentation more than healthy evolution, and for this reason too naturally inclined to welcome without proper judgment those who, in the name of independence, flatter unsatisfied pride and in truth prepare the paths to anarchy." Jules Carde, Direction des Affaires Politiques, letter to the Ministère des Colonies, June 26, 1928, *La Dépêche africaine* folder, Archives Nationales, Section d'Outre-Mer, Service de Liaison avec les Originaires des Territoires de la France d'Outre-Mer (abbreviated henceforth as SLOTFOM), series V, box 2 (abbreviated henceforth as "V, 2").

23. As with other journals, this attention took many forms. On the one hand, there was coverage of the experiences of African American soldiers in the war: see "Black French Troops in Germany," *Messenger* 2, no. 7 (July 1919): 65; "Two Frenchmen on the Negro Troops," *Messenger* 5, no. 2 (Feb. 1923): 592–593; William N. Colson, "Propaganda and the American Negro Soldier," *Messenger* 2, no. 7 (July 1919): 24–25; Colson, "The Social Experience of the Negro Soldier Abroad," *Messenger* 2, no. 10 (Oct. 1919): 26–27. On the other hand, there were broader interventions concerning the possibilities and pitfalls of internationalism in the period: see "Internationalism," *Messenger* 2, no. 8 (August 1919): 5–6; "Three Schools of Internationalist Thought," *Messenger* 2, no. 12 (December 1920): 169–170; A. Philip Randolph, "Internationalitis," *Messenger* 3, no. 2 (July 1921): 216; William S. Nelson, "The International Viewpoint," *Messenger* 6, no. 7 (July 1924): 222–223. At the same time, one might note an especial concern with the French context, too: see "Americanism in France," *Messenger* 4, no. 9 (September 1922): 477; "France and the Negro," *Messenger* 5, no. 9 (September 1923): 806.

24. Michel Foucault, *The Archeology of Knowledge,* trans. A. M. Sheridan Smith (New York: Pantheon, 1972), 131. The original is *L'Archéologie du savoir* (Paris: Gallimard, 1969), 172–173.

25. C. L. R. James, "Preface" (1938), in *The Black Jacobins: Toussaint L'Ouverture and the San Domingo Revolution,* 2nd ed. (New York: Vintage, 1963), xi.

26. Brent Hayes Edwards, "The Uses of *Diaspora,*" *Social Text* 66 (spring 2001): 45–73.

27. Stuart Hall, "Race, Articulation, and Societies Structured in Dominance" (1980), reprinted in *Black British Cultural Studies: A Reader,* ed. Houston A. Baker, Manthia Diawara, and Ruth H. Lindeborg (Chicago: University of Chicago Press, 1996), 33.

28. Ibid., 38.

29. Other work touching on the importance of the term in Birmingham cultural studies includes Jennifer Daryl Stack, "The Theory and Method of Articulation in Cultural Studies," in *Stuart Hall: Critical Dialogues in Cultural Studies,* ed. David Morley and Kuan-Hsing Chen (New York: Routledge, 1996), 112–130; and the interview with Hall, "On Postmodernism and Articulation," 131–150, in the same volume. Fredric Jameson offers a more idiosyncratic genealogy of the term (in his review essay "On 'Cultural Studies,'" *Social Text* 34 [1993]: 30–33), but elegantly notes the ways the term implies a "poetic" between the structural and the discursive (32).

30. Stuart Hall, "Cultural Identity and Diaspora," in *Identity, Community, Culture, Difference,* ed. Jonathan Rutherford (London: Lawrence and Wishart, 1990), 235.

31. Tommy Lott, "Black Cultural Politics: An Interview with Paul Gilroy," *Found Object* 4 (fall 1994): 56–57.

32. Earl Lewis, "To Turn as on a Pivot: Writing African Americans into a History of Overlapping Diasporas," *American Historical Review* 100 (June 1995): 765–787.

33. Senghor, "Problématique de la Négritude" (1971), in *Liberté III: Négritude et civilisation de l'universel* (Paris: Seuil, 1977), 274. The translation is my own.

34. Historian Ranajit Guha is one of the few scholars writing in English who regularly makes recourse to the term *décalage,* using it to indicate a structural overlap or discrepancy, a period of "social transformation" when one class, state bureaucracy, or social formation "challenges the authority of another that is older and moribund but still dominant." Guha, *Dominance without Hegemony: History and Power in Colonial India* (Cambridge: Harvard University Press, 1997), 13, 157. See also Guha, *Elementary Aspects of Peasant Insurgency in Colonial India* (Durham, N.C.: Duke University Press, 1999), 173, 330.

35. Senghor, "Problématique de la Négritude," 278.

36. Hall, "Race, Articulation, and Societies Structured in Dominance," 41.

1. Variations on a Preface

1. Jane Nardal, letter to Alain Locke, December 27, 1927, Alain Locke Papers, box 164–74, folder 25, Moorland-Spingarn Manuscript Division, Howard University. Unless otherwise indicated, all translations are my own.

2. Du Bois, "The Negro Mind Reaches Out," *Foreign Affairs* 3, no. 3 (1924), collected in *The New Negro* (1925; reprint, New York: Atheneum, 1989), 412–413.

3. Alain Locke, letter to Jane Nardal, n.d., Alain Locke Papers.

4. Nardal, "L'internationalisme noir," *La Dépêche africaine* 1 (February 1928): 5.
5. Paulette Nardal, "Eveil de la conscience de race," *La Revue du monde noir* 6 (1932): 25.
6. Du Bois, "The Negro Mind Reaches Out," 386.
7. Locke, "Le Nègre nouveau," trans. Louis and Renée Guilloux, *Europe* 102 (June 15, 1931): 289–300.
8. Naoki Sakai, *Translation and Subjectivity: On "Japan" and Cultural Nationalism* (Minneapolis: University of Minnesota Press, 1997), 13.
9. Gates, "The Trope of a New Negro and the Reconstruction of the Image of the Black," *Representations* 24 (fall 1988): 129–157; Levine, "The Concept of the New Negro and the Realities of Black Culture," in *The Unpredictable Past: Explorations in American Cultural History* (New York: Oxford University Press, 1993), 86–106.
10. Williams, *Keywords: A Vocabulary of Culture and Society* (New York: Oxford University Press, 1976), 20, 15.
11. Ibid., 11.
12. Raymond Williams, "Keywords," in *Politics and Letters: Interviews with New Left Review* (London: New Left Books, 1979), 177.
13. Edouard Glissant, *Le Discours antillais* (Paris: Seuil, 1981), 30. A partial translation by J. Michael Dash has been published as *Caribbean Discourse: Selected Essays* (Charlottesville: University of Virginia Press, 1989), 16. Subsequent citations will be indicated with page numbers for the French and English editions (in that order) in parentheses in the text. I have modified many of the English translations.
14. Franck L. Schoell, "La 'Renaissance Nègre' aux Etats-Unis," *La Revue de Paris* (January 1, 1929): 158.
15. Stovall calls Paris a "Gateway to Africa" in *Paris Noir: African Americans in the City of Light* (Boston: Houghton Mifflin, 1996), 97.
16. Jack D. Forbes, *Africans and Native Americans: The Language of Race and the Evolution of Red-Black Peoples* (1988; reprint, Carbondale: University of Illinois Press, 1993). Page numbers for subsequent citations will be indicated in parentheses in the text.
17. See Simone Delesalle and Lucette Valensi, "Le Mot 'Nègre' dans les dictionnaires français d'Ancien Régime: histoire et lexicographie," *Langue Française* 15 (September 1972): 79–104.
18. See Lucette Valensi, "Nègre/Negro: recherches dans les dictionnaires français et anglais du XVIIème au XIXème siècles," in *L'Idée de race dans la pensée politique française contemporaine,* ed. Pierre Guiral and E. Temime (Paris: Editions du Centre National de la Recherche Scientifique, 1977), 157–170. Other comparative works focusing on the development of racial terminology

in English include H. L. Mencken, "Designations for Colored Folk," *American Speech* (October 1944): 161–174; James W. Ivy, "Le fait d'être nègre dans les Amériques," *Présence africaine* 24–25 (February–May 1959): 123–131; Nathan Hare, "Rebels without a Name," *Phylon* 23, no. 3 (fall 1962): 271–277; Harold R. Isaacs, "A Name to Go By," in *The New World of Negro Americans* (Cambridge: MIT Press, 1963), 62–72; Richard B. Moore, *The Name "Negro": Its Origin and Evil Use,* ed. W. Burghardt Turner and Joyce Moore Turner (1960; reprint, Baltimore: Black Classic Press, 1992).

19. Serge Daget, "Les mots *esclave, nègre, Noir,* et les jugements de valeur sur la traite négrière dans la littérature abolitionniste française de 1770 à 1845," *Revue française d'histoire d'outre-mer* 60 (1973): 518. Daget notes that this project was largely ineffectual in the abolitionist movement.

20. Fanon, "Antillais et Africains," in *Pour la révolution africaine* (Paris: Maspero, 1964), 26; translated by Haakon Chevalier as "West Indians and Africans," in *Toward the African Revolution: Political Essays* (New York: Grove Press, 1988), 21 (modified).

21. Toni Morrison, *Playing in the Dark: Whiteness and the Literary Imagination* (Cambridge, Mass.: Harvard University Press, 1992), 6.

22. The phrase "legitimation by reversal" is adopted from Gayatri Chakravorty Spivak, "Race before Racism and the Disappearance of the American: Jack D. Forbes' *Black Africans and Americans: Color, Race and Caste in the Evolution of Red-Black Peoples,*" *Plantation Society* 3, no. 2 (1993): 89.

23. With a certain amount of fanfare, the *New York Times* finally gave in to Du Bois's crusade and granted the word "Negro" a capital "N" in a patronizing Op-Ed—but only on March 15, 1930, much later than we might expect. See Isaacs, *The New World of Negro Americans,* 65. This came no less than nearly a hundred and fifty years after English sealed the link between "Negro" and "slave" precisely by removing that very capital "N"—early translations of the Spanish *negro* had been written as "Negro" in English from the mid-1500s until the end of the eighteenth century. (See Ivy, "Le fait d'être nègre dans les Amériques," 125.) For critics of *Negro* such as Richard B. Moore, however, the futility and inconsequentiality of such "petty" struggles to "fine-tune" or rehabilitate the designation represent a supreme irony.

24. Cousturier took it upon herself to tutor a number of the soldiers in French in her home, lamenting the abysmal quality of language instruction in the military. "The word *nègre* has not remained a simple vocable of practical usage," she writes, "and is not used for real objects [*ne saurait s'appliquer à des objets réels*]. As poetically as the word 'dove' [*colombe*], which evokes white peace, innocence, divine love, for us the word 'nègre' effectively symbolizes inversely brutal frenzy, satanic ugliness and other nocturnal nightmares." As Cous-

turier saw it, her black pupils were ultimately just *des hommes* like any others. She goes on to say that she thinks of the African soldiers as *inconnus*, "unknown," because they have been so consistently misnamed and misused. Cousturier, *Des Inconnus chez moi* (Paris: Éditions la Sirène, 1920), 9.

25. A. James Arnold, *Modernism and Negritude: The Poetry and Poetics of Aimé Césaire* (Cambridge: Harvard University Press, 1981), 36.

26. On this congress and Senghor's speech, see Willi Munzenberg, "Pour une conférence coloniale," *La Correspondence internationale* 91, no. 6 (August 14, 1926): 1011; "La question nègre devant le Congrès de Bruxelles," *La Voix des Nègres* (March 1927): 1; "A Black Man's Protest," *Living Age* 332 (May 15, 1927): 866–868.

27. For more detail on Senghor's activities, see Philippe de Witte, *Les Mouvements nègres en France, 1919–1939* (Paris: L'Harmattan, 1985); J. Ayodele Langley, *Pan-Africanism and Nationalism in West Africa, 1900–1945* (London: Oxford University Press, 1973); J. S. Spiegler, *Aspects of Nationalist thought among French-Speaking West Africans, 1921–1939* (Ph.D. diss., Oxford University, 1968); *Lamine Senghor: vie et oeuvre* (Dakar: Front Culturel Sénégalais, 1979); Robert Cornevin, "Du Sénégal à la Provence: Lamine Senghor (1889–1927), pionnier de la négritude," *Provence historique* 25, no. 99 (January–March 1975): 69–77; Tiemoko Garan Kouyaté, "La ligue est en deuil: son très dévoué président Senghor Lamine est mort," *La Race nègre* 5 (May 1928); Brent Hayes Edwards, "The Shadow of Shadows," *Positions* (forthcoming winter 2003). I should note that Lamine Senghor was not related to Négritude founder Léopold Sédar Senghor.

28. Lamine Senghor, "Le mot 'Nègre'," *La Voix des Nègres* 1 (January 1927): 1. Although the article is signed "Le Comité" of the Comité de Défense de la Race Nègre, it was written exclusively by Senghor, as it is nearly identical to an article called "Le réveil des Nègres" that he had previously published under his own name in *Le Paria* (The pariah), the journal of the French Communist branch of colonial radicals, the Union Intercoloniale. (See Senghor, "Le réveil des Nègres," *Le Paria* 38 [April 1926]: 1–2.) For other considerations of this essay, see Christopher Miller, "Involution and Revolution: African Paris in the 1920s," in *Nationalists and Nomads: Essays on Francophone African Literature and Culture* (Chicago: University of Chicago Press, 1998), 30–37; Philippe de Witte, *Les Mouvements nègres en France, 1919–1939* (Paris: L'Harmattan, 1985), 143–146.

29. Jack D. Forbes, "The Manipulation of Race, Caste and Identity: Classifying Afroamericans, Native Americans and Red-Black People" *The Journal of Ethnic Studies* 17, no. 4 (winter 1990): 5. In her review, Gayatri Spivak is some-

what critical of the application of "caste" to this context. See Spivak, "Race before Racism and the Disappearance of the American," 87.

30. Miller, "Involution and Revolution," 36–37.

31. At the time, a segregated balcony in a theater was called "nigger heaven." The phrase also figuratively depicts the way Harlem "hangs" out over the rest of Manhattan. Carl Van Vechten, *Nigger Heaven* (New York: Knopf, 1926), translated as *Le Paradis des Nègres* (Paris: Editions Kra, 1927). For two sides of the U.S. response, see W. E. B. Du Bois's caustic review in "Books," *Crisis* 33 (1926): 81–82; and James Weldon Johnson's more positive "Romance and Tragedy in Harlem—A Review," *Opportunity* 4 (1926): 316–317, 330. For commentary on this controversy, see George Hutchinson, *The Harlem Renaissance in Black and White* (Cambridge: Harvard University Press, 1995), 166–167; David Levering Lewis, *When Harlem Was in Vogue* (New York: Oxford University Press, 1981), 182–189.

32. Roark Bradford, *Ol' Man Adam an' His Chillun, Being the Tales They Tell about the Time When the Lord Walked the Earth Like a Natural Man* (New York: Harper and Brothers, 1928). I would like to thank Robert O'Meally for drawing my attention to this collection.

33. Ibid., x.

34. Ibid., x–xi.

35. Ibid., xii.

36. Langston Hughes, *The Big Sea* (1940; reprint, New York: Thunder's Mouth, 1986), 78–79.

37. Spivak, "Race before Racism," 84, 85.

38. See Winston James, "Migration, Racism and Identity: The Caribbean Experience in Britain," *New Left Review* 193 (May–June 1992): 49–55.

39. Gratiant, "Mulâtres . . . pour le bien et le mal," *L'Etudiant noir* 1 (March 1935): 5–7. This essay has been reprinted in Gratiant, *Fables créoles et autres écrits,* ed. Isabelle Gratiant et al. (Paris: Stock, 1996), 701–710.

40. Ibid., 7.

41. See Henry Louis Gates, Jr., "Preface to Blackness: Text and Pretext," in *Afro-American Literature: The Reconstruction of Instruction,* ed. Dexter Fisher and Robert Stepto (New York: Modern Language Association, 1978), 44–69.

42. David Scott, preface to "The Archaeology of Black Memory: An Interview with Robert A. Hill," *Small Axe* 5 (March 1999): 83.

43. See William L. Andrews, *To Tell a Free Story: The First Century of Afro-American Autobiography, 1769–1865* (Urbana: University of Illinois Press, 1986).

44. Du Bois, "Forethought," *The Souls of Black Folk,* in Du Bois, *Writings* (New York: Library of America, 1986), 359. Here I am adopting the title phrase of

Paul de Man's *Allegories of Reading: Figural Language in Rousseau, Nietzsche, Rilke, and Proust* (New Haven: Yale University Press, 1979).

45. Toni Morrison, "The Site of Memory," in *Inventing the Truth: The Art and Craft of Memoir,* ed. William Zinsser (Boston: Houghton Mifflin, 1987), 109–110.

46. Du Bois, 359.

47. Robert Stepto, *From behind the Veil: A Study of Afro-American Narrative* (Urbana: University of Illinois Press, 1979), 52.

48. On the epigraphs to *The Souls of Black Folk,* see Eric Sundquist, *To Wake the Nations: Race in the Making of American Literature* (Cambridge: Harvard University Press, 1993), 490–493.

49. Stepto, 62.

50. See for example the sections on the novel in Stepto, *From behind the Veil* and Sundquist, *To Wake the Nations;* and also Aldon Nielsen's "James Weldon Johnson's Impossible Text: *The Autobiography of an Ex-Colored Man,*" in *Writing between the Lines: Race and Intertextuality* (Athens: University of Georgia Press, 1994), 172–184. Houston Baker, Jr., goes so far as to claim that "in a sense, *The Autobiography of an Ex-Colored Man* is a fictional rendering of *The Souls of Black Folk.*" Baker, *Singers of Daybreak: Studies in Black American Literature* (Washington, D.C.: Howard University Press, 1974), 22.

51. Richard Yarborough, "The First-Person in Afro-American Fiction," in *Afro-American Literary Study in the 1990's,* ed. Houston A. Baker and P. Redmond (Chicago: University of Chicago Press, 1989), 118.

52. James Weldon Johnson, *The Autobiography of an Ex-Colored Man* (1927; reprint, New York: Vintage, 1989), xxxix. Page numbers of subsequent citations will be indicated parenthetically in the text.

53. Interestingly, the book was received as a valid autobiographical document, and Johnson did not officially claim authorship until 1915. See Eugene Levy, *James Weldon Johnson: Black Leader, Black Voice* (Chicago: University of Chicago Press, 1973), 161.

54. Du Bois, 364, 365.

55. Nielsen, 173–174.

56. Nielsen, 178.

57. Johnson, "Race Prejudice and the Negro Artist," *Harper's Magazine* 157 (1928), reprinted in *The Selected Writings of James Weldon Johnson, vol. 2: Social, Political and Literary Essays,* ed. Sondra Kathryn Wilson (New York: Oxford University Press, 1995), 397.

58. Nielsen, 173.

59. Gerald Early, "Introduction" *My Soul's High Song: The Collective Writings of Countee Cullen, Voice of the Harlem Renaissance* (New York: Doubleday, 1991), 33.

60. Here is an inexhaustive, chronological sampling of the unprecedented explosion of anthologies and collections of "Negro materials" in English, French, and German after World War I. To give a sense of the breadth of this activity, I have included popular, literary, anthropological, musicological, and historical works (some collections would fall under more than one of these categories). *Anthologie nègre,* ed. Blaise Cendrars (Paris: Editions de la Sirene, 1921); *Petits Contes nègres pour les enfants des blancs,* ed. Cendrars (Paris: Denoël, 1921); *Atlantis: Volksmärchen und Volksdichtungen afrikans,* 12 volumes, ed. Leo Frobenius (Jena: E. Diederichs, 1921–1928); *Afrikanische Märchen,* ed. C. Meinhof (Jena: E. Diederichs, 1921); *The Book of American Negro Poetry,* ed. James Weldon Johnson (New York: Harcourt Brace, 1922); *Negro Folk Rhymes, Wise and Otherwise,* ed. Thomas Talley (New York: Macmillan, 1922); *L'Ame nègre,* ed. Maurice Delafosse (Paris: Payot, 1922); *La Poésie chez les primitifs,* ed. E. Hurel (Brussels: Goemaere, 1922); *Negro Poets and Their Poems,* ed. Robert Kerlin (Washington, D.C.: Associated Press, 1923); *Congo Life and Jungle Stories,* ed. J. H. Weeks (London: Religious Tract Society, 1923); *An Anthology of Verse by American Negroes,* ed. Newman Ivey White and Walter Clinton Jackson (Durham, N.C.: Trinity College Press, 1924); Fernando Ortiz, *Glosario des Afronegrismos* (Havana: El Siglo, 1924); *The New Negro,* ed. Alain Locke (New York: Albert and Charles Boni, 1925); *Negro Orators and Their Orations,* ed. Carter G. Woodson (Washington, D.C.: Associated Publishers, 1925); *The Negro and His Songs,* ed. Howard W. Odum and Guy B. Johnson (Chapel Hill: University of North Carolina Press, 1925); *On the Trail of Negro Folk Songs,* ed. Dorothy Scarborough (Cambridge: Harvard University Press, 1925); *The Book of American Negro Spirituals,* ed. James Weldon Johnson and J. Rosamond Johnson (New York: Viking, 1925); *Die Schilluk: Geschichte, Religion und Leben eines Niloten-Stammes,* ed. Wilhelm Hofmayr (Mödling bei Wien: Verlag der Administration des Anthropos, 1925); *The Mind of the Negro, as Reflected in Letters Written during the Crisis, 1800–1860,* ed. Carter G. Woodson (Washington, D.C.: Association for the Study of Negro Life and History, 1926); *The Blues—An Anthology,* ed. W. C. Handy and Abbe Niles (New York: Albert and Charles Boni, 1926); *Negro Workaday Songs,* ed. Odum and Johnson (Chapel Hill: University of North Carolina Press, 1926); *Primitive Negro Sculpture,* ed. Paul Guillaume and Thomas Munro (1926; reprint, New York: Hacker Art Books, 1968); *Among the Bantu Nomads,* ed.

J. T. Brown (London: Seeley, Service and Co., 1926); *Four Negro Poets,* ed.
Locke (New York: Simon and Schuster, 1927); *Caroling Dusk: An Anthology
of Verse by Negro Poets,* ed. Countee Cullen (New York: Harper and Brothers,
1927); *Ebony and Topaz: A Collectanea,* ed. Charles S. Johnson (New York:
Opportunity, 1927); *L'Art nègre: l'art animiste des noirs d'Afrique,* ed. Georges
Hardy (Paris: H. Laurens, 1927); *La Littérature populaire à la côte des esclaves:
contes, proverbes, devinettes,* ed. R. Trautmann (Paris: Institut d'Ethnologie,
1927); *A Decade of Negro Self-Expression,* ed. Locke (Charlottesville: John F.
Slater Fund, 1928); *Le Nègre qui chante,* ed. Eugène Jolas (Paris: Cahiers
Libres, 1928); *Anthology of American Negro Literature,* ed. V. F. Calverton
(New York: Modern Library, 1929); *Neue Märchen aus Afrika,* ed. A. Mislich
(Leipzig: R. Voigtländers, 1929); *Akan-Ashanti Folk-Tales,* ed. R. S. Rattray
(Oxford: Clarendon Press, 1930); *African Stories,* ed. A. D. Helser (New
York: Fleming H. Revell, 1930); *Diaeli, le livre de la sagesse noire,* ed. André
Demaison (Paris: H. Piazza, 1931); *Proverbes et maximes peuls et toucouleurs
traduits, expliqués et annotés,* ed. H. Gaden (Paris: Institut d'Ethnologie,
1931); *Ce que content les Noirs,* ed. O. de Bouveignes (Paris: P. Lethielleux,
1935); *Negro: An Anthology,* ed. Nancy Cunard (1934; reprint, New York:
Negro Universities Press, 1969).

   Regarding the history of anthologies in African American literature, see
John S. Lash, "The Anthologist and the Negro Author," *Phylon* 7, no. 1
(1947): 68–76; Kenneth Kinnamon, "Anthologies," in *The Oxford Companion to African American Literature,* ed. William L. Andrews, Frances Smith
Foster, and Trudier Harris (New York: Oxford University Press, 1997), 22–
28; Theodore O. Mason, Jr., "The African-American Anthology: Mapping
the Territory, Taking the National Census, Building the Museum," *American
Literary History* 10, no. 1 (1998): 185–198.

61. Mason, "The African-American Anthology," 187.
62. Ibid., 192.
63. The phrase "allographic preface" is adopted from Gerard Genette, *Paratexts:
    Thresholds of Interpretation,* trans. Jane E. Lewin (Cambridge: Cambrige Uni-
    versity Press, 1997), 161, 263–275.
64. See Gayatri Chakravorty Spivak, "Translator's Preface," in Jacques Derrida,
    Of Grammatology (Baltimore: Johns Hopkins University Press, 1976), ix–xiii.
65. James Weldon Johnson, *Along This Way: The Autobiography of James Weldon
    Johnson* (1933; reprint, New York: Penguin, 1990), 374–375. On the publi-
    cation of *The Book of American Negro Poetry,* see Levy, *James Weldon Johnson,*
    304–305.
66. "Preface to the First Edition," *The Book of American Negro Poetry* (rev. 2nd

ed., New York: Harcourt Brace Jovanovich, 1931), 9. Page numbers for subsequent references will be indicated parenthetically in the text.

67. Immanuel Wallerstein, "The National and the Universal: Can There Be Such a Thing as World Culture?" in *Culture, Globalization and the World-System: Contemporary Conditions for the Representation of Identity,* ed. Anthony D. King (Minneapolis: University of Minnesota, 1997), 100.

68. Paul Gilroy, *The Black Atlantic: Modernity and Double Consciousness* (Cambridge: Harvard University Press, 1993), 36. Interestingly, Gilroy takes this phrase without comment from a context that inflects it rather differently, Zygmut Bauman's "The Left as the Counterculture of Modernity," *Telos* 70 (winter 1986–1987): 81–93.

69. Johnson, *Along This Way,* 375.

70. Ibid., 375. He notes that "the word was coined, so far as I know, by Sir Harry H. Johnston," and says that it acquired a "slightly derisive sense" in the 1920s when it was adopted by H. L. Mencken.

71. Jacques Derrida, *Dissemination,* trans. Barbara Johnson (Chicago: University of Chicago Press, 1981), 17.

72. Johnson, "Preface to the Revised Edition," *The Book of American Negro Poetry,* 3.

73. Ibid., 5. On Johnson's prefaces to *God's Trombones* and *The Book of American Negro Spirituals* and his arguments about "Negro dialect," see Brent Hayes Edwards, "The Seemingly Eclipsed Window of Form: James Weldon Johnson's Prefaces," in *The Jazz Cadence of American Culture,* ed. Robert O'Meally (New York: Columbia University Press, 1997), 580–601.

74. Derrida, *Dissemination,* 36.

75. Baba Diarra, "Réponse d'un ancien tirailleur sénégalais à M. Paul Boncour," *La Race nègre* 1 (June 1927): 158.

76. Philippe de Witte, *Les Mouvements nègres en France,* 157.

77. Miller, "Involution and Revolution," 44.

78. Fanon writes for instance that the Antillean "knows that what the poets call *divine crooning* [*roucoulement divin*] (that is: Creole) is only a middle term between pidgin-nigger [*petit-nègre*] and French." Fanon, "The Negro and Language," in *Black Skin, White Masks,* trans. Charles Lam Markmann (New York: Grove, 1967), 20 (modified). The original is "Le noir et le langage," in *Peau noire, masques blancs* (Paris: Seuil, 1952), 15.

79. Cousturier, *Des Inconnus chez moi,* 103. The excerpt in the paper is "Notre page littéraire: un général sauvage, de Lucie Cousturier," *La Race nègre* 1 (June 1927): 3. On *petit nègre,* see also Myron Echenberg, *Colonial Conscripts: The Tirailleur Sénégalais in French West Africa, 1857–1960* (Ports-

mouth, N.H.: Heinemann, 1991), 15, 115–116. The *petit nègre* instruction manual used during the war was the sublimely titled *Le Français tel que le parlent nos tirailleurs sénégalais* (French as our African soldiers speak it) (1916).

80. De Witte, *Les Mouvements nègres en France,* 158.

81. Lacascade, *Claire-Solange, âme africaine* (Paris: Eugène Figuière, 1924), 95. Page numbers of subsequent quotes will be indicated parenthetically in the text.

82. Maryse Condé, *La Parole des femmes, essai sur les romanciers des Antilles de langue française* (Paris: L'Harmattan, 1979), 28–31.

83. See Jack Corzani, *La Littérature des Antilles-Guyane françaises, vol. 3: la Négritude* (Fort-de-France: Editions Desormeaux, 1978), 211–213. I have located no information on Lacascade aside from this anecdote.

84. *Pas fais guiolle kiou poule, da chè* translated literally means "Don't make a face like a hen's ass, my dear."

85. See Peter Ostwald, *Schumann: The Inner Voices of a Musical Genius* (Boston: Northeastern University Press, 1985), 115; Frederick Niecks, *Robert Schumann* (London: J. M. Dent, 1925), 176.

86. Du Bois, "The Sorrow Songs," *The Souls of Black Folk,* 538–539. Other slightly different versions of this anecdote are "The Shadow of Years," chapter 1 in *Darkwater: Voices from within the Veil* (1920; reprint, New York: Dover, 1999), 3; "The Concept of Race," chapter 5 in *Dusk of Dawn: An Essay toward an Autobiography of a Race Concept* (1940), in *Writings* (New York: Library of America, 1986), 638; and *The Autobiography of W. E. B. Du Bois: A Soliloquy on Viewing My Life from the Last Decade of Its First Century* (New York: International Publishers, 1968), 62.

87. Ousmane Socé, *Karim, roman sénégalais* (1935; reprint, Paris: Nouvelles Editions Latines, 1948).

88. For the often overlooked translations by the fathers of Négritude, see Sterling Brown, "Les Hommes Forts" (Strong Men), trans. Aimé Césaire, *Charpentes* 1 (June 1939): 52–53 [the issue features poetry from around the world, although there is no U.S. rubric: the translation of Brown's poem is listed along with poems by Senghor and Léon-Gontran Damas under "Afrique noire"]; Léopold Sédar Senghor, "Trois poètes négro-américains," *Poésie 45* 23 (February–March 1945): 32–44 [the selection offers translations and the English originals of Jean Toomer, "Song of the Sun" and "Georgia Dusk"; Langston Hughes, "Our Land," "An Earth Song," and "Minstrel Man"; and Countee Cullen, "Heritage"]. On Hughes's own work as translator, see Alfred J. Guillaume, Jr., "And Bid Him Translate: Langston Hughes' Translations of Poetry from French," *The Langston Hughes Review* 4, no. 2 (fall 1985): 1–23; John F.

Matheus, "Langston Hughes as Translator," in *Langston Hughes: Black Genius,* ed. Therman B. O'Daniel (New York: William Morrow, 1971), 157–170.

89. Langston Hughes, *Fine Clothes to the Jew* (New York: Knopf, 1927).

90. Regarding reviews of *Fine Clothes to the Jew,* see *Langston Hughes: Critical Perspectives Past and Present,* ed. Henry Louis Gates, Jr., and K. A. Appiah (New York: Amistad, 1993); and Hughes, *The Big Sea: An Autobiography* (1940; reprint, New York: Thunder's Mouth Press, 1986), 264.

91. Howard Mumford Jones, *Chicago Daily News* (June 29, 1927), in *Langston Hughes: Critical Perspectives,* 67.

92. Arnold Rampersad, *The Life of Langston Hughes, vol. 1: I, Too, Sing America* (New York: Oxford University Press, 1986), 141.

93. Hughes, "The Weary Blues," *The Weary Blues* (1926), collected in *The Collected Poems of Langston Hughes,* ed. Arnold Rampersad (New York: Knopf, 1994), 50.

94. Hughes, "Young Gal's Blues," in *Fine Clothes,* 83.

95. Martin Williams, "Recording Limits and Blues Form," in *The Art of Jazz: Essays on the Nature and Development of Jazz,* ed. Williams (New York: Grove, 1959), 91–94.

96. Hughes, "Baby," "Shout," in *Fine Clothes,* 61, 49.

97. Jahan Ramazani, *Poetry of Mourning: The Modern Elegy from Hardy to Heaney* (Chicago: University of Chicago Press, 1994), 153.

98. Hughes, "Hey" and "Hey! Hey!" in *Fine Clothes,* 17, 89. Indeed, Hughes would republish these poems as a single two-stanza poem, "Night and Morn," in his book *The Dream Keeper* (New York: Knopf, 1932).

99. Ramazani, *Poetry of Mourning,* 140–143.

100. Hughes, *The Big Sea,* 264.

101. Hughes, "Songs Called the Blues," *Phylon* 2 (second quarter 1941): 143.

102. Hughes, "Magnolia Flowers," "Mulatto," "Red Silk Stockings," *Fine Clothes,* 70, 71–72, 73.

103. Langston Hughes, "Jazz Band in a Parisian Cabaret," in *Fine Clothes,* 74.

104. Hughes, *The Big Sea,* 162.

105. See Hughes, *The Big Sea,* 158–163, 171–183; Craig Lloyd, *Eugene Bullard: Black Expatriate in Jazz-Age Paris* (Athens: University of Georgia Press, 2000), 90–100; William A. Shack, *Harlem in Montmartre: A Paris Jazz Story between the Great Wars* (Berkeley: University of California Press, 2001), 33; Bricktop [Ada Smith Ducongé] with James Haskins, *Bricktop* (New York: Atheneum, 1983), 84–103; Rampersad, *The Life of Langston Hughes, vol. 1,* 85.

106. Hughes, *The Big Sea,* 162.

107. I have adopted the phrase "amphibious spaces" from Stepto, *From behind the Veil,* 102.

108. Hughes, "The Cat and the Saxophone (2 A.M.)," *The Weary Blues* (1926), collected in *The Collected Poems,* 89. Rampersad gives the source of the lyric in his endnote, 624.

109. Hughes, "Jazz as Communication," in *The Langston Hughes Reader* (New York: G. Braziller, 1958), 492.

110. Significantly, the poem was originally titled "To a Negro Jazz Band in a Parisian Cabaret" when published in the *Crisis* in 1925; the revised title in *Fine Clothes* allows the phrase to be read both as an apostrophe and as a descriptive. Hughes, "Jazz Band in a Parisian Cabaret," *Crisis* (December 1925): 67. See Rampersad's note in *The Collected Poems,* 620.

111. Duke Ellington, "The Encyclopedia of Jazz," foreword to Leonard Feather, *The Encyclopedia of Jazz* (New York: Bonanza Books, 1960), 15.

112. Hughes, "Songs Called the Blues," 145.

113. See Jacques Derrida, "Schibboleth, pour Paul Celan," in *Midrash and Literature,* ed. Geoffrey Hartman and S. Budick (New Haven: Yale University Press, 1986), 324–325.

2. On Reciprocity: René Maran and Alain Locke

1. René Maran, *Batouala* (Paris: Albin Michel, 1921). Page numbers of subsequent citations to this edition will be indicated parenthetically in the text. Nearly two decades later, Maran published a thoroughly revised "definitive edition" (Paris: Albin Michel, 1938).

2. Maran, *Batouala,* trans. Adele Szold Seltzer (New York: Thomas Selzter, 1922). The English translation was also published in London by Jonathan Cape in 1922. A different, somewhat better translation of the "definitive edition" appeared in the 1970s: see Maran, *Batouala: A True Black Novel,* trans. Barbara Beck and Alexandre Mboukou (Washington, D.C.: Black Orpheus, 1972). Hubert Harrison, "M. Maran's *Batouala,* a French-African Tale: Work of a Negro Novelist as It Impresses a Negro Reviewer—Prize Story of a Land That Has Known the Abuses of Civilization," *New York World* (August 20, 1922), collected in *A Hubert Harrison Reader,* ed. Jeffrey B. Perry (Middletown, Conn.: Wesleyan University Press, 2001), 334.

3. Charles Chesnutt, Letter to Benjamin Brawley, March 24, 1922, Moorland-Spingarn Collection, Howard University, quoted in Michel Fabre, "René Maran, the New Negro and Negritude," *Phylon* 36, no. 3 (September 1975): 341. Alain Locke, "The Colonial Literature of France," *Opportunity* 1 (November 1923): 331. Interestingly, in an extremely uncommon link, Locke's

essay was published nearly simultaneously in Marcus Garvey's the *Negro World* (December 15, 1923): 6. Alain Locke, "Negro Youth Speaks," in *The New Negro,* ed. Alain Locke (1925; reprint, New York: Atheneum, 1968), 51.

4. "More about René Maran," *Opportunity* 1 (January 1923): 31. Jessie Fauset, "No End of Books," *Crisis* (March 1922), collected in *The Chinaberry Tree and Selected Writings,* ed. Mary Jane Knopf (Boston: Northeastern University Press, 1995), 346. See also Fauset, "'Batouala' is translated," *Crisis* 24 (September 1922): 218–219.

5. "The Whole World Is Reading It!" *Crisis* 23 (March 1922): 208–209.

6. Robert Machray, "The Negro Problem of France," *Negro World* (May 5, 1923); William H. Ferris, "The Significance of René Maran," *Negro World* (March 11, 1922); J. A. Rogers, review, *Negro World* (Sept. 23, 1922). See also "Speech by Marcus Garvey" (August 1, 1922), in *The Marcus Garvey and UNIA Papers, vol. 4: 1 Sept. 1921–2 Sept. 1922,* ed. Robert A. Hill (Berkeley: University of California Press, 1985).

7. W. E. B. Du Bois, "The Negro Mind Reaches Out," *Foreign Affairs* 3, no. 3 (1924), collected in *The New Negro,* 392.

8. See Michel Fabre, "Autour de Maran," *Présence africaine* 86 (second trimester 1973): 171.

9. Maran, *Batouala,* 11–12; Maran, *Batouala,* trans. Seltzer, 10 (modified).

10. Toni Morrison, "Unspeakable Things Unspoken: The Afro-American Presence in American Literature," in *Modern Critical Views: Toni Morrison,* ed. Harold Bloom (New York: Chelsea House, 1990), 210.

11. Spivak, "Three Women's Texts and a Critique of Imperialism," in *'Race,' Writing and Difference,* ed. Henry Louis Gates, Jr. (Chicago: University of Chicago Press, 1986), 279.

12. *Anthologie nègre,* ed. Blaise Cendrars (Paris: Editions de la Sirene, 1921). An expanded edition was published a few years later (Paris: Au Sans Pareil, 1927). This second edition was translated into English under the title *The African Saga,* trans. Margery Bianco (1927; reprint, New York: Negro Universities Press, 1969).

13. Maran, "Le Professeur Alain Leroy Locke," *Présence africaine* 4 (1949): 137. Also see Fabre, "René Maran, the New Negro and Negritude," 350.

14. Edward W. Said, *Orientalism* (New York: Vintage, 1978).

15. Leiris, quoted in Steins, *Blaise Cendrars: bilans nègres* (Paris: Lettres Modernes, 1977), 10.

16. Cendrars, "Notice," *Anthologie nègre,* n.p.

17. Steins, *Blaise Cendrars,* 18.

18. On the *indigénat,* see Jean Suret-Canale, *French Colonialism in Tropical Af-*

rica, 1900–1945, trans. Till Gottheiner (New York: Pica Press, 1971), 331–336. The original is *Afrique noire, vol. 2: l'ère coloniale, 1900–1945* (Paris: Editions Sociales, 1964).

19. See Sarraut's *La Mise en valeur des colonies françaises* (Paris: Payot, 1923).

20. For discussions of this developing discipline in France, see Raoul Girardet, *L'Idée coloniale en France de 1871–1962* (Paris: La Table Ronde, 1972), 231–233; Herman Lebovics, "Identity Conflicts: Folklore and National Heritage," *True France: The Wars over Cultural Identity, 1900–1940* (Ithaca: Cornell University Press, 1992), 135–162.

21. Michel Leiris, "Du Musée d'Ethnographie au Musée de l'Homme," *La Nouvelle Revue française* 299 (August 1938): 344–345; Paul Rivet, "Organisation d'un musée d'ethnologie," *Museum* 1, no. 1–2 (July 1948): 68–69, 111–112; Georges Henri Rivière, "My Experience at the Musée d'Ethnologie," in *Proceedings of the Royal Anthropological Institute of Great Britain and Ireland for 1968* (London: Royal Anthropological Institute, 1969), 17–21.

22. Maurice Delafosse, "Sur l'orientation nouvelle de la politique indigène dans l'Afrique noire," *Renseignements coloniaux* 6, supplement to *L'Afrique française* (1921), 145; quoted in Raymond Leslie Buell, *The Native Problem in Africa,* vol. 2 (New York: MacMillan, 1928), 88–89 (modified). On his complex career, see *Maurice Delafosse: entre orientalisme et ethnographie: l'itinéraire d'un africainiste (1870–1926),* ed. Jean-Loup Amselle and Emmanuelle Sibeud (Paris: Maisonneuve and Larose, 1998).

23. Buell, *The Native Problem in Africa,* vol. 2, 85.

24. Maurice Delafosse, *Les Civilisations négro-africaines* (Paris: Librairie Stock-Delamain, 1925); André Demaison, *Diaeli, le livre de la sagesse noire* (Paris: Editions d'Art H. Piazza, 1931); Louis Huot, "L'âme noire: l'homme primitif centre-africain," *Mercure de France* 560 (October 15, 1921): 372–405; Lucien Levy-Bruhl, *La Mentalité primitive* (Paris: Librairie Félix Alcan, 1923); Robert Delavignette, *Les Paysans noirs* (Paris: Stock, 1931); Leo Frobenius, *Histoire de la civilisation africaine,* trans. H. Back and D. Ermont (Paris: Gallimard, 1936).

25. Delafosse, quoted in Buell, 88–89.

26. Alice L. Conklin, *A Mission to Civilize: The Republican Idea of Empire in France and West Africa, 1895–1930* (Stanford: Stanford University Press, 1997), 175.

27. M. le Gouverneur Général to MM. les Lieutenants-Gouverneurs, "Circulaire confidentielle au sujet du Congrès panafricain de Bruxelles et de Paris," September 17, 1921, quoted in Conklin, 190.

28. These reports are collected in the Archives Nationales: "Rapport des colonies sur l'état d'esprit des populations indigènes: la repercussion des congrès pan-

africains de Bruxelles et de Paris (1921)," Archives Nationales de la République du Sénégal (hereafter ANS) Archives du gouvernement général de l'Afrique occidentale française, *fonds moderne,* series 21G, folder 124. Cf. also "Garveyisme," ANS series 21G, folder 126.

29. Demaison, *Diaeli, le livre de la sagesse noire,* 3.

30. Delafosse, *Les Noirs de l'Afrique* (Paris: Payot, 1922), 3–4.

31. Ibid., 157.

32. Ibid., 159–160.

33. Girardet, *L'Idée coloniale en France,* 236–238.

34. René Maran, "French African Literature," *Encyclopaedia Britannica,* 14th ed. (1929), 755.

35. Leiris, *L'Age d'homme* (Paris: Gallimard, 1939), 162. In Africa, though, Leiris would depart from such a position; see *L'Afrique fantôme* (1934; reprint, Paris: Gallimard, 1981) and his interview with Michael Haggerty, "L'autre qui apparaît chez vous," *Jazz Magazine* 325 (January 1984): 33–36.

36. Michael Haggerty, "Georges Henri Rivière: 'un mariage d'amour,'" *Jazz Magazine* 325 (January 1984): 48–49; J. F. Leroux-Dhuys, "Georges Henri Rivière, un homme dans le siècle," in *La Muséologie selon Georges-Henri Rivière,* ed. Anne Gruner Schlumberger (Paris: Dunod, 1989), 16–17.

37. Rivière, "Roland Hayes," *Les Continents* 3 (June 15, 1924): 2; "Lettre d'un provincial," *Les Continents* 8 (September 1, 1924): 2.

38. Leroux-Dhuys, 17.

39. Ibid., 17. Also see Brent Hayes Edwards, "The Ethnics of Surrealism," *Transition* 78 (1999): 84–91.

40. Paul Gaultier, "Du jazz-band au roman nègre," *Revue politique et littéraire (Revue bleue)* (January 21, 1922); reproduced in *Jazz Magazine* 325 (January 1984): 37.

41. Paul Souday, "Livres," *Le Temps* (December 15, 1921).

42. Girardet, *L'Idée coloniale en France,* 240.

43. Angoulvant, "Préface" to Gaston Joseph, *Koffi, roman vrai d'un Noir* (Paris: Editions du Monde Nouveau, 1922), 7. The novel was translated as *Koffi: The Romance of a Negro* by E. A. Wood (London: J. Bale, 1923).

44. The Tharaud brothers make much of the fact that Demaison not only lived "in the jungle among the blacks of l'Afrique Occidentale," but also was an expert in African languages, immersing himself in African culture to the point that he was able in *Diato,* "so lively and so colorful, to translate the complication that naturally escapes the notice of the visitor simply passing through." In "Préface," Demaison, *Diato, roman de l'homme noir qui eut trois femmes et en mourut* (Paris: Albin Michel, 1923).

45. Delafosse, *Broussard ou les états d'âme d'un colonial, suivis de ses propos et opin-*

ions (Paris: Emile Larose, 1923), 173; quoted in Iheanachor Egonu, "Le Prix Goncourt de 1921 et la 'querelle de Batouala,'" *Research in African Literatures* 11, no. 4 (winter 1980): 533.

46. Among others, see René Trautmann, *Au pays de 'Batouala': noirs et blancs de l'Afrique* (Paris: Payot, 1922); and J. Blanche, *Vrais noirs et vrais blancs d'Afrique au XXe siècle* (Orléans: Maurice Caillette, 1922). Maran later extended the debate in the anthropological context by publishing his own "non-fiction" version of many of the tales and customs represented in *Batouala*. Maran, "Légendes et coutumes nègres de l'oubangui-chari: choses vues," *Les Œuvres libres* 147 (1933): 325–381.

47. It is not the first, though. That distinction belongs to Ahmadou Mapaté Diagne's short didactic novel for children, *Les Trois Volontés de Malic* (Paris: Larousse, 1920). On Diagne, see Christopher Miller, "Unfinished Business: Colonialism in Sub-Saharan Africa and the Ideals of the French Revolution," in *The Global Ramifications of the French Revolution,* ed. Joseph Klaits and Michael H. Haltzel (New York: Woodrow Wilson Center Press/Cambridge University Press, 1994), 105–126.

48. G. Barthémey, "Batouala," *Les Annales coloniales* 24, no. 1 (January 2, 1923); Henri Bidou, "Parmi les livres," *La Revue de Paris* (January–February 1922): 400–405. A few of the reviews in English reflect this charge that *Batouala* was "propaganda"; see Julia Wood, "Black Shame and France," *New York Times* (April 30, 1922).

49. Fabre points out that "the phrase 'contemporary African' was used again and again" to describe Maran in American reviews of the novel. Arna Bontemps praised "this first novel by an African to receive the great French prize" (Bontemps interview, March 16, 1972, quoted in Fabre, "René Maran, the New Negro and Negritude," 342). Similarly, Robert Machray writes that Maran is a "pure African Negro" in "The Negro Problem of France," *Negro World* (May 5, 1923). Interestingly, Ernest Hemingway, writing for the *Toronto Star Weekly,* gave the novel an accurate and positive review, noting that Maran's defenders "have rallied to him and asked the politicians to take the novel as a work of art which it is: great art, except for the preface, which is the only bit of propaganda in the work." Hemingway, "A Prize-Winning Book is Centre of Storm," *Toronto Star Weekly* (March 25, 1922): 3.

50. Fauset, "No End of Books," 346. But see Fauset's smart commentary on the faults of the original English translation: "'Batouala' Is Translated," *Crisis* 24 (September 1922): 218–219.

51. Maran, "Souvenirs d'un ancien Prix Goncourt," *Bingo, l'illustré africain* 73 (February 1959): 13.

52. The best consideration of the French critical response to *Batouala* is Egonu,

"Le Prix Goncourt de 1921 et la 'querelle de Batouala,'" 529–545. Fabre, in "René Maran, the New Negro and Negritude," considers the African American response in a general sense, while the most thorough take on the many reviews in the *Negro World* is Tony Martin's *Literary Garveyism* (Dover, Mass.: Majority Press, 1983), 95–99. For criticism on the story itself rather than the reception of *Batouala* as a cultural force, one might begin with Lilyan Kesteloot, *Les Écrivains noirs de langue française: naissance d'une littérature* (Brussels: Université Libre, 1963), 83–90; Femi Ojo-Ade, *René Maran, the Black Frenchman: A Bio-Critical Study* (Washington, D.C.: Three Continents, 1984), 47–52; Keith Cameron, *René Maran* (Boston: Twayne, 1985), 14–41; Manuel Gahisto, "La genèse de *Batouala*," in *Hommage à René Maran* (Paris: Présence Africaine, 1965), 93–155.

53. Asad, "The Concept of Cultural Translation in British Social Anthropology," in *Writing Culture: The Poetics and Politics of Ethnography*, ed. James Clifford and George Marcus (Berkeley: University of California Press, 1986), 160.

54. Demaison, "Préface," in *Diato* n.p.; Jérôme and Jean Tharaud, "Préface," in *La Randonnée de Samba Diouf* (Paris: Librairie Plon, 1922), 3–4.

55. Asad, "The Concept of Cultural Translation," 160.

56. In fact, one of the main complaints in reviews of *Batouala* was that the novel contained too many unfamiliar African words. This response was common both in Paris (the review in *La Nouvelle Revue française* complained about the abundance of "vocables nègres") and in English-language reviews of the translation. When an episode from the novel appeared in the journal the *Living Age,* for example, the accompanying commentary complained that the African words were a "nuisance." See "'Batouala' and the Winner of the Prix Goncourt," *Living Age* 312 (February 4, 1922): 307–309. Also see Egonu, "Le Prix Goncourt de 1921 et la 'querelle de Batouala,'" 536–537.

57. Chantal Zabus, *The African Palimpsest: Indigenization of Language in the West African Europhone Novel* (Amsterdam: Rodopi, 1991), 157–158.

58. Maran, letter to M. Burel, November 6, 1922, correspondence file, René Maran papers, collection of Michel Fabre, Paris.

59. Locke, "The Colonial Literature of France," 331.

60. Ibid., 334.

61. Ibid., 331.

62. Although Freud and Locke both employ a metaphor of inscription to suggest the workings of the psyche, the differences between these models are significant. Freud is describing the "hypothetical" structure of perceptual and mnemic systems in the individual psyche. Locke's image, on the other hand, is both more ambitious and more loosely formulated: it aims to describe a model of the impression of cultural, even ideological, data onto a collective

psyche, the "public mind." Locke's confusing proposition of an etching that erases implies that racist ideology can be wiped clean or corrected—apparently it can be erased without leaving a trace. For Freud, on the contrary, the attraction of the novelty "mystic writing-pad" *(Wunderblock)* is precisely its ability to "provide both an ever-ready receptive surface and permanent traces of the notes that have been made upon it." Sigmund Freud, "A Note upon the 'Mystic Writing-Pad'" (1925), collected in *General Psychological Theory,* ed. Philip Rieff (New York: Collier, 1963), 209.

63. Bruce Robbins, "Comparative Cosmopolitanism," *Social Text* 31–32 (1992): 178.

64. Frantz Fanon, *Peau noire, masques blancs* (Paris: Seuil, 1952), 170–171. The English edition is *Black Skin, White Masks,* trans. Charles Lam Markmann (New York: Grove, 1967), 211 (modified).

65. Locke, "The Colonial Literature of France," 331.

66. McKay, *A Long Way from Home* (New York: Harcourt Brace Jovanovich, 1937), 313.

67. See Egonu, "Le Prix Goncourt de 1921 et la 'querelle de Batouala,'" 530.

68. Egonu, 531–533, 537. On the "failed assimilation" critique, see ibid., 534–535.

69. J. L., "La logique noire," *Le Temps* (February 18, 1922). It should be noted that the author, though he writes *les nègres,* always puts *"les blancs"* in quotes, as though to question at the level of grammar the word's status as a category. So "white" is, in linguistic terms, the "marked" category—what normally would not even have to be named, in other words—and, of course, this is because "white" is defined as "not *nègre*"; it is located precisely by the differentiation of the Other.

70. For example, Batouala's drunken speech about the "evilness" *(méchanceté)* and "duplicity" of the French *(des blancs)* is similar to the rhetoric in the preface: the *blancs,* he says in a long soliloquy, "lie for nothing. They lie with method and memory, they lie the way one breathes. . . . Us? We're less than animals, we're the lowest of the low. They're killing us slowly" (75–77).

71. Chidi Ikonné's candid and thorough essays on Maran are one example of the criticism that chooses to read Maran through this "doubled" logic, attempting to explain it—usually biographically—as a fault that damns *Batouala* to ambivalence or self-contradiction. See "René Maran and the New Negro," *Colby Library Quarterly* 15, no. 4 (December 1979): 224–239; "René Maran, 1887–1960: A Black Francophone Writer between Two Worlds," *Research in African Literatures* 5, no. 1 (spring 1974): 5–22; and especially "What is 'Batouala'?" *Journal of African Studies* 3, no. 3 (fall 1976): 373–391.

72. Senghor, "René Maran, précurseur de la Négritude," in *Hommage à René Maran* (Paris: Présence Africaine, 1965), 11, 13.

73. Maran, "French Colonial Policy: Open Letters," *Opportunity* 2 (September 1924): 201.

74. Ibid., 262.

75. Maran, "La France et ses Nègres," *L'Action coloniale* 5, no. 90 (September 25, 1923): 1.

76. Maran, "French Colonial Policy: Open Letters," 201.

77. Maran, "La France et ses Nègres," 1.

78. Also see his article "Un appel aux écrivains combattants: comment on traite nos frères noirs," *La Rumeur coloniale, La Rumeur financière* 445 (January 28, 1929).

79. Maran, letter to M. Burel, November 6, 1922; Maran, *Un Homme pareil aux autres* (Paris: Editions Arc-en-Ciel, 1947).

80. Maran, "La France et ses Nègres," 1.

81. Léon Treich, "René Maran," *Le Soir* 116 (May 14, 1960): 2.

82. See Ikonné, "René Maran and the New Negro," 232–233.

83. Walter F. White, *L'Etincelle,* trans. Marguerite Humbert-Zeller (Paris: Plon, 1928).

84. On the journal's brief but important publication history, see Iheanachor Egonu, "*Les Continents* and the Francophone Pan-Negro Movement," *Phylon* 42 (September 1981): 245–254; J. Ayodele Langley, "The Movement and Thought of Francophone Pan-Negroism: 1924–1936," chapter 8 in *Pan-Africanism and Nationalism in West Africa, 1900–1945: A Study in Ideology and Social Classes* (London: Oxford University Press, 1973), 286–300; J. S. Spiegler, "Kojo Tovalou-Houénou and *Les Continents,*" chapter 3 in *Aspects of Nationalist Thought among French-Speaking West Africans, 1921–1939* (Ph.D. diss., Oxford University, 1968), 50–80.

85. See "Le bon apôtre," *Les Continents* 11 (October 15, 1924). I suggest that Maran penned the article not only judging from the piece's tone, but also because the scandal was quickly portrayed as a personal battle between the two men—or "Maranism vs. Diagnism," as *Les Continents* described it.

86. "Le procès fantôme," *Les Continents* 13–14 (November 15–December 1, 1924).

87. Hughes, "The Negro" and "A Black Pierrot," *Les Continents* 5 (July 15, 1924). The original sources are "The Negro," *Crisis* (January 1922): 113; "A Black Pierrot," *Amsterdam News* (April 4, 1923): 12. See *The Collected Poems of Langston Hughes,* ed. Arnold Rampersad (New York: Knopf, 1994), 612n24, 614n31.

88. See for example "Maranism vs. Diagnism," *Les Continents* [English section] 13–14 (November 15–December 1, 1924): 1–2. The section includes the "first list of the American members of the Ligue Universelle pour la Défense de la Race Noire," with six subscriptions, all for individuals in Chicago (most likely a reflection of Tovalou Houénou's speaking tour through the Midwest that fall).

89. "La presse noire d'Amérique," *Les Continents* 15 (December 15, 1924). For U.S. awareness of the periodical, see Gwendolyn Bennett, "The Ebony Flute," *Opportunity* 5 (August 1927): 243. On August 25, 1924, Du Bois wrote to Maran: "I have read 'Les Continents' with great pleasure. I hope it will live and I hope that the forward-looking Negroes of America and the world can be brought into close cooperation with your league." W. E. B. Du Bois Papers, University of Massachusetts-Amherst.

90. "Au Caméléon," *Les Continents* 3 (June 15, 1924).

91. Announcement of Roland Hayes benefit concert, June 19 and June 25, 1924, *Les Continents* 3 (June 15, 1924).

92. It is not clear when Du Bois and Maran met, but they knew each other before 1924. The next year, Maran would serve as a judge (along with H. G. Wells, Charles Chesnutt, Sinclair Lewis, and Mary White Ovington) in the short story division of the Amy E. Spingarn Prizes in Negro Literature and Art, organized by the *Crisis.*

93. Du Bois, letter to Maran, August 25, 1924, W. E. B. Du Bois Papers. This letter comes in the midst of a strange exchange between the two. Maran, having recommended Tovalou Houénou, then wrote Du Bois in English on August 15 to warn him that the Dahomean was an "escroc" (the word *escroc* in French means a "swindler" or "conman") and shouldn't be trusted. Four days later, Maran wrote again, saying that although there had been a "few difficulties of private order" with regard to Tovalou Houénou, his prior warning should be disregarded.

94. Claude McKay, "What Is and What Isn't," *Crisis* 27 (April 1924): 259. On Tovalou Houénou, see also the later article by Eslanda Goode Robeson, "Black Paris," *Challenge* 1, no. 4 (January 1936): 12–18.

95. "Convention Report" (New York, August 20, 1924), in *The Marcus Garvey and UNIA Papers, vol. 5: September 1922–August 1924,* ed. Robert A. Hill (Berkeley: University of California, 1983), 762.

96. "Convention Report" (New York, August 18, 1924), in *The Marcus Garvey and UNIA Papers,* 750.

97. Kenneth W. Warren, "Appeals for (Mis)recognition: Theorizing the Diaspora," in *Cultures of United States Imperialism,* ed. Amy Kaplan and Donald E. Pease (Durham: Duke University Press, 1993), 395.

98. "Discours prononcé le 19 Aout, 1924, au Congrès Annuel de l'Association Universelle pour l'Avancement de la Race Noire, pas S. A. le Prince Kojo Tovalou Houénou, Président de la Ligue Universelle pour la Défense de la Race Noire, Directeur Fondateur du Journal 'Les Continents,'" *Negro World* (September 13, 1924). The speech was also excerpted in "Paris, coeur de la race noire," *Les Continents* 9 (September 15, 1924). See also "Notre directeur en Amérique: du Liberty Hall au Carnegie Hall et à Philadelphie," *Les Continents* 9 (September 15, 1924); "Notre directeur en Amérique: de New York à Chicago," *Les Continents* 15 (December 15, 1924).

99. "Convention Reports" (New York, August 31, 1924), in *The Marcus Garvey and UNIA Papers*, 823.

100. Tovalou Houénou, letter to Du Bois, September 3, 1924, W. E. B. Du Bois Papers.

101. As one might expect, there is a great deal written by and about Tovalou Houénou, such as Tovalou Houénou, "Le problème de la race noire," *Negro World* (May 1924): 15, and *Negro World* (May 17, 1924): 17; Tovalou Houénou, "L'esclavagiene [*sic*] colonial," *Negro World* (June 14, 1924): 13; "The Prince of Dahomey Arrives from France," *Negro World* (August 23, 1924): 7. For articles culled directly from issues of *Les Continents,* see John H. Whitaker, "Une crise politique aux Philippines," *Negro World* (June 14, 1924): 13; Georges-Henri Rivière, "Deux heures avec Roland Hayes," *Negro World* (August 16, 1924): 17; "Réponse du Professeur Locke à René Maran," *Negro World* (September 20, 1924): 14; "Après l'ouverture du Congrès de New York: le Prince Kojo Tovalou Houénou en Amérique," *Negro World* (September 20, 1924): 14; "Rapport de Madame Lucie Cousturier," *Negro World* (September 27, 1924): 14.

102. "Hon. Marcus Garvey, Writing from France, Discusses Treatment Accorded Negroes There and in Other Countries of the World," *Negro World* (August 11, 1928).

103. "Report of Speech by Marcus Garvey," *Chicago Tribune* (October 6, 1928), Paris edition, collected in *The Marcus Garvey and Universal Negro Improvement Association Papers, vol. 7: November 1927–August 1940,* ed. Robert A. Hill (Berkeley: University of California Press, 1983), 278. See also "Garvey in Paris Speaks to Famed Club de Faubourg," *Negro World* (October 27, 1928): 1; "Garvey Corrects False Press Report of What Took Place at Faubourg Club, Paris," *Negro World* (November 10, 1928): 1.

104. Daniel Legrand, "L'agitateur au Faubourg: le conférencier Marcus Garvey, dont les geôles américaines n'ont pas refroidi l'ardeur, rêve de conduire ses frères de couleur jusqu'à la Société des Nations," *La Dépêche coloniale et maritime,* (October 9, 1928): 1. SLOTFOM, 3, 65.

105. Maran, letter to Locke, quoted in Ikonné, "René Maran and the New Negro," 234.

106. Locke, "The Black Watch on the Rhine," *Opportunity* 2 (January 1924): 6–9. Page numbers for further references will be indicated parenthetically in the text.

107. Maran, "Lettre ouverte au professeur Alain-Leroy Locke, de l'Université d'Howard (Etats-Unis)," *Les Continents* 3 (June 15, 1924): 1; Maran and Locke, "French Colonial Policy: Open Letters," *Opportunity* 2 (September 1924): 261–263. Page numbers for subsequent references to the *Opportunity* exchange will be indicated parenthetically in the text.

108. It is unclear whether Maran is aware of Locke's 1923 article "The Colonial Literature of France," in which Locke reviews not only Maran's own *Batouala,* but also the Tharauds' *La Randonnée de Samba Diouf,* Gaston Joseph's *Koffi* (1923), Cousturier's *La Forêt du Haut-Niger* (1923), and Llewellyn Powys's *Ebony and Ivory* (1922).

109. Locke, "Apropos of Africa," *Opportunity* 2 (February 1924): 37.

110. Locke, 37 (emphasis added).

111. Locke, "The Colonial Literature of France," *Opportunity* 1 (November 1923): 331.

112. Locke, "Apropos of Africa," 40. This is of course the theme that reappears in Locke's introduction to the anthology he compiled later that year: "As with the Jew, persecution is making the Negro international." Locke, "The New Negro," in *The New Negro,* 14.

113. Locke told the *Chicago Defender* that "[a]mong the progressive movements of today none is more important than the work of the league of nations. Its basic principles of the equality of nations, of self-determination of peoples, and the moral responsibility of governments before the court of world opinion, are the only basis upon which we can hope for a world free of the oppressions and exploitations of the old order of things, the only program that may successfully avoid race war on a scale even bigger than the war we called the World war." Locke, "America Must Aid in Affairs of Africa: Philosopher Sees New Era for Continent," *Chicago Defender* (October 22, 1927), sec. II: 1.

114. For Locke's notion of reciprocity, see also his "The Contribution of Race to Culture," *The Student World* 23 (1930): 349–353; collected in *The Philosophy of Alain Locke: Harlem Renaissance and Beyond,* ed. Leonard Harris (Philadelphia: Temple University Press, 1989), 201–206.

115. Locke, "Apropos of Africa," 37.

116. Ibid., 37.

117. Ibid., 38.

118. Ibid., 38.

119. Warren, 405.

120. See René Maran, "Gandhi," trans. Edna Worthley Underwood, *Opportunity* 3 (February 1925): 40–42; Maran, "The Harriet Beecher Stowe of France" [on Lucie Cousturier], trans. Edna Worthley Underwood, *Opportunity* 3 (August 1925): 229–231; Maran, "Two Book Reviews" [on Albert Londres, *Terre d'ebene;* Claire Goll, *Le Nègre Jupiter enlève Europa*], trans. Rayford W. Logan, *Opportunity* 7 (December 1929): 379–380, 394; Maran, "French Colonization—What It Might Have Been," trans. Francis Hammond, *Opportunity* 14 (1936): 57, 63.

121. David Levering Lewis, *When Harlem Was in Vogue* (New York: Oxford University Press, 1981), 95.

122. Here are just a few examples aside from Locke's "The Colonial Literature of France": "More about René Maran," *Opportunity* 1 (January 1923): 30 [this article was reprinted in part from *Brentano's Book Chat* (Thanksgiving 1922)]; William H. Baldwin, "Africa—A Study in Misunderstanding," *Opportunity* 1 (February 1923): 5–6, 28; "Claude MacKay before the Internationale," *Opportunity* 1 (September 1923): 258–259; "The Color Line in Paris," *Opportunity* 1 (September 1923): 287–288; "Fair France," *Opportunity* 1 (October 1923): 317–318; Alain Locke, "As Others See Us" [on Franck Schoell, *La Question des Noirs aux Etats-Unis*], *Opportunity* 2 (April 1924): 109–110.

123. "African Art" issue, *Opportunity* 2 (May 1924). The other poem is Langston Hughes's "Our Land"; the three appear on p. 142. The pivotal influence of French and German art criticism on Locke's thinking is described in Matgorzata Irek, "From Berlin to Harlem: Felix von Luschan, Alain Locke, and the New Negro," in *The Black Columbiad: Defining Moments in African American Literature and Culture,* ed. W. Sollors and M. Diedrich (Cambridge: Harvard University Press, 1994), 174–184; Mark Helbling, "African Art: Albert C. Barnes and Alain Locke," *Phylon* 43 (March 1982): 57–67; and Locke, "Europe Discovers Negro Art," in *Negro Art: Past and Present* (1936; reprint, New York: Arno, 1969), 34–42. One might also note that Locke met both Barnes and Guillaume in Paris.

124. Cullen, "The Dance of Love (After Reading René Maran's *Batouala*)," *Opportunity* 1 (April 1923): 30. The other poem in this issue is Leslie Pinckney Hill, "Voyaging," 23.

125. Kojo Tovalou Houénou, "The Problem of Negroes in French Colonial Africa," *Opportunity* 2 (July 1924): 203–207. This lecture was originally delivered in February 1924 at the Ecole Interalliée des Hautes Etudes Sociales in Paris.

126. Locke, "La jeune poésie africo-américaine," *Les Continents* 8 (September 1, 1924).

127. Jacques Derrida, "Semiology and Grammatology," in *Positions* (Chicago: University of Chicago Press, 1981), 20.

128. Edward Said, *Culture and Imperialism* (New York: Knopf, 1993).

129. Locke, "Internationalism—Friend or Foe of Art?" *World Tomorrow* (March 1925): 75–76. Subsequent page numbers for this reference are noted in text in parentheses.

130. Maran's work in *Opportunity* is cited earlier. For other translations from the French, see for example: Louis Charbonneau, "Fièvres d'Afrique," trans. Edna Worthley Underwood, *Opportunity* 4 (April 1926): 114–115, 138; "Legend of Ngurangurane" [from Blaise Cendrars, *Anthologie nègre*], trans. Violette de Mazie, *Opportunity* 4 (May 1926): 153–55, 170; Dantès Belle-garde, "Haiti under the Rule of the United States," trans. Rayford W. Logan, *Opportunity* 5 (December 1927): 354–357; Frederic Marcelin, "Jan-Jan: A Haitian Idyll," trans. Suzanne Sylvain, *Opportunity* 6 (January 1928): 16–18, 27; Jenner Bastien, "Haiti and Haitian Society," trans. Countee Cullen, *Opportunity* 6 (June 1928): 176–177; Dantès Bellegarde, "The American Occu-pation of Haiti," trans. J. A. Rogers, *Opporunity* 8 (December 1929): 10–12; Fernand Grogh, "Negroisms," trans. Countee Cullen, *Opportunity* 8 (April 1930): 124–125.

I should note that it is equally possible to trace such an interest in the pages of the other major "Harlem Renaissance" journal, the *Crisis.* This is es-pecially due to the work of Jessie Fauset as literary editor in the 1920s. See Yvette Guilbert, "Joseph and Mary Come to Bethlehem," trans. Jessie Fauset, *Crisis* 21 (December 1920): 72–73; Amédée Brun, "The Pool," trans. Fauset, *Crisis* 22 (September 1921): 205; Oswald Durand, "To a Foreign Maid," trans. Fauset, *Crisis* 25 (February 1923): 158; G. D. Perier, "Kirongozi" (from *Curiosités congolaises*), trans. Fauset, *Crisis* 27 (March 1924): 208–209; Frank L. Schoell, "La question des Noirs aux Etats-Unis" (selections), trans. Fauset, *Crisis* 28 (June 1924): 83–86; Af Carl Kjersmeier, "Negere som digtere" [Negroes as poets], trans. E. Franklin Frazier, *Crisis* 30 (August 1925): 186–189.

131. Benedict Anderson, *Imagined Communities* (1983; 2nd ed., New York: Routledge, 1991), 33.

132. Ibid., 25.

133. Gayatri Chakravorty Spivak, "The Politics of Translation," in *Outside in the Teaching Machine* (New York: Routledge, 1993), 179.

134. Lawrence Venuti, *The Scandals of Translation: Towards an Ethics of Difference* (New York: Routledge, 1998), 69.

135. Warren, "Appeals for (Mis)recognition," 393.
136. Johannes Fabian, *Time and the Other: How Anthropology Makes Its Object* (New York: Columbia University Press, 1983), 31.
137. In Locke's work in particular, this bias reveals itself in his notions of expressive forms. Indeed, in introducing the notion of a "cosmopolitan humanism," Locke pictures it as trickling down from high art to popular art and to "the masses": "In other forms of art and art appreciation, aesthetic cosmopolitanism has been achieved, but fiction has always seemed to reflect the narrower, more stunted values, and to have absorbed the worst provincialisms and prejudices of the Caucasian and European bias. However emancipated the elite, the masses will never respond to the broader view until it expresses itself in the forms of the popular taste and the arts of the masses. Thus the importance, and the peculiar social importance, of a broadening view in drama and fiction—the popular arts. When they begin to reflect cosmopolitan humanism, then to the wakeful eye the great day of humanity almost dawns." Only fiction and drama are "popular" here—film and popular music (and "recording technology") are apparently not even worthy of mention. Locke, "The Colonial Literature of France," 331.
138. Damas, "Misère noire," *Esprit* 7, no. 81 (June 1939): 333–354. Page numbers for further references will be cited parenthetically in the text.
139. Fabian, 34.

3. *Feminism and* L'Internationalisme Noir: *Paulette Nardal*

1. Eslanda Goode Robeson, "Black Paris," part II, *Challenge* 1, no. 5 (June 1936): 11–12. Tellingly, Nardal adds that "[t]he only forbidden subject, the only taboo, is politics, because it is dangerous."
2. "Ce que nous voulons faire" ("Our Aim"), *La Revue du monde noir* 1 (1931): 1–2.
3. The phrase "cultural intermediary" comes from Michel Fabre, "Autour de Maran," *Présence africaine* 86 (second trimester 1973): 169–170. Senghor did not meet Langston Hughes until he visited the United States after World War II. See Mercer Cook, "Afro-Americans in Senghor's Poetry," *Hommage à Léopold Sédar Senghor, homme de culture* (Paris: Présence Africaine, 1976), 152; Janet G. Vaillant, *Black, French, and African: A Life of Léopold Sédar Senghor* (Cambridge: Harvard University Press, 1990), 91–92; Senghor, "Problématique de la Négritude," in *Liberté III: Négritude et civilisation de l'universel* (Paris: Seuil, 1977), 274. English-language contributions to the journal include Langston Hughes, "I, Too," *La Revue du monde noir* 3 (1931): 34; Claude McKay, "To America," *La Revue du monde noir* 1 (1931): 38; McKay, "Spring in New Hampshire," *La Revue du monde noir* 3 (1931):

34; John Matheus, "Fog," *La Revue du monde noir* 1 (1931): 39–52; Cugo Lewis, "T'appin" [originally in Locke's *The New Negro*], *La Revue du monde noir* 4 (1932): 44–47; Walter White, excerpt from "The Fire in the Flint," *La Revue du monde noir* 5 (1932): 37–43; Clara W. Shepard, "Tuskegee Normal and Industrial Institute," *La Revue du monde noir* 2 (1931): 15–18; Shepard, "The Utility of Foreign Languages for American Negroes," *La Revue du monde noir* 4 (1932): 28–31.

4. Senghor, "Femme noire," *Chants d'ombre* (1945), in Senghor, *The Collected Poetry*, trans. Melvin Dixon (Charlottesville: University of Virginia Press, 1991), 270.

5. Keith Warner, interview with Damas, in *Critical Perspectives on Léon-Gontran Damas*, ed. Warner (Washington, D.C.: Three Continents, 1988), 24.

6. In Senegal, Senghor named Nardal an Officier des Palmes Académiques, Chevalier de la Légion d'Honneur, et Commandeur de l'Ordre National de la République du Sénégal. When Nardal died in 1985, Césaire, as *député-maire* in Fort-de-France, Martinique, arranged an elaborate funeral cortege in the city, and a square was renamed after her. See Louis-Thomas Achille, "In Memoriam: Paulette Nardal," *Présence africaine* 133–134 (1985): 291.

7. Quoted in Hymans, *Léopold Sédar Senghor: An Intellectual Biography* (Edinburgh: Edinburgh University Press), 36.

8. "Eveil de la conscience de race" ("Awakening of Race Consciousness"), *La Revue du monde noir* 6 (April 1932): 25. Page numbers for subsequent citations from this essay will be noted in the text in parentheses.

9. It should be evident that the phrase *congénères attardés* (translated as "retarded brothers") does not refer to mental deficiency, but to the "backward" or "delayed" intellectual state of "fellow blacks" *(congénères)* around the world. In addition, the gendered pronouns in the French make it clear that the "they" *(elles)* in the first part of the passage are female, while the "students coming up for degrees" *(étudiants)* can be both male and female.

10. Jane Nardal to Alain Locke, December 27, 1927. Alain Locke Papers, box 164-74, folder 25, Moorland-Spingarn Manuscript Division, Howard University.

11. Cooper, "The Social Conditions of the French-American Colonies: The Class Structure (1925)," and "Black Slavery and the French Nation," in *The Voice of Anna Julia Cooper, Including A Voice from the South and Other Important Essays, Papers, and Letters*, ed. Charles Lemert and Esme Bhan (Lanham: Rowman and Littlefield, 1998), 272–279, 280–290. See also "The Third Step: Cooper's Memoir of the Sorbonne Doctorate (1945–1950?)," in the same volume, 320–330.

12. See Louis Daniel Hutchinson, *Anna Julia Cooper: A Voice from the South* (Washington, D.C.: Smithsonian Institution Press, 1981), 139.

13. On Anna Julia Cooper's career and transatlantic work, see Mary Helen Washington's introduction to Cooper, *A Voice from the South, by a Black Woman of the South* (1892; reprint, New York: Oxford University Press, 1988); Leona C. Gabel, *From Slavery to the Sorbonne and Beyond: The Life and Writings of Anna J. Cooper* (Northampton, Mass.: Dept. of History of Smith College, 1982); David W. H. Pellow, "Anna J. Cooper: The International Dimensions," in *Recovered Writers/Recovered Texts: Race, Class, and Gender in Black Women's Literature,* ed. Dolan Hubbard (Knoxville: University of Tennessee, 1997), 60–74.

14. A good introduction to this history is Michel Fabre, *From Harlem to Paris: Black American Writers in France, 1840–1980* (Urbana: University of Illinois Press, 1991), especially chapters 3, 8, 9, and 10. See also Nellie Bright's essay "Black," *Opportunity* 5 (November 1927): 331–334, collected in *Harlem's Glory: Black Women Writing, 1900–1950,* ed. Lorraine E. Roses and Ruth E. Randolph (Cambridge: Harvard University Press, 1996), 241–248.

15. Leila Rupp's work briefly considers the International Council of Women of the Darker World and the Women's International League for Peace and Freedom, as well as issues of "feminist orientalism" in attempts to include women from the colonized world in international feminist organizations. See *Worlds of Women: The Making of an International Women's Movement* (Princeton: Princeton University Press, 1997), 73–80. Most works on French women between the wars tend to gloss over the colonial issue: see Mary Louise Roberts, *Civilization without Sexes: Reconstructing Gender in Postwar France, 1917–1927* (Chicago: University of Chicago Press, 1994); James E. McMillan, *Housewife or Harlot: The Place of Women in French Society, 1870–1940* (New York: St. Martin's, 1981); Dominique Desanti, *La Femme au temps des années folles* (Paris: Stock, 1984). Works more specifically on French feminism are also marred by this gap: see Christine Bard, *Les Filles de Marianne: histoire des féminismes 1914–1940* (Paris: Fayard, 1995); Paul Smith, *Feminism and the Third Republic: Women's Political and Civil Rights in France, 1918–1945* (Oxford: Clarendon, 1996); Siân Reynolds, *France between the Wars: Gender and Politics* (London: Routledge, 1996).

16. Countee Cullen, "The Dark Tower," *Opportunity* 5 (February 1927): 53.

17. Joan Wallach Scott, *Only Paradoxes to Offer: French Feminists and the Rights of Man* (Cambridge: Harvard University Press, 1996), 8–9.

18. The term "profeminist" comes from Joy James, "Profeminism and Gender Elites: W. E. B. Du Bois, Anna Julia Cooper, and Ida B. Wells-Barnett," in

Transcending the Talented Tenth: Black Leaders and American Intellectuals (New York: Routledge, 1997), 35. In terms of work on gender and black internationalism more generally, one counterexample is the fine recent scholarship of Barbara Bair on issues of gender and black internationalism: see "True Women, Real Men: Gender, Ideology, and Social Roles in the Garvey Movement," in *Gendered Domains: Re-Thinking Public and Private in Women's History*, ed. Dorothy O. Helly and Susan Reverby (Ithaca: Cornell University Press, 1992), 154–166; "Pan-Africanism as Process: Adelaide Casely Hayford, Garveyism, and the Cultural Roots of Nationalism," in *Imagining Home: Class, Culture and Nationalism in the African Diaspora*, ed. Sidney Lemelle and Robin D. G. Kelley (New York: Verso, 1994), 121–144.

19. See W. E. B. Du Bois's summary article, "The Pan-African Congresses: The Story of a Growing Movement," *Crisis* (October 1927): 263–264.

20. Cynthia Neverdon-Morton, *Afro-American Women of the South and the Advancement of the Race, 1895–1925* (Knoxville: University of Tennessee Press, 1989), 198–199; Leila Rupp, *Worlds of Women*, 75.

21. Deborah McDowell, "New Directions for Black Feminist Criticism," *Black American Literature Forum* 14, no. 4 (winter 1986): 157, quoted in Carole Boyce Davies, *Black Women, Writing and Identity: Migrations of the Subject* (New York: Routledge, 1994), 131.

22. Cheryl Wall, *Women of the Harlem Renaissance* (Bloomington: Indiana University Press, 1995), xiv.

23. Bennett, "Tokens," in *Ebony and Topaz: A Collectanea*, ed. Charles Johnson (New York: Opportunity, 1927): 149–150; "Wedding Day," *Fire!!* (November 1926): 25–28.

24. Bennett, "The Ebony Flute," *Opportunity* 5 (September 1927): 277.

25. On Josephine Baker and *La Voix des Nègres*, see Bennett, "The Ebony Flute," *Opportunity* 5 (March 1927): 90. Regarding *Le Courrier des Noirs*, see "The Ebony Flute," *Opportunity* 5 (September 1927): 277.

26. Bennett, "The Ebony Flute," *Opportunity* 5 (August 1927): 243.

27. See Fabre, *From Harlem to Paris*, 120. Bennett's journals are housed at the Schomburg Center, New York Public Library.

28. Joy James critiques Paul Gilroy's 1993 *The Black Atlantic* on this score in *Transcending the Talented Tenth*, 57.

29. Langston Hughes wrote that "Jessie Fauset at the *Crisis*, Charles Johnson at *Opportunity*, and Alain Locke in Washington, were the three people who midwifed the so-called New Negro Literature into being." Hughes, *The Big Sea* (1940; reprint, New York: Thunder's Mouth, 1986), 218. Tellingly, one never sees this term applied in scholarship on the careers of Johnson or Locke, but it is a common descriptive in introductions to Fauset's work, as in

Abby Arthur Johnson, "Literary Midwife: Jessie Redmon Fauset and the Harlem Renaissance," *Phylon* 39, no. 2 (June 1978): 143–153. Melvin Dixon, evidently echoing Hughes's characterization, has written more recently that "the Nardal sisters were the unsung heroines of the negritude movement, midwives to the birth of black consciousness in French literature." Dixon, introduction to Senghor, *The Collected Poetry,* xxvii.

30. Robert Bone, *The Negro Novel in America* (1958; reprint, New Haven: Yale University Press, 1965), 101.

31. Wall, *Women of the Harlem Renaissance,* 48. Another argument for the importance of the essays is Erica L. Griffin, "The 'Invisible Woman' Abroad: Jessie Fauset's New Horizon," in *Recovered Writers/Recovered Texts,* 75–89.

32. Hughes, *The Big Sea,* 247.

33. Fauset, "Tracing Shadows," *Crisis* 10 (September 1915): 247–251; "Dark Algiers the White," *Crisis* 29 (April–May 1925): 255–258; "Nationalism and Egypt," *Crisis* 19 (April 1920): 310–316; "Yarrow Revisited," *Crisis* 29 (1925): 107–109.

34. Fauset, "Nationalism and Egypt," 310.

35. Ibid., 316.

36. See Wall, *Women of the Harlem Renaissance,* ch. 2; McDowell, "The Neglected Dimension of Jessie Redmon Fauset," in *Conjuring: Black Women, Fiction, and Literary Tradition,* ed. Marjorie Pryse and Hortense Spillers (Bloomington: Indiana University Press, 1985), 86–104; Hull, *Color, Sex, and Poetry: Three Women Writers of the Harlem Renaissance* (Bloomington: Indiana University Press, 1987), 7–12.

37. Fauset, Foreword, *The Chinaberry Tree and Other Writings,* ed. Mary Jane Knopf (Boston: Northeastern University Press, 1995), xxxi.

38. Fauset, "Impressions of the Second Pan-African Congress," *Crisis* 22 (November 1921), collected in *The Chinaberry Tree and Other Writings,* 367–382. Page numbers of further references to this essay will be indicated in the text in parentheses.

39. Compare Du Bois's discussion of the congress in "A Second Journey to Pan-Africa," *New Republic* 29 (December 7, 1921): 39–42.

40. Fauset, "What Europe Thought of the Pan-African Congress," *Crisis* 22 (November 1921): 66.

41. McDowell, "The Neglected Dimension of Jessie Redmon Fauset," 87, 88.

42. Fauset, "Yarrow Revisited," 108.

43. Wall, *Women of the Harlem Renaissance,* 38.

44. Fauset, "This Way to the Flea Market," *Crisis* 29 (February 1925): 163.

45. Here is the whole passage: "A laughing youngster offering us a box of shoeblacking, opened the box and pretended to lick it, closing his eyes in an ec-

stasy because it was so good. 'So shoe-blacking your favorite dish now,' bantered my Alsatian, 'and how does it taste?' 'It's all right, my old one,' grinned back the boy, 'you'd better buy some for mademoiselle!'" Fauset, "This Way to the Flea Market," 163. Page numbers of subsequent references to this essay will be indicated in the text in parentheses.

46. Pierre Loving, interview with Fauset, "We're in Paris Because . . . ," in *The Left Bank Revisited: Selections from the Paris Tribune, 1917–1934,* ed. Hugh Ford (University Park: Penn State University Press, 1972), 47.

47. Wall, *Women of the Harlem Renaissance,* 35.

48. Fauset to Spingarn, January 25, 1922, Joel Spingarn Collection, New York Public Library, quoted in Wall, *Women of the Harlem Renaissance,* 58. Fauset did, however, go on to translate articles and poetry for the *Crisis.*

49. Carby, *Reconstructing Womanhood: The Emergence of the Afro-American Woman Novelist* (New York: Oxford University Press, 1987), 166.

50. Ibid., 168.

51. Nella Larsen, *Quicksand* (1928), collected in *Quicksand and Passing,* ed. Deborah E. McDowell (New Brunswick: Rutgers University Press, 1986), 1–135. On this point also see Carby, 173.

52. Farah Jasmine Griffin, *"Who Set You Flowin'?" The African-American Migration Narrative* (New York: Oxford University Press, 1995), 155.

53. Fauset, *Comedy: American Style* (1933; reprint, New York: G. K. Hall, 1995), 183.

54. Fauset, "Nostalgia," *Crisis* 22 (August 1921): 155. Page numbers of subsequent references will be indicated parenthetically in the text.

55. Gates, "The Trope of a New Negro and the Reconstruction of the Image of the Black," *Representations* 24 (fall 1988): 132.

56. Susan Stewart, *On Longing: Narratives of the Miniature, the Gigantic, the Souvenir, the Collection* (Durham: Duke University Press, 1993), 23.

57. Du Bois, *Dusk of Dawn: An Essay toward an Autobiography of a Race Concept* (1940; reprint, New York: Library of America, 1986), 639.

58. Paulette Nardal, "En Exil," *La Dépêche africaine* 19 (December 15, 1929): 6. Subsequent page numbers for this reference are noted in the text in parentheses.

59. In the 1920s, the Algerian city Bechar was known in French as Colomb-Béchar. See *Larousse du XXe siècle,* ed. Paul Augé (Paris: Libraire Larousse, 1929), 346 s.v. "Colomb-Béchar."

60. This passage uses the verb *éveiller* to describe the "obscure emotion" of "African" consciousness, thus prefiguring Nardal's "Eveil de la conscience de race" in *La Revue du monde noir* two years later. This rhetoric of "awakening" would characterize Nardal's take on racial identity during the next decade,

even as late as the article she wrote about Italy's invasion of Ethiopia in 1935. There, she characterizes black internationalism as "un élan purement sentimental, irraisonné, véritable réflexe racial du semblable vers le semblable" ("a purely sentimental, unreasoned surge, a veritable racial reflex of like towards like"). Ethiopia's "sorrow" *(malheur)*, Nardal continues, has been able to "reawaken" *(réveiller)* in peoples of African descent around the world the "secret nostalgia" for a "mysterious bond [*lien*] of race that, suddenly, brings all colonized Negroes, no matter how loyalist, assimilated, and conformist, together with these 'savages.'" Paulette Nardal, "Levée des races," *La Périscope africain* 318 (October 15, 1935): 2.

61. "L'âme Nègre en exil. . . . au bal antillais," Odéon Records catalog (1930), reproduced in Jean-Pierre Meunier and Brigitte Léardée, *La Biguine de l'Oncle Ben's: Ernest Léardée, raconte* (Paris: Editions Caribéennes, 1989), 157.

62. Theodor W. Adorno, "The Form of the Phonograph Record" (1934), trans. Thomas Y. Levin, *October* 55 (winter 1990): 58.

63. Stewart, *On Longing*, 135.

64. Karl Marx, *Capital*, vol. 1 (1867), trans. Ben Fowkes (New York: Vintage, 1977), 165.

65. A. James Arnold, *Modernism and Negritude: The Poetry and Poetics of Aimé Césaire* (Cambridge: Harvard University Press, 1981), 11.

66. Steins, "Jeunesse Nègre," *Neohélicon* 4, nos. 1–2 (1976): 98.

67. Steins, "Black Migrants in Paris," in *European-Language Writing in Sub-Saharan Africa,* vol. 1, ed. Albert S. Gerard (Budapest: Academiai Kiado, 1986), 363.

68. Steins, "Brown France vs. Black Africa: The Tide Turned in 1932," *Research in African Literatures* 14, no. 4 (winter 1983): 477–478.

69. Ibid., 477.

70. For an introduction to Gratiant, see Patrick Chamoiseau and Raphaël Confiant, *Lettres créoles: tracées antillaises et continentales de la littérature: Haïti, Guadeloupe, Martinique, Guyane, 1635–1975* (Paris: Hatier, 1991), 109–111; and especially Jack Corzani, *La Littérature des Antilles-Guyane françaises, vol. 3: la Négritude* (Fort-de-France: Editions Desormeaux, 1978), 222–235.

71. Steins, "Brown France vs. Black Africa," 478.

72. Nardal, "L'internationalisme noir," *La Dépêche africaine* 1 (February 1928): 5.

73. Steins, "Black Migrants in Paris," 363.

74. Satineau writes for instance that "[c]ertainly the colonizing methods of the civilized nations are far from perfect; but colonization in itself is a necessary human undertaking. . . . [I]n the present state of things, the autonomy of the colonies can neither facilitate nor hasten the evolution of the latecomer races [*races retardataires*]." See Satineau, "Notre but—notre programme" *La*

Dépêche africaine 1 (February 1928): 1. See also his "La défense des libertés coloniales," *La Dépêche africaine* 7 (September 1928); "Le Communisme et l'opinion indigène," *La Dépêche africaine* 29–30 (October–November 1930). Paul Guillaume, "Opinion sur l'art nègre," *La Dépêche africaine* 17 (October 15, 1929): 4. See also his "L'art nègre et l'esprit de l'époque," *La Dépêche africaine* 1 (February 1928): 6. Noble Sissle, "Why Jazz Has Conquered the World: It Is the Tonic for the Depressed Condition of the War Weary World," *La Dépêche africaine* [English page] 7 (September 1928). Félix Couchoro, "Le mari parjuré, conte africain," *La Dépêche africaine* 4 (June 1928): 4; "La reconnaissance chez les noirs," *La Dépêche africaine* 6 (August 1928): 6; "Folklore africain: la providence," *La Dépêche africaine* 17 (October 15, 1929): 4; Charles Bellan, "Sauvons nos colonies," *La Dépêche africaine* 1 (February 1928): 1. See also Robert Wibaux, "Elites noires," *La Dépêche africaine* 13 (April 1929): 1. Dantès Bellegarde, "L'occupation de Haïti et ses conséquences économiques," *La Dépêche africaine* 21 (February 15, 1930): 4. One article on activities in Harlem is "Nos triomphes," *La Dépêche africaine* 21 (February 15, 1930): 1.

75. Madame Winter Frappier de Montbenoît, "Les métis des colonies," *La Dépêche africaine* 25 (June 15, 1930): 2. See also her "Les femmes de couleur devant la colonisation," *La Dépêche africaine* 23 (April 15, 1930): 2.

76. Besson, "La femme et l'action coloniale," *La Dépêche africaine* 6 (August 1928): 7. A recent history of this approach to feminism is Cynthia Enloe's *Bananas, Beaches and Bases: Making Feminist Sense of International Politics* (London: Pandora, 1989).

77. Scott, *Only Paradoxes to Offer,* xii, 3.

78. Sylvia Wynter, "Beyond Miranda's Meanings: Un/silencing the 'Demonic Ground' of Caliban's 'Woman,'" in *Out of the Kumbla: Caribbean Women and Literature,* ed. Carole Boyce Davies and Elaine Savory Fido (Trenton: Africa World Press, 1990), 355–372. Wynter writes: "And the central point I want to make in this After/Word is that the contradiction inserted into the consolidated field of meanings of the ostensibly 'universal' theory of feminism by the variable *'race* . . . points toward the emergent 'downfall' of our present 'school like mode of thought' . . . in the same way as feminist theory itself had earlier, inserted the contradiction of the variable *gender* into the ostensibly 'universal' theories of Liberal Humanism and Marxism-Leninism" (356–357).

79. Balibar writes: "The phenomenon of 'depreciation' [*minorisation*] and 'racialization' [*racisation*] which is directed simultaneously against different social groups which are quite different in 'nature' . . . does not represent a juxtaposition of merely analogous behaviors and discourses applied to a potentially

indefinite series of objects independent of each other, but *a historical system of complementary exclusions and dominations which are mutually interconnected.* In other words, it is not in practice simply the case that an 'ethnic racism' and a 'sexual racism' (or sexism) exist in parallel; racism and sexism function together, and in particular, *racism always presupposes a sexism.*" Balibar, "Racism and Nationalism," in Balibar and I. Wallerstein, *Race, Nation, Class: Ambiguous Identities,* trans. Chris Turner (New York: Verso, 1991), 49 (translation modified). The original is *Race, nation, classe: les identités ambiguës* (Paris: La Découverte, 1988), 71.

80. Robeson, "Black Paris," part II, 9.

81. Ibid., 9.

82. Ibid., 10.

83. Besides Paulette, Alice, Cécyl, and Jane, the other sisters were Andrée (who became a pianist), Emilie (who worked as an accountant), and Lucie (who was a math and physics teacher). Interview with Alice Nardal Eda-Pierre, Dec. 3, 1997, Fort-de-France, Martinique. See also Louis-Thomas Achille, "In Memoriam: Paulette Nardal," 292.

84. Paulette Nardal, *Martinique,* in *Guides des colonies françaises: Martinique, Guadeloupe, Guyane, St. Pierre-Miquelon* (Paris: Société d'Editions Géographiques, Maritimes et Coloniales, 1931).

85. John H. Paynter *Fifty Years After* (New York: Margent Press, 1940), 63–64, 66. See also Michel Fabre, *From Harlem to Paris,* 142.

86. This biographical information comes from my conversation with Alice Nardal Eda-Pierre, from Robeson's "Black Paris" essay, and from the entry "Paulette Nardal," in *Fort-de-France: les hommes d'hier dans nos rues d'aujourd'hui,* ed. Marie-Eugénie André et al. (Fort-de-France: Editions Femmes Actuelles, n.d.).

87. Robeson, 10.

88. Nardal, quoted in Michel Fabre, "Autour de Maran," *Présence africaine* 86 (second trimester 1973): 167.

89. Achille, preface to *La Revue du monde noir (1931–32),* reprint edition (Paris: Jean-Michel Place, 1992), xv.

90. Paulette Nardal was stridently Catholic, as were some of the organizations she was affiliated with, such as the Union Féminine Civique et Sociale. She contributed to explicitly religious publications as well, e.g., her article "L'évolution familiale et sociale des femmes noires," *Univers, bulletin catholique international* 3, no. 26 (September 1937): 120–122.

91. See Hull, *Color, Sex, and Poetry,* 5; and David Levering Lewis, *When Harlem Was in Vogue,* (New York: Oxford University Press, 1981) 123, 127–128, 156–157, on salons and "literary evenings" in New York, as well as Boston

(the Quill Club), Philadelphia (the Black Opals group), Washington, D.C. (around Georgia Douglas Johnson, and the journal the *Stylus* at Howard University), and Cleveland.

92. For information on Georgia Douglas Johnson's salons, see Ronald M. Johnson, "Those Who Stayed: Washington's Black Writers of the 1920's," *Records of the Columbia Historical Society* 50 (1980): 484–499; Claudia Tate, introduction to *The Selected Works of Georgia Douglas Johnson* (New York: G. K. Hall, 1997), xxix–xxxii; Hull, *Color, Sex, and Poetry,* 165; and George B. Hutchinson, "Jean Toomer and the 'New Negroes' of Washington," *American Literature* 63, no. 4 (December 1991): 683–692.

93. Johnson, "Those Who Stayed," 488–489.

94. Hull, *Color, Sex, and Poetry,* 165; Johnson, "Those Who Stayed," 496–497.

95. Charles Michael Smith, "Bruce Nugent: Bohemian of the Harlem Renaissance," in *In the Life: A Black Gay Anthology,* ed. Joseph Beam (Boston: Alyson Publishers, 1986), 211–212.

96. Lewis, *When Harlem Was in Vogue,* 127.

97. Ibid., 121.

98. Johnson, "Those Who Stayed," 494.

99. Hughes, *The Big Sea,* 216–217, 206–207.

100. Achille, preface to *La Revue du monde noir,* xv.

101. Scott, *Only Paradoxes to Offer,* 174.

102. Hortense Spillers, "Mama's Baby, Papa's Maybe: An American Grammar Book," *Diacritics* 17, no. 3 (summer 1987): 65.

103. Régis Antoine, *Les Ecrivains français et les antilles, des premiers pères blancs aux surréalistes noirs* (Paris: G. P. Maisonneuve et Larose, 1978), 352, 379–380.

104. Ibid., 209.

105. Richard D. E. Burton, "'Maman-France Doudou': Family Images in French West Indian Colonial Discourse," *Diacritics* 23, no. 3 (fall 1993): 81.

106. Antoine, *Les ecrivains français et les antilles,* 353.

107. Ibid., 353.

108. Ibid., 379–380.

109. Oruno Lara, *Question de couleurs (blanches et noirs): roman de moeurs* (Paris: Nouvelle Librairie Universelle, 1923). On Lara's career, see Antoine, 322–323; and Maryse Condé, *La civilisation du bossale: réflexions sur la littérature orale de la Guadeloupe et de la Martinique* (Paris: L'Harmattan, 1978), 57–59.

110. Lara, *Question de couleurs,* 18.

111. Ibid., 36.

112. Ibid., 106–107.

113. Interestingly, Lara himself goes on to undertake precisely this kind of task:

see Oruno Lara, *Histoire de la Guadeloupe (1492–1920)* (Paris: Nouvelle Librairie Universelle, 1923).

114. Phyllis Rose, *Jazz Cleopatra: Josephine Baker in Her Time* (New York: Doubleday, 1989), 148. The interior quote comes from the administrator and writer Robert Delavignette, *Freedom and Authority in French West Africa* (London: Oxford University Press, 1950), a translation of Delavignette's 1946 *Service africain.*

115. Tyler Stovall, *Paris Noir: African Americans in the City of Light* (Boston: Houghton Mifflin, 1996), 90.

116. Clifford, "Histories of the Tribal and the Modern," in *The Predicament of Culture: Twentieth-Century Ethnography, Literature, and Art* (Cambridge: Harvard University Press, 1988), 197.

117. Rose, *Jazz Cleopatra,* 146.

118. Ibid., 147.

119. Wall, *Women of the Harlem Renaissance,* 105.

120. Paul Morand, *Magie noire* (1928), in *Nouvelles complètes,* vol. 1, ed. Michel Collomb (Paris: Gallimard, 1992). The novel was translated by Hamish Miles as *Black Magic* (New York: The Viking Press, 1929). Page numbers of subsequent references to the French and English editions (in that order) will be indicated in the text in parentheses.

121. Michel Collomb, introduction to Morand, *Nouvelles complètes,* 1026.

122. Du Bois, "The Negro in Literature," *Crisis* 36 (November 1929): 376.

123. See for instance René Maran, "Paul Morand et les Nègres," *Le Monde* (September 19, 1928); Georges Joseph-Henri, "Magie noire," *La Revue du monde noir* 1 (1931): 57–60.

124. Damas, "Misère noire," *Esprit* 81 (June 1939): 352.

125. Nardal, "Pantins exotiques" [Exotic puppets], *La Dépêche africaine* 8 (October 1928): 2.

126. Morand, "L'age du Nègre: à propos de 'Magie noire,'" *Candide* 226 (July 12, 1928): 4.

127. Jean-Claude Klein, "Borrowing, Syncretism, Hybridisation: The Parisian Revue of the 1920's," in *Popular Music 5: Continuity and Change,* ed. Richard Middleton (Cambridge: Cambridge University Press, 1985), 181.

128. "Le Concert de 6 Octobre à la Salle Hoche," *La Dépêche africaine* 9 (November 1928): 1.

129. Paulette Nardal, "Le Nouveau Bal Nègre de la Glacière," *La Dépêche africaine* 14 (May 30, 1929): 3.

130. Alain Boulanger, liner notes to "Musique of Martinique, 1929–50" (Sussex, England: Interstate Music Ltd., 1985), Fly CD 947. Some of these crossover

figures are covered in Chris Goddard, *Jazz Away from Home* (New York: Paddington Press, 1979). Jean-Pierre Meunier calls the resulting hybrids "musique métisée" (mixed music) in his thorough liner notes to the compact disc "Biguine: biguine, valse et mazurka créoles (1929–1940)" (Paris: Frémaux et Associés, 1993), FA 007.

131. The Bal is described in Ernest Léardée's autobiography, *La Biguine de l'Oncle Ben's,* 151.

132. J. A. Rogers, "The French Harlem," New York *Amsterdam News* (April 4, 1928) sec. II, 1.

133. Andrée Nardal, "Notes on the Biguine Créole," *La Revue du monde noir* 2 (1931): 51–52.

134. George F. Paul, "The Gayest Dance in Gay Paree!" *Abbott's Monthly* (August 1928).

135. David Levering Lewis, *W. E. B. Du Bois: The Fight for Equality and the American Century, 1919–1963* (New York: Henry Holt, 2000), 221.

136. Countee Cullen, "The Dark Tower," *Opportunity* 6 (September 1928): 271–273. Page numbers for further references will be indicated parenthetically in the text. Cullen's "The Dark Tower" ran from *Opportunity* 4 (December 1926) until *Opportunity* 6 (September 1928). Later, Cullen also wrote a European travel column for the *Crisis:* see "Countee Cullen to His Friends," *Crisis* 36 (April 1929): 119; "Countee Cullen on French Courtesy," *Crisis* 36 (June 1929): 193; "Countee Cullen in England," *Crisis* 36 (August 1929): 270; "Countee Cullen on Miscegenation," *Crisis* 36 (November 1929): 373.

137. Nardal, "Musique Nègre: antilles et aframérique," *La Dépêche africaine* 25 (June 1930): 5.

138. Rogers, "The French Harlem."

139. Léardée, *La Biguine de l'Oncle Ben's,* 146.

140. Georgia Douglas Johnson, autobiographical statement, *Opportunity* 5 (July 1927): 204.

141. Nardal, "Le nouveau Bal Nègre de la Glacière," *La Dépêche africaine* 14 (May 30, 1929): 3.

142. *L'Etudiant noir, journal de l'Association des Etudiants Martiniquais en France* (March 1935). Page numbers for subsequent citations will be indicated parenthetically in the text.

143. Damas, "Notre génération," quoted in Lilyan Kesteloot, *Les Ecrivains noirs de langue française: naissance d'une littérature* (Brussels: Institut de Sociologie de l'Université Libre de Bruxelles, 1963), 91.

144. See Edward O. Ako, "*L'Etudiant Noir* and the Myth of the Genesis of the Negritude Movement," *Research in African Literatures* 15, no. 3 (fall 1984):

341–353; Martin Steins, "Jeunesse noire," *Neohelicon* 4, nos. 1–2 (1976): 91–121.

145. Césaire's essay "Nègreries" is discussed and reproduced in Georges Ngal, *Aimé Césaire: un homme à la recherche d'une patrie* (1975; reprint, Paris: Présence Africaine, 1994).

146. Scott, *Only Paradoxes to Offer*, 8.

4. Vagabond Internationalism: Claude McKay's Banjo

1. Claude McKay, *Banjo: A Story without a Plot* (1929; reprint, New York: Harcourt Brace Jovanovich, 1957). Page numbers for subsequent citations will be indicated in the text in parentheses.

2. See Wayne F. Cooper, *Claude McKay: Rebel Soujourner in the Harlem Renaissance: A Biography* (Baton Rouge: Louisiana State University Press, 1987), 214–215, 232, 259–260. McKay, "What Is and What Isn't," *Crisis* 27, no. 6 (April 1924): 259–262.

3. McKay, *Banjo,* trans. Ida Treat and Paul Vaillant-Couturier (Paris: Rieder, 1931). Page numbers for subsequent citations from this translation will be indicated in the text in parentheses, with the indicator "Fr." It is not insignificant for the Francophone reception of McKay that *Banjo* was his first book to be translated: *Home to Harlem* (published in English in 1928) would follow in 1932, and *Banana Bottom* (published in English in 1933) in 1934. McKay, *Quartier noir,* trans. Louis Guilloux (Paris: Rieder, 1932); *Banana Bottom,* trans. F. W. Laparra (Paris: Rieder, 1934).

4. McKay, "To America," *La Revue du monde noir* 1 (1931): 34; "Spring in New Hampshire," *La Revue du monde noir* 3 (1931): 38. The excerpt from *Banjo* is titled "L'étudiant antillais vu par un noir américain," *Légitime Défense* 1 (1932; reprint, Paris: Jean-Michel Place, 1978): 13–14. All subsequent citations refer to this edition. All translations from the journal are my own.

5. Etienne Léro, "Misère d'une poésie," *Légitime Défense* 1 (1932): 12.

6. René Depestre, "Entretien avec Aimé Césaire," in *Bonjour et adieu à la négritude* (Paris: Seghers, 1980), 73; translated by Maro Riofrancos as "An Interview with Aimé Césaire," in Césaire, *Discourse on Colonialism* (New York: Monthly Review, 1972), 71.

7. Léon-Gontran Damas, "Hoquet," *Piments* (1937), in *Piments/Névralgies* (Paris: Présence Africaine, 1972), 38; "Naissance et vie de la Négritude" (1968), in *Léon-Gontran Damas: l'homme et l'œuvre,* ed. Daniel Racine (Paris: Présence Africaine, 1983), 185. In the same volume, see also Racine, "Entretien avec Léon-Gontran Damas" (1977), 200.

8. Senghor, "Le Problème culturel en A.O.F." (September 1937), collected in

Liberté I: négritude et humanisme (Paris: Seuil, 1964), 21. The divergences between Senghor's version and the French published translation (and the excerpt in *Légitime Défense*) are subtle but interesting. Senghor speaks of the "roots of our race" in the place of the book's "racines de notre peuple" [roots of our people]—neither of which is quite consonant with McKay's phrase "our native roots." (One imagines that the French word for "native"—*indigène*—would have rather different connotations for Senghor in a French West African colony than in McKay's Marseilles.) Senghor also evokes "notre profond fond" ("our deep reserves") instead of the published translation's "notre propre fonds" (our own funds) (Fr 258).

9. Ousmane Socé, *Mirages de Paris* (1955; reprint, Paris: Nouvelles Editions Latines, 1964), 145. See also Christopher Miller, "Hallucinations of France and Africa," *Nationalists and Nomads: Essays on Francophone African Literature and Culture* (Chicago: University of Chicago Press, 1998), 59–65.

10. Martin Duberman, *Paul Robeson* (New York: Alfred A. Knopf, 1988), 207–209.

11. See for example Pierre MacOrlan, *Rues secrètes* (1934; reprint, Paris: Arléa, 1989), 137; Pierre Guerre, preface to *Marseille* (Paris: Arts et Métiers Graphiques, 1962), 11.

12. Cooper, *Claude McKay*, 255. On the section of the port destroyed during the war, see André Bouyala d'Arnaud, *Evocation du vieux Marseille* (Paris: Les Editions de Minuit, 1959). Also see Michel Fabre's informative afterword to his revised translation of *Banjo* (Marseille: André Dimanche, 1999), 317–331.

13. McKay, "A Negro Writer to His Critics," *New York Herald-Tribune Books* (March 6, 1932), collected in *The Passion of Claude McKay: Selected Poetry and Prose, 1912–1948,* ed. Wayne F. Cooper (New York: Schocken Books, 1973), 136–137. The French critic is Gabriel Bertin, "Avec Banjo et les 'Frères du Port,'" *Cahiers du Sud* 141 (June 1932): 397.

14. Latnah's background is left unclear: she is often described as "Oriental" (e.g., 169), although without any more specificity. She reminds Malty of an Indo-Caribbean girl he knew as a schoolboy (30–31), and there are also hints that she is Indian, or Arab (32). Malty flatly says, "I don't know whether she is Arabian or Persian or Indian" (10).

15. André Levinson, "De Harlem à la Cannebière," *Figures américaines* (Paris: Editions Victor Attinger, 1929), 190.

16. Georges Friedmann, preface to *Banjo* [1931 French translation], 14; Gwendolyn Bennett, "Our Book Shelf," *Opportunity* 7 (August 1929): 254.

17. Etienne Léro, Thélus Léro, René Ménil, Jules-Marcel Monnerot, Michel

Pilotin, Maurice-Sagas Quitman, August Thésée, Pierre Yoyotte, "Avertisse-ment" [Declaration], in *Légitime Défense* 1 (1932): 1.

18. *Légitime Défense* was not immediately banned in Martinique, however, as has often been asserted. The acting governor of the colony, the Guyanese Félix Eboué, was criticized for his inaction both by the colonial administration and by the white and creole elite on the island. Brian Weinstein, *Eboué* (New York: Oxford University Press, 1972), 140.

19. See "Les Origines: *Légitime Défense*," part I of Kesteloot, *Les Écrivains noirs de langue française: naissance d'une littérature* (Brussels: Université Libre, 1963), 25–87. For critiques of Kesteloot, see Martin Steins, "Black Migrants in Paris," in *European-Language Writing on Sub-Saharan Africa,* vol. 1, ed. Al-bert S. Gerard (Budapest: Academiai Kiado, 1986), 354; Steins, *Les Antécé-dents et la genèse de la négritude senghorienne* (Ph.D. diss., Université de Paris III, 1981), 557–563; Iheanachor Egonu, "*Les Continents* and the Franco-phone Pan-Negro Movement," *Phylon* 42, no. 3 (September 1981): 245. In her emphasis on *Légitime Défense,* Kesteloot was influenced most of all by Léon-Gontran Damas, who claims to have been involved with the group around *Légitime Défense* (though none of his work is included in the journal, and his name is not among the signatures). See "Leon Damas: Interviewed Feb. 18, 1977," *Journal of Caribbean Studies* 1, no. 1 (winter 1980): 70–71.

20. René Ménil, "Généralités sur 'l'écrivain' de couleur antillais," *Légitime Défense* 1 (1932): 7.

21. Ibid., 8.

22. "Avertissement," 2.

23. Richardson, introduction to *Refusal of the Shadow: Surrealism and the Carib-bean,* ed. Richardson, trans. Richardson and Krzysztof Fijalkowski (London: Verso, 1996), 5.

24. Ibid., 5.

25. Césaire, interview with Georges Ngal, April 1967, in Ngal, *Aimé Césaire: un homme à la recherche d'une patrie* (1975; reprint, Présence Africaine, 1994), 59.

26. Césaire, interview with Régis Antoine, July 17, 1974, quoted in Antoine, *Les Ecrivains français et les Antilles: des premiers pères blancs aux surréalistes noirs* (Paris: G. P. Maisonneuve et Larose, 1978), 375.

27. Réné Ménil, preface (1978 reissue), *Légitime Défense* 1 (1932), n.p.

28. Ménil, "Nulle part," *Légitime Défense* 1 (1932): 18.

29. Antoine, *Les Ecrivains français et les Antilles,* 364–376.

30. Jules Monnerot was the father of Jules-Marcel Monnerot, the student linked with *Légitime Défense* who would later be aligned with Georges Bataille's

Collège de Sociologie before becoming a conservative Gaulliste after World War II. Stéphane Rosso was a Guadeloupean born in 1889, active with Senghor's Ligue and with the journal *La Race nègre* in the late 1920s before his return to the Antilles. During the celebrations of the 300-year anniversary of the French conquest of the Antilles, Rosso wrote an incendiary work called *Le Tricentenaire des Antilles* (1935), denouncing the mystification of colonialism, calling for a socialist revolt on the islands, and envisioning the creation of an "independent federation of the Antilles." See Jack Corzani, *La Littérature des Antilles-Guyane françaises vol. 3: la Négritude* (Fort-de-France: Ed. Desormeaux, 1978), 222, 244–246; Richard D. E. Burton, "Between the Particular and the Universal: Dilemmas of the Martinican Intellectual," in *Intellectuals in the Twentieth-Century Caribbean, vol. 2: Unity in Variety: The Hispanic and Francophone Caribbean,* ed. Alistair Hennessy (London: Macmillan, 1992), 197–200.

31. In *Home to Harlem,* Ray gives Jake a long lesson in Haitian and Ethiopian history. In fact, Ray originally comes to the States in exile from the U.S. occupation of Haiti, where his father had been jailed and his brother murdered by U.S. marines. McKay, *Home to Harlem* (1928; reprint, Boston: Northeastern University Press, 1987), 131–139, 155–156. See also John Lowney's insightful "Haiti and Black Transnationalism: Remapping the Migrant Geography of *Home to Harlem,*" *African American Review* 34, no. 3 (fall 2000): 413–429.

32. Martin Steins, *Les Antécédents et la genèse de la négritude senghorienne* (Paris: Université Paris III, Thèse d'Etat, 1981), 588–589.

33. Ibid., 589.

34. Ibid., 588.

35. McKay, *A Long Way from Home* (1937; reprint, New York: Harcourt Brace Jovanovich, 1970), 277.

36. See Winston James, *Claude McKay: The Making of a Black Bolshevik, 1889–1923* (Ithaca: Cornell University Press, forthcoming), and James, *Holding Aloft the Banner of Ethiopia: Caribbean Radicalism in Early Twentieth-Century America* (New York: Verso, 1998), 165–166. The quote comes from McKay, "The Negro Communist and his Race," *Bolshevik* (December 2, 1922), quoted in appendix 2 to McKay, *The Negroes in America* (1923), trans. from the Russian by Robert Winter, ed. Alan McLeod (Port Washington, N.Y.: Kennikat Press, 1979), 89.

37. Albert Londres, *Marseille, porte du Sud* (Editions de France, 1927), 54.

38. Dewey R. Jones, "Dirt," *Chicago Defender* (July 27, 1929): 12. Jones may be alluding to an exchange in the "Story-telling" chapter, where Ray, explaining that he wants to write about black life in Marseilles, quotes the proverb "Let

down your bucket where you are," and Goosey jokes: "You might bring up a lot of dirt." Ray counters: "Many fine things come out of dirt—steel and gold, pearls and all the rare stones your nice women must have to be happy" (115–116).

39. Levinson, "De Harlem à la Cannebière," 190.

40. Karl Marx, *The Eighteenth Brumaire of Louis Bonaparte* (1852), collected in *Surveys from Exile: Political Writings,* vol. 2, trans. Ben Fowkes, ed. David Fernbach (New York: Penguin, 1973), 197.

41. Peter Linebaugh, "All the Atlantic Mountains Shook," *Labour/Le Travailleur* 10 (autumn 1982): 88. Page numbers for subsequent references will be given in the text. On this point, also see Linebaugh and Marcus Rediker, *The Many-Headed Hydra: Sailors, Slaves, Commoners, and the Hidden History of the Revolutionary Atlantic* (Boston: Beacon Press, 2000).

42. See Linebaugh, 108 ff., for a consideration of slavery in this connection.

43. Robin D. G. Kelley, introduction to *Race Rebels: Culture, Politics, and the Black Working Class* (New York: The Free Press, 1994), 8. See also Chris Booker, "Lumpenization: A Critical Error of the Black Panther Party," in *The Black Panther Party Reconsidered,* ed. Charles E. Jones (Baltimore, Md.: Black Classic Press, 1998), 337–363; and especially Frantz Fanon, *The Wretched of the Earth,* trans. C. Farrington (New York: Grove Press, 1963), 129–137.

44. Stuart Hall, Chas Critcher, Tony Jefferson, John Clarke, and Brian Roberts, *Policing the Crisis: Mugging, the State, and Law and Order* (New York: Holmes and Meier, 1978), 352–353.

45. McKay, *Home to Harlem,* 155.

46. McKay, *A Long Way from Home,* 4.

47. One might note a certain homoeroticism in this portrait of black male drifters, of course. There are a few scenes such as the moment when the boys are surrounded on the Place de la Bourse by a "troop of painted youths" who dance around them "with queer gestures and queerer screams" (196), but they are fleeting in *Banjo.* This element becomes explicit in a manuscript McKay attempted to write in 1930 and thereafter, called "The Jungle and the Bottoms" and then "Romance in Marseilles." In this book (centered on the story of the Nigerian who was the base of the Taloufa character in *Banjo*), there is an entire chapter devoted to a homosexual couple. See "Romance in Marseilles," McKay Papers, Schomburg Center for Research in Black Culture, New York; Wayne Cooper, *Claude McKay,* 237, 267–269.

48. McKay to W. A. Bradley, November 1, 1929, James Weldon Johnson Collection, Beinecke Rare Book Library, Yale University. See Michel Fabre, *From Harlem to Paris: Black American Writers in Paris, 1840–1980* (Urbana: University of Illinois Press, 1991), 109.

49. Du Bois, "The Browsing Reader," *Crisis* 36 (July 1929): 324.

50. Michel Fabre, *From Harlem to Paris,* 110.

51. Since McKay spoke French passably, but perhaps not well enough to feign a newspaper editorial, it seems reasonable to assume that this article is quoted from an actual French periodical of the period. (Earlier, *Banjo* quotes from *La Race Nègre*—in English, however [75–76].) But I have not been able to locate the article (it would take some luck, as we are given neither the date nor the source).

52. The music and lyrics to "The West Indies Blues" are reproduced in *The Marcus Garvey and Universal Negro Improvement Association Papers, vol. 5: Sept. 1922–Aug. 1924,* ed. Robert Hill (Berkeley: University of California Press, 1986), 801n14, 803–804. See also Ted Vincent, *Keep Cool: The Black Activist Who Built the Jazz Age* (London: Pluto Press, 1995), 129–130.

53. André Suarès, *Marsiho* (Marseille: B. Grasset, 1933), quoted in Michel Fabre, postface to *Banjo* (Marseille: André Dimanche, 1999), 321.

54. Robert Bone, *The Negro Novel in America* (1958; reprint, New Haven: Yale University Press, 1965), 69, 71.

55. See Brent Edwards, "The Ethnics of Surrealism," *Transition* 78 (1999): 84–135.

56. Georges Bataille, "The Use Value of D. A. F. de Sade (An Open Letter to My Current Comrades)," in *Visions of Excess: Selected Writings 1927–39,* ed. Allan Stoekl (Minneapolis: University of Minnesota Press, 1985), 99.

57. On "elusive" in Johnson, see Brent Edwards, "The Seemingly Eclipsed Window of Form: James Weldon Johnson's Prefaces," in *The Jazz Cadence of American Culture,* ed. Robert G. O'Meally (New York: Columbia University Press, 1998), 586, 589–590.

58. Photographs file, Claude McKay Papers, James Weldon Johnson Collection, Beinecke Rare Book Library, Yale University. The phrase on the card is usually associated with an infamous advertising campaign for Banania, a chocolate-flavored breakfast drink, that used drawings of a grinning black soldier in the typical uniform of the World War I *tirailleurs sénégalais* and the phrase: "Y'a bon Banania." See Anne Donadey, "'Y'a bon Banania': Ethics and Cultural Criticism in the Colonial Context," *French Cultural Studies* 11 (2000): 9–29; *NégriPub: l'image des noirs dans la publicité,* ed. R. Bachollet, J.-B. Debost, A.-C. Lelieur, and M.-C. Peyrière (Paris: Somogy, 1992). The English approximation I have suggested follows Charles Lam Markmann's version of Frantz Fanon's *Black Skin, White Masks,* which translates "Y'a bon Banania" with "Sho' good!" (unfortunately, without the French, this translation captures the connotation but conceals the particular context of French stereotypes that Fanon is analyzing). *Black Skin, White Masks* (New York:

Grove, 1967), 34; published originally as *Peau noire, masques blancs* (Paris: Seuil, 1952), 27.

59. McKay to Bradley, March 11, 1927, quoted in Cooper, *Claude McKay,* 235–236.

60. "La Vie de nos sections," *La Race nègre* 3, no. 2 (February–March 1930): 3.

61. The French government surveillance of M'Baye's bar during the period shows an especial interest in these activities. See for example the report on Tiemoko Garan Kouyaté's recruiting visit by the agent Fouqué, report of January 23, 1930, Archives Nationales, SLOTFOM, III, 111, "Ligue de Défense de la Race Nègre"; on M'Baye's links to Vietnamese and North African sailors, see Fouqué, report of February 10, 1930; unsigned reports, March 11 and 18, 1930, SLOTFOM III, 111.

62. Advertisement for the Comptoir Marseillais, *La Race nègre* (March 1929): 3.

63. McKay, *A Long Way from Home,* 279. The reviewer of *Banjo* who claimed to know the milieu in Marseilles also writes of M'Baye's "rare discretion" and "charming modesty." Gabriel Bertin, "Avec Banjo et les 'Frères du Port,'" 397.

64. McKay, *A Long Way from Home,* 278.

65. Ibid., 279.

66. Ibid., 278. This building is extensively described in chapter 14 of McKay's manuscript for "Romance in Marseilles." There, the Nigerian character Lafala meets a labor organizer named Etienne St. Dominique, a "mulatto" former student from Martinique. They are tailed by a pair of spies as they go to visit the Seamen's Building, where St. Dominique tells the Nigerian about the "class struggle for a new society." (The description of St. Dominique is so vivid that one wonders whether McKay might have met other black activists in Marseilles—one thinks immediately of the similarly named Camille St. Jacques, also associated with *La Revue nègre* in that period.) See "Romance in Marseilles," Claude McKay collection, Schomburg Center for Research in Black Culture, New York Public Library, 98–105.

67. McKay, *A Long Way from Home,* 278, 288.

68. Lamine Senghor, *La Violation d'un pays* (Paris: Bureau d'Editions de Diffusion et de Publicité, 1927).

69. McKay, *A Long Way from Home,* 278.

70. For the descriptives *à couleur d'ébène* and *les bronzés,* see for instance *La Violation d'un pays,* 26, 29.

71. Christopher Miller, "Involution and Revolution: Black Paris in the 1920s," in *Nationalism and Nomads: Essays on Francophone African Literature and Culture* (Chicago: University of Chicago Press, 1995), 25. Vaillant-Couturier, "Préface," *La Violation d'un pays,* n.p.

72. Ibid., 25. See also Ahmadou Mapaté Diagne, *Les Trois Volontés de Malic* (Paris: Larousse, 1920).

73. J. S. Spiegler, "Aspects of Nationalist Thought among French-Speaking West Africans, 1921–1939" (Ph.D. diss., Oxford University, 1968), 125–126.

74. Miller, "Involution and Revolution," 28.

75. Ibid., 26, 27.

76. Ibid., 25.

77. Papa Samba Diop, *Ecriture romanesque et cultures régionales au Sénégal: des origines à 1992* (Frankfurt: IKO Verlag, 1993–95), 155–156, quoted in Miller, "Involution and Revolution," 25. See also Diop, "Un texte sénégalais inconnu: *La Violation d'un pays* (1927) de Lamine Senghor," *Komparatistische Hefte* 9–10 (1984): 123–128.

78. Spiegler, "Aspects of Nationalist Thought among French-Speaking West Africans," 121.

79. "Bibliographie," *La Race nègre* 1 (June 1927): 2.

80. Valliant-Couturier, "Préface," *La Violation d'un pays,* n.p.

81. I have taken up this argument in more detail elsewhere, specifically in terms of Senghor's relationship to his Vietnamese counterpart Nguyen Ai Quoc (Ho Chi Minh), a writer also experimenting with the proper form of radical prose. See Edwards, "The Shadow of Shadows," in *Rethinking Black Marxism,* ed. Edwards, Nikhil Singh, and Penny Von Eschen (Durham: Duke University Press, forthcoming).

82. Du Bois, *Dark Princess: A Romance* (1928; reprint, Jackson: University Press of Mississippi, 1995).

83. Joy James, "Profeminism and Gender Elites: W. E. B. Du Bois, Anna Julia Cooper, and Ida B. Wells-Barnett," *Transcending the Talented Tenth: Black Leaders and American Intellectuals* (New York: Routledge, 1997); Patricia Morton, "The All-Mother Vision of W. E. B. Du Bois," in *Disfigured Images: The Historical Assault on Afro-American Women* (New York: Greenwood, 1991), 55–65.

84. Rampersad, *Art and Imagination of W. E. B. Du Bois* (Cambridge: Harvard University Press, 1976), 204. Another work that raises some of these questions around the status of fiction in Du Bois's work is Kenneth Warren, "An Inevitable Drift? Oligarchy, Du Bois, and the Politics of Race between the Wars," *boundary 2* 27, no. 3 (fall 2000): 153–170. And see Edwards, "Introduction: The 'Autonomy' of Black Radicalism," *Social Text* 67 (summer 2001): 3–4.

85. See Alys Eve Weinbaum, "Reproducing Racial Globality: W. E. B. Du Bois and the Sexual Politics of Black Internationalism," *Social Text* 67 (summer 2001): 15–41.

86. Du Bois, "The Negro Mind Reaches Out," *Foreign Affairs* 2, no. 3 (1925), reprinted in *The New Negro* ed. Locke (1925; reprint, New York: Atheneum, 1968), 408–409.

87. Du Bois, *Dusk of Dawn: An Essay toward an Autobiography of the Race Concept* (1940), collected in *Writings* (New York: Library of America, 1986), 751.

88. Ovington, quoted in Rampersad, *Art and Imagination of W. E. B. DuBois,* 165.

89. Du Bois, *Dusk of Dawn,* 758.

90. Ibid., 643–644.

91. Du Bois, "Little Portraits of Africa," *Crisis* (April 1924), collected in *W. E. B. Du Bois: A Reader,* ed. David Levering Lewis (New York: Henry Holt, 1995), 668.

92. Rampersad, *Art and Imagination of W. E. B. DuBois,* 215.

93. Du Bois, *Dark Princess,* n.p.

94. Senghor, *La Violation d'un pays,* 30–31.

95. Warren, "An Inevitable Drift?" 158.

96. McKay, *A Long Way from Home,* 300.

97. *Cosmopolitics: Thinking and Feeling beyond the Nation,* ed. Pheng Cheah and Bruce Robbins (Minneapolis: University of Minnesota Press, 1998); Aihwa Ong, *Flexible Citizenship: The Cultural Logics of Transnationality* (Durham: Duke University Press, 1999).

98. McKay, *A Long Way from Home,* 302, 304.

5. Inventing the Black International: George Padmore and Tiemoko Garan Kouyaté

1. T. Ras Makonnen, *Pan-Africanism from Within,* ed. Kenneth King (Nairobi: Oxford University Press, 1973), 155. Further page references will be indicated parenthetically in the text.

2. Cedric Robinson, *Black Marxism: The Making of the Black Radical Tradition* (London: Zed Press, 1983), 373. Robinson does not quote the last sentence of the paragraph, as I have, perhaps in deference to its vexing incongruity.

3. Cedric Robinson, "Black Intellectuals at the British Core, 1920s–1940s," in *Essays on the History of Blacks in Britain,* ed. Jagdish S. Gundara and Ian Duffield (Aldershot: Avebury, 1992), 173.

4. Such a critique is elaborated by J. Ayodele Langley, *Pan-Africanism and Nationalism in West Africa, 1900–1945* (London: Oxford University Press, 1973), 286–288. Also see George Shepperson, "Pan-Africanism and 'pan-Africanism': Some Historical Notes," *Phylon* 23, no. 4 (winter 1962): 355–356.

5. C. L. R. James, "Black Intellectuals in Britain," in *Colour, Culture and Consciousness: Immigrant Intellectuals in Britain,* ed. Bhikhu Parekh (London: G. Allen and Unwin, 1974), 154, 162.

6. Hubert Henry Harrison, "A New International," in *When Africa Awakes* (1920; reprint, Baltimore: Black Classic Press, 1997), 111–112.

7. See Jeffrey B. Perry, "The International Colored Unity League and the Way Forward," in *A Hubert Harrison Reader,* ed. Jeffrey B. Perry (Middletown, Conn.: Wesleyan University Press, 2001), 397–398; and "Program and Principles of the International Colored Unity League," *Voice of the Negro* 1, no. 1 (April 1927): 4–6, reprinted in *A Hubert Harrison Reader,* 399–402.

8. Harrison, "Wanted—A Colored International," in *A Hubert Harrison Reader,* 228.

9. See Lenin, "Theses on the National and Colonial Questions," in *The Communist International, 1919–1943: Documents,* ed. Jane Degras (London: Frank Cass, 1956), 142; and the Indian Marxist M. N. Roy's debate with Lenin regarding the role of the national bourgeoisies, in Roy, "Supplementary Theses on the National and Colonial Question," *The Selected Works of M. N. Roy, vol. 1, 1917–1922,* ed. Sibnaraya Ray (Oxford: Oxford University Press, 1987), 174–178.

10. Robinson, "Coming to Terms: The Third World and the Dialectic of Imperialism," *Race and Class* 22, no. 4 (1981): 369.

11. Nathaniel Mackey, "Interview with Edward Kamau Brathwaite," *Hambone* 9 (winter 1991): 44; Brathwaite, "Metaphors of Underdevelopment: A Proem for Hernan Cortez," *New England Review and Bread Loaf Quarterly* 7, no. 4 (summer 1985): 460.

12. James Hooker, *Black Revolutionary: George Padmore's Path from Communism to Pan-Africanism* (New York: Praeger, 1967), 30.

13. Padmore, letter to Du Bois, February 17, 1934. W. E. B. Du Bois Papers, University of Massachusetts–Amherst.

14. See for instance George Padmore, "Bankruptcy of Negro Leadership," *Negro Worker* 1, no. 12 (December 1931): 5; Padmore, *The Life and Struggles of Negro Toilers* (London: Red International of Labor Unions, 1931), 124.

15. C. L. R. James, *Nkrumah and the Ghana Revolution* (London: Allison and Busby, 1977), 75.

16. Hooker, *Black Revolutionary,* 26. St. Clair Drake characterizes Padmore as "an institution all by himself" in "A Report on the Brown Britishers," *Crisis* 56 (June 1949): 188.

17. C. L. R. James, "Notes on the Life of George Padmore," *Nation* [Trinidad] (c. 1960), in *The C. L. R. James Reader,* ed. Anna Grimshaw (New York: Blackwell, 1992), 290.

18. Roi Ottley, *No Green Pastures* (New York: Charles Scribner's Sons, 1951), 62.

19. Some sources of these rumors include James, "Notes on the Life of George Padmore." Undated typescript, 2. Padmore Library, Accra, Ghana. Copy in the collection of the Schomburg Center for Research in Black Culture. (There is some overlap between these "Notes" and the article by James of the same title, collected in *The C. L. R. James Reader.* But the unpublished "Notes" is much longer and much more detailed.) Russell Warren Howe, "George Padmore," *Encounter* 75 (December 1959): 53; Roi Ottley, *No Green Pastures,* 66.

20. Letter from the French Consulary Agent (Bathurst) to the Gouverneur Général of French West Africa, May 7, 1930, Archives Nationales de la République du Sénégal (ANS), Archives du gouvernement général de l'Afrique Occidentale Française, *fonds moderne.* Series 17G folder 58.

21. On the events in Bathurst, see Edward T. Wilson, *Russia and Black Africa before World War II* (New York: Holmes and Meier, 1974), 240–241 (an account that does not mention Padmore's presence).

22. Unsigned report, September 19, 1933; report of Agent Joe, November 3, 1933, "Union des Travailleurs Nègres" folder, Archives Nationales, Section d'Outre-Mer, SLOTFOM, III, 53.

23. James, *Nkrumah and the Ghana Revolution,* 65.

24. This biographical information comes in part from the entry for Kouyaté in the *Dictionnaire biographique du movement ouvrier français, 1914–1939,* ed. Jean Maitron and Claude Penneiter (Paris: Les Editions Ouvrières, 1988), vol. XLI, 249–250. The best single evaluation of his career is found in J. S. Spiegler, *Aspects of Nationalist Thought among French-Speaking West Africans, 1921–1939* (Ph.D. diss., Oxford University, 1968), 166 ff. Philippe de Witte echoes some of Spiegler's arguments in his solid historical overview, *Les Mouvements nègres en France, 1919–1939* (Paris: L'Harmattan, 1985), especially 171–210, 277–320, 381–386.

25. See Wilson, *Russia and Black Africa,* 179–181; Hooker, *Black Revolutionary,* 12.

26. See de Witte, *Les Mouvements nègres,* 189; Wilson, *Russia and Black Africa,* 232.

27. Kouyaté, "Vox africae," *La Race nègre* 2, no. 1 (March 1929): 1.

28. "Vers l'élaboration d'un programme," *La Race nègre* 2, no. 1 (March 1929): 1.

29. See Marcus Garvey, "L'Afrique aux Africains," *La Race nègre* 1, no. 4 (November–December 1927): 2; "Le Nègre à travers la presse," *La Race nègre* 1, no. 4 (November–December 1927): 3.

30. "Discours du Camarade Kouyaté au Congrés de la Ligue [Contre Impérialisme]," *Ouvrier nègre* 2, no. 4 (August 1929): 28.

31. Letter from the Commissaire central (Bordeaux) to the Directeur de la Sureté Générale, March 19, 1930, "Ligue de Défense de la Race Nègre" folder, SLOTFOM III, 111.

32. de Witte, *Les Mouvements nègres*, 172.

33. Wilson, *Russia and Black Africa*, 231–232, 236. See also Report of Agent Paul, May 25, 1930, SLOTFOM V, 3; "Au Caméroun: une colonie torpille," *La Race nègre* 4, no. 2 (September 1930).

34. Report of Agent Fouqué, January 23, 1930, SLOTFOM III, 111.

35. Report of Agent Fouqué, March 1930, SLOTFOM III, 36. Quoted in de Witte, *Les Mouvements nègres*, 198–199.

36. *Le Reveil coloniale* 3 (May 1930), in SLOTFOM III, 74. Quoted in de Witte, *Les Mouvements nègres*, 203.

37. Wilson, *Russia and Black Africa*, 177.

38. Ibid., 185, 200.

39. Hooker, *Black Revolutionary*, 17. See also the obituaries for Nzula and Macauley: "Albert Nzula," *Negro Worker* 4, no. 1 (May 1934): 9; "The Death of Comrade Macauley," *Negro Worker* 1, no. 10–11 (October–November 1931): 42. See Wilson, *Russia and Black Africa*, 240–243, on the career of Small, and 243–244, on Macauley.

40. Padmore, "Our Aims," *International Negro Workers' Review* 1, no. 1 (January 1931): 3.

41. A. Losovsky, "Greetings to Negro Workers," *Negro Worker* 1 (1928), reprinted in *Negro Worker* 1 (January 1931): 7.

42. Wilson, *Russia and Black Africa*, 214–215.

43. C. L. R. James, "Notes on the Life of George Padmore," in *The C. L. R. James Reader*, 290.

44. Wilson, *Russia and Black Africa*, 220.

45. Ibid., 201, 224–225. See for example Kouyaté, "Black and White Seamen Organize for Struggle," *Negro Worker* 1, no. 12 (December 1931):19–20; "La grève nationale de marins," *Le Cri des Nègres* 4–5 (November–December 1931): 1; "Solidarity between White and Coloured Sailors," *Negro Worker* 2, no. 3 (March 1932).

46. "Alerte! camarades Nègres la répression s'accentue," *Le Cri des Nègres* 2 (September 1932): 1. See also de Witte, *Les Mouvements nègre*, 287.

47. "World Congress of Seamen," *Negro Worker* 2, no. 6 (June 1932): 23. On international organizing around the Scottsboro case and specifically Ada Wright's tours in Europe during the early 1930s, see James A. Miller, Susan D. Pennybacker, and Eve Rosenhaft, "Mother Ada Wright and the International Campaign to Free the Scottsboro Boys, 1931–1934," *American Histor-*

ical Review (April 2001): 387–430, especially 418. See also Stéphane Rosso, "Au 'Paradis Américain,'" *Le Cri des Nègres* 1 (August 1931): 1–2.

48. Padmore, "Comment vivent les fermiers nègres en Amérique," *La Race nègre* 4, no. 1 (July 1930): 2.

49. For one example in the series: François Coty, "Contre le communisme: les intellectuels noirs aux ordres de Moscou," *L'Ami du peuple* (January 27, 1930). A number of these articles were collected in a book the following year titled *Sauvons nos colonies: le péril rouge en pays noir.* Kouyaté responded to Coty's attacks in "François Coty, directeur de 'l'ami du peuple' a calomnié," *La Race nègre* 3, no. 2 (February–March 1930): 1.

50. Spiegler, *Aspects of Nationalist Thought,* 178. See also de Witte, *Les Mouvements nègre,* 210–216.

51. "The Change in the Name of Our Journal ('The Negro Worker')," *Negro Worker* 1, no. 3 (March 1931): n.p.

52. On *Le Cri des Nègres* and Africa, see Spiegler, *Aspects of Nationalist Thought,* 181–183. Articles on the exposition include a series of pieces by Saumane titled "L'exposition coloniale internationale: son véritable sens," *Le Cri des Nègres* 1–3 (August–October 1931): 1; V.D., "L'exposition anti-impérialiste," *Le Cri des Nègres* 3 (October 1931): 1. Both the LDRN and the UTN were involved in the protests that culminated in an "Anti-Colonial Exposition" organized by the League Against Imperialism at the Pavillion des Soviets in Paris. The protest exhibition was underfunded, hurriedly assembled, sparsely attended, and largely ignored. There is an increasing amount of scholarship on the Exposition Coloniale (and some coverage on the Exposition Anti-Coloniale): one might begin with Sylviane Leprun, *Le Théâtre des colonies* (Paris: L'Harmattan, 1986); Herman Lebovics, *True France: The Wars over Cultural Identity, 1900–1943* (Ithaca: Cornell University Press, 1992), 51–97; Christopher L. Miller, "Hallucinations of France and Africa," in *Nationalists and Nomads: Essays on Francophone African Literature and Culture* (Chicago: University of Chicago Press, 1998), 55–89.

53. Padmore, *Les Ouvriers nègres et l'intervention armée antisoviétique* (excerpt), *Le Cri des Nègres* 2 (September 1931): 3. This is a French translation of Padmore, *Negro Workers and the Imperialist War—Intervention in the Soviet Union* (Hamburg: Red International of Labor Unions, 1931).

54. Wilson, *Russia and Black Africa,* 212.

55. James, "Notes on the Life of George Padmore," typescript, 15–16.

56. Report of Agent Désiré, July 15, 1927, SLOTFOM, II, 5; report of Agent Coco, June 8, 1929, SLOTFOM II, 19.

57. Letter from the Communist International ITUC-NW [Padmore] to the

Confédération Générale de Travail Unitaire [CGTU] of the Parti Communiste Française, July 21, 1931, "CGTU" folder, SLOTFOM III, 31. Quoted in de Witte, *Les Mouvements nègre,* 285.

58. Unsigned reports, October 28 and 30, 1932, "Le Cri des Nègres" folder, SLOTFOM, V, 23. Quoted in Spiegler, *Aspects of Nationalist Thought,* 187.

59. de Witte, *Les Mouvements nègre,* 205.

60. Spiegler, *Aspects of Nationalist Thought,* 175.

61. James, "George Padmore, Black Marxist Revolutionary—A Memoir," *At the Rendezvous of Victory* (London: Allison and Busby, 1984), 255.

62. Spiegler, *Aspects of Nationalist Thought,* 190.

63. "Fascist Terror against Negroes in Germany," *Negro Worker* 3, nos. 4–5 (April–May 1933): 2. See also Jan Valtin (pseudonym of Richard Krebs), *Out of the Night* (New York: Alliance Book Corporation, 1941), 400–404.

64. See Hakim Adi, *West Africans in Britain, 1900–1960: Nationalism, Pan-Africanism and Communism* (London: Lawrence and Wishart, 1998), 39–42, 57–76.

65. Unsigned report, June 22, 1933, SLOTFOM III, 79. Quoted in de Witte, *Les Mouvements nègre,* 305–306.

66. See René Depestre, "An Interview with Aimé Césaire" (1967), in Césaire, *Discourse on Colonialism* (1972; reprint, New York: Monthly Review, 2000), 86; Régis Antoine, *La Littérature franco-antillais: Haïti, Guadeloupe et Martinique* (Paris: Editions Karthala, 1992), 260 (quoting an interview with Ménil); Bernard Dadié, "Senghor, mon parrain," in *Hommage à Léopold Sédar Senghor: homme de culture* (Paris: Présence Africaine, 1976), 209; Léopold Sédar Senghor, "Problématique de la Négritude" (1971), in *Libertés III: Négritude et civilisation de l'universel* (Paris: Seuil, 1977), 276; Gilbert Gratiant, "Mulâtres . . . pour le bien et le mal," *L'Etudiant noir* 1 (March 1935): 7. Also see "La vie des étudiants nègres," *La Race nègre* 2, no. 1 (March 1929): 2, which devotes an entire page to the lives and needs of students and calls for a "groupe d'étudiants nègres de la ligue"; J. Bourgarel, "Pour une association unique d'étudiants nègres," *Le Cri des Nègres* new series 3 (November–December 1933): 1; "Chez les étudiants martiniquais," *Le Cri des Nègres* new series 24 (January 1936): 3.

67. On Léro, see Report of Agent Désiré, August 17, 1932, SLOTFOM II, 11.

68. Report of Agent Paul, June 23, 1933, SLOTFOM II, box 19.

69. "Nouvelles dans les associations sœurs: afrique occidentale," *L'Etudiant martiniquais* new series 1 (May 1934): 2.

70. Léopold Senghor, "Association des Etudiants Ouest-Africains," *Le Cri des Nègres* new series 8 (August 1934): 2.

71. Unsigned reports, July 21 and 25, 1933, SLOTFOM III, 53.

72. "Expulsion of Kouyaté," *L'Humanité* (October 31, 1933), reprinted in *Negro Worker* 4, no. 1 (May 1934): 32. The *Liste noire* of the French Communist Party was more blunt: "Chassé du parti pour attitude désagrégatrice, anticommunisme et indélicatesse" ("Kicked out of the Party for disintegrative attitude, anticommunism and indelicacy"). *Liste noire* 2 (1933), quoted in *Dictionnaire biographique,* 250.

73. "Communiqué: l'exclusion de Kouyaté," *Le Cri des nègres* new series 3 (November–December 1933).

74. "Le 'Cri des Nègres' seul organe des travailleurs nègres: *Soutenez-le!*" *Le Cri des Nègres* new series 4 (January 1934): 1.

75. Hooker, *Black Revolutionary,* 37. He also recounts an anecdote about Kouyaté's death (apparently told to Nancy Cunard by Jules Marcel Monnerot, the intellectual linked to *Légitime Défense* in the early 1930s): that the Germans had killed him for the misappropriation of funds they had given him to produce anti-French propaganda. However, this rather flimsy, third-hand hearsay has never been corroborated by the historians who have attempted to investigate Kouyaté's mysterious death (see Spiegler, *Aspects of Nationalist Thought,* 190).

76. See Spiegler, *Aspects of Nationalist Thought,* 173, 190n5.

77. Padmore, *Controversy* (July 1937), quoted in Hooker, *Black Revolutionary,* 31.

78. "Au Revoir," *Negro Worker* 3, no. 8–9 (August–September 1933): 18.

79. "Expulsion of George Padmore from the Revolutionary Movement," *Negro Worker* 4, no. 2 (June 1934): 14.

80. Helen Davis, "Rise and Fall of George Padmore as a Revolutionary Worker," *Negro Worker* 4, no. 4 (August 1934): 17, 21. See also "A Betrayer of the Negro Liberation Struggle," *Negro Worker* 4, no. 3 (July 1934): 6–10.

81. "Le 'Cri des Nègres' seul organe des travailleurs nègres: *soutenez-le!*" 1.

82. Kouyaté, letter to the UTN, November 4, 1933, SLOTFOM III, 53.

83. Padmore, "An Open Letter to Earl Browder," *Crisis* 42 (October 1935): 302, 315.

84. Padmore, "Expelled Red Scores Party," *Amsterdam News* (June 17, 1934): 1. Padmore sent versions of the letter to Browder and other communiqués from Paris to black U.S. newspapers: see "Exposure of Communists Is Promised," *Amsterdam News* (July 28, 1934): 1; "Padmore Hits Soviets Again," *Amsterdam News* (September 15, 1934): 1.

85. On the variances in the etymology of "psychosis" in psychiatry and psychoanalysis, see Jean Laplanche and J.-B. Pontalis, "Psychosis," in *The Language of Psycho-Analysis,* trans. Donald Nicholson-Smith (New York: Norton, 1973), 369–372. See also Fanon, "Colonial War and Mental Disorders," *The*

Wretched of the Earth, trans. Constance Farrington (New York: Grove, 1963), 251–252. For Fanon's analysis of the colonial condition as neurosis, see generally *Black Skin, White Masks,* trans. Charles Lam Markmann (New York: Grove, 1967).

86. Fanon, *The Wretched of the Earth,* 217–218 (modified). The original is *Les Damnés de la terre* (1961; reprint, Paris: Maspero, 1968), 150.

87. François Girard, "The Anti-Fascist Movement in France," *New Statesman and Nation* (September 7, 1935): 300. The battles were also covered extensively in the journal *Commune,* the review published by the Association of Revolutionary Writers and Artists: see Louis Aragon, "Fevrier," *Commune* 9 (May 1934): 894–896; "Les Ouvriers de Paris à l'assaut du ciel" [The workers of Paris assault the heavens] *Commune* 5–6 (January–February 1934): 487–490.

88. Adolphe Mathurin, interview with Spiegler, *Aspects of Nationalist Thought,* 209n4. Regarding the link to Diop see Spiegler, 289n2.

89. "Expulsion of George Padmore from the Revolutionary Movement," *Negro Worker* 4, no. 2 (June 1934): 14.

90. Report of Agent Moïse, February 3, 1934, SLOTFOM, III, 53.

91. "Kouyaté, Tiemoko Garan," in *Hommes et destins: dictionnaire biographique d'outre-mer,* vol. 1, ed. Robert Cornevin (Paris: Publications de l'Académie des Sciences d'Outre-Mer, 1975), 327.

92. Hooker, *Black Revolutionary,* 34.

93. See the biographical note to George Padmore, "Ethiopia and World Politics," *Crisis* 42 (May 1935): 138.

94. James, "Notes on the Life of George Padmore," typescript, 27.

95. Hooker, *Black Revolutionary,* 45.

96. In June 1935, British officials in West Africa were even under the impression that Kouyaté and Padmore had founded an organization called the "Pan-African Brotherhood" that sent out "a manifesto on behalf of Ethiopia" criticizing the Italian invasion. See S. K. B. Asante, *Pan-African Protest: West Africa and the Italo-Ethiopian Crisis, 1934–1941* (London: Longman, 1977), 52. I have seen no other indication of such an organization, however.

97. Makonnen, *Pan-Africanism from Within,* 159. Langley even asserts that when Padmore formed the International African Service Bureau in March 1937, the executive committee included Kouyaté as the sole Francophone member (representing the French Sudan). Langley, *Pan-Africanism and Nationalism,* 337–338. I have seen no confirmation of this claim, however.

98. Padmore, letter to Bunche, July 27, 1937, Ralph Bunche Papers, General Correspondence, folder 13, box 10b, Schomburg Center for Research in Black Culture, New York Public Library.

99. There is some confusion around the precise time line of James's research for *The Black Jacobins*. In the one document where he recounts the book's genesis, James implies that although he had visited France as early as 1933, he spent "three or four months" in the archives in Paris in the second half of 1936. See James, "Lectures on the Black Jacobins 1: How I Wrote the Black Jacobins," *Small Axe* 8 (September 2000): 70. Also see Robert Hill, "In England, 1932–8," in *C. L. R. James: His Life and Work*, ed. Paul Buhle (London: Allison and Busby, 1986), 67–68.

100. James, "George Padmore, Black Marxist Revolutionary—A Memoir," 258.

101. Alan Mackenzie, "Radical Pan-Africanism in the 1930s: A Discussion with C. L. R. James," *Radical History Review* 24 (fall 1980): 73.

102. Spiegler, *Aspects of Nationalist Thought*, 240.

103. Letter from Kouyaté to Baldwin, April 18, 1929, SLOTFOM III, 24.

104. "Extrait des délibérations et des décisions initiales des réunions des 4 nov. et 9 dec. 1933," in "Congrès Mondial Nègre" folder, SLOTFOM III, 34. All subsequent quotes from the Congress materials come from this source.

105. Padmore apparently had Kouyaté's text translated around the middle of that month. Unsigned report, December 13, 1933, SLOTFOM III, 34.

106. James, "Notes on the Life of George Padmore" typescript, 54.

107. Reports of Agent Paul, October 7, 1932, and July 25, 1933, SLOTFOM II, 19.

108. Walter Benjamin, "The Task of the Translator" (1923), in *Illuminations*. ed. Hannah Arendt, trans. Harry Zohn (New York: Schocken, 1969), 80.

109. Ibid., 79, 74–75.

110. V. N. Volosinov, *Marxism and the Philosophy of Language* (1929), trans. Ladislav Matejka and I. R. Titunik (Cambridge: Harvard University Press, 1986), 23, 22.

111. George Padmore, "Call for Pan-African Parley in Paris Drafted by British Colonial Leaders," *Chicago Defender* (March 17, 1945): 18. For Du Bois's response to Padmore's call (at first he suggests the Congress should be held in Africa, but later acquiesces to the idea of Paris), see *The Correspondence of W. E. B. Du Bois, vol. 3: Selections 1944–63*, ed. Herbert Aptheker (Amherst: University of Massachusetts Press, 1978), 56 ff. See also David Levering Lewis, *W. E. B. Du Bois: The Fight for Equality and the American Century, 1919–1963* (New York: Henry Holt, 2000), 501, 512–513; Penny M. Von Eschen, *Race against Empire: Black Americans and Anticolonialism, 1937–1957* (Ithaca: Cornell University Press, 1997), 50–53.

112. Makonnen, *Pan-Africanism from Within*, 166, 170.

113. One error in Padmore's *Pan-Africanism or Communism?* is his assertion that Faure was "banished to the Sahara for the duration of the war," which con-

jures images of the nationalist leader languishing in the desert (313). In fact, Faure was arrested in Paris in December 1939, when the LDRN was officially dissolved. He was transferred for trial to the Ivory Coast, where a local court sentenced him as a "threat to the security of the state" to five years in prison. He served time in the Ivory Coast (including seven months solitary confinement) and then in Bamako, Mali; on his release in 1944, he recuperated in Saint Louis, Senegal, and then returned to Paris, where again he was closely watched by government surveillance. He did publish an interesting article based in part on his experiences: "French Terror in Negro Africa," trans. James W. Ivy, *Crisis* 54 (April 1947): 108–110, 124–125. (One wonders whether Padmore—who was writing for *Crisis* during this period—arranged for Faure's essay to be translated.) The biographical account comes from this article and from Spiegler, *Aspects of Nationalist Thought,* 256.

114. "Note sur la propagande révolutionnaire intéressant les pays d'outre mer," February 20, 1928, SLOTFOM III, 144.

115. The Institut Nègre plan brought together a slice of black intellectuals in Paris (Kouyaté, Léo Sajous, Emile Faure) and some Antillean professionals: the dentist Hélène Jadfard and the lawyers André Breton and Samuel Stéphany. See "Note sur la propagande révolutionnaire intéressant les pays d'outre mer," March 19, 1930, SLOTFOM III, 81; Report of Agent Désiré, March 15, 1930, SLOTFOM III, 24; "Comité universel de l'Institut Nègre de Paris," ANS 17G 53.

116. "Le générosité française sous la IIIe République," *La Race nègre* (September 1927): 1.

117. Padmore, "Subjects and Citizens in French Africa," *Crisis* 47 (March 1940): 76.

118. Makonnen, *Pan-Africanism from Within,* 156. The quote refers to a meeting of the Rassemblement Coloniale, a group discussed later in this chapter.

119. Hooker, "The Impact of African History on Afro-Americans, 1930–1945," *Black Academy Review* (spring–summer 1972): 45.

120. James, "Notes on the Life of George Padmore." Typescript, 50.

121. Helen Davis, "The Rise and Fall of George Padmore as a Revolutionary Fighter," *Negro Worker* 4, no. 4 (August 1934): 17. See also James R. Hooker, "Africa for Afro-Americans: Padmore and the Black Press," *Radical America* 2, no. 4 (1968): 61–80.

122. Africanus [George Padmore], "Un noir accuse," *Vu* (March 3, 1934): 28. On Padmore's use of the pseudonym, see Reports of Agent Moïse, February–April 1934, SLOTFOM, III, 53. Padmore also seems to have used this pseudonym for publication in English: see for example the especially caustic "The Empire This Month," *Controversy* 24 (September 1938).

123. On the Comte de Beaumont and the earlier *fête nègre,* see Bernard Gendron, "Jamming at Le Bœuf: Jazz and the Paris Avant-Garde," *Discourse* 12, no. 1 (fall–winter 1989–90): 10.

124. Report of Agent Paul, March 10, 1933, and Report of Agent Joe, March 10, 1933, SLOTFOM III, 34. Report of Agent Joe, March 17, 1933, and unsigned report, June 17, 1933, SLOTFOM III, 53.

125. Spiegler, *Aspects of Nationalist Thought,* 150. One example of the use of this phrase is in Siragnouman, "La necessité de nous organiser," *La Race nègre* 1, no. 1 (June 1927): 4.

126. Kouyaté, "La trahison du clerc Paul Morand," *La Race nègre* 1, no. 6 (October 1928): 2–3. Subsequent page references will be indicated parenthetically in the text.

127. Spiegler, *Aspects of Nationalist Thought,* 155.

128. Some early issues featured a column titled "Notre page littéraire." See Lucie Cousturier, "Un général sauvage," *La Race nègre* 1, no. 1 (June 1927) [an excerpt from her book *Des Inconnus chez moi*]; André Gide, "L'oeuvre de la colonisation," *La Race nègre* 1, no. 3 [an excerpt from *Voyage au Congo*]. See also Jeanne Marqués, "A ma pauvre négresse," *La Race nègre* 1, no. 5 (May 1928). The November–December 1927 issue (1, no. 4) reprints Jean-Louis Finot's review of Philippe Soupault's novel *Le Nègre* from *La Revue mondiale.*

129. Julien Benda, *The Treason of the Intellectuals,* trans. Richard Aldington (1928; reprint, New York: Norton, 1969). For a discussion of Benda see Edward Said, *Representations of the Intellectual* (New York: Vintage, 1994), 5–8.

130. Report of Agent Désiré, February 13, 1934, SLOTFOM II, 11. There is a marginal note in different handwriting on this report, indicating that the journalist's name was "Johnson."

131. "Aux Etats-Unis d'Amérique: l'activité des nègres," *La Race nègre* 1, no. 3 (September 1927): 1.

132. See Marcus Garvey, "L'Afrique aux Africains," *La Race nègre* 1, no. 4 (November–December 1927): 2; "Le Nègre à travers la presse," *La Race nègre* 1, no. 4 (November–December 1927): 4 [translation of an article from the *Negro World*]; "Le réveil des Nègres francais," *La Race nègre* 2, no. 1 (March 1929): 3 [a translation of an article from the *Pittsburgh Courier,* reviewing issue 1, no. 3 of *La Race nègre*]. Another issue translated a brief article on Harlem by Carl Van Vechten that makes specific note that the "Negro quarter" possessed its own journals (mentioning the *Crisis, Opportunity,* and the *Messenger*); see Van Vechten, "La cité nègre," *La Race nègre* 1, no. 4 (November–December 1927): 5.

133. Report of Agent Désiré, September 17, 1927, SLOTFOM II, 5.

134. On Amy Jacques Garvey, see especially Winston James, *Holding Aloft the*

Banner of Ethiopia: Caribbean Radicalism in Early Twentieth-Century America (New York: Verso, 1998), 141–155.

135. Lapido Solanke, letter to Kouyaté, October 1, 1927, SLOTFOM II, 5. The paper reprinted a long open letter that had appeared in *Wasu:* see "Lettre du président de l'Union des Etudiants de l'Ouest-Africain de la Grande Bretagne à l'editeur de 'WASU,' publiée par cette intéressante revue," *La Race nègre* 1, no. 4 (November–December 1927): 1; "Adresse du Président J. B. Danquah à l'éditeur de la revue 'Watu' [*sic*]," *La Race nègre* 2, no. 1 (March 1929): 3.

136. Spiegler, *Aspects of Nationalist Thought,* 160n6.

137. Garvey, letter to Kouyaté, January 31, 1928 (French translation), in "Note sur la propagande révolutionnaire intéressant les pays d'outre mer," February 20, 1928, SLOTFOM III, 144.

138. Amy Jacques Garvey, *Garvey and Garveyism* (Kingston, Jamaica: Amy Jacques Garvey, 1963), 182. Theodore Vincent claims that Garvey's CDRN membership card is in the papers of Amy Jacques Garvey. See Vincent, *Black Power and the Garvey Movement* (Berkeley: Ramparts Press, 1971), 176; Rupert Lewis, *Marcus Garvey: Anti-Colonial Champion* (Trenton: Africa World Press, 1988), 160. I should note that, along with the confrontation with René Maran and Kojo Tovalou Houénou I mentioned in chapter 2, there is also evidence of contact between Garvey and the group around *La Dépêche africaine* in this period. Another surveillance report mentions that his mailing address during his visit was the address of *La Dépêche africaine.* Unsigned report, December 18, 1928, SLOTFOM III, 81.

139. Copy of letter from Kouyaté to Marcus Garvey, report of Agent Désiré, July 10, 1928, SLOTFOM III, 24.

140. Report of Agent Désiré, October 1, 1927, SLOTFOM II, 5; "Note sur la propagande révolutionnaire intéressant les pays d'outre mer," October 31, 1927, SLOTFOM III, 67.

141. Kouyaté, letter to James Weldon Johnson, c. September 1928, SLOTFOM III, 24.

142. Ligue de Défense de la Race Nègre, circular, June 14, 1929, SLOTFOM III, 111.

143. "La vie des étudiants nègres," *La Race nègre* (April 1929): 2. See also "La vie des étudiants nègres," *La Race nègre* (March 1929): 2.

144. Report of Agent Désiré, December 1928, SLOTFOM III, 111.

145. Letter from Kouyaté to Du Bois (May 2, 1929), SLOTFOM III, 111. Langley found a copy of this letter in the Archives Nationales du Dahomey (Porto Novo), sent from the ministere des colonies to the governeur générale of French West Africa. See Langley, *Pan-Africanism and Nationalism,* 312. He

suggests that the letter was intercepted by the French police and thus never delivered. In fact, though, the surveillance reports in the Archives Nationales often include handwritten copies or typescripts of such letters, implying that the originals were indeed sent. And indeed, there is a copy of the letter in the Du Bois files conserved at the University of Massachusetts.

146. There is a great deal of historical work on the Italo-Ethiopian conflict: see Robert G. Weisbord, "British West Indian Reaction to the Italian-Ethiopian War: An Episode in Pan-Africanism," *Caribbean Studies* 10, no. 1 (April 1970): 34–41; Weisbord, "Black America and the Italian-Ethiopian Crisis: An Episode in Pan-Negroism," *Historian* 34, no. 2 (February 1972): 230–241; S. K. B. Asante, *Pan-African Protest: West Africa and the Italo-Ethiopian Crisis, 1934–1941* (London: Longman, 1977); Cedric J. Robinson, "The African Diaspora and the Italo-Ethiopian Crisis," *Race and Class* 27, no. 2 (Autumn 1985): 51–65; William R. Scott, *The Sons of Sheba's Race: African-Americans and the Italo-Ethiopian War, 1935–1941* (Bloomington: Indiana University Press, 1993); Joseph E. Harris, *African-American Reactions to War in Ethiopia, 1936–1941* (Baton Rouge: Louisiana State University Press, 1994); Kevin A. Yelvington, "The War in Ethiopia and Trinidad 1935–1936," in *The Colonial Caribbean in Transition: Essays on Post-Emancipation Social and Cultural History,* ed. Bridget Brereton and Yelvington (Gainesville: University Press of Florida, 1999), 189–225.

147. Makonnen, *Pan-Africanism from Within,* 116–117.

148. Wilson, *Russia and Black Africa,* 368n27. Also see Adami, "International Conference of Negroes and Arabs," *International Press Correspondence* 16, no. 24 (May 23, 1936): 659.

149. On the Rassemblement Coloniale, see Spiegler, *Aspects of Nationalist Thought,* 251–253.

150. Makonnen, *Pan-Africanism from Within,* 156.

151. See for example René Maran, "Le conflit italo-ethiopien et la France," *Bec et Ongles* 123 (October 19, 1935): 3–4; Maran, "La guerre italo-ethiopien et le problème coloniale," *Bec et Ongles* 124 (October 26, 1935): 3–4.

152. "Activité du comité de défense d'Ethiopie," *Africa* 1 (December 1, 1935): 3; "Au Faubourg," *Bec et Ongles* 123 (October 19, 1935): 12. Kouyaté's articles include "Il est préférable de mourir libre que de vivre comme esclaves," *El Ouma* (August–September 1935); "Silence aux négriers complices de Mussolini," *El Ouma* (October 1935).

153. "Activité du comité de défense d'Ethiopie," 3.

154. Paulette Nardal, "On nous prie d'insérer," *Le Cri des Nègres* 4, no. 17 (June 1935): 2.

155. Paulette Nardal, "Levée des races," *Le Périscope africain* 318 (October 15, 1935): 2. The article was provided to *Le Périscope* by the Agence Metromer, a news service run in Paris by the Dahomean Augustin Azango. See Spiegler, *Aspects of Nationalist Thought,* 268.

156. "Hommage aux bonnes volontés," *La Race nègre* new series, no. 1 (January–February 1936): 3. On the IAFE, see George Padmore, *Pan-Africanism or Communism* (1956; reprint, Garden City, N.J.: Doubleday, 1971), 123.

157. James, *Nkrumah and the Ghana Revolution,* 64; Robert A. Hill, "In England, 1932–1938," in *C. L. R. James: His Life and Work,* ed. Paul Buhle (London: Allison and Busby, 1986), 74–75. As I mentioned earlier, Langley also contends that Kouyaté was a member of the IASB.

158. James, *Nkrumah and the Ghana Revolution,* 64–65.

159. Immanuel Geiss, *The Pan-African Movement: A History of Pan-Africanism in America, Europe, and Africa,* trans. Ann Keep (New York: Africana Publishing Co., 1974), 387–388; J. Ayodele Langley, *Pan-Africanism and Nationalism,* 343.

160. Makonnen, *Pan-Africanism from Within,* 120.

161. "Editorial," *International African Opinon* 1, no.1 (July 1938): 2. Page numbers of subsequent citations will be indicated parenthetically in the text. The famous claim that "la négritude, non plus un indice céphalique, ou un plasma, ou un soma, mais mesurée au compas de la souffrance" [Negritude, no longer a cephalic index, or plasma, or soma, but measured by the compass of suffering] appears in Aimé Césaire, *Cahier d'un retour du pays natal* (Notebook of a return to my native land) (1947), trans. Clayton Eshelman and Annette Smith in *Aimé Césaire: The Collected Poetry* (Berkeley: University of California Press, 1983), 76.

162. Makonnen, *Pan-Africanism from Within,* 117.

163. Leila Seleau, "The French Colonies under the Popular Front," *International African Opinion* 2 (August 1938): 5.

164. Padmore mentions *Africa* in his aforementioned letter to Bunche, July 27, 1937.

165. Spiegler, *Aspects of Nationalist Thought,* 276.

166. Kouyaté, "A nos lecteurs!" *Africa* 1 (December 1, 1935): 1.

167. "The Literary Scene," *International African Opinion* 1 (July 1938): 14; Hughes, "Poem on Scottsboro," *International African Opinion* 2 (August 1938); C. L. R. James, "The Voice of Africa," *International African Opinion* 2 (August 1938): 3; Claude McKay, "If We Must Die," *International African Opinion* 6 (February–March 1939); Paul Potts, "Hello, Langston Hughes" and J. R. Ralph Casimir, "O Africa," *International African Opinion* 7 (May–June 1939): 5.

168. "What Is the International African Service Bureau?" in C. L. R. James, *A History of Negro Revolt,* in *Fact* 18 (September 1938): 95.

169. Ralph Ellison, "The World and the Jug," in *Shadow and Act* (New York: Random House, 1964), 132.

170. Makonnen, *Pan-Africanism from Within,* 117.

171. Robinson, "Coming to Terms," 369. See also Brent Hayes Edwards, "The 'Autonomy' of Black Radicalism," *Social Text* 67 (summer 2001): 1–13.

172. Padmore, "The White Man Is Killing Africa," in *Negro: An Anthology,* ed. Nancy Cunard (London, 1934), 854.

173. James, *Nkrumah and the Ghana Revolution,* 69.

Coda: The Last Anthology

1. See Frederick G. Vogel, *World War I Songs: A History and Dictionary of Popular American Patriotic Tunes, with Over 300 Complete Lyrics* (Jefferson, N.C.: McFarland and Co., 1995), 99, 325. A copy of the published score is held in the Sam De Vincent Collection, subseries 2.4, box 49, Armed Forces: World War One, Archives Center, Museum of American History, Smithsonian Institution.

2. Richard A. Long, "An Interview with George Schuyler," *Black World* 25, no. 4 (February 1976): 77.

3. Reid Badger, *A Life in Ragtime: A Biography of James Reese Europe* (New York: Oxford University Press, 1995), 7.

4. "On Patrol in No Man's Land," *James Reese Europe's 369th U.S. Infantry "Hell Fighters" Band: The Complete Recordings* (Memphis Archives CD MA 7020, 1996), 13.

5. Badger, *A Life in Ragtime,* 207. See also Arthur W. Little, *From Harlem to the Rhine: The Story of New York's Colored Volunteers* (New York: Covici-Friede, 1936).

6. John J. Niles, *Singing Soldiers* (New York: Charles Scribner's Sons, 1927). Niles, in keeping with conventional usage (even in the major newspapers) of the period, does not capitalize the word "negro." Page numbers for subsequent references will be indicated parenthetically in the text.

7. Ted Vincent, *Keep Cool: The Black Activists Who Built the Jazz Age* (London: Pluto Press, 1995), 152–160. On the UNIA and music, see especially Vincent, 106–144.

8. See Sonny Boy and his Pals, "France Blues," in *The Blues Line: A Collection of Blues Lyrics,* ed. Eric Sackheim (New York: Mushinsha, 1969), 306.

9. Vincent, *Keep Cool,* 11. Vincent also cites a song called "The 15th Regiment" that was penned in honor of James Reese Europe's success by Andy Razaf (Razafinkeriefo), the poet and lyricist who would later work with musicians

such as Eubie Blake and Fats Waller on tunes including "Ain't Misbehavin'," "S'posin'," and "Honeysuckle Rose."

10. The original edition of *Negro: An Anthology* was published by Wishart in London in 1934. There are two reprint editions: a complete facsimile edition published by the Negro Universities Press in New York in 1969, and a severely abridged version (cut nearly in half) assembled by Hugh Ford in 1970 (reprinted by Continuum in New York in 1996). Unless otherwise noted, subsequent citations will include parenthetical reference to the pagination of the 1969 facsimile reprint edition.

11. Susan Stanford Friedman, "Nancy Cunard (1896–1965)," in *The Gender of Modernism: A Critical Anthology,* ed. Bonnie K. Scott (Bloomington: Indiana University Press, 1990), 63.

12. Jane Marcus, "Bonding and Bondage: Nancy Cunard and the Making of the Negro Anthology," in *Borders, Boundaries, and Frames: Cultural Criticism and Cultural Studies,* ed. Mae Henderson (New York: Routledge, 1995), 36.

13. Marcus, "Bonding and Bondage," 35.

14. Raymond Michelet, "Nancy Cunard," in *Nancy Cunard: Brave Poet, Indomitable Rebel, 1896–1965,* ed. Hugh Ford (Philadelphia: Chilton Book Company, 1968), 128.

15. Jacques Derrida, *Mal d'archive: une impression freudienne* (Paris: Galilée, 1995); *Archive Fever: A Freudian Impression,* trans. Eric Prenowitz (Chicago: University of Chicago Press, 1996), 91.

16. Arlette Farge, *Le Goût de l'archive* (Paris: Seuil, 1989), 10.

17. See Hugh Ford, "Introduction," *Negro: An Anthology,* ed. Cunard, abridged ed. (1970; reprint, New York: Continuum, 1996), xvii.

18. Andrée Nardal, "Etude sur la biguine créole," *La Revue du monde noir* 2 (1931): 51–53.

19. See *Beckett in Black and Red: The Translations for Nancy Cunard's Negro (1934),* ed. Alan Warren Friedman (Lexington: University Press of Kentucky, 2000).

20. Material in *Negro* that originally appeared in the *Negro Worker* includes Charles Alexander, "Negro Workers Starving in Cuba" (483); "Race Prejudice in England" (554–555); an untitled excerpt from the paper (562); and "Letter from a Native Worker in South Africa" (792–793).

21. On Cunard's links to *Le Cri* and to Padmore, see Philippe de Witte, *Les Mouvements nègres en France, 1919–1939* (Paris: L'Harmattan, 1985), 302. When she contributed a poem to the *Negro Worker* in 1933, Padmore introduced her as "a staunch friend and champion of the Negro masses." Cunard,

"Lincoln's Grinding Verbiage," the *Negro Worker* 3, nos. 8–9 (August–September 1933): 32. See also the book they wrote in collaboration a decade later, *White Man's Duty* (Manchester: Panaf Services, 1945). For the UTN Scottsboro fundraising party, see the unsigned report dated June 17, 1933, SLOTFOM III, 53.

22. Report of Agent Désiré, February 2, 1932, SLOTFOM II, 11.

23. Nancy Cunard, "An African Call to Duty," *New Times and Ethiopia News* (October 21, 1939): 3. By this time Kouyaté's politics had greatly moderated, to the point of being almost unrecognizable. He gave her a "Proclamation to the Negroes of French West Africa" he had written, which argues that "all the treaties signed by France, our 'Mère Patrie,' are ours as well. Her commitments are ours. . . . We, the black peoples of French Africa, esteem that we are responsible for her honour, her prestige, her word that is given, her future before man, God and history."

24. Locke, letter to Cunard (April 14, 1934), quoted in Marcus, "Bonding and Bondage," 56.

25. Michael North, *The Dialect of Modernism: Race, Language and Twentieth-Century Literature* (New York: Oxford University Press, 1994), 191.

26. Ibid., 191, 192.

27. Ibid., 191. See Hurston, "The Eatonville Anthology," *Messenger* (September–November 1926), collected in Hurston, *Folklore, Memoirs, and Other Writings* (New York: Library of America, 1995), 813–825.

28. Theodore O. Mason, Jr., "The African-American Anthology: Mapping the Territory, Taking the National Census, Building the Museum," *American Literary History* 10, no. 1 (1998): 193.

29. Cunard, letter to Hugh Ford, 1964, quoted in Anne Chisholm, *Nancy Cunard* (New York: Knopf, 1979), 191.

30. Ford, "Introduction," xxi.

31. Jacques Derrida, "Des Tours de Babel," trans. Joseph F. Graham, in *Difference in Translation,* ed. Graham (Ithaca: Cornell University Press, 1985), 166.

32. Cunard, letter to Claude McKay, January 28, 1932, quoted in *Beckett in Black and Red,* xix.

33. Cunard, circular regarding *Negro* [then titled *Color*], April 1, 1931, quoted in Ford, "Introduction," xvii. *Negro* was dedicated to Henry Crowder, Cunard's longtime African American lover.

34. In a subtle reading, North writes that it is the black vernacular voice that concludes Hurston's "Eatonville Anthology" ("Stepped on a tin, mah story ends") that frames or "enclose[s] the whole anthology" and that "it is only within this voice . . . that the anthology can leap from seemingly factual ac-

counts of real people, to parabolic folktales to stories in which animals talk, and then simply saunter off without concluding." North, 188.

35. See Mason's consideration of the African American anthology in relation to the census, the map, and the museum, in "The African-American Anthology."

36. Ford, "Introduction," xxvii.

ACKNOWLEDGMENTS

This book has spread its debts across many continents. I could not have undertaken this project without the support of a broad foundation of friends in the United States, Europe, the Caribbean, and Africa, who in one way or another kept me sane and healthy as the project took form and lumbered or sped through its phases. I am deeply grateful for all the kindness, patience, commiseration, and cajoling they provided—not to overlook the more practical hospitality of the many beds and couches they lent. In Paris and Dakar: Thierno (Gilles) Soulemane Bâ, Valérie Castan, Antoine Effroy, Emmanuelle Ertel, Lynn Festa, Pamela Golbin, Amélia Radrigan, Antoine Rajon, Amadou Tapsoba, Patrick Tricoit, Dominique Vincent, Anne Wirz, Olwen Wolfe, and especially Bénédicte Alliot and Janet Yesk. In Marseille and Aix-en-Provence: Damien Bonelli, Emmanuel Effroy, Monique Patris, Nico and Manu Patris, Mike Vann, and Uli Wolters. In Fort-de-France: Dawn Fulton, Jacques Eda-Pierre, and especially the late Alice Nardal, who was gracious enough to invite me to her home and speak with me about her family at the end of 1997. In France, her daughter Christiane Eda-Pierre also weathered my enthusiasm during a number of long-distance phone calls, and allowed me to reproduce some of the wonderful photos of the Nardal sisters in her possession. There are too many to name in New York and elsewhere in the United States, but I would especially like to thank Roberto Calasanz, Yvette Christiansë, Emily Coates, Rodney Crump, Laura Harris, Rayna Kalas, Katya Kazakina, Peter Mendelsund, Rosalind Morris, Fred Moten, Jorge Pérez, Anne Protopappas, Ellen Przybyla, Marina Rustow, Tara Susman, Mike Vazquez, and Robert Weston.

I met Michel and Geneviève Fabre in 1995, when I was living for a year and a half in France through the assistance of a foreign research grant from Columbia University. I do not know how to thank them sufficiently for their generosity since then. Michel Fabre put me in touch with a number of other scholars, shared his extraordinary personal library with me, allowed me access to a number of manuscripts in his possession, and gave me indispensable advice too many times to count on everything from issues of methodology to details of bibliography.

A number of librarians and curators have helped me navigate the intricacies of the archival research this project has required. Michèle Le Pavec of the Bibliothèque Nationale went out of her way to help me track down some elusive items. The curators at the Schomburg Center for Research in Black Culture in New York have assisted me time and time again, especially when I was a scholar-in-residence there on a post-doctoral fellowship funded by the National Endowment of the Humanities in 1997–1998; I would particularly like to thank Diana Lachatanere, André Elizée, and Howard Dodson. I also am grateful for the assistance of librarians at the Moorland-Spingarn Collection at Howard University, the James Weldon Johnson Papers at the Beinecke Library at Yale University, and especially the Centre des Archives d'Outre-Mer in Aix-en-Provence. In addition, I thank Henry Louis Gates, Jr., Richard Newman, and Lisa Thompson for their encouragement during my year in 1996–1997 as a scholar-in-residence at the W. E. B. Du Bois Institute for Afro-American Research at Harvard University.

The process of revision over the past four years has benefited in particular from the scholars who read some or all of the book at one point or another. Many responded with thorough (sometimes unflinching) comments, criticisms, and suggestions. In particular, I thank Marcellus Blount, Daphne Brooks, Maryse Condé, Michael Denning, Ann Douglas, Kevin Gaines, Phillip Brian Harper, David Kazanjian, Wahneema Lubiano, Nathaniel Mackey, Jane Marcus, Randy Martin, Chandan Reddy, Cedric Robinson, David Lionel Smith, Werner Sollors, Penny Von Eschen, Kenneth Warren, and Kevin Yelvington. In facing the impossible necessities of translation, I relied on a number of friends and colleagues for a second ear; Gil Anidjar, Simon Kohn, Nora Nicolini, and Bénédicte Alliot helped with some particularly thorny points. Nora Nicolini undertook the heroic task of proofreading the French in the text. (All translations are my own unless otherwise indicated.) The book's fabric was also shaped, indelibly if fleetingly, by two who have passed on: François Manchuelle, who (when I popped into his office unexpectedly in 1995) gave me crucial bibliographic leads as well as pointers about the Archives Nationales; and Joe Wood, whom I knew for many years but never knew well until we hooked up in 1999 for a few lively bull sessions about the politics of diaspora.

At Rutgers, the support from my colleagues has been heartening and sometimes transformative. Many have given useful feedback on sections of the book, including Herman Bennett, Chris Brown, Elin Diamond, Daphne Lamothe, and Cheryl Wall. Richard Dienst, Donald Gibson, and Bruce Robbins read an earlier version of the entire manuscript, and how much it has changed is a sign of their influence. The Black Atlantic/African Diaspora Seminar at the Rutgers Center for Historical Analysis has been a vital space for me to think about this project throughout the past five years, and I have presented three parts of chapters to that audience. I am especially grateful to Mia Bay, David Brown, Wesley Brown, Abena Busia, Belinda Edmondson, Renée Larrier, Jennifer Morgan, and Deborah White. I would also like to thank my students at Rutgers, especially my graduate students in my seminar "Black Cultural Studies: Issues and Approaches" in the fall of 1998, where some of my thinking about diaspora crystallized.

Portions of the book have been presented as lectures at other institutions, including the Yale University Afro-American Studies Department, the Princeton University Social History Workshop, the City University of New York Graduate Center, the New York University History Department, and the Université de Paris VII. I am grateful for the comments of the audiences on those occasions. In addition, parts of the prologue and chapters 2 and 4 previously appeared in different form in the journals *Social Text* and *Transition,* and in the collection *Temples for Tomorrow: Looking Back at the Harlem Renaissance,* edited by Geneviève Fabre and Michel Feith (Indiana University Press, 2001).

Lindsay Waters, my editor at Harvard University Press, has been remarkably patient with what must have seemed at times the glacial progress of the manuscript. Tom Wheatland has walked me, baby step by baby step, through the labyrinth of the publishing process. Hilary Selby Polk copyedited the book with a sharp eye and offered a wealth of excellent substantive suggestions.

I have had the extraordinary fortune of being able to draw on a few scholars who have always found the time to give me advice about my scholarship, about publishing, and about academia in general. Robin Kelley, Farah Griffin, and Patricia Williams have given me more than I could ever know how to thank them for—with their time, their openness, and their wisdom. Gayatri Chakravorty Spivak has shaped my thinking in ways I'm still discovering. But I also treasure our small follies: working dinners on the fly, drives downtown, grocery runs, bad bad movies. From that first afternoon I peeked into his office at Barnard College, Robert O'Meally has taught me and supported me and pushed me in too many ways to count. His Center for Jazz Studies at Columbia remains one of the centers of my intellectual life, and Bob and Jacqui Malone have welcomed me into their home, lent me books, played me records, and taken me to concerts. These debts cannot be repaid. All I can do is to take them as models for the ways I approach teaching and mentoring my own students.

Above all, this book was written and rewritten in the company of family and a few fellow travelers. Nikhil Singh and Alys Weinbaum have been my best collaborators, comrades, readers, and friends, now too far away but always there for the steps this project has taken. My parents, my sister Michelle, and my grandmothers Angella Hayes and Esther Gordy Edwards have granted me everything and welcomed me home no matter how far I roamed. Une seule m'a donné plus que tout: Nora Nicolini, martillo mío. Vos has esperado tanto el fin, cuando éste sería solamente otro mueble. Tu as patienté, au-delà—Ceci n'est pas ton livre, mais il s'écrit.

INDEX

Achille, Louis-Thomas, 4, 119, 152, 154, 155, 158
Adorno, Theodor, 145
Africa (journal), 8, 250, 302
Algeria, 29, 143, 144, 237, 250, 273, 284, 297, 298
Aliker, André, 196
Amsterdam News, 8, 173, 271, 286
Anderson, Benedict, 115–116
anthologies, 43–44, 70–72, 310–311, 317–318, 331n60; prefaces of, 38, 45, 46–50, 315
Antoine, Régis, 159, 195
archive, 7–10, 311
Asad, Talal, 84, 85, 86
Association des Etudiants Martiniquais, 154, 178–179, 265

Baker, Josephine, 133, 154, 169, 171, 287; relationship with Rivière, 79–80; impact on Paris fashion, 130; in context of French colonialism, 161–163
Baldwin, Roger, 276–277
Balibar, Etienne, 152
Bal Nègre (dance hall in Paris), 145, 169, 170, 173–177
Bataille, Georges, 223–224
beguine, 116, 145–146, 171–177, 218. *See also* jazz
Bellegarde, Dantès, 132, 149
Benda, Julien, 289
Benjamin, Walter, 8, 189, 281–282
Bennett, Gwendolyn, 98, 100, 129, 132–133, 157, 190
Berlin, 42–43, 254

blues, 60–68, 89, 90, 158, 309
Bradford, Roark, 34
Bradley, William Aspenwall, 210, 226
Brathwaite, Edward Kamau, 245
Breton, André, 192–193, 194
"Bricktop" (Ada Smith), 4, 64, 66, 79, 100, 169
Buell, Raymond Leslie, 74
Bullard, Eugene, 4, 63, 66
Bunche, Ralph, 276

Candace, Gratien, 32, 284
Carby, Hazel, 140–141
Cendrars, Blaise, 44, 70, 71–73, 82, 86
Césaire, Aimé, 23, 24, 38, 59, 193, 243, 284, 286, 300; and Négritude movement, 28, 121, 122; and *L'Etudiant Noir,* 36, 178, 179–180; on the Nardal sisters, 147, 156; on *Banjo,* 187, 211; on *Légitime Défense,* 194; on *Le Cri des Nègres,* 266
Chicago Defender, 8, 200, 283, 286
Clifford, James, 162, 169
colonialism, French, 6, 9, 94, 96–97, 99, 230; reflected in language, 26–33; and gender, 54, 56–57, 80–81, 159, 161–163, 184–186; threatened by black internationalism, 70–71, 75–76, 83; and stereotypes, 71–72, 73, 158–159, 167–171; and *indigénat,* 73, 95; and assimilation, 73–74, 86–87, 124, 128, 147, 193; and association, 74–75; and metonymy, 146, 158, 161–163; compared to British, 161, 238–239, 241–242, 283–284, 285